TOURISM IN CENTRAL ASIA

Cultural Potential and Challenges

Advances in Hospitality and Tourism Book Series

Editor-in-Chief:
Mahmood A. Khan, PhD
Professor, Department of Hospitality and Tourism Management,
Pamplin College of Business,
Virginia Polytechnic Institute and State University,
Falls Church, Virginia
email: mahmood@vt.edu

BOOKS IN THE SERIES:

Food Safety: Researching the Hazard in Hazardous Foods
Editors: Barbara Almanza, PhD, RD, and Richard Ghiselli, PhD

Strategic Winery Tourism and Management: Building Competitive Winery Tourism and Winery Management Strategy
Editor: Kyuho Lee, PhD

Sustainability, Social Responsibility and Innovations in the Hospitality Industry
Editor: H. G. Parsa, PhD
Consulting Editor: Vivaja "Vi" Narapareddy, PhD
Associate Editors: SooCheong (Shawn) Jang, PhD, Marival Segarra-Oña, PhD, and Rachel J. C. Chen, PhD, CHE

Managing Sustainability in the Hospitality and Tourism Industry: Paradigms and Directions for the Future
Editor: Vinnie Jauhari, PhD

Management Science in Hospitality and Tourism: Theory, Practice, and Applications
Editors: Muzaffer Uysal, PhD, Zvi Schwartz, PhD, and Ercan Sirakaya-Turk, PhD

Tourism in Central Asia: Issues and Challenges
Editors: Kemal Kantarci, PhD, Muzaffer Uysal, PhD, and Vincent Magnini, PhD

TOURISM IN CENTRAL ASIA
Cultural Potential and Challenges

Edited by
**Kemal Kantarci, PhD, Muzaffer Uysal, PhD,
and Vincent P. Magnini, PhD**

Apple Academic Press

TORONTO   NEW JERSEY

Apple Academic Press Inc.	Apple Academic Press Inc.
3333 Mistwell Crescent	9 Spinnaker Way
Oakville, ON L6L 0A2	Waretown, NJ 08758
Canada	USA

©2015 by Apple Academic Press, Inc.

First issued in paperback 2021

Exclusive worldwide distribution by CRC Press, a member of Taylor & Francis Group
No claim to original U.S. Government works

ISBN 13: 978-1-77463-366-3 (pbk)
ISBN 13: 978-1-77188-055-8 (hbk)

Library of Congress Control Number: 2014944730

Library and Archives Canada Cataloguing in Publication

Tourism in Central Asia: cultural potential and challenges/edited by Kemal Kantarci, PhD, Muzaffer Uysal, PhD, and Vincent P. Magnini, PhD.

(Advances in hospitality and tourism book series)
Includes bibliographical references and index.
ISBN 978-1-77188-055-8 (bound)
1. Tourism--Asia, Central. I. Kantarci, Kemal, author, editor II. Uysal, Muzaffer, author, editor III. Magnini, Vincent P., author, editor IV.
Series: Advances in hospitality and tourism book series

| G155.A742T69 2014 | 338.4'791580443 | C2014-904835-1 |

Apple Academic Press also publishes its books in a variety of electronic formats. Some content that appears in print may not be available in electronic format. For information about Apple Academic Press products, visit our website at **www.appleacademicpress.com** and the CRC Press website at **www.crcpress.com**

ABOUT THE EDITORS

Kemal Kantarci, PhD

Kemal Kantarci, PhD, is an Associate Professor of Tourism Management at Akdeniz University, Antalya, Turkey. His teaching and research interests are destination management and marketing, tourism geography, and tourism marketing. He also works as a consultant to public and private sector organizations. He has published several papers in international and national journals and proceedings. His studies are mainly focused on tourism opportunities and challenges in Central Asian and Balkan countries. Dr. Kantarci has visited Virginia Polytechnic Institute and State University, USA, as Visiting Professor and worked as a full-time lecturer at Ahmet Yesevi University, Kazakhstan. He currently teaches in the areas of tourism management, tourism geography, destination development, and tourism policy and planning.

Muzaffer Uysal, PhD

Muzaffer Uysal, PhD, is a Professor of Tourism in the Department of Hospitality and Tourism Management at Pamplin College of Business of Virginia Polytechnic Institute and State University Blacksburg, Virginia, USA. He has extensive experience in the travel and tourism field, authoring or co-authoring a significant number of articles in tourism, hospitality, and recreation journals, proceedings, book chapters, and monographs, and several books related to tourism research methods, tourist service satisfaction, tourism and quality-of-life, creating experience value in tourism, consumer psychology in tourism, and hospitality settings. He is a member of the International Academy for the Study of Tourism and the Academy of Leisure Sciences and serves as co-editor of *Tourism Analysis: An Interdisciplinary Journal*. He has received a number of awards for research and excellence in international education, and teaching. His current research interests center on tourism demand/supply interaction, tourism development, and QOL research in tourism.

Vincent P. Magnini, PhD

Vincent Magnini, PhD, is an Associate Professor of Hospitality Management in the Department of Hospitality and Tourism Management at Pamplin College of Business of Virginia Polytechnic Institute and State University, Blacksburg, Virginia, USA. His research interests reside mainly in the area of service management. He is as an associate editor to the *Cornell Hospitality Quarterly* and also serves on the editorial boards of a number of other journals, including the *International Journal of Hospitality Management*, the *Journal of Hospitality and Tourism Research*, and the *Journal of Travel Research*. His recent book, titled *Performance Enhancers: Twenty Essential Habits for Service Businesses*, is being widely read across a variety of service sectors.

CONTENTS

LIST OF CONTRIBUTORS

Kemal Kantarci
Akdeniz University, Alanya Faculty of Business, Department of Tourism Management. Kestel/Alanya –Antalya Turkey

Vincent Magnini
Hospitality and Tourism Management, Pamplin College of Business,Virginia Polytechnic Institute and Sate University, Blacksburg, VA 24060, USA

Muzaffer Uysal
Hospitality and Tourism Management, Pamplin College of Business, Virginia Polytechnic Institute and Sate University, Blacksburg, VA 24060, USA

Pınar Akçalı
Middle East Technical University, Department of Political Science and Public Administration, Universiteler Mahallesi Dumlupinar Bulvari No: 1, 06800 Ankara, Turkey

Azhar Baisakalova
4, Abai av., #312, 050010 Almaty, Kazakhstan, KIMEP University, Almaty, Kazakhstan

Kazim Develioglu
Akdeniz University, Alanya Faculty of Business, Alanya –Antalya, Turkey

Vladimir Garkavenko
2, Abai av., #340, 050010 Almaty, Kazakhstan, KIMEP University, Almaty, Kazakhstan

Slavomír Horák
The Institute of International Studies, Faculty of Social Sciences, Charles University in Prague, Vrsni 35, Prague 8, 182 00 Czech Republic

Ismail Mangaltepe
Istanbul University, Ordu Cad. No. 196, 34459 Beyazit – İstanbul, Turkey

Ayhan Pala
Hoca Ahmet Yesevı International Turkish-Kazakh University, Turkistan/161200, Kazakhstan

Gozde Sazak
Istanbul University, Kanlica Cad. No. 2 Cubuklu, Istanbul, Turkey

Professor Simon Milne
School of Hospitality and Tourism, Auckland University of Technology, New Zealand

Guillaume Tiberghien
PhD Candidate in Tourism, Auckland University of Technology, Private Bag 92006 I Auckland 1142 I New Zealand, PhD Candidate in Tourism, Auckland University of Technology

Mualla Uydu Yucel
Istanbul University, Chief of the General Turkish History Program, Ordu Cad. No. 196, 34459 Beyazıt – İstanbul, Turkey

Saulesh Yessenova
Department of Anthropology, ES 602, University of Calgary, 2500 University Drive NW, Calgary, Alberta, Canada T2N 1N4

Munevver Ebru Zeren
Istanbul University, Ordu Cad. No. 196, 34459 Beyazıt – İstanbul, Turkey

LIST OF ABBREVIATIONS

ASSR	Autonomous Soviet Socialist Republic
B2B	Business to Business
B2C	Business to Consumer
CA	Central Asia
CBT	Community-Based Tourism
CI	Competitiveness Index
CIS	Commonwealth Independent States
CRC	Cooperative Research Center's
CRS	Computer Reservation System
CSR	Corporate Social Responsibility
DNT	Den Norske Turist Forening
ETPACK	Ecological Tourism and Public Awareness in Central Kazakhstan
FDI	Foreign Direct Investment
FEVAD	Federation du E-commerce et de la Vente à Distance
GDP	Gross Domestic Product
GDS	Global Distribution Systems
IBPP	Institution Building Partnership Program
ICT	Information and Communication Technology
IRR	Internal Rate of Return
KCBTA	Kyrgyz Community Based Tourism Association
KITF	Kazakhstan International Tourism Fair
KTA	Kazakhstan Tourism Association
NABU	Nature and Biodiversity Conservation Union
NII	National Institute of Informatics
OLI	Ownership–Location–Integration
RSFSR	Russian Soviet Federated Socialist Republic
SMES	Small and Medium-Size Enterprises
SSR	Soviet Socialist Republic
T&T	Travel & Tourism
TIRET	Turkish-Islamic Republic of Eastern Turkestan
TNCs	Transnational Corporations

TSE	Travel Agent Sector in Singapore
TTIA	Turkish Tourism Investors Association
UNWTO	United Nations World Tourism Organization
USP	Unique Selling Point
WEF	World Economic Forum
WTO	World Tourism Organization

PREFACE

There has been a proliferation of tourism books in the past two decades dealing with several aspects of the global phenomenon of tourism activities. Although there has been some work from tourism researchers that has examined tourism issues in select countries of Central Asia such as Kazakhstan, Kyrgyzstan, Uzbekistan, Turkmenistan and Tajikistan, scholarly publications addressing tourism development opportunities and challenges in Central Asia are few in number in comparison to the attention afforded to tourism development in many other regions of the world. There is no question that there is still more work needed to bring tourism issues and challenges to light that are likely to impact these countries. This book is an attempt to house key writings on this topic in a single resource.

The origin of this book idea dates back several years. One of the editors, Dr. Kemal Kantarci, who has made his research focus on Central Asian tourism development for the past 10 years, has also had a number of visits to the region and spent two years conducting field research and teaching in the region. During his sabbatical in 2010 in the Department of Hospitality and Tourism Management – Virginia Polytechnic Institute and State University (Virginia Tech), USA and working with Dr. Muzaffer Uysal and Dr. Vincent Magnini, the idea was further developed and moved into implementation. It took almost four years to bring it to light! By doing so, we hope that researchers will afford increased attention to further researching tourism development and understanding the nature of challenges and opportunities that exist in Central Asia. One of the main goals of this edited book for scholars and practitioners is to realize the importance of these newly emerging destinations in Central Asia and their unique potential as upcoming world destinations.

Existing studies and reports consistently mention that the Central Asian countries are unique destinations in that they are exotic and offer a wide variety of rich cultural and heritage attractions and possess natural beauty and great hospitality. Over thousands of years these Central Asian countries have served as a bridge between the West and the East. Furthermore, due to the heightened interest in the Silk Road project after the collapse of the Soviet Union, the Central Asian countries began gaining more attention from researchers, potential investors as well as tour operators, and thus visitors. Such signs signify that these countries have tremendous potential for tourism development. However, turning these opportunities and potential into reality is likely to be a result of long, expensive, and complicated processes.

In this book, we invited over 15 researchers who have the knowledge and expertise to energize further examination and attention to the topic of tourism development with its potential and challenges. The passion of our contributors regarding this subject area shines throughout the book. They infuse their passion into their writings when communicating their expertise regarding their respective topics.

We hope that you will find this book useful and consider it an initial effort to shed light on the topic of tourism development in modern-day Central Asia. It is our desire that the outcomes of this book would help increase our current knowledge base as well as spawn further inquiry. Consistent with the view of methodological pluralism, the chapters of this book can stimulate both qualitative and quantitative studies designed to examine tourism development along the modern Silk Road.

The contribution of this book to our current knowledge was made possible by the contributors who shared their time, talent, and expertise in these pages. As editors, we established only one boundary for the contributors: the chapter had to offer insight into tourism development in the Silk Road region of the Central Asian countries. As you will see, their passion and knowledge shine through in their writings. Lastly, we are grateful for the support and encouragement of Apple Academic Press and Series Editor Dr. Mahmood Khan for helping to shape this book to reach its current form.

**— Kemal Kantarci, PhD, Muzaffer Uysal, PhD,
and Vincent P. Magnini, PhD**

CHAPTER 1

EXPLORING TOURISM POTENTIAL IN CENTRAL ASIA

KEMAL KANTARCI, MUZAFFER UYSAL, and VINCENT MAGNINI

CONTENTS

INTRODUCTION

For thousands of years, Central Asia has played the critical role of connecting the East with the West and vice versa. This region contains the most direct trade route between China and Europe, termed the Silk Road, which has been documented since Roman times (e.g., Akayev, 2001; Airey and Shackley, 1997). Although the list of Silk Road countries stretches across Asia to the Middle East and from the Middle East on to Europe. Covering nearly 28 countries, the relevance of the Silk Road as a tourism project is gaining more importance in the Central Asian countries such as Kyrgyzstan, Kazakhstan, Uzbekistan, Turkmenistan and Tajikistan (Kantarci and Develioglu, 2013). For example, the study "the New Silk Road: Mediators and Tourism Development in Central Asia" by Werner (2005) focuses on the role of different actors (such as tour operators, hosts, and guests) as mediators, who actively market and promote tourist destinations for the development of tourism for Kyrgyzstan and Kazakhstan. The study by Vogel et al. (2003), on the other hand, explored if the former glory and success of the historical Silk Road could be rejuvenated as a new e-Silk Road in order to further develop e-commerce for the attractions, cultural and heritage resources of the Silk Road cities and countries. The authors concluded the e-Silk Road as promising but challenging with numerous opportunities for research. The region's rich heritage invokes opportunities but also makes salient an ongoing need for cultural preservation and special sensitivity that may be less necessary in other contexts. It is clear that the historical prominence of the Silk Road has renewed significance in global e-commerce and travel and is also receiving attention from researchers representing different fields of academic studies.

One of the most unique e-projects is the attempt to form the Digital Silk Roads project (http://dsr.nii.ac.jp/about.html.en) that was initiated by the National Institute of Informatics of Japan (called NII) in conjunction with UNESCO in April 2001. Since then, the project has held meetings, conferences and archived the vast amount of cultural resources that exist in and around the Silk Road cities and countries from the ancient to the current in a form without deterioration, and inherit those resources for the future. The specific aim of the project is to investigate various methods, starting from the digitization of real cultural artifacts, and the construction of digital archives, to the exhibition of digital cultural resources over the network and annotation to digital cultural resources based on collaborative work. The end result is to improve accessibility to those cultural and heritage resources for many people to actually see and use those resources (for further information on this: Progress by the Digital Silk Roads Project by Ono et al., 2006).

Dating back to ancient civilization, this region of the world has a rich, interesting, and meaningful heritage worthy of our attention. Even today, living oral epic traditions are still remarkably rich along the Silk Roads, both on the Desert Route and the Maritime Route and documenting these epic traditions are also being undertaken by researchers (e.g., Honko, 1996).

For example, the Manas epos of Batyr-khan Manas, an estimated 553,000 lines in total, reveals the formation, life struggles, and triumphs of the Kyrgyz people and represents the highpoint of a widespread Central Asian oral culture. There has been some effort to use the Manas epos and heritage products in the creation of both a national identity and destination image in the positioning of Kyrgyzstan in the global market place (e.g., Schofield and Maccarrone-Eaglen, 2011; Thompson, 2004; Thompson, Schofield, Foster and Bakieva, 2006). Central Asia spans from central Siberia in the north to Afghanistan, Iran, and Pakistan to the south. The west is framed by the Caspian Sea and by China in the east (Buyers, 2003). Today, the five countries most often included in the definitions of the region include the five republics of the former Soviet Union: Kazakhstan (pop. 16.6 million), Kyrgyzstan (5.5 million), Tajikistan (7.6 million), Turkmenistan (5.1 million), and Uzbekistan (29.5 million), for a total population of approximately 65 million (http://en.wikipedia.org/wiki/Central_Asia; accessed December 2, 2013). Not surprisingly, foreign direct investment (FDI) in this region depends heavily upon earlier trade relations as well as the extent of cultural distance between home and host country (Culpan and Akcaoglu, 2003). For example, Turkey's geographic and cultural proximity to Central Asian countries appears to give Turkish tourism firms an advantage over competitor firms looking to penetrate from other markets (Kantarci, 2007a). FDI, however, is trickling in from a number of European and Asian countries with other regions such as the Americas represented to a much lesser extent.

Tourism development in the region depends upon the confluence of numerous push and pull factors, representing both demand and supply sides of tourism planning, development, and activities. Push factors in tourism represent the demand side and include items such as the socioeconomic conditions of the home countries from which a tourist originates (e.g., Papatheodorou, 2001; Uysal, 1998). Pull factors, on the other hand, are vast and include many of the topics that will be discussed throughout the chapters of this book. Examples of pull factors are the comfort levels of host country accommodations, conditions of host country transportation infrastructure, natural and scenic beauty, quality of historical and cultural attractions, and perceptions of safety and security (Uysal et al., 2008). As with tourism development in any region of the world, a myriad of pull factors influence the speed and level at which tourism is being developed in Central Asia (Kantarci, 2006).

Recently, we have seen a number of studies that have examined some aspects of tourism and its variants in Central Asian countries. These studies emphasized areas such as sustainability of tourism services and strategies (Beheshti et al., 2013), ecosystem services and pricing strategies (Samimi and Kraudzun, 2013), distribution channel strategies for attracting foreign tourists for Tajikistan (Beheshti and Zare, 2013); image making (Schatz, 2008), tourism development problems and tourist attraction clusters (Zholdasbekov, 2011) for Kazakhstan, factors determining the characteristics of the tourism sector (Edwards, 2010) for Turkmenistan, perceptions of Central Asia travel conditions, general and tourism specific investment conditions, perceptions and images for Kyrgyzstan, Kazakhstan, Uzbekistan, and Turkmenistan (Kantarci, 2006, 2007a, 2007b).

Small heritage tourism attractions and development case studies were also found in the literature for Turkmenistan (Edwards, 2010) and Uzbekistan (Airey and Shackley, 1997). Issues that deal with human resources in the area of skills needed, training and tourist skills inventory in the tourism sector were also examined for Kyrgyzstan and Uzbekistan (Baum, 2007; Baum and Thompson, 2007). Furthermore, the study by Zhidkoblinova (2013) exclusively focused on the notion that further tourism development in Kazakhstan on the world market would certainly require concerted efforts from policymakers that could help form the nature of specific regulations of economic relations and measures of state support in the country. On the other hand, Palmer's (2007) work considered ethnic equality and stakeholder involvement in relation to tourism as a tool to build national identity in Kyrgyzstan. Kulnazarova (2010) in her dissertation points out that because of the limited energy resources and the impairment of industrialization in Kyrgyz Republic, the country regards tourism as the locomotive of development that has the comparative advantage structure, as one of the most important sectors that would contribute to its developing economy. However, her study also mentions that in order to tap into the natural, cultural and heritage resources of the country there has to be a concerted effort on the part of all the stakeholders in the tourism sector, including the government and the private sector. Furthermore, in its current form and structure, the tourism sector lacks the capacity to accommodate tourists with high quality of services compounded with inappropriate pricing strategies that are not consistent with the level of services in the tourism sector, confirming that the tourism sector poses both opportunities and also tremendous challenges. In addition, safety and security matters are also factors that impact the image of the country as a destination.

Almost all the studies mentioned the fact that the Central Asian countries are unique in that they are exotic and newly emerging destinations, offer a wide variety of rich cultural and heritage attractions and possess natural beauty and great hospitality but in some instances may lack good infrastructure for basic tourism amenities, trained personnel and more importantly lack channels of distributions and suffer from inaccessibility to some areas apart from major cities. Due to the Silk Road project and their abundance of cultural and natural resources, the Central Asian countries are gaining more attention and heightened interest from potential investors as well as tour operators and thus visitors, all signifying that these countries have tremendous potential for tourism development. However, turning these opportunities and potential into a reality is likely to be a result of long, expensive, and complicated processes (Uysal and Kantarci, 2007).

As you will read in the coming chapters, it has not been an easy road for tourism development in Central Asia. Many pull factors, particularly road infrastructure and accommodation quality, have been hurdles for the area's development. Government corruption and bureaucratic red tape have also been formidable challenges encountered by those attempting to develop successful tourism businesses in the region. On the other hand, other pull factors such as natural beauty and visible remnants of the regions rich cultural heritage are patiently waiting to be noticed and appreciated by the masses. Thus, by advancing our knowledge of such pull factors, and by enhancing our comprehension of the region's heritage in general, we can better understand the current opportunities and challenges regarding tourism development in the area.

CONTRIBUTION OF THIS BOOK

As we know, the global tourism landscape continually changes. Political, economic, cultural, and technological forces interplay to determine where and when tourists travel. That is, the confluence of these forces shape push and pull factors. While challenges still exist and will always exist to some extent in every tourism market, many factors appear to indicate that the Central Asia region (also termed the Silk Road region) is ripe for future tourism development. The region is rich with historical, cultural, and natural beauty that could provide significant utility to many potential visitors.

This book is an attempt to house key writings on this topic in a single resource. Publications addressing tourism development opportunities and challenges in Central Asia are few in number in comparison to the attention afforded to tourism development in many other regions of the world. More specifically, a number of books address tourism development in other world regions [such as, Europe: McCabe, Minnaert, and Diekmann (2011); North America: Chandana (2003); South America: Santana (2001); South-east Asia: Hitchcock, King, and Parnwell (2009)], but Central Asia has received little explicit attention. This project was initiated to address this void. In summary, we intend to make this book a major bibliographic resource for all academic researchers and practitioners interested in issues dealing with the development of tourism, its potential and challenges, and policy and regulatory issues in Central Asian countries.

OVERVIEW OF THE CONTENTS

More than 15 prominent researchers have contributed their time and talent to this project. We invited those researchers who have the knowledge and expertise to energize further examination and attention to the topic of tourism development along the Silk Road to be contributors. The passion of the contributors regarding this subject area shines through in the coming chapters. They infuse their passion into their writings when communicating their expertise regarding their respective topics.

The first two contributions, Chapter 2 (Baisakalova and Garkavenko) and Chapter 3 (Tiberghien, Garkavenko and Milne) provide detailed analyzes of tourism development in Kazakhstan. As outlined by the authors, Kazakhstan, with its abundant natural and cultural resources, has a great potential in boosting tourism by developing different segments of tourism, such as ecotourism, educational and cultural tourism, business tourism and adventure tourism. There is a strong and ambitious political will to become a tourist "Mecca" in Central Asia.

Chapter 4 (Sazak) eloquently describes the beauty and unique cultural heritage of Bukhara as described by the author as 'Princess Bukhara.' Located in Uzbekistan, Bukhara was considered by many to be the intellectual center of the Islamic World during the golden age of Saminids and was considered one of the main centers of world civilization for thousands of years. This chapter, therefore, details the rich history of the city until present day. The museums, traditional handcrafts, and jewelry that exist today are also described in this chapter as they provide a glance at the robust history and traditions of the city.

Chapter 5 (Mangaltepe) explicates the heritage, as well as opportunities and challenges in the current tourism sector in Khiva. Khiva is a city of about 50,000 residents located in the Xorazm Province of Uzbekistan. The chapter details the city's exciting heritage and includes items such as trade route and religious traditions. Information regarding modern archeological digs is also included to help paint a picture of this once robust city. Today there are more than 400 historical monuments in the region, many of which are located in Khiva.

In Chapter 6, Zeren describes the oasis city of Merv located in the Mary province of Turkmenistan. Surrounded by the Karakum desert, Merv has been of major strategic value throughout the chronology of the Silk Road. As described by Zeren, Merv "is an oasis city established on the delta of the Murag River which takes roots from the Afghan mountains and vanishes up north in the Karakum desert." It has even been claimed by some that Merv was briefly the largest city in the world in the twelfth century. This chapter, therefore, examines not only history, but also culture as reflected in architecture and handcrafts.

In Chapter 7, Yucel intricately details the heritage of Samarkand, a city of approximately a half a million residents located in Uzbekistan. Samarkand is one of the oldest inhabited cities in the world founded around 700 BC. The chapter describes the heritage, culture and current tourist attractions in this 'Queen of All Cities.' Under the proper conditions, there is little question regarding the tourism potential of this majestic city. Tourists from across the globe would enjoy and appreciate this robust beauty anchored with nearly three thousand years of history.

Chapter 8 takes an interesting turn by exploring how cinema can be used to aid in branding a destination. The author, Yessenova, states that her article examines a particular cinema project: the epic film "Nomad" (2005). A grandiose state-sponsored endeavor, this film was designed to introduce Kazakhstan, its people, and its history to the world and to brand the country as a creative modern economy. Tragically once it was released, "Nomad" made little or no splash in the public consciousness becoming unsuccessful not only internationally, but also domestically. It left the query 'why did this costly cinematic effort fail?' This article specifically addresses the question: at what juncture of conception or production did the film lose its viewers? To this end the author discusses the film's story situating it within both Kazakh past and present cultural milieus so as to explain both the state's branding choices and missed opportunities.

In Chapter 9, Develioglu and Kantarci use the World Economic Forum's "Travel & Tourism Competitiveness Index" to map out how the Silk Road countries can be more competitive and sustainable in the long run. More specifically, they cluster and compare the countries based on Travel & Tourism Competitiveness Index variables. Cluster analyzes revealed that two clusters can be derived as a result. Diffusion of clusters imply that Cluster 1 countries mostly consist of Central Asian Countries, whose competitiveness performance have been found relatively lower compared to Cluster 2 countries.

Next, in Chapter 10, Horák details some of the red tape and bureaucratic challenges associated with the current development of tourism in Central Asia. Many issues are examined such as challenges with obtaining travel visas, problems associated with the registration of foreigners, and other bureaucratic inefficiencies as well. The chapter uses observations and unstructured interviews at Central Asian border crossings to illustrate some of these challenges. Such challenges need to be understood and mitigated in order for development in the region to reach its fullest potential.

For Chapter 11, Akcali describes the opportunities and obstacles associated with further developing the tourism sector in post-Soviet Kyrgyzstan. The first portion of the chapter provides a synopsis of the Kyrgyzstan from geographic, economic and social perspectives. The latter portion of the chapter addresses how these macro and situational forces provide both opportunities and obstacles for the nation's tourism development efforts. This chapter communicates to readers the rich and promising potential pertaining to tourism development in Kyrgyzstan.

In Chapter 12, Garkvenko and Tiberghien analyze information and communication technology (ICT) diffusion in Kazakhstan as it relates to tourism in the country. The chapter focuses on the Internet presence of tourism players as well as how tourism commodities are distributed via the web. The authors detail how the level of ICT adoption by the travel industry in Kazakhstan varies substantially according to sector and even within sectors, but is mostly lower than the practices in western countries; thus, there is significant potential for further development.

Next, Chapter 13 by Kantarci focuses on the perceptions of foreign investors on the tourism market with respect to both general investment conditions and tourism specific investment conditions in Central Asia including Kyrgyzstan, Kazakhstan, Uzbekistan, and Turkmenistan. Based on the empirical findings, the chapter makes the argument that those emerging markets such the ones that were covered in the study should develop creative and sustainable investment incentives and plans to promote their respective countries. Drawing such investment is critical to the region's development from a tourism point-of-view.

Lastly, the Chapter 14 offers a chronology of Central Asia covering its history from ancient times to the modern day. As described by the author Pala, the events that occurred on this ancient continent form an important part of world history. The chronology will help those studying the political, economic and cultural history as well as other aspects of the region to grasp the subject matter from all perspectives. It presents political history and cultural history together and thus shows in which political conditions certain cultural artifacts arose. It is this rich history that serves as the foundation for the present. Thus, an enhanced understanding of this history aids in carving the most desirable path going forward.

READERSHIP AND DESIRED OUTCOMES

A variety of readers can benefit from this book. First, academic researchers interested in the topic of tourism development in this region of the world can use this book not only to advance their current knowledge, but also as a springboard to generate further research questions investigating tourism potential/challenges. Second, practitioners working in hotel and destination development can enhance their understanding of this region. The cultural distance between developers' headquartered in other regions and the tourism development opportunities in Central Asia can be vast, thus, this book is a convenient resource that can be used to help bridge this distance. Third, students (future hospitality and tourism sector leaders) will benefit from the information contained herein as they prepare for careers in the sector. Reading this book might help reduce students' ethnocentrism and self-reference criterion because discussions of how culture is anchored with history often serves as a frame for better cultural understanding which in turn aids business decision making.

We hope that you will find this book useful and consider it an initial effort to shed light on the topic of tourism development in modern-day Central Asia. Each of the chapters herein perhaps provide more questions than answers which will lead to further development of the literature covering this rich and interesting topic. Consequently, desired outcomes of this project include increasing our current knowledge base as well as spawning further inquiry. Consistent with the view of methodological pluralism, the chapters of this book can spawn both qualitative and quantitative studies designed to examine tourism development along the modern Silk Road.

ACKNOWLEDGMENT

The contribution of this book to our current knowledge was made possible by the contributors who shared their time, talent, and expertise in these pages. As editors, we established only one boundary for the contributors: the chapter had to offer insight into tourism development in the Silk Road region of the Central Asian countries. Being that English is not the native tongue of most of the authors, their contributions required significant effort and polishing. To restate from above, however, you will see their passion and knowledge shine through in their writings. Lastly, we are grateful for the support and encouragement of Apple Academic Press and Series Editor Dr. Mahmood Khan for helping to shape this book to reach its current form. Enjoy!

KEYWORDS

- **Central Asia**
- **Culture and Heritage**
- **Emerging Destinations**
- **Push and Pull Factors**
- **Tourism Development**
- **Tourism Potential**

REFERENCES

Airey, D., Shackley, M. (1997). "Tourism Development in Uzbekistan." *Tourism Management*, 18(4), 198–208.

Akayev, A. (2001). *Kyrgyzstan.* Australia: Asia Pacific Press.

Beheshti, S., Zare, I. (2013). "Distribution Channel Strategies for Attraction of Foreign Tourists." *Middle-East Journal of Scientific Research*, 13(3), 280–287.

Beheshti, S., Yavari, M., Nekounam, J., Ghesary, T., Ahmadi, M. (2013). "Services and Goods Strategic marketing Mixture Model to Develop Tourism in Tajikistan." *Life Science Journal*, 10(5), 627–632.

Baum, T. (2007). "Skills and the Hospitality Sector in a Transition Economy: The Case of Front Office Employment in Kyrgyzstan." *Asia Pacific Journal of Tourism Research*, 12(2), 89–102.

Baum, T., Thompson, K. (2007). "Skills and labor markets in Transition: A Tourism Skills Inventory of Kyrgyzstan, Mongolia, and Uzbekistan." *Asia Pacific Journal of Human Resources*, 45, 2235–2255.

Buyers, L. (2003). *Central Asia in Focus.* New York: Nova Science Publishers, Inc.

Chandana J. (2003) "Sustainable tourism development in Canada: practical challenges." *International Journal of Contemporary Hospitality Management,* 15 (7), 408–412

Culpan, E., Akcaoglu, E. (2003). "An examination of Turkish direct investments in central and eastern Europe and the Commonwealth of Independent States." In S.T. Marinova and M.A. Marinov (Eds.), Foreign Direct Investment in Central and Eastern Europe (pp. 181–197). USA: Ashgate.

Edwards, J. (2010). Tourism in Turkmenistan. In Noel Scott, Jafar Jafari (Ed) *Tourism in the Muslim World (Bridging Tourism Theory and Practice).* Emerald Group Publishing, UK. Pp. 121–139.

Hitchcock, M., King, V., Parnwell, M. (2009). *Tourism in South-east Asia: Challenges and New Directions.* University of Hawaii Press: Hilo, Hawaii. http://dsr.nii.ac.jp/about.html.en: accessed December 27, 2013.

Honko, L. (1996), Oral Tradition, 11(1), 1–17. http://journal.oraltradition.org/files/articles/11i/5_introduction_11_1.pdf. Retrieved December 25, 2013.

Kantarci, K and Develioglu, K. (2013). The Impact of Travel & Tourism Competitiveness factors on Tourism Performance: The Case of Silk Road Countries. International Conference on Economic and Social Studies (ICESoS), Sarajevo, Bosnia and Herzegovina, May 10–11, 2013, pp. 1–5.

Kantarci, K. (2006). "Perceptions of Central Asia travel conditions: Kyrgyzstan, Kazakhstan, Uzbekistan, and Turkmenistan." *Journal of Hospitality and Leisure Marketing,* 15(2), 55–71.

Kantarci, K. (2007a). "Perceptions of foreign investors on the tourism market in Central Asia including Kyrgyzstan, Kazakhstan, Uzbekistan, and Turkmenistan." *Tourism Management,* 28, 820–829.

Kantarci, K. (2007b). "The Image of Central Asia Countries: Kyrgyzstan, Kazakhstan, Uzbekistan, Turkmenistan." *Tourism Analysis,* 12, 307–318.

Kulnazarova, A. (2010). Orta Asya Geçic Ekonomilerinde Turizm Sektörünün Mevcut Durumu Ve Gelisme Olanaklari: Kirgizistan Örnegi. Unpublished Dissertation, Balikesir University, Department of Tourism and Hotel Management, Balikesir, Turkey, pp. 248.

McCabe, S., Minnaert, L., and Diekmann, A. (2011). *Social Tourism in Europe: Theory and Practice.* Channel View Publications: Bristol, UK.

Ono, K., Yamamoto, T., Kamiuchi, Kitamoto, T., Andres, F., Sato, S., Andaroodi, F. (2006). Progress of the Digital Silk Roads Project. R&D Project Report, Progress in Informatics, 1, 93–141.

Palmer, N. (2007). "Ethnic Equality, National Identity and Selected Cultural Representation in Tourism promotion: Kyrgyzstan, Central Asia." *Journal of Sustainable Tourism,* 15(6), 645–662.

Papatheodorou, A. (2001). "Why people travel to different places." *Annals of Tourism Research,* 28(1), 164–179.

Santana, G. (2001). *Tourism in South America.* Routledge, London.

Samimi, C., Kraudzun, T. (2013). Ecosystem Services in the Eastern Pamirs of Tajikistan: can a Price be ascertained? http://www.mtnforum.org/content/ecosystem-services-eastern-pamirs-tajikistan-can-price-be-ascertained. Retrieved on December 20, 2013.

Schatz, E. (2008). "Transnational image making and soft authoritarian Kazakhstan." *Slavic Review,* 50–62.

Schofeild, P., Maccarrone-Eaglen, A. (2011). Nation in Transition: Tourism and national Identity in the Kyrgyz Republic. In *Tourism and national Identities: An International Perspective,* edited by E. Frew and L. White, Routledge, London, U.K. pp. 105–120.

Thompson, K. (2004). "Post-colonial Politics and Resurgent Heritage: The Development of Kyrgyzstan's Heritage Tourism Product." *Current Issues in Tourism,* 7(4–5), 370–382.

Thompson, K., Schofield, P., Foster, N., Bakieva, G. (2006). Kyrgyzstan' s 'Manas' epos Millennium Celebrations: Post-colonial Resurgence of Turkic Culture and the Strategic Marketing of Cultural Tourism. In *Festivals, Tourism and Social Change.* Channel View Publications, Clevedon, pp. 172–190. U.K.

Uysal, M. (1988). The Determinants of Tourism Demand: A Theoretical Perspective. In *The Economic Geography of Tourism,* edited by D. Ioannidis and K. Debbage. Routledge. London., pp. 79–95.

Uysal, M., Kantarci, K. (2007). An Integrated Approach to Image, Investment and Travel Conditions in CA Countries. In *New Perspectives and Values in World Tourism and Tourism Management in the Future,* edited by A. Aktas, M. Kewsgin, E. Cengiz, and E. Yenidip. Detay Yayincilik Ltd, Sti. Ankara—Turkey, 138–146.

Uysal, M., Li, X., Sirakaya-Turk, E. (2008). Push-Pull Dynamics in Travel Decisions. In *the Handbook of Hospitality & Tourism Marketing*, edited by H. Oh and A. Pizam, Published by Elsevier, 412–438.

Werner, C. (2005). "The New Silk Road: Mediators and Tourism Development in Central Asia." *Ethnology,* 42(2), 141–159.

Vogel, D., Davison, R., Gricar, J., Harris, R., Sorentino, M. (2003). eTransformation of the Silk Road: Rejuvenating a Historical Trade Network. 16th eCommerce Conference eTransformation. Bled, Sloveniam June 9–11, 2003.

Zhidkoblinova, K. (2013). "State Policy of Tourism Industry Development in the Republic of Kazakhstan." *World Applied Services Journal*, 23(8), 1079–1084.

Zholdasbekov, A. (2011). "Modern Aspects of The Tourist Industry Development Problem In Kazakhstan." *UTMS Journal of Economics*, 2(2), 207–212.

CHAPTER 2

COMPETITIVENESS OF TOURISM INDUSTRY IN KAZAKHSTAN

AZHAR BAISAKALOVA and VLADIMIR GARKAVENKO

CONTENTS

INTRODUCTION

The tourism industry is one of the most rapidly developing economic sectors worldwide. For many countries it is not only the main source of income but also the engine for the growth of other related industries and emergence of new jobs. According to the UN World Tourism Organization (UNWTO), today every seventh job in the world is in the tourism sector.[1] The cost of its creation is significantly lower than of other economy sectors. In 2011, the number of international tourist arrivals grew by nearly 4% to 983 million. UNWTO helps developing countries to benefit from sustainable tourism. Starting with 2010, profit growth of the world tourism is about 7%, and at present it is shifting to Asian nations.[1]

Kazakhstan has been a member of the UNWTO since 1993. UNWTO General Secretary Francesco Frangialli noted that Kazakhstan has made significant progress in promoting its image as an attractive, tourism-friendly and dynamic Eurasian destination. He also emphasized Kazakhstan's enormous potential for cultural and nature-based tourism due to its geographic attributes, its amazing history and its location on the Silk Road (KITF Catalogue, 2008). "Kazakhstan has very good prospects for tourism from Europe because the country gets better and better known and has much to offer!" (Langedijk, 2012).

The strong President and state, multiethnicity, political stability, religious tolerance and persistent economic growth make Kazakhstan an attractive place to gather world forums on different aspects of modern life. In 2009, Kazakhstan hosted the 18th UNWTO General Assembly that showed the active involvement and contribution of Kazakhstan to the international tourism community. The annual Kazakhstan International Tourism Fair (KITF) was launched in 2001 and nowadays it is the leading travel event for inbound and outbound tourism in Kazakhstan. Since 2008 Annual Economic Forums gather leading international economists, analysts and experts in Astana—the new capital of Kazakhstan. The OECD chairmanship of Kazakhstan in 2010 was concluded with inclusion of the country in the OSCE Summit held in Astana at the end of the year. In 2011, Kazakhstan successfully hosted the 7th Asian Winter Games and was highly appraised by international experts. In 2012, 80 five delegations from 40 countries participated in the 4th Session of leaders of international and traditional religions in Astana. Nominating Astana for hosting EXPO 2017 will further promote the country on the international arena and should result in millions of inbound tourists. The 2017 Winter Universiade will also be held in Kazakhstan, in the former capital of the country—the city of Almaty. As can be seen, there is a strong and ambitious political will to become a tourist "Mecca" in Central Asia.

Economic indicators of the tourism industry of Kazakhstan show a positive trend: today there are about 1200 small and medium size business enterprises in the tourism sector in Kazakhstan. Each year between four to 5 million inbound tourists visit the country (Tourism in Kazakhstan, 2012). Kazakhstan's competitive advantage lays in its exotic culture, the natural environment (ecotourism), increasing business activities (business tourism) and sports and adventure tourism. Most Europeans and Americans value authentic Nomad Kazakh culture and vast virgin territories (Langedijk, 2012). Under the State program of forced industrial and innovative development for 2010–2014, new roads, railways, guesthouses and hotels are being constructed, while older resorts are being renovated. Furthermore, Kazakhstan has new border posts on railways with China and Turkmenistan.[2] Finally, Kazakhstan will form a vital part of the Western Europe-Western China International Transit Corridor when it becomes operational. Mega projects such as the "Great Silk Way" and the "West Europe—West China" transport corridor passing through five regions of Kazakhstan (Almaty, Zhambyl, South-Kazakhstan, Kyzylorda and Aktobe regions) promise to further the development of tourism clusters along these routes (Nazarbayev, 2012). The country's authorities consider tourism to be one of the most important industries for the development of the Kazakh economy.

This study aims to understand the main issues and challenges the tourism industry faces in Kazakhstan today, explore competitiveness of local tourism companies and the dynamics of changes in international competitiveness of the country. The following research questions are addressed:

- What are the main issues and challenges the tourism industry faces in Kazakhstan today?
- What are the determinants of competitiveness of the local tourist firms—one of the key actors in the tourism cluster core?
- How can the competitiveness of the tourism industry be promoted in Kazakhstan? What measures should be undertaken by central and local governments in order to attract more tourists to Kazakhstan?
- What are the dynamics of change in international competitiveness of the tourism industry of Kazakhstan?

- What are the public policies and instruments in the field of tourism development?

THEORETICAL OVERVIEW

BASIC CONCEPTS

Tourism takes on an important role as a strategy for local development by generating jobs, increasing the income of workers and stimulating capital investments through new business opportunities, which result in the establishment of new organizations, including SMEs, among other advantages (Cuncha and Cuncha, 2005). The development of tourism can also bring negative impacts to the economic, social and environmental sustainability of the local community, such as noise, water and visual pollution, invasion of protected areas, etc. The central hypothesis in Cuncha and Cuncha (2005) is that tourism activity should be one of the main sources of sustainable regional development, with positive effects on the creation of jobs, the generation of income, and improvements in the quality of local life. Tourism stimulates other economic activities: entertainment, trade, transport, lodging, crafts, supporting services and amenities and the development of infrastructure: roads, airports, sanitation, energy, etc.

Nations or regions compete in offering the most productive environment for business (Porter, 2005). Competitive strategies for industry players and tourism destinations include four key principles of competitive success: (1) put consumers first; (2) be a leader in quality; (3) develop radical innovations; and (4) strengthen the player's strategic position within the industry's value chain (Leiper, 2004). There are three sources of competitive advantage:

1. differentiation advantage allows the firm to offer customers products and services with greater benefits;
2. cost advantage allows the firm to lower the costs of using its own assets and to reduce its payments to suppliers by reducing the costs of delivering a particular benefit to customers or by reducing supplier costs;
3. transaction advantage allows the firm to discover new combinations of customers and suppliers that create greater value (Porter, 1985; Spulber, 2009).

Porter's (1990) definition of competitiveness is "the ability of entrepreneurs (of a country) to design, produce and market goods and services, the price and nonprice characteristics of which form a more attractive package than that of competitors." Competitiveness is determined by the productivity with which a nation, region, or cluster uses its human, capital, and natural resources. The productivity of "local" industries is of fundamental importance to competitiveness, not just that of trade industries. To improve a location's competitiveness, all elements affecting the context for productivity and innovation in individual firms and clusters have to be looked at: regions need to activate their clusters, address crosscutting weaknesses in their general business environments, create an institutional structure to focus on competitiveness beyond the life cycle of specific administrations, and define an overall understanding of the unique value they intend to provide relative to other locations (Ketels, 2003; Porter, 1998). Clusters are defined as groups of organizations that work in a defined economic sector and a geographically limited environment; this permits the generation of a series of operative synergies that constitute sources from which to extract competitive advantages (Porter, 1998).

Cuncha and Cuncha (2005) developed the concept that a tourism cluster is a group of companies and institutions bound up to a tourism product or group of products. Such companies and institutions are spatially concentrated and have vertical (within the tourism productive chain) and horizontal relationships (involving factor, jurisdiction and information exchange between similar agents dealing with a tourism product offer). They show an intern configuration that generally includes:

- the concentration of tourism service companies: restaurants, accommodations, transport services, crafts, travel agencies etc.;
- sectors providing support to tourism services;
- suitable and low-cost infrastructure (roads, energy, sanitation, health services, etc.);
- companies and institutions that provide specialized qualification, information and financial capital;
- intern agents organized into class associations; and
- government agencies and other regulating bodies that impact tourism agglomerations.
- Interactions within tourism clusters can bring benefits such as (Cuncha and Cuncha, 2005):

- entrepreneurial cooperation, work productive specialization, collective infrastructure, service specialization;
- the increased ability to negotiate collectively with suppliers of inputs and components;
- the development of new models, production processes and organizations;
- the exchange of technical and market information; and
- consortiums for buying and selling goods and services, as well as joint marketing campaigns.

Interaction and synergy arising from joint actions lead to competitive advantages over the isolated actions of companies (Nordin, 2003).

PORTER'S CLUSTER THEORY

In 2004, the President of the Republic of Kazakhstan in his Address to the People of Kazakhstan emphasized the importance of defining priorities for diversification of the Kazakh economy and further development of the country based on the analysis of the country's competitive advantages and identifying the most promising subregional and regional clusters. Although so far the efforts to create clusters in the countries of the former Soviet Union were not successful,[3] the decision was made to implement a pilot project on organizing a tourism cluster in Almaty city and Almaty oblast, which was prepared by representatives of the Center for Marketing and Analytical Research, the tourist community, and leading tour operators in cooperation with experts from the American consulting company "J.E. Austin Associates Inc." headed by an outstanding economist, Michael Porter. They recommended diversifying Kazakhstan's economy by focusing on the development of seven clusters with tourism being one of them.

National competitiveness was put on the agenda by the President of Kazakhstan in 2005. In the same year, the World Economic Forum included the country in the Global Competitiveness Report. In 2011–2012, Kazakhstan's rank in the WEF rating list was 72 (out of 142 countries),[6] while in 2005–2006 it was 61 (out of 117 countries). In 2005, an assessment of the Kazakhstan business environment using Porter's diamond model was presented at the conference "Kazakhstan competitiveness and cluster development" (Porter, 2005), where the role of SMEs in cluster development was emphasized. Porter (1990) introduced his "diamond" model as an analytical tool to assess the general quality of the business environment at the national, regional, or local level. The diamond includes four elements: factor conditions (e.g., physical infrastructure, skills, etc.), demand conditions (e.g., sophistication of local customers, product and consumer regulation), the context for strategy and rivalry (e.g. taxation structure, competition laws, and the strategies of competing local companies), and the presence of related and supporting industries (e.g., the breadth and depth of the cluster).

Analyzing the business environment in Kazakhstan, Porter (2005) emphasized positive aspects such as good basic workforce skills, low electricity costs, modern airport infrastructure and a large pool of investment capital. Negative aspects included weaknesses in the physical infrastructure, shortage of managerial skills and entrepreneurship, lack of advanced technical skills, significant barriers for smaller companies to obtain credit.

The tourist cluster structure based on the Porter's recommendations for Kazakhstan defines the core (tourist operators, travel agencies, accommodation providers, etc.), key partners (food, service, trade, entertainment, communications, etc.), regulatory bodies, consumers, auxiliary partners, financial and legal service, and resources (objects of active and passive leisure) (Mukanov, 2012). Kaygorodtsev (2009) identified three groups of tourism cluster participants. The first group includes tourist and travel agencies and organizations providing basic tourist services such as accommodation, catering and transportation. The second group includes control and administrative authorities (border police, customs, quarantine services, police, banks); sports facilities (stadiums, sports grounds, swimming pools, tennis courts); businesses and cultural institutions (museums, theaters, cinemas, exhibitions, galleries, dance clubs); tour operators, guides and instructors, producers of souvenirs; the media; public utilities and public services (baths, laundries, dry cleaners, photo studios); trading enterprises (shops, markets, rental); communications companies, although their participation is minimized with the advent of wireless remote communication. The third group of cluster participants involves industrial and agricultural enterprises producing food, clothing, and other consumer goods.

Porter (2005) argues that the public and private sectors should play different but interrelated roles in creating a productive economy. Government policy has an impact on all elements of the cluster-specific diamond. It often has responsibilities for large parts of the infrastructure, it sets key rules and regulations affecting competition and demand, and it affects the cluster presence through, for example, recruiting companies from other locations to make investments (Porter, 1998). The government is an important factor in shaping the business environment as well as the companies, universities, and many other institutions. The government's role in cluster initiatives is of facilitator and participant. The most successful cluster initiatives are public-private partnerships. Effective cluster-based development needs to be based on an assessment of the most critical barriers that hold back productivity improvements and innovation (Porter, 2005).

METHODOLOGY

HYPOTHESES

Based on a review of the literature on the research topic the following hypotheses are formulated and tested:
1. There is a positive relationship between competitiveness of the firm, its age, the propensity of the firm to innovate and the number of cluster actors in its network.
2. There is a positive trend in the international competitiveness of Kazakhstan.

RESEARCH METHODS

The research adopts a mixed methods approach based on a combination of qualitative and quantitative approaches. Data sources include international and national tourism statistical data, official state documents, mass media publications and Internet. Empirical data on the competitiveness of tourism companies were collected through a survey of tourist and travel organizations located in the city of Almaty. The city of Almaty—the former capital of the Republic of Kazakhstan—is the biggest city in the country and has a relatively good infrastructure and attractions meeting different tastes and purposes of tourists. Almaty is the commercial center of Kazakhstan, providing about 20% of Kazakhstan's GDP. The city has a relatively good infrastructure and attractions meeting different tastes and purposes of tourists as well as flight connections to most major tourism destinations. About 50% of all travel and tourism organizations are located in Almaty and they serve about 50% of all tourists in Kazakhstan (Tourism in Kazakhstan, 2012). According to the National Program on the Tourism Development in the Republic of Kazakhstan in the period of 2007–2011 a pilot tourism cluster was also planned to be developed in the city of Almaty and Almaty oblast (National Program, 2006).

Questionnaires for this trend study were distributed among tourist firms in 2009 and 2011. There are 23 questions in the questionnaire. The collected data contain information on the respondents' status, age and gender, firm employment size and age, firm competitors, cooperation with support and related industries, firm development prospects, educational level of employees by gender, professional needs of the firm, perception of firm prospects, annual revenue, annual output, propensity to innovate, number of inbound and domestic tourists by tourism purpose, information on tour operators, barriers to business growth and development, relationship with public inspection bodies and participation of the firm in activities within the framework of corporate social responsibility (CSR). The surveyed companies were selected randomly from the Almaty City Business Directory Online.[5] The sample size was 50 in 2009 and 48 in 2011. However, sample sizes differ for different research questions depending on the missing data.

The competitiveness of the travel and tourism industry and its relationship with basic indicators such as business environment, infrastructure, laws and regulations, and resources is analyzed using statistical data provided in the Travel & Tourism Competitiveness Reports of the World Economic Forum (e.g., Bălan, Balaure and Veghes, 2009). Papp and Raffay (2011) suggested distinguishing between competitive position and competitive potential of the country. According to the authors, the competitive position refers to the competitive performance, which can be measured by statistical data; the competitive potential relates to what the destination could achieve, with the appropriate development of the facilities and management activities. The dynamics of changes in international competitiveness of Kazakhstan, its competitive position and competitive potential are examined based on the statistical data in the Travel & Tourism Competitiveness Reports of the World Economic Forum (2007–2009 and 2011).

Data analysis is conducted with SPSS (version 19) for descriptive statistics, factor analysis and correlations.

RESULTS OF THE LONGITUDINAL STUDY

SURVEY OF LOCAL TOURIST COMPANIES IN 2009 AND 2011

The results of the survey including firm age, gender composition of the tourist firms' employees, their education and language skills are shown in Table 1.

TABLE 1   Descriptive Statistics of Survey Results

Variable	2009	2011
Mean age of the surveyed tourist firms (years)	5.4	6.3
Proportion of firms with age from one to two years (%)	18	19
Proportion of firms with age from three to seven years (%)	60	38
Proportion of firms with age of more than seven years (%)	22	43
Medians for the number of female employees in the firm	5	4
Medians for the number of male employees in the firm	2	1
The percentage of female employees in tourist firms (%)	67	84
The percentage of male employees in tourist firms (%)	30	16
Women with higher education (%)	90	82
Men with higher education (%)	85	85
Women with higher education in tourism (%)	45	30
Men with higher education in tourism (%)	32	13
The proportions of women with English language knowledge (%)	47	38
The proportions of women with Kazakh language knowledge (%)	54	49
The proportions of men with English language knowledge (%)	40	41
The proportions of men with Kazakh language knowledge (%)	42	67

Table 1 shows that from 2009 to 2011 the mean age of the surveyed tourist firms increased by one year. The percentage of firms from three to seven years of age decreased by nearly 20%, while the percentage of firms more than seven years of age increased by the same value. The percentage of male employees in tourist firms decreased. Women's qualifications in terms of education and language skills also worsened.

The data on respondents' status presented in Table 2 confirms the fact that the firms' owners and managers are reluctant to complete questionnaires as compared with rank-and-file employees.

TABLE 2   Distribution of Respondents by Status

Respondent's status (%)	2009	2011
Owner	7.7	8
Director	7.7	22
Manager	75	64
Other	9.6	2
Non-response	—	4

The needs assessment of the labor market revealed that although the former Soviet Union population was famous for its good educational level, today knowledge in marketing, tourism, public relations, human resource management, IT, marketing, business management, advertising, psychology, restaurants and hospitality, and foreign languages are in high demand to adapt to the market economy environment. In particular, in the 2009 survey, 46 percent of firms expressed the need for staff training, 16 percent—qualification improvement, 34 percent—retraining, and 12 percent needed consulting services basically in the listed fields. Most respondents were optimistic about the future prospects of their firms: 80 percent expected firm growth, 18 percent expected no change, and 2 percent were going to close or to merge with another enterprise. Among external barriers, competitors and inspection by numerous state inspection agencies were examined. Only about 7 percent of firms mentioned large tourist enterprises as the most serious competitors, 47 percent—medium size firms, and 46 percent—small firms. It should be noted that most of the tourist firms are small, with less than ten employees.

The respondents' answers to the open-ended question "What measures should be undertaken by central and local governments in order to attract more tourists to Kazakhstan?" demonstrate concerns about the need in improving tourism infrastructure, roads, and service quality—these problems are addressed to local governments. From the central government the respondents expect more effective activities directed at advertising the country's tourism potential around the world. Among measures to be undertaken by the "Other," "Better service quality" was also prioritized.

In order to attract more tourists to Almaty city and its surroundings the respondents emphasized the need in maintenance of cleanness in the city, towns and their streets, improving service quality by providing value for money, improving infrastructure, repairing and building new roads, using alternative transportation, expanding parking zones, improving access to the main tourist objects/roads and building new or refurbishing existing hotels which are close to the tourist objects. The major issues for tourists' complaints are based on low service quality (including hotels and transportation) and unjustified high hotel prices. It is interesting to note that based on the survey results the percentage of firms participating in CSR related activities increased from 48% in 2009 to 52% in 2011.

Comparison of respondents' answers in 2009 and 2011 reflects the changes in the tourism industry environment, firm's managers and tourists' perceptions. Globalization leads to the emergence of new challenges and requires higher standards of service in the tourism industry: tourists are becoming more demanding today.

DYNAMICS OF CHANGES IN INTERNATIONAL COMPETITIVENESS

In order to mitigate the impact of changes in the methodology between 2007 and 2008 and in the number of countries included in Travel & Tourism Competitiveness Reports of the World Economic Forum, the authors examined the trend in the relative position using percentile ranks instead of actual ranks (Travel & Tourism Competitiveness Reports, 2007, 2008, 2009 and 2011). The results of the analysis are presented in Table 3 below.

TABLE 3 The Travel & Tourism Competitiveness Index: Kazakhstan

						SUBINDEXES			
		OVERALL INDEX		T&T regulatory framework		T&T business environment and infrastructure		T&T human, cultural and natural resources	
Country coverage	Year	Rank	Percen-tile rank	Rank	Percentile rank	Rank	Percentile rank	Rank	Percentile rank
124	2007	82	66	81	65	81	65	90	73

TABLE 3   *(Continued)*

		OVERALL INDEX		T&T regulatory framework		T&T business environment and infrastructure		T&T human, cultural and natural resources	
Country coverage	Year	Rank	Percentile rank	Rank	Percentile rank	Rank	Percentile rank	Rank	Percentile rank
130	2008	91	70	61	47	96	74	112	86
133	2009	92	69	60	45	96	72	121	91
139	2011	93	67	65	47	88	63	123	88
Trend in standing relative to the year 2007		Approx. the same (−1) relative standing		Positive (+18)		Positive (+2)		Negative (−15)	

Source: The Travel & Tourism Competitiveness Reports 2007, 2008, 2009 and 2011. World Economic Forum.
Authors' calculation and interpretation of percentiles and their trends.

Table 3 shows that from 2007 to 2011 the calculated percentile rank of the Overall Travel & Tourism (T&T) Competitiveness Index of Kazakhstan did not significantly change while percentile ranks of the T&T regulatory framework and the T&T business environment and infrastructure subindices went up, and the T&T human, cultural and natural resources subindex rank decreased. In order to clarify what the strengths and weaknesses of the travel and tourism industry in Kazakhstan are, the sub indexes' pillars are further considered in detail.

The first pillar rank out of the five pillars of the T&T regulatory framework sub index of the Travel & Tourism Competitiveness Index—Policy rules and regulations—can be improved as a result of enforcement of well-protected property rights, rules attracting FDI in the tourism sector, and simplified visa requirements. The second pillar—Environmental sustainability—lacks strong and well enforced environmental legislation with a specific focus on developing the tourism sector in a sustainable way, decreasing pollution and protecting the environment. The third pillar rank—Safety and security—can be improved by increasing the effectiveness and reliability of police services in providing protection from crime and violence and reducing the number of road traffic accidents. The international rank of the fourth pillar is rather competitive (the 9th) due to the traditionally good quality of health and hygiene in the country. The rank and score of the fifth pillar—Prioritization of Travel & Tourism—increased due to increased government expenditure on the sector, hosting and participating in key international tourism fairs (the 50th rank), and increased comprehensiveness of the annual T&T data (the 28th rank).

The results of the analysis of the T&T business environment and infrastructure sub index of the Travel & Tourism Competitiveness Index indicate positive trends for the percentile ranks of three pillars. There is great potential for further progress by improving a) the quality of air transport infrastructure and expanding the international air transport network (the 6th pillar: Air transport infrastructure), b) the quality of port infrastructure and the quality and density of roads (the 7th pillar: Ground transport infrastructure), c) the competitiveness of hotel prices—providing value for money (the 10th pillar: Price competitiveness in the T&T industry).

The results of the analysis of the T&T human, cultural and natural resources sub index of the Travel & Tourism Competitiveness Index do not reveal improvements for the ranks of its four pillars. There is great space for the development of T&T human resources (the 11th pillar) and the affinity of travel and tourism (the 12th pillar). A significant focus should be placed on the natural resources (the 13th pillar): the protected areas (ranked 114th) and the quality of the natural environment (ranked 126th). Cultural resources (the 14th pillar) also have low T&T competitiveness in terms of the number of World Heritage cultural sites, creative industries, international fairs and exhibitions held in the country, and sports stadiums capacities.

RESULTS OF THE LONGITUDINAL STUDY: HYPOTHESIS TESTING

Hypothesis 1: There is a positive relationship between competitiveness of the firm, its age, the propensity of the firm to innovate and the number of cluster actors in its network. To define the underlying determinants of firm competitiveness factor analysis was used. The eigenvalue-greater-than-one criterion was used in identifying four factors. The principal component solution using the Varimax with Kaiser Normalization rotation method resulted in the rotated component matrix (rotation converged in five iterations) where the first three factors have high loadings (greater than 0.7) on the number of employees, their education and language skills. The fourth factor has high loadings on the firm age (0.653), the total number of the tourism cluster participants the tourist company cooperates with (0.774), and the total number of innovations introduced (0.686). The fourth factor can be interpreted as competitiveness of the firm as the variables associated with this concept have the highest loadings. It is positively correlated with these three variables with correlation coefficients of 0.653, 0.774 and 0.686, respectively. Therefore, Hypothesis 1 is not rejected.

The innovativeness of tourism firms basically relates with the introduction and use of modern information technology in their work, and multiple interactions among the tourism cluster actors result in competitive advantages for the firms (Porter 1998; Camprubi, Guia, and Comas 2008), supporting Porter's (1998) theory that in this case "1 + 1 ≠ 2." Nordin (2003) also claims that interaction and synergy arising from joint actions lead to competitive advantages over the isolated actions of companies.

Hypothesis 2. There is a positive trend regarding the international competitiveness of Kazakhstan.

As it is shown above, positive trends are observed for seven pillars out of 14. Percentile ranks are above 50 for two pillars: health and hygiene (the 6th) and ICT infrastructure (the 44th). Table 4 shows the change in Kazakhstan's position in 2008, 2009 and 2011 relative to its position in the year of 2007. As can be seen, the sum of positive changes is greater than the sum of negative changes for 14 pillars of the Overall Competitiveness Index for all years from 2008 to 2011.

TABLE 4 The Trend in International Competitiveness of Kazakhstan in 2007–2011

	SUBINDEXES							
	OVERALL INDEX		**T&T regulatory framework**		**T&T business environment and infrastructure**		**T&T human, cultural and natural resources**	
Year	Percentile rank	Change relative to 2011	Percentile rank	Change relative to 2011	Percentile rank	Change relative to 2011	Percentile rank	Change relative to 2011	Overall change relative to 2011
2007	66	-1	65	19	65	2	73	–16	5
2008	70	3	47	0	74	11	86	–2	8
2009	69	2	45	–2	72	9	91	2	10
2011	67	0	47	0	63	0	88	0	0

Source: The Travel & Tourism Competitiveness Reports 2007, 2008, 2009 and 2011. World Economic Forum.
Authors' calculation and interpretation of percentiles and their trends.

We can conclude that there is a positive trend in the international competitiveness of Kazakhstan. Hence, Hypothesis 2 is not rejected.

OVERVIEW OF THE MAIN FINDINGS

COMPETITIVENESS OF LOCAL TOURIST COMPANIES

Most of the travel and tourism organizations in Kazakhstan are small firms. The contribution of small and medium-size enterprises (SMEs) to achieving and sustaining growth and performance in national economies is increasingly recognized. SMEs play a critical role in the development of employment, innovation, and social and economic growth (Baisakalova, 2003). "In order to create a viable and resilient economy, we consistently implemented difficult structural reforms, built up our export potential and began to diversify by creating significant incentives for the development of the noncommodity sector of the economy, and small and medium business."[7] In 2011, Travel & Tourism was expected to directly support 99,048,000 jobs or 3.4% of total employment in Kazakhstan (Travel & Tourism Economic Impact: Kazakhstan, 2011).

The longitudinal study shows that most of the tourism firms are female-led small firms with a good workforce. In spite of the high educational level of the labor force small enterprises are in great need of training, retraining, and consulting services in marketing, tourism, public relations, human resource management, IT, marketing, business management, advertising, psychology, restaurants and hospitality, and foreign languages. Today, among the main determinants of new firm survival, relevant expert consultancy, easy access to information, managerial competence, and sufficient marketing knowledge should be provided.

The respondents showed increases in profit and delivery of tourist products from 2006 through 2008. In 2009, these indicators as well as the total number of tourists decreased. It is interesting to note that the total number of tourists decrease is explained by the reduction in the number of outbound tourists. However, since 2006, the numbers of inbound and domestic tourists have steadily increased by about 1.5 and 6 times, respectively. In 2009, the number of tourists fell down three times in cultural and cognitive tourism, in business tourism—two times, in ecotourism—by 20 percent, and in health tourism it remained at about the same level as in 2008. In 2009, financial indicators of the firms worsened due to the decreased number of outbound tourists. Meanwhile the financial crises of 2007–2010 significantly activated domestic tourism. Inbound tourism slightly increased over the last four years. One of the reasons is that Almaty is a host for many international events. Most of the surveyed firms are optimistic about their future as the Government takes efforts to improve the business environment and the physical structure, and to further develop the tourism cluster.

The sample data shows that the competitiveness of local firms is positively correlated with their age, innovativeness, and network size. The higher extent of innovativeness is inherent to firms, which interact with many other companies in the related and supporting industries. The higher the propensity of the firm to innovate, the more the number of actors they cooperate with and the higher is the likelihood of its survival and growth. Most of the respondents are optimistic about the future prospects of their firms expecting a firm's growth. This reflects the fact that the external environment in the country is improving. The problems are caused by lack of credits for small and medium enterprises, lack of investments in reconstruction and building of public infrastructure, and complicated visa issue procedures. In future research it is interesting to explore the relationship between corporate social responsibility (CSR) and competitiveness.

INTERNATIONAL COMPETITIVENESS OF THE KAZAKHSTANI TOURISM INDUSTRY

The country's authorities consider tourism to be one of the most important industries for the development of the Kazakh economy. Tourism in the country remains underdeveloped, and retains significant future growth potential. Authorities in the country have looked to promote tourism in a variety of ways, such as through passing legislation and committing to development programs. Under the State Program of Forced Industrial and Innovative Development for 2010–2014, new roads, railways and guesthouses are being constructed.

Porter (2005) emphasized good basic workforce skills, low electricity costs, modern airport infrastructure and the large pool of investment capital as competitive advantages of Kazakhstan; weaknesses in the physical infrastructure, shortage of managerial skills and entrepreneurship, lack of advanced technical skills, and significant barriers for smaller companies to obtain credit were identified as competitive disadvantages of the country. Since 2005 utility tariffs significantly went up, competitiveness was lost in this field; there is also little progress in coping with competitive disadvantages today. However, positive results can be observed in the communication infrastructure and in the higher education system where new majors required for the tourism cluster activating are opened.

Among demand conditions for the competitive tourism cluster development improved regulation on IT and environmental quality as well as better standards-setting and certification organization should be mentioned. The context for firm strategy and rivalry has not changed significantly and the problem of the establishment of favorable business environment is still on the public agenda. Related and supporting industries in the tourism cluster are developing due to numerous international events being held in Almaty.

According to Bălan, Balaure and Veghes (2009) the overall competitiveness of the world's 25 top tourist destinations is strongly associated with the business environment and infrastructure ($r = 0.97$), the specific regulatory framework ($r = 0.86$), and the human, cultural and natural resources ($r = 0.83$). They also found that associations between the specific pillars and the overall competitiveness of the regulatory framework appear to be strong in the cases of safety and security ($r = 0.83$), environmental sustainability ($r = 0.82$), health and hygiene ($r = 0.78$), and policy rules and regulations ($r = 0.73$). The first two indicators—safety and security and environmental sustainability—deserve serious attention as they are below the 100th rank for Kazakhstan. Simplifying visa requirements and procedures is also a daunting issue to resolve. In order to clarify what are the strengths and weaknesses of the travel and tourism industry in Kazakhstan the pillars of the sub indexes are further considered in detail.

The first pillar rank out of the five pillars of the T&T regulatory framework sub index of the Travel & Tourism Competitiveness Index—Policy rules and regulations—can be improved as a result of enforcement of well-protected property rights, rules attracting FDI in the tourism sector, and simplified visa requirements. The second pillar—Environmental sustainability—lacks strong and well enforced environmental legislation with a specific focus on developing the tourism sector in a sustainable way, decreasing pollution, and protecting the environment. The third pillar rank—Safety and security—can be improved by increasing effectiveness and

reliability of police services in providing protection from crime and violence, and reducing the number of traffic accidents. The rank of the fourth
pillar is rather competitive (the 9th) due to the traditionally good quality of
health and hygiene in the country. The rank and score of the fifth pillar—
Prioritization of Travel & Tourism—went up by eight points and 0.47,
respectively, due to increased government expenditure on the sector and
hosting and participating in key international tourism fairs (the 50th rank),
and increased comprehensiveness of annual T&T data (the 28th rank).

The results of the analysis of the T&T business environment and infrastructure sub index of the Travel & Tourism Competitiveness Index indicate positive trends for the percentile ranks of three pillars. There is great
potential for further progress by improving a) the quality of air transport
infrastructure and expanding the international air transport network (the
6th pillar: Air transport infrastructure), b) the quality of port infrastructure
and the quality and density of roads (the 7th pillar: Ground transport infrastructure), c) the competitiveness of hotel prices—providing value for
money (the 10th pillar: Price competitiveness in the T&T industry).

The results of the analysis of the T&T human, cultural and natural
resources sub index of the Travel & Tourism Competitiveness Index do
not reveal improvements for the ranks of its four pillars. There is great
space for the development of T&T human resources (the 11th pillar) and
the affinity of travel and tourism (the 12th pillar). Significant focus should
be placed on the natural resources (the 13th pillar): the protected areas
(ranked 114th) and the quality of the natural environment (ranked 126th).
Cultural resources (the 14th pillar) also have low T&T competitiveness in
terms of the number of World Heritage cultural sites, creative industries,
international fairs and exhibitions held in the country, and sports stadiums
capacities.

The focus should be first of all on the improvement of affinity for
T&T (the 91st percentile rank), development of the T&T human, cultural
and natural resources (the 88th percentile rank), and environmental sustainability (the 93rd percentile rank). An analysis of indicators of pillars
(T&T Competitiveness Report, 2011) shows that significant focus should
be placed on the natural resources (the 13th pillar): the protected areas
(ranked 114th) and the quality of the natural environment (ranked 126th);
cultural resources (the 14th pillar) also have a low T&T competitiveness
score (1.5 out of 7) in terms of the number of World Heritage cultural sites,
creative industries, international fairs and exhibitions held in the country,

and sports stadiums capacities. To improve the overall competitiveness of the tourism industry ground transportation infrastructure, tourism infrastructure and hotel price competitiveness should be of main concern as they represent the pillars pulling down the overall competitiveness of the business environment and infrastructure.

Although the current rank of Kazakhstan in the WEF Travel & Tourism Competitiveness ranking list is only 93rd corresponding to the 67th percentile (Table 3), the country has great potential to be among the top 50 competitive countries in the tourism industry due to the efforts undertaken by state decision makers. There is a positive trend in international competitiveness of Kazakhstan as demonstrated above in Table 4.

THE MAIN ISSUES AND CHALLENGES OF TOURISM INDUSTRY IN KAZAKHSTAN

Kazakh authorities take all efforts to become a center of tourism in the Central Asian region by passing tourism legislation and development programs in order to realize the country's tourism potential and to promote a competitive tourism cluster. The pressing challenge for the country is to create a modern tourism infrastructure that meets international standards. The public-private partnership envisages *creating incentives for private investments in the development of the tourism cluster* as well as using state funds[8]. Within the framework of the public-private partnership 16 thousand kilometers of roads will be built and repaired by the year of 2020.[9] To attract foreign business investors in the tourism industry for the reconstruction of existing and creation of new tourist facilities and accommodation, visa procedures have been simplified for citizens of economically developed and politically stable countries—for 34 countries it will not be required; in addition, one window service will be provided for them (Nazarbayev, 2012).

To improve the level of training of human resources in the tourism industry, the Government of Kazakhstan established scholarships within the "Bolashak" Program. There are also positive changes in promoting the tourism image of the country throughout the world. In 2010, Kazakhstan opened an official online tourism portal providing information about the country as a tourist destination and giving opportunity to potential visitors to book hotels, flights, and tours. International mass media and different international tourism events are also used for advertising the tourism potential of the country.

An analysis of the current status of the tourism industry in Kazakhstan (e.g., Kaygorodtsev, 2009; Langedyjk, 2012; Macerinskiene and Sakhanova, 2011; Mukanov, 2012; Manaseryan, 2012; Naizabekov and Kunchayev, 2009) and the results of the present study reveal that tourism in the country remains underdeveloped in spite of favorable conditions for competitive cluster development and significant future growth potential. According to Kaygorodtsev (2009), this situation results from administrative barriers (lengthy procedures for obtaining permits in the border zone, a long registration procedure for foreign tourists); ineffective promotion of tourist product into the world market; lack of financing; lack of tourism infrastructure that meets international requirements, including poor road condition and lack of communication means; lack of coordination of intra and interdepartmental activities on the development of tourism infrastructure; lack of skilled professionals, including guides who speak foreign languages. Langedyjk (2012) also indicates that there is a shortage in guides with excellent knowledge and with foreign language skills, lack of good accommodations, in particular outside the main cities, and visa problems. He suggests legislating one Central Asian Tourism Visa in order to attract more tourists and investors to Kazakhstan. Low quality of tourist services and infrastructure, and inadequately high prices in hotels also do not lead to increase in inbound and local tourists, the latter often preferring foreign countries to have value for money instead of contributing to domestic tourism growth.

CONCLUSION

Kazakhstan can significantly improve its competitiveness by diversifying its economy, in particular, by developing the competitive tourism clusters in different regions of its vast territory with rich tourism potential. Although the country's rank is rather low today there is a persistent positive trend in the dynamics of changes in the international competitiveness of Kazakhstan since 2007 (Table 4). It is expected that the implementation of the State Program of Forced Industrial and Innovative Development for 2010–2014 will contribute to the development of Kazakhstan's tourist facilities in accordance with international standards found in the western countries. Authorities in the country intend to promote tourism through passing tourism legislation and committing to development programs. Public policies are directed at improving the business environment, marketing strategy, public-private partnership, promoting tourism cluster initiatives and effective implementation of already approved programs and policies in the tourism industry.

The surveyed tourism firms provided valuable information on the issues and challenges that the tourism industry faces in Kazakhstan today, such as poor tourism infrastructure, roads, and service quality, lack of relevant knowledge in tourism related fields, lack of advertising the tourism potential within the country and around the world. They believe that eliminating barriers such as visa obtaining procedures, and providing incentives for innovations and knowledge development can also contribute to the growth of inbound and domestic tourism, which are prioritized in Kazakhstan. The study also supports Porter's theory that innovativeness and interactions among the tourism cluster actors result in competitive advantages for the firms.

In future study it is interesting to explore the relationship between CSR and competitiveness of the firm. Jespersen, Kothuis and Tran (2012) argue that there is little knowledge on the meaning of CSR for small and medium size enterprises (SMEs) in developing countries: the data on CSR and competitiveness for SMEs are scarce providing only anecdotal evidence of the relationship between CSR and competitiveness, e.g., Singh, Garg and Deshmukh (2008) and Luken and Stares (2005) found a positive relationship between CSR and competitiveness. Our study also demonstrates correlation between the percentage of firms involved in CSR activities (from 48% in 2009 to 52% in 2011) and international competitiveness of the country.

In the context of the reviewed literature and the results of the present study the following recommendations for further development of the competitive tourism industry can be made:

- improve tourism infrastructure (hotels, resorts, roads, etc.);
- use incentives to foster international standards of management and service quality;
- improve quality of specialized education by creating new syllabi with an emphasis on the needs of the tourism industry; arrange re/ training for tourism staff;
- encourage collaboration among tourism cluster participants towards achievement of mutually beneficial goals and objectives in effective and efficient ways;

- increase the investment attractiveness of the tourism industry; promote the image of the country at the regional and international level; create professionally designed brochures, catalogs, maps and other tourism materials for domestic and international tourists; create informative three-lingual tourism organizations' websites with efficient "highways" via links that allow the users to obtain all the information they need; and
- provide financial support to entrepreneurs to develop tourism clusters not only in big cities but also in rural areas, which have great tourism potential, especially in authentic cultural-cognitive tourism.

NOTES

[1] http://www.unwto.org/facts/menu.html accessed on November 2, 2012.
[2] http://www.euromonitor.com/travel-and-tourism-in-kazakhstan/report accessed on October 28, 2012.
[3] http://www.kursiv.kz/ accessed on November 22, 2012.
[4] http://www.weforum.org/ttcr08browse/index.html accessed on March 9, 2009.
[5] Almaty City Business Directory Online. Accessed on July 29, 2011 at http://www.infokz.com/base/eng/index.php?type=firms&sscd=256&p=13.
[6] http://reports.weforum.org/global-competitiveness-2011–2012/
[7] Kazakhstan President Nursultan Nazarbayev's State of the Nation Address, March 6, 2009, available at www.akorda.kz/en
[8] http://www.inform.kz/eng/article/2497736 accessed 26 September 2012
[9] Kazakhstanskaya Pravda (2012), May 23 (national newspaper)

KEYWORDS

- **Cluster theory**
- **Competitiveness**
- **Kazakhstan**
- **Longitudinal study**
- **Tourism**

REFERENCES

Almaty City Business Directory Online. Accessed on July 29, 2011 at http://www.infokz.com/base/eng/index.php?type=firms&sscd=256&p=13

Baisakalova, A. B. (2003). The significance of small firms for the Kazakhstan economy. *The Central Asian Journal*, 3, 37–47.

Bălan, D., Balaure, V., Veghes, C. (2009). Travel & Tourism Competitiveness of the World's Top Tourism Destinations: an Exploratory Assessment. *Annales Universitatis Apulensis Series Oeconomica*, 11(2), 979–987.

Camprubi, R., Guia, J., J. Comas. (2008). Destination Networks and Induced Tourism Image. *Tourism Review*, 63 (2), 47–58.

Chupakhina, N. (2007). *Strategic Importance of the management System Improvement.* Accessed at http://referent.mubint.ru/8/6357 on June 2, 2012.

Cuncha, K.S., Cuncha, J. C. (2005). Tourism cluster competitiveness and sustainability: proposal for a systemic model to measure the impact of tourism on local development. *Brazilian Administration Review,*.2 (2), 47–62. PR, Brazil.

Jespersen, S., Kothuis B., Tran, A. N. (2012). Corporate Social Responsibility and Competitiveness for SMEs in Developing Countries: South Africa and Vietnam, *Focales 16*, France: Montligeon.

Ketels, Ch. H. M. (2003). The development of the cluster concept—present experiences and further developments. Prepared for *NRW conference on clusters*, Duisburg, Germany, 5 Dec 2003. Harvard Business School, USA.

Kaygorodtsev, A. A. (2009). Prospects of cluster tourisms development in East Kazakhstan. Accessed at http://g-global.aef.kz/en/economy/public/detail.php?id=46960 on November 24, 2012.

KITF 2008 Catalogue (2008). Almaty, Kazakhstan.

Langedijk, A. (2012). A favorable law and business environment in Kazakhstan to attract tourists from Europe. Kazakhstan Reizen. The Netherlands. Accessed at http://www.aef.kz/upload/iblock/961/Ardjan%20Langedijk.pdf on October 26, 2012.

Leiper, N. (2004). *Tourism Management (3rd Ed.)*, Malaysia: Pearson Education Australia.

Luken, R., Stares, R. (2005. "Small Business Responsibility in Developing Countries: A Threat or an Opportunity?" *Business Strategy and the Environment*, 14, 38–53.

Macerinskiene, I., Sakhanova, G. (2011). National Economy Competitiveness of Kazakhstan Republic. *Inzinerine Ekonomika-Engineering Economics,* 22(3), 292–299.

Manaseryan, T. (2012). *Kazakhstanskaya Pravda* (national newspaper). March 29.

Mukanov, A. (2012). Features of the tourist cluster development in the Republic of Kazakhstan. *European Science and Technology*, 1, 171–176.

Naizabekov, G., Zh. Kunchayev. (2009). On the cluster development concept. *Transit Economy*, 124–126. Almaty, Kazakhstan.

Nazarbayev, N. A. (2005). Address to People of Kazakhstan. Available at http://www.akorda.kz

Nazarbayev, N. A. (2012). Concluding Speech at the 25th session of the Council of Foreign Investors. Accessed at http://www.akorda.kz/ru/page/zaklyuchitelnoe-slovo-prezidenta- respubliki-kazakhstan-nazarbaeva-n-a-na-25-m-zasedanii-soveta-inostrannykh-in on December 2, 2012.

Nordin, S. (2003). Tourism Clustering and Innovation. ETOUR. *European Tourism Research Institute*. Ostersund, Sweden.

Papp, Z., Á. Raffay. (2011). Factors Influencing the Tourism Competitiveness of Former Socialist Countries. *Journal of Studies and Research in Human Geography*, 5.2, 21–30. Accessed at www.humangeographies.org.ro on December 23, 2012.

Porter, M.E. (1985). *Competitive Advantage: Creating and Sustaining Superior Performance*. New York: Free Press.

Porter, M. E. (1990). *The Competitive Advantage of Nations*, New York: The Free Press.

Porter, M. E. (1998a). Clusters and the New Economics of Competition, *Harvard Business Review*, 76(6), 1998.

Porter, M. E. (1998b). *On Competition*. Boston: Harvard Business School Press.

Porter, M. E. (2005). Kazakhstan's Competitiveness: Roadmap Towards a Diversified Economy. Presentation in Almaty, Kazakhstan, 26 January 2005.

RK Law #211. (2001). *On tourist activities in the Republic of Kazakhstan* (with amendments as of April 1, 2007).

Singh, R. K., Garg, S. K., Deshmukh, S. G. (2008). Strategy Development by SMEs for Competitiveness: A Review, *Benchmarking: An International Journal*, 15(5), 525–547.

Spulber, D. F. (2009). *Economics and Management of Competitive Strategy*. World Scientific Publishing Co. Pte. Ltd. Accessed at http://www.worldscibooks.com/business/7171.html on December 10, 2012.

State Program on the Tourism Development in the Republic of Kazakhstan in 2007–2011. (2006). Viewed, http://www.akorda.kz/www/www_akorda_kz.nsf/ on April 24, 2009.

Tourism in Kazakhstan: 2004–2008. (2009). National Statistical Data. Ed. Zh. I. Omarov. Astana, Kazakhstan.

Tourism in Kazakhstan: 2007–2011. (2012). National Statistical Data. Ed. A.A. Smailov. Astana, Kazakhstan.

The Travel & Tourism Competitiveness Report (2007–2011). World Economic Forum.

World Tourism Organization (WTO). (1995). Concepts, definitions and Classifications for Tourist Statistics: A Technical Manual.

Zholdasbekov, A. (2011). Modern aspects of the tourist industry development problem in Kazakhstan. *UTMS Journal of Economics,* 2 (2), 207–212.

CHAPTER 3

AUTHENTICITY AND ECOCULTURAL TOURISM DEVELOPMENT IN KAZAKHSTAN: POTENTIAL AND CHALLENGES

GUILLAUME TIBERGHIEN, VLADIMIR GARKAVENKO, and SIMON MILNE

CONTENTS

INTRODUCTION

The question of authenticity is central to much literature on cultural heritage and tourism development (Chhabra, 2005; Cohen, 1988; Kolar and Zabkar, 2010; Reisinger and Steiner, 2006; Wang, 2000). As tourism grows the authentic undergoes change via a process of commodification evolving into new forms of cultural expression that engage both the tourist and the local community in a newly globalized form of culture (Prideaux and Timothy, 2008). The attribute 'authentic' "is usually given to something that is genuine and original, that can be certified by evidence, or remains true to a tradition" (Smith and Duffy, 2003, p. 14). Whereas the tourism industry tends to provide its own definitions of the traditional or typical, it is thus important to assess various stakeholders' perceptions of authenticity of ecocultural tourism practices as they tend to be negotiated through what is locally perceived as authentic and what tourists and developers view as key travel experiences (Smith and Duffy, 2003).

One of the issues at stake for visitors when they visit culturally and environmentally remote regions is how the concept of authenticity is understood and applied to local tourism practices. Wallace and Russell (2004, p. 236) argue that "eco-cultural tourism reflects present-day practice, but also acts as a model for how cultural and eco-tourism could be employed by local people to build an empowered, sustainable future in similar settings." What tourists usually see is the performative aspect of local cultures – a 'performed authenticity' created, staged and carried out for external consumption (MacCannell, 1976). It is important therefore to place this 'authenticity' in the context of how and why the tourism industry defines and presents its version of the genuinely local in both ecological and cultural aspects of tourism experience (Jamal and Hill, 2002, 2004).

As heritage is inherently a contested phenomenon (Keir, 2010), especially when communities are comprised of multiple ethnic groups, belief systems, cultures and social norms, the concept of authenticity applied to Kazakhstani cultural heritage has become particularly relevant to the specialists and developers of cultural and sustainable tourism in the country. Insofar, the country of Kazakhstan is not a well known tourism destination, either globally or within Central Asia. Although the number of inbound tourists is relatively small (The Agency of Statistics of the Republic of Kazakhstan, 2012), the country possesses numerous ecocultural tourism attractions based on its past Soviet times, nomadic culture and a variety of unique landscapes. The reconstruction of national traditions and the renaissance of a local nomadic folklore have been central to the restoration of a lost identity since the independence of Kazakhstan in 1991 (Laruelle, 2008). The political focus of the President of the country, Noursoultan Nazarbayev, is to foster a local craft-making industry for local and international tourists that participate in a 'return to nomadic traditions.' This contemporary collective imagery has, for example, "largely restored the figure of the 'Nomad' that has become a fetish theme in Marketing" (Laruelle, 2008, p. 14). During the 1920s and 1930s, the cultural landscapes of Kazakhstan have undergone a tremendous process of transformation from being shaped by pastoral nomadic activities into agrarian and industrial land (Svanberg, 1999). In particular, the nomadic lifestyle that was prevailing in the beginning of the 1930s was slowly transformed during Soviet Times into a seminomadic lifestyle which incorporated many new commodified cultural habits and changes in nomadic traditions (Laruelle, 2008).

Our empirical analysis will encounter an overview of various community members, policymakers and tourism developers' perceptions of authenticity of ecocultural tours in Kazakhstan. In particular, several aspects of the tours including the Kazakhstani landscapes, local home-stays and cultural artifacts (food and craft-making) are considered. It is then followed by an examination of how these different perceptions of authenticity can be used to position Kazakhstan as a tourism destination and develop its brand equity on the international tourism market. A review of these perceptions of authenticity reveals how the concept of authenticity can influence some of the impacts associated with tourism development in the region and in particular be used in the country branding strategy. Additionally, this chapter is designed to enhance tourism operators' understanding of various stakeholders' perceptions of authenticity to improve local tourism product development when attracting new visitors in the country. Finally, conclusions and recommendations underlying the factors that influence sustainable tourism development in the country are made for local tourism providers and policymakers.

AUTHENTICITY CONCEPTS AND DEFINITIONS

AUTHENTICITY AND THE COMMODIFICATION OF CULTURE

While the issue of authenticity affects the discourse of cultural and heritage tourism, defining what is genuine, traditional or real can be a puzzling issue. Smith and Duffy (2003, p. 133) argue that "as authenticity can be defined in terms of the existence of alternative (non-modern) forms of life or of untouched wilderness, then the very presence of the tourist makes such experiences problematic." Richter and Harrison (1992) consider the politics of representation in authenticity, particularly in cultural and heritage sites and attraction are of critical importance in the development of indicators of authenticity. For Jamal and Hill (2004, p. 369), "the dynamically constitutive nature of heritage is a similarly important consideration for other national and public spaces characterized by emergent economies, globalizing cultures and hybrid populations" like it is the case for Kazakhstan.

As postmodern society is characterized by fragmentation, confusion, emptiness, alienation and by a crisis of morality and identity, people have become concerned with identity, meaning and values (Cova, 1999), as well as nostalgia and history (Goulding, 2000). The perception of a 'real' travel experience can be dependent upon the notion of a genuine local experience, which raises the issue of what is defined as traditional, original and local. In the following sections, three dimensions and aspects for addressing authenticity in cultural heritage tourism defined by Jamal and Hill (2002) were applied to Kazakhstani cultural heritage and ecocultural tourism practices (Tiberghien, et al., 2012).

OBJECTIVE AUTHENTICITY

The objective approach highlights that the authentic experience is achieved thanks to the recognition of the authenticity of visited objects of the experience that are consumed. According to Wang (1999), objective authenticity refers to the authenticity of originals; consequently the objective authenticity of a lived experience corresponds to the authenticity of the objects of the experience. For MacLeod (2006, p. 182) objective authenticity "is placed on objects made from what is considered to be authentic materials and by indigenous craftspeople or on events and rituals that we perceive as being traditional emanations of genuine cultures."

Original objects provide genuine touristic experiences for those who recognize the authenticating signs (MacLeod, 2006). The commercialization of culture and standardization of tourism experiences oppose the originals to the ones that are perfectly replicated: what MacCannell (1976) calls 'staged authenticity.' MacCannell's work reveals the complexity of the term authenticity and its multiple uses. Tourist settings can be viewed "as a continuum, with the first and front-most region being the one that is most for show purposes and the sixth or backmost region being the one that is most authentic and motivates touristic consciousness (MacCannell, 1976, p. 102). According to Jamal and Hill (2004, p. 355), "the dialectic of authenticity, reflects an ontological anxiety of existence about what we are and what is genuine and objectively true about the human condition." Accordingly, "an authentic historic event or site is one that has been scientifically and objectively situated in the original time period, setting materials of the era" (Jamal and Hill, 2002, p. 84). Objective authenticity places emphasis on both the integrity of the materials and the context within which an object is made (MacLeod, 2006). In Kazakhstan, visual arts have existed in the country in the form of rock drawings, or petroglyphs, since the Neolithic Age. The archaeological landscapes of 'Tamgaly' portraying nomadic petroglyphs were added by UNESCO on the list of World Heritage sites in September 2005, and are nowadays visited as 'authentic' cultural tourism products by local and international visitors.

CONSTRUCTIVE AUTHENTICITY

Constructive authenticity is relative and negotiable (Cohen, 1988) and context dependent (Salamone, 1997). For Mcleod (2006, p. 184), authenticity is a *dynamic process* that changes over time, as "reality is a constructed phenomenon created in our own minds, which are influenced by our personal worldview and external social, cultural and political factors." Thus, the notions of what is authentic are not static but evolve over time and are relative and negotiated. According to Wang (1999, p. 355) "authenticity is thus a projection of tourists' own beliefs, expectations, preferences, stereotyped images and consciousness onto toured objects, particularly toured Others." From this perspective, authenticity can be linked to an experience of collective identifications made by the individual. The analysis of rituals and the research on how such experiences are constituted can reveal how authenticity is influenced by subjective and collective views on consensus, creativity and existentialism in the tourist role (Olsen and Timothy, 2002). Constructed authenticity can also be the result of projected dreams, stereotyped images or expectations from the consumed objects or what Culler (1981) calls 'symbolic authenticity.'

Generally speaking, authenticity depends on the needs of society in terms of tradition and origins, even if those are invented (Hobsbawm and Ranger, 1983), on the cultural background and the interpretation of history (Bruner, 1994). The objects and events of a particular time period may be appropriated to construct a story (or a myth) that conforms to the economic, social and political interests in a particular domain (Bruner, 1994). The national flag of the Republic of Kazakhstan portrays a blue-sky color with a picture of a golden sun with 32 rays in its center and a soaring steppe eagle under them. The blue color of the flag suggests cultural and ethnical unity of different nations and the indivisibility of the state while the sun represents the source of life and energy. The steppe eagle or golden eagle takes a special place in the nomads' view of the world and symbolizes liberty, independence, and self-accomplishment.

As Jamal and Hill (2002, p. 87) suggest, "authenticity is not a quality of objects themselves, but one that is ascribed to them, often by those with the authority to do so." Residents consume and renegotiate tourist images to create a new form of authenticity for themselves. The tourists themselves are also involved in this process, what Cohen (1988) describes as the creation of 'emergent authenticity.'

THE POST-MODERN AUTHENTICITY OF CONSUMING EXPERIENCE

Authors have also argued for a more existential approach to the question of authenticity (Hughes, 1995; Wang, 1999) where the individuals create a sense of truth within themselves. Cohen (1988) highlights the question of how to generate a perception of authenticity taking into account new expectations of consumers in terms of lived experience. If a certain authenticity can be revealed from a consuming experience, the search for postmodern authenticity is translated from a day-to-day search for experiences (Cova and Cova, 2002) in a postmodern era in which the consumers are looking for an authenticity that is lost. Wang suggests that "as a contrast to the everyday roles, the tourist is linked to the ideal of authenticity" (Wang, 1999, p. 360). Whereas the object can be undoubtedly inauthentic, the experience that results from the consuming can be in this case *existentially authentic* and reveal a sense of truth within visitors. According to the philosophy of existence, the idealistic view of authenticity states that human existence finds it sense only in the affirmation of him, its true nature and its autonomy (Taylor, 1991).

MacLeod (2006, p. 187) details that "tourists involved in active participation rather than observation are more likely to experience a sense of existential authenticity" and if tourists can feel they are both part of the local community and experiencing culture themselves" (Ooi, 2002). Tourism activities that involve a close association with the countryside such as camping, hiking or cycling are therefore popular because they allow individuals to test themselves and rediscover their essential selves. These tourists are seeking authenticity within themselves rather than in toured places or objects. As Wang (1999, p. 364) states, "tourists are not merely searching for authenticity of the 'Other.' They also search for an authenticity of, and between, themselves. The toured objects can be just a means or medium by which tourists are called together, and then an authentic interpersonal relationship between them can be experienced subsequently." The experience of drinking tea in a yurt camp and embarking in an ecocultural tour in Central Kazakhstan allows tourists to test themselves and rediscover their essential selves. Meanwhile, tourists have a sense of existential authenticity by sharing this experience with the seminomadic livestock breeding communities (Schreiber, 2008).

ECOCULTURAL TOURISM, COUNTRY BRANDING AND SENSE OF PLACE IN KAZAKHSTAN

Ecocultural tourism can be presented as a concept in which ecological and cultural aspects of a landscape are combined to create experiences for tourists. Hobsbawn and Ranger (1983) and MacCannell (1992) consider that the increasing nostalgia for the past felt primarily by citizens of developed countries is linked to the need to flee modernity and get back to a simpler way of life in the countryside. In removing oneself far from any crowded place, the ecotourist yearns for a specialized, exclusive experience (Wallace & Russell, 2004). By making a connection between cultural tourism and ecotourism in this way, Wallace and Russell further argue that combining these two types of tourism allow indigenous people for empowerment of their tourism practices and define accordingly their 'sense of place.'

SENSE OF PLACE AND COUNTRY BRANDING IDENTITY

According to Anholt (2007), the nation's brand is the combination of various elements that make up the image of the country as a whole and includes its culture, history, people, government, and business. National branding is the practice of building a positive reputation of a particular country and its people in the international community. Saunders (2008) claims that unlike commercial brands, nation brands are unique and cannot be replicated. Dinnie (2008) has identified that the most effective approach for building a nation brand is 'cultural branding,' that involves the blending of cultural and social aspects of the country for the creation of a brand image. Others argue that the development of a country's brand should be done through the development of various areas such as tourism and exports, and significant attention should be paid to the natural resources and landscapes (Kotler and Gertner, 2002; Porter, 1998).

Konecnik and Go (2008, p. 177) highlight that "place identity can contribute importantly to the creation and sustenance of a distinctive competitive edge." When referring to Smith (1989) about the 'extraordinary' part of the tourism experience visitors are in search for, Konecnik and Go further mention that "raising awareness of the historical nature of the concept of culture is relevant in the process of identity formation at both global and local levels." The Kazakhstani brand identity building should thus not only be driven by the political side, but should also satisfy a broad range of stakeholders implied in ecocultural tourism development in the country. A supply side, governmental and managerial perspective on country branding is therefore justified as the concept of authenticity applied to the Kazakhstani brand identity strategy involves community members and a local insight.

As modern tourists want to experience 'a sense place' when visiting a destination, therefore experiential and symbolic benefits play as functional benefits in a destination brand's identity (Keller 1993). Kapferer (1998, p. 71) additionally highlights that "before knowing how we are perceived, we must know who we are." Surveying 'the supply side' when conceptualizing the country's branding strategy is thus particularly relevant, in particular for a 'young' country like Kazakhstan who does not have a clear brand image yet. Brand identity can also be conceptualized by the country's culture (De Chernatony, 1999), which in turn "drive its desired positioning, personality and subsequent relationships, all of which are later presented to reflect the stakeholders' actual and aspirational self-images" (Konecnik and Go, 2008, p. 179). In line with Govers and Go (2004) for whom the destination image needs to be projected by the destination management organization, this book chapter discusses various concepts and definitions of authenticity applied to ecocultural tourism development in the country. Conclusions will be made on how Kazakhstan can incorporate the notion of authenticity to develop its tourism destination' brand identity as well as enhance the sustainability of its ecocultural tourism products and services.

AUTHENTICITY AND SUSTAINABLE ECOCULTURAL TOURISM DEVELOPMENT IN KAZAKHSTAN

ECOCULTURAL TOURISM DURING THE SOVIET ERA

According to the voluntary Society for Proletarian Tourism that emerged in the late 1920s, "a tourist was a traveler who embarked on a purposeful journey, a circuit using the traveler's own physical powers, by foot, boat, bicycle, or horseback" (Gosudarstvennyi arkhiv Rossiiskoi federatsii (GARF), 1930). "Beginning in 1939, Soviet citizens could earn the badge 'Turist SSSR' by completing a six-day trip and demonstrating skills in pitching a tent, lighting a fire, and orienteering using a compass" (Na sushe i na more, 1935). Koenker (2003, pp. 658–659) details that during Soviet Union time, "travelers in search of pleasure could take excursions; and tourism was meant to involve work, the enhancement of one's intellectual and physical capital, but not leisure [...]. Travelling was synonymous to escape from collective norms and patterns, to discover new territories, new experiences, to be the first to encounter a mountain peak, a waterfall, a hidden lake, or an unknown ethnic group." Koenker (2003, p. 661) further informs when referring to various periodicals during the Soviet era that the nation-building of tourism and travel was also created from "patriotic tours of civil war and world war battle-fields, excursions to the house-museums of famous revolutionary leaders and cultural figures, as well as visits to exemplary industrial and agricultural sights."

INTERNATIONAL TOURISM DEVELOPMENT

Hall (1991, p. 80) details that until the mid-1950s, tourist facilities in the USSR were primarily social-class oriented and developed for domestic tourists who generally vacationed with workers from the same collective or trade union. Werner (2003, p. 147) when referring to Shaw (1991) specifies that "throughout the Soviet period, health spas (sanatoria) and children's Pioneer camps were the most common destinations for domestic tourists [...]. In contrast, foreign tourists, including those from socialist countries, generally went on sightseeing tours of cities." International tourism in Kazakhstan has changed since the end of the Soviet period due to the country's economical shift to a market-economy and the development of foreign trade. The modernization of Kazakhstani lifestyles and international tourism development has led to an increase in the number of visitor arrivals, with visitors primarily looking for Silk Road, adventure and extreme tours (Werner, 2003).

CURRENT ECOCULTURAL COMMUNITY-BASED TOURISM DEVELOPMENT

The country has faced drastic changes in its cultural, economic and political situation since its independence in 1991. Economic changes as well as major political event (the OSCE Summit in November 2010) and international sports competitions (the 7th Asian Winter Games in February 2011) are forcing the country to look more closely at the development of its tourism industry. Kazakhstan holds numerous assets to become a major player in a dynamic tourism policy in Central Asia and already offers a wide range of different types of tourism: educational and entertainment tours, ethnic as well as ecotourism. In particular, it was mentioned by the Minister of Tourism and Sport of the Republic of Kazakhstan during the hosting of the 18th World Tourism Organization assembly hold in the capital city Astana in September 2009 that, "today tourists seek new ideas and travel destinations and are interested in original culture and history of nomad civilizations as well as ecological and active tourism" (Dosmukhambetov, 2009). This approach was reinforced by the Delegation of the European Union of the Republic of Kazakhstan, which stated that "ecological tourism is considered one of the *priority directions* for the development of the

country (Delegation of the European Union to the Republic of Kazakhstan, 2010). Consequently, the Institution Building Partnership Program
(IBPP) of the European Union launched in September 2008 the Ecological
Tourism and Public Awareness in Central Kazakhstan (ETPACK) project, which explored the development of community, based ecotourism
promoted by national and international third sectors (the German Nature
and Biodiversity Conservation Union (NABU) and the Kazakhstani NGO
'Ecomuseum Karaganda.'

'KYZYLARAI' ECOCULTURAL TOUR, CENTRAL KAZAKHSTAN

Central Kazakhstan (Karaganda region) is also known as "The heart of
Kazakhstan" and has an area of 398.800 km². Central Kazakhstan is a land
of ancient nomadic civilizations, boundless steppe expanses and natural
diversity. Since ancient times, these lands have been known by their po-
etic name "Sary-Arka." The mountains of Central Kazakhstan (Karkara-
ly, Ulytau, Kyzylarai) are noticeable because of their "clean lakes, fresh
pine air and unique wildlife and have always played an important role
as signposts for travelers along the Silk Road as an oasis for rest and re-
cuperation" (ETPACK, 2010a). The Korgalzhyn Nature Reserve, which
includes the Lake Tengiz and several other smaller lakes, was assigned
as a UNESCO Natural World Heritage Site due to the local wetlands and
steppe biodiversity.

The Kyzylarai ecocultural tour has been developed by the ETPACK
project and is looking into the development of community based ecotourism in Central Kazakhstan promoted by national and international organizations. The two-year project started in September 2008 and was financed
up to 160.000 Euros (80% of the total budget) by the Institution Building Partnership Program (IBPP) of the European Union. The German Nature and Biodiversity Conservation Union (NABU) and the Kazakh NGO
'Ecomuseum Karaganda' cooperated to realize the project and provided
the needed co-financing. During the project implementation, three ecosites
with a network of home-stays and one souvenir production of traditional
handicrafts were built up in Karaganda region (Ulytau, Kyzylarai and
Kent) and a small ecotourism operator "Nomadic Travel Kazakhstan" is
now marketing the tourism products of the ecosites, tours and souvenir
products. The tour Kyzylarai (3 days) goes through a combination of

ecocultural elements: pine forests which grow on the granite rocks and present particular interest for scientists being the most southern place of the pine habitat in the Central Kazakhstan ecosystem, the granite sepulchers of "Begazy" and rock paintings dating from the Bronze age, stone statues of the Turkic period and mausoleums of the period of the Kazakh-Jungar wars dating from the XVIII century. The local population managed to preserve skills of producing articles out of felt and numerous national fermented milk products: 'koumiss" (horse milk), "shubat" (camel milk) and local dairy products that are made available to the visitors. The tour brochure notes "such combination of pristine nature, ancient historical monuments and well-preserved way of life of the local population makes the "Kyzylarai" ecocultural tour a great place to visit for those who like to explore something new and interesting for themselves" (ETPACK, 2010b).

RESEARCH METHODOLOGY

Besides documentation and secondary data including travel brochures, interviews represented the most important information sources. The study employed 15 semi-structured interviews using open-ended questions with various stakeholders who were directly and indirectly involved with the development of ecocultural tourism and Community-Based Tourism (CBT) in Kazakhstan. Different members (the director, marketing and logistics specialists) of the tourism operator 'Nomadic Travel Kazakhstan' selling ecocultural tours, international and local NGOs including the German Nature and Biodiversity Conservation Union, 'Ecomuseum Karaganda' and 'Avalon historic-geographical society' were interviewed. The fieldwork has taken place in Almaty, Karaganda and Astana cities as well as ecovillages developed in Kazakhstan. International experts in nomadic culture and ecocultural tourism selected from their publications about tourism and ecotourism development in Kazakhstan have been included in the panel. The political side was represented by government officials from the Ministry of Tourism and Sport of Kazakhstan as well as the promotional director of the Kazakhstan Tourism Association (KTA) responsible for the development of ecocultural tourism in the country. Community members selling local souvenirs, running local guesthouses and working in partnership with the operator "Nomadic Travel Kazakhstan" in the ecosite of Kyzylarai, constituted the remaining of the interviewees.

Notes were taken during the interviews and subsequent analysis of the interviews was employed to identify themes of interest including identifying ecological and cultural aspects of the Kazakhstani culture that can be incorporated into an authentic ecocultural tourism experience for local and international visitors. The interviewees were probed with additional questions such as how the perception of authenticity could be incorporated into the branding of ecocultural tours developed in the country. As culture is produced by individual residents, especially small-scale artisans and artists who offer heir crafts for sale for tourists, the researchers decided to interview in particular the 'insiders' who jointly represent the destination culture (Anholt 2002; Konecnik 2002).

The "Kyzylarai" ecocultural tour in Central Kazakhstan has been chosen as a case study for the chapter. "Because authenticity is a socially, individually constructed and evaluated perception or experience and because managers can influence authenticity" (Kolar and Zabkar, 2010, p. 654), the researchers have adopted a constructivist paradigm as a managerially more adequate position. As the researchers had limited available information about the population from which the sample will be taken, nonprobability sampling was used for the research, in particular purposive or judgmental sampling method that is used in situations in which an expert uses judgment in selecting cases with a specific purpose in mind (Neuman, 2009). This method has been chosen to select unique cases that are especially informative about the development of ecocultural tourism projects in Kazakhstan. A multiple stakeholders approach (experts in nomadic culture, home stay providers and tourism developers) allowed the researcher to interview all the different groups of population involved in the development of the Kyzylarai ecocultural tour detailed further in the paper.

RESEARCH FINDINGS

According to the main stakeholders interviewed, the notion of authenticity is linked with the ecocultural tourism practices and tours offered in the country. As former nomads used to live in harmony with the nature in a sustainable way, their nomadic lifestyles are deeply engrained with the steppe landscapes and this combination creates a unique tourism experience for international visitors who often had no previous knowledge about the traditional nomadic culture before arriving in the country. In particular, the tour 'Kyzylarai' is matching the definition of ecocultural tourism, mixing ecological and cultural aspects of the Kazakhstani landscapes.

THEMES IDENTIFIED TO BE POTENTIALLY AUTHENTIC FOR KAZAKHSTAN BRANDING STRATEGY

Three themes detailed below were identified by the respondents to be potentially authentic for local and international visitors when undertaking an ecocultural tour in the country (Tiberghien et al., 2012).

THE "GEOGRAPHICAL IMAGINATION"

Culture and scenery are inextricably integrated in the expectations and perceptions of locals and tourists alike (Buckley et al., 2008). From a geographical perspective, it is useful to argue for greater attention to the situated place and space in which the object is experienced (Crouch, 2000). All the different stakeholders have been interviewed regarding their perception of the scenery [for example, whether Kazakhstani landscapes can be viewed as "abstract mental landscapes," (Ringer, 1998)], the environment as well as the wild life encountered during the 'Kyzylarai' ecocultural tour in Central Kazakhstan.

According to the tourism operator "Nomadic Travel Kazakhstan," objective authenticity can be found in the cultural landscapes (steppes landscapes) that are witnessed by the visitors. This perception is shared by local home-stay providers for whom steppes landscapes are recognized to be one of the most authentic themes for local and international tourists. The archeological site of 'Begazy' from the Bronze Age included in the 'Kyzylarai' tour is offering a unique opportunity for visitors to witness ancient authentic historical sites. As the tourism brochure mentions on the official website of 'Nomadic Travel Kazakhstan' operator, "historical heritage is presented in a quite interesting way: monumental granite sepulchers of Begazy and rock paintings, dating from the Bronze age, stone statues of the Turkic period and mausoleums of the period of the Kazakh-Jungar wars. Such an amazing combination of pristine nature, ancient historical monuments and rather well-preserved way of life of the local population makes the 'Kyzylarai' ecosite a great place to visit for those who like to explore something new and interesting for themselves" (Nomadic Travel Kazakhstan, 2012).

PERFORMATIVE SPACES AND THE POLITICS OF CULTURAL SITES

According to the main stakeholders involved in the development of eco-cultural tours, the notions of ecocultural tourism and authenticity have a real meaning together as most of the villages in Central Kazakhstan are still looking the same as they were since the 1930s. On the contrary to some open-air museums developed by the Ministry of Tourism and Sport of Kazakhstan in the region of Balkash Lake and Burabai (Baravoie), local villages that are part of the 'Kyzylarai' tour are perceived as authentic either from the home-stay providers or the tour operator "Nomadic Travel Kazakhstan" points of views. The local populations "have managed to preserve skills of producing articles out of felt and numerous national fermented milk products: 'kumyz,' 'shubat' and 'kurt'" (Nomadic Travel Kazakhstan, 2012). In particular, some of the home-stay providers are highlighting the fact that more yurts (mobile dwellings from nomadic times known as gers in Mongolia) should be set in the steppes as they are matching some of the visitor's expectations when traveling in Central Kazakhstan. The visitors' stay in the guest houses sharing a 'nomadic life-style' and interacting with the local population is strongly participating in the authenticity of their tourism experiences.

The researchers looked at different dimensions of authenticity experienced by local and international visitors regarding traditional Kazakhstani nomadic food (ingredients, links to the past, as well as new food traditions) made available to the tourists during the 'Kyzylarai' tour. According to the tourism operators interviewed, the experiential part of the tourist experience can be found in the sharing of traditional meals ('beshbarmak,' 'kuyrdak') based on horse meat and prepared by the host people which are the same since generations as well as being able to witness traditional games like horses festivals and hunting during the feasts periods. When mentioning *'understand you can find happiness from simple things'* in the 'Ecotourism Resources of Kazakhstan' brochure, the official Kazakhstan Tourism Association (KTA) welcomes visitors to experientially participate and share the life of the local populations during the 'Kyzylarai' tour.

The traditional 'Dastarkhan' (table filled with horse meat dishes) allow visitors to discover the traditional way of cooking within the village and experience an authentic meal with the host populations. As tourists involved in active participation rather than observation are more likely to experience a sense of existential authenticity, Ooi (2002) notes that there is more chance of this happening if cultural mediators absent themselves and allow tourists to feel they are both part of the local community and experiencing culture bodily. For some of the home stay providers, 'national traditional food is the best expression of our culture, and the meals we are preparing for the visitors are still prepared in the same way generation after generation.' The experience itself is, from MacCannel (1976) point of view, not 'staged' as the home-stay providers are serving Kazakh meals according to the traditions of the ancestors.

CRAFTS PURCHASED BY TOURISTS

Hand-made crafts in the forms of 'Kilems' and 'Korpes' (carpets) made of fur materials are proposed during the 'Kyzylarai' tour for tourists on demand. The crafts are following the embroideries and ornaments from ancient times but are now mostly made out from cotton instead of camel textile. The souvenir articles are individually owned by local villagers and members in the village who sell a choice of hand crafted souvenirs including hand-made fur carpets, fur products in the form of slippers and mobile phones boxes. Some of these crafts are seen as reproductions of some ancient traditional crafts, some shops also sell ethnic tee-shirts and slippers with Kazakhstani ornaments that can participate in experiential authentic tourism experiences when they are worn by the visitor's outside of the village or back home.

STAKEHOLDER'S PERCEPTION OF AUTHENTICITY AS A MARKETING TOOL FOR ECOCULTURAL TOURISM ATTRACTIONS AND DESTINATIONS

SHAPING KAZAKHSTANI BRAND IDENTITY

We have examined how tourism spaces in this region of central Kazakhstan can be constructed by community members, policymakers and tourism developers regarding the question of authenticity and ecocultural tours in Central Kazakhstan. On particular relevance of this study is that tourism stakeholders shouldn't distort the reality but provide a depiction of the true social and economic situation in the destination (Britton, 1979; Silver, 1993) that redefines the social meanings of places, though creating an image of the country that would be exposed to the international arena. As Milne, Grekin, and Wolley (1998, pp. 102–103) highlight, "cultural landscapes are viewed and shaped as commodities that can be consumed by potentially malleable consumers. The construction of tourist landscapes in peripheral regions and areas where indigenous peoples live has focused on the fact that this commodification process involves the elaborate creation of 'fantasy'."

After the collapse of the Soviet Union, Kazakhstan, as a new state, has faced a need to identify itself in the eyes of the world community and to differentiate itself. Saunders (2008, p. 67) states that the Kazakhstani government has put much effort into creating a "unique, recognizable, and credible national brand" and has indeed approached the process of forming a national brand strategically. According to Marat (2009) the country's government has so far monopolized the process by limiting the participation of the domestic audiences in the development of its country brand image. The government chose to position the country as a resourceful, stable and multiethnic country located in a fairly unstable region of the world, which also serves as a crossroad between West and East, combining diverse cultures and beliefs (Marat, 2009; Saunders, 2008). In order to promote this image, Kazakhstani government has adapted the message "Kazakhstan—the Heart of Eurasia" that highlights the country's favorable geographical location and the efforts of the government to be recognized for its vast territories, rich natural resources and political stability (Marat, 2009).

A NEED FOR REBRANDING THE COUNTRY'S IMAGE

According to Saunders (2008), the Kazakhstani government plans to change the target audience of the advertising campaign and try to attract a younger public by focusing more on cultural and tourism aspects rather than political issues. One example is the OSCE chairmanship, which Kazakhstan obtained in 2010 and the reason for applying for chairmanship, as Marat (2009) claims, was to prove that Kazakhstan managed to be the home for numerous cultures and ethnicities. Furthermore, Kazakhstan also hosted the Asian Olympic Games in 2011 and applied to host the Winter Olympic Games in 2014; all of these activities of being actively involved in the hosting of international events have helped the process of establishing the country's brand in the international market.

Kahn (2006) points out that the process of rebranding, as a mean to gain a better global reputation, is a complicated process that needs changes related to changing and reforming policies and legislation as well as improving infrastructure, reducing unemployment and poverty rates. For Crouch (2000, p. 65), as cultural and heritage places and spaces are always "in the making" through the construction of meaning and participatory activities, it is important to "generate a variety of personal, heritage and identity relationships including sense of ownership or emotional attachment, empowerment, value, and feeling" (Jamal and Hill, 2004, p. 25). As Kazakhstan keeps defining the dynamic nature of its cultural heritage and the potential of its ecocultural tourism practices to attract new visitors, it is important to consider the notion of authenticity as a contributing factor in the country's rebranding strategy (Tiberghien et al., 2012).

STAKEHOLDER'S PERCEPTIONS OF AUTHENTICITY TO ENHANCE SUSTAINABLE ECOCULTURAL PRODUCT DEVELOPMENT

RECENT TOURISM DEVELOPMENTS

Werner (2003, p. 142) details that tour operators' enduring work to develop adequate tourist accommodations, create tourist itineraries, and influence government institutions that support and regulate tourism in Central Asia participates in cultivating a positive image of a new tourist destination [...]. In this perspective, the role of tourism mediators became particularly important as Kazakhstan is not very well known in the Western tourist-generating countries."

As stated by the delegation of the European Union in Kazakhstan (2010), one of the potential types of tourism that deserve more development is linked to the preservation of traditional cultures and environment protection. Community-based tourism is regarded as a tool for natural and cultural resource conservation and community development and is closely associated with ecotourism (Davison et al., 2002). Furthermore,

Community-based approaches are central to many tourism development plans around the world and as Milne and Ateljevic (2001) emphasize, "there is a growing realization that localized cooperations, trust and net-working are essential ingredients in providing the right mix for success-ful tourism development." According to some of the home-stay providers interviewed, the collection of waste in the villages in order to keep them clean for tourists was organized since 2010. The ecosites in the region of 'Kyzylarai' are included in ecological zones by the official regional envi-ronment office. A high level of awareness regarding ecological issues is achieved through seminars conducted by KTA who organizes ecological crafts-making workshops that participate in the revival of Kazakh tradi-tions. KTA is also involved in the attribution of certification procedures to the best guest houses in the villages, a process that makes the home-stay providers more conscious about the different visitors' expectations and activities while on the ecosites.

SUSTAINABILITY AND PROFITABILITY OF THE ECOCULTURAL TOURS

Financial sustainability and the participation of different stakeholders are crucial for the long-term future of ecocultural tourism. Graburn (1995) argues that the need to provide financial gain can change priorities in cul-tural tourism from education to entertainment as the desire for nostalgia translates to profit. Although the principles of sustainability are financially relevant, they may be perceived from a local perspective as imperialist and orientalist views of development (Errington and Gewertz, 1989; MacCan-nell, 1999; Tucker, 1997; Wallace and Russell, 2004). Milne et al. (1998, p. 104) argue that "shifts in the structure and organization of the tourism industry can change the relationship between the producers and consum-ers of tourism products and how the meanings of the tourist experience are negotiated by various agencies."

The way cultural products are perceived is as much about the politics of representation of the Kazakhstani culture from the host population as about selling and sharing authentic cultural experiences with descendants of Kazakhstani population who have been living in the villages since three or four generations (Tiberghien and Garkavenko, 2010). According to the deputy director of 'Nomadic Travel Kazakhstan' operator, the limitation of the applicability of the notion of authenticity in Kazakhstani practices is to be found in the tourism business structures and the purpose of building the ecocultural sites themselves. For the home stay providers' interviewed, sustainability and profit are two notions that do not contradict each other whereas the main stakeholders involved in the development of the ecosites advocate primarily the preservation of the local traditions and environmental biodiversity.

CONCLUSION

This chapter presented the contributions of the perception of authenticity to the development of ecocultural tourism practices undertaken in Central Kazakhstan through the lenses of different stakeholders involved in ecocultural tourism projects in the country.

According to Reisinger and Steiner (2006) and Wang (1999), objectivist and modernist authors argue that there is an evident, objective basis for judging authenticity. Conversely, constructivists suggest that tourists' experiences or perceptions can be authentic even when they are perfectly aware that the setting has been contrived (Cohen, 1988). This debate around authenticity revolves around the question of what can be authentic. Kolar and Zabkar (2010, p. 653) suggest that from a managerial point of view, "tourism managers should devote more attention to subtle and deeply ingrained societal changes that exist outside the tourism market yet which essentially shape tourist behavior and experiences."

Jamal and Hill (2004, p. 369) assert that "by understanding the philosophical and methodological assumptions being made about authenticity, researchers and practitioners may be able to develop effective frameworks for the study of authenticity, and for the management of heritage tourism." The three dimensions of authenticity (objective, constructive and existential) explored in this chapter are important for local tourism providers as the country keeps defining the dynamic nature of its cultural heritage and the potentialities for ecocultural tourism practices. The 'Kyzylarai' ecocultural tour in Central Kazakhstan can inspire ecocultural tourism practices in other Kazakstani landscapes where local populations are aiming for sustainable tourism practices involving different stakeholders (Tiberghien & Garkavenko, 2012). The potential of ecocultural tourism as a tool for empowerment and development of a tourism region is dependent on many different stakeholders' points of views. Similarly to Wallace and Russell

(2004, p. 251) advocate, funding may be the most practical constraint, and "outside funding, such as from nongovernmental organizations or national, regional and local governments may be first required to develop and maintain ecocultural tourism in the short-term."

Kazakhstan recently celebrated its 20 years of gaining independence and the country has come a long way since the collapse of the Soviet Union. The country faced numerous challenges in the search for self-identification and in determining their place in the global arena. The national image of Kazakhstan has been a subject of concern for the country's government and a lot of resources and effort has been put into developing a strong country image, however, the brand is still in its infancy stage (Saunders, 2008). In order to develop a truly effective and recognizable national brand, local tourism providers should include the concept of authenticity in Kazakhstan's country branding strategy as a mean to propose a unique tourism destination on the international market. This approach applied to Kazakhstani ecocultural tourism practices can help shaping the nation's brand identity and position the country as a destination that favors tourism experiences based on crafted tours emphasizing genuine Kazakhstani cultural heritage.

KEYWORDS

- **Authenticity**
- **Challenges**
- **Commodification**
- **Country branding**
- **Ecocultural tourism development**
- **Kazakhstan**
- **Potential**

REFERENCES

Anholt , S. (2002). Foreword. *Journal of Brand Management, 9*(4–5), 229–239.

Anholt, S. (2007). *Competitive Identity: The New Brand Management for Nations, Cities and Regions*. New York: Palgrave Macmillian.

Britton, S. (1979). Some notes on the geography of tourism. *The Canadian Geographer, 23*(3), 276-282.

Bruner, E. (1994). Abraham Lincoln as authentic reproduction: A critique of postmodernism. *American Anthropologist, 96*, 397–415.

Buckley, R., Ollenburg, C., & Zhong, L. (2008). Cultural landscape in Mongolian tourism. *Annals of Tourism Research, 35*(1), 47–61. doi:10.1016/j.annals.2007.06.007

Chhabra, D. (2005). Defining authenticity and its determinants: Towards an authenticity flow model. *Journal of Travel Research, 44*(1), 64-68. doi:10.1177/0047287505276592

Cohen, E. (1988). Authenticity and commoditization in tourism. *Annals of Tourism Research, 15*(3), 371–386. doi:10.1016/0160-7383(88)90028-X

Cova, B. (1999). From Marketing to Societing: When The Link Is More Important than the Thing. In D. Brownlie, M. Saren, R. Wensley, & R. Whittington (Eds.), *Rethinking Marketing: Towards Critical Marketing Accountings* (pp. 64–83). London: Sage Publications.

Cova, V., & Cova, B. (2002). Les particules expérientielles de la quête d'authenticité du consommateur. *Décisions Marketing, 28*(Sept.–Dec.), 33–42.

Crouch, D. (2000). Places around us: Embodied lay geographies in leisure and tourism. *Leisure Studies, 19*, 63–76. doi:10.1080/026143600374752

Culler, J. (1981). Semiotics of Tourism. *American Journal of Semiotics, 1*, 127–140.

Davison, R. M., Harris, R., & Vogel, D. R. (2002). E-Commerce for Community-Based Tourism in developing countries Symposium conducted at the meeting of the Community Based Ecotourism in Southeast Asia, Bangkok.

De Chernatony, L. (1999). Brand management through narrowing the gap between brand identity and brand reputation. *Journal of Marketing Management, 15*(1-3), 157-179. doi:10.1362/026725799784870432

Delegation of the European Union to the Republic of Kazakhstan. (2010). *Ecotourism in Kazakhstan*. Retrieved 15 August 2010, from http://ec.europa.eu/delegations/kazakhstan

Dinnie, K. (2008). *Nation Branding: Concepts, Issues, Practice*. Burlington: Butterworth-Heinemann.

Dosmukhambetov, T. (2009). *Tourism potential of Kazakhstan*. Retrieved 9 September 2009, from http://www.mts.gov.kz

Errington, F., & Gewertz, D. (1989). Tourism and Anthropology in a Postmodern World. *Oceania, 60*, 37–54.

ETPACK. (2010a). *Ecological Tourism and Public Awareness in Central Kazakhstan*. Retrieved 16 August 2010, from http://etpack.ecotourism.kz/proekt/index.php

ETPACK. (2010b). *Map of "Kyzylarai" eco-cultural tour in Central Kazakhstan*. Retrieved 16 August 2010, from http://etpack.ecotourism.kz/cognitive/kyzylarai-the-highest-the-oldest

Gosudarstvennyi arkhiv Rossiiskoi federatsii (GARF). (1930). Central Soviet for Tourism and Excursions. *1*(1).

Goulding, C. (2000). The commodification of the past, postmodern pastiche, and the search for authentic experiences at contemporary heritage attractions. *European Journal of Marketing, 34*(7), 835–853. doi:10.1108/03090560010331298

Govers, R., & Go, F. (2004). Cultural identities constructed, imagined and experienced: A 3-gap tourism destination image model. *Tourism (13327461), 52*(2), 165–182.

Graburn, N. H. (1995). Tourism, Modernity and Nostalgia. In A. S. Ahmed & C. Shore (Eds.), *The Future of Anthropology: Its Relevance to the Contemporary World* (pp. 158–178). London: The Athlone Press.

Hall, D. R. (1991). *Tourism & economic development in Eastern Europe & the Soviet Union.* New York: Belhaven Press.

Hobsbawm, E., & Ranger, T. (1983). *The Invention of Tradition.* Cambridge: Cambridge University Press.

Hughes, G. (1995). Authenticity in tourism. *Annals of Tourism Research, 22*(4), 781–803. doi:10.1016/0160-7383(95)00020-X

Jamal, T., & Hill, S. (2002). The home and the world: (Post)touristic spaces of (in)authenticity. In G. Dann (Ed.), *The Tourist as Metaphor of the Social World* (pp. 77–107). Wallingford: CABI Publishing.

Jamal, T., & Hill, S. (2004). Developing a Framework for Indicators of Authenticity: The Place and Space of Cultural and Heritage Tourism. *Asia Pacific Journal of Tourism Research, 9*(4), 353–372. doi:10.1080/1094166042000311246

Kahn, J. (2006). A Brand–New Approach. *Foreign Policy, 157*(92).

Kapferer , J. N. (1998). *Strategic Brand Management.* London: Kogan Page Publishers.

Keir, M. (2010). Living pasts: Contested Tourism Authenticities. *Annals of Tourism Research, 37*(2), 537–554.

Keller , K. L. (1993). Conceptualizing, measuring and managing customer-based brand equity. *Journal of Marketing, 57*(1), 1–22.

Koenker, D. P. (2003). Travel to Work, Travel to Play: On Russian Tourism, Travel and Leisure. *Slavic Review, 62*(4), 657-665.

Kolar, T., & Zabkar, V. (2010). A consumer-based model of authenticity: An oxymoron or the foundation of cultural heritage marketing? *Tourism Management, 31*(5), 652–664. doi:10.1016/j.tourman.2009.07.010

Konecnik , M. (2002). The image as a possible source of competitive advantage of the destination -The case of Slovenia. *Tourism Review, 57*(1/2), 6–12.

Konecnik, M., & Go, F. (2008). Tourism destinations brand identity: The case of Slovenia. *Brand Management, 15*(3), 177-189. doi:10.1057/palgrave.bm.2550114

Kotler, P., & Gertner, D. (2002). Country as Brand, Product, and Beyond: A Place Marketing and Brand Management Pespective. *Journal of Brand Management, 9*(4), 249-261.

Laruelle, M. (2008). Enjeux identitaires et nomadisme. *Le courrier des pays de l'Est, 3*(1067), 14–18.

MacCannell, D. (1976). *The tourist: A new theory of the leisure class.* London: MacMillan.

MacCannell, D. (1992). *Empty Meeting Grounds: The Tourist Papers.* London and New York: Routledge.

MacCannell, D. (1999). *The tourist: A new theory of the leisure class.* New York: Schocken (original work published 1976): University of California press.

MacLeod, N. (2006). Cultural tourism: Aspects of Authenticity and Commodification. In M. Robinson & M. Smith (Eds.), *Cultural Tourism in a changing world: politics, participation and (re)presentation* (pp. 177–179). London: Channel View Publications.

Marat, E. (2009). Nation Branding in Central Asia: A New Campaign to Present Ideas about the State and the Nation. *Europe-Asia Studies, 61*(7), 1123-1136.

Milne, S., & Ateljevic, I. (2001). Tourism, economic development and the global-local nexus: theory embracing complexity. *Tourism Geographies, 3*(4), 369-393. doi:10.1080/146166800110070478

Milne, S., Grekin, J., & Woodley, S. (1998). Tourism and the construction of place in Canada's eastern Arctic. In G. Ringer (Ed.), *Destinations,Cultural landscapes of tourism*. New York: Routledge.

Na sushe i na more. (1935, July 1935). *13*(6).

Neuman, W. L. (2009). *Social research methods: Qualitative and quantitative approaches* (7th ed.). Boston: Pearson Education.

Nomadic Travel Kazakhstan. (2012). *Kyzylarai – The Highest, The Oldest*. Retrieved 3 February 2012, from http://www.nomadic.kz/index.php?option=com_content&view=article&id=7%3Akyzylarai-5&catid=1%3A11-cognitive-tours&Itemid=8&lang=en

Olsen, D. H., & Timothy, D. J. (2002). Contested Religious Heritage: Differing Views of Mormon Heritage. *Tourism Recreation Research, 27*(2), 7–15.

Ooi, C. (2002). *Cultural Tourism and Tourism Cultures: The Business of Mediating Experiences in Copenhagen and Singapore*. Copenhagen: Copenhagen Business School Press.

Porter. (1998). *The Competitive Advantage of Nations*. New York: Palgrave Macmillan

Prideaux, B., & Timothy, D. J. (2008). Themes in Cultural and Heritage Tourism in the Asia Pacific Region. In B. Prideaux, D. J. Timothy, & K. Chon (Eds.), *Cultural and Heritage Tourism in Asia and the Pacific* (pp. 1–14). New York: Routledge.

Reisinger, Y., & Steiner, C. J. (2006). Reconceptualizing object authenticity. *Annals of Tourism Research, 33*(1), 65–86. doi:10.1016/j.annals.2005.04.003

Richter, L. K., & Harrison, D. (1992). Political instability and tourism in the Third World. In D. Harrison (Ed.), *Tourism and the Less Developed Countries* (pp. 35–46). New York: John Wiley & Sons.

Ringer, G. (1998). *Destinations: Cultural Landscapes of Tourism*. London: Routledge.

Salamone, F. (1997). Authenticity in tourism: The San Angel Inns. *Annals of Tourism Research, 24*, 305–321. doi:10.1016/S0160-7383(97)80003-5

Saunders, R. A. (2008). Buying into Brand Borat: Kazakhstan's Cautious Embace of Its Unwanted "Son." *Slavic Review, 67*, 63–80.

Schreiber, D. (2008). *Kazakhstan, Nomadic Routes From Caspian to Altai*. Hong Kong: Odyssey Books and Guides Publications.

Shaw, D. J. B. (1991). National Studies: The Soviet Union. In D. R. Hall (Ed.), *Tourism and Economic Development in Eastern Europe and the Soviet Union* (pp. 119-141). New York: Belhaven Press.

Silver, I. (1993). Marketing authenticity in third world countries. *Annals of Tourism Research, 20*(2), 302–318. doi:10.1016/0160-7383(93)90057-A

Smith, M., & Duffy, R. (2003). *The Ethics of Tourism Development* (2nd ed.). London: Sage Publications.

Smith, V. L. (1989). *Hosts and guests: the anthropology of tourism*. Philadelphia, Pennsylvania: University of Pennsylvania Press.

Svanberg, I. (1999). The Kazak Nation. In I. Svanberg (Ed.), *Contemporary Kazakhs: Cultural and Social Perspectives* (pp. 1–16). Surrey: Curzon Press.

Taylor, C. (1991). *The Ethics of Authenticity*. Cambridge, MA: Harvard University Press.

The Agency of Statistics of the Republic of Kazakhstan. (2012). *Number of inbound visitors in Kazakhstan (2008–2012)*. Retrieved 31 October 2013, from http://www.eng.stat.kz/digital/Tourism/Pages/default.aspx

Tiberghien, G., & Garkavenko, V. (2010, August 2010). Authenticity and eco-cultural tourism in New Zealand: the case of Whakarewarewa thermal village. Proceedings of the 1st International Eco-tourism Conference in Kazakhstan, Karaganda, Central Kazakhstan.

Tiberghien, G., & Garkavenko, V. (2012, April 2012). Eco-cultural tourism development and perception of authenticity in Kazakhstan: A supply side analysis. Proceedings of the 9th Kimep International Research Conference (KIRC 2012), Almaty, Kazakhstan.

Tiberghien, G., Garkavenko, V., & Ashirbekova, M. (2012). Authenticity and eco-cultural tourism development in Kazakhstan: A country branding approach. *European Journal of Tourism, Hospitality and Recreation (EJTHR), 4*(1), 29-43

Tucker, H. (1997). The Ideal Village: Interactions through Tourism in Central Anatolia. In S. Abram, J. Waldren, & D. V. L. Macleod (Eds.), *Tourists and Toursim: Identifying People and Places* (pp. 107–128). Oxford: Berg Publishers.

Wallace, G., & Russell, A. (2004). *Eco-cultural tourism as a means for the sustainable development of culturally marginal and environmentally sensitive regions*. New Delhi: Sage Publications.

Wang, N. (1999). Rethinking authenticity in tourism experience. *Annals of Tourism Research, 26*(2), 349–370. doi:10.1016/S0160-7383(98)00103-0

Wang, N. (2000). *Tourism and modernity: A sociological analysis*. Amsterdam: Pergamon.

Werner, C. (2003). The New Silk Road: Mediators and Tourism Development in Central Asia. *Ethnology, 42*(2), 141–159.

CHAPTER 4

BUKHARA: THE PRINCESS OF CITIES

GÖZDE SAZAK

CONTENTS

INTRODUCTION

Let us start to depict Bukhara by reciting the Basmala, "Bismillahirrahmanirrahim": "In the name of Allah, most Gracious, most Merciful."

"In all other parts of world light descends upon earth; from holy Bukhara it ascends" (Blunt, 1973). To comprehend Bukhara's soul truly, one needs to know her body first. Bukhara is like her elder sister Samarkand in several ways, yet she is quite different. Samarkand represents wealth and power, whereas Bukhara is the center of science and spirit. It is best to imagine her as a 16-year-old maiden with long dark hair. On her head, she is wearing a colorfully embroidered **silken cap** (Fig. 1). On the cap, there is **holy jewelry** (Fig. 2) shaped as a bird of paradise. On her forehead rests her turquoise, opal, topaz, and pearl ornamented glamorous **börk** (crown) (Fig. 3). There are a kettle and birds symbolizing hospitality and fertility on top of the cap. Her looks are compassionate and determined owing to the **pendants** (Fig. 4) swinging from her temples down to her neck. Keys to heaven hang from the end of one pendant and a dagger protecting her chastity from the other. She stands upright wearing a **silver belt** (Fig. 5) and an **ikat** (dress) that is scarcely embroidered signifying her nobility and modesty. While the cylindrical turquoise **amulet** (Fig. 6) on her neck protects her heart, the **arm talisman** (Fig. 7) around the upper part of her right arm protects the strength of her fist. Noble Bukhara is a faithful and brave princess who rides her horse valiantly in her colorful **boots** (Fig. 8). As a Muslim tradition, in everyday life the Basmala is often recited before performing each task in order for it to be propitious. The reason why we used Basmala at the beginning of this paper is the same. The spirituality of the city Bukhara requires a Basmala before studying it. Even Tamerlane, one of the greatest conquerors of the world, visited Bukhara not on horseback but on foot, out of his respect to this glorious city.

The city Bukhara is one of the oldest settlements in Central Asia. It is located in modern-day Uzbekistan. It lays between the rivers Amu Darya (ancient Oxus) and Syr Darya (ancient Jaxartes) in the ancient Mawarannahr (Transoxiana) region in the Zarafshan Oasis (Fig. 9). Bukhara is hot in summers and freezing cold in winters. Traveler Ujfalvy described Bukhara as follows:

"...do not assume that this plain land is deprived of poetry. The steppe, dried out and dusted in summers and autumns, snow-white in winters, is elegantly cool in springs. It is flourished with red, yellow, and blue flowers, covered with

long grass... Apple, pear, pomegranate, almond, and pistachio trees rise in the gardens where melons that Tamerlane is delighted in grow. In the same gardens, there are hundred-year-old gazebos surrounded by grapevines and scent of roses that conquered the heart of Babur..." (Gorshenina and Rapin, 2008).

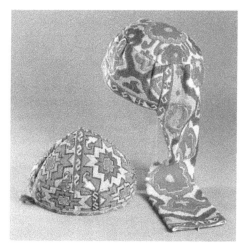

FIGURE 1   Silk Cap (Uzbekistan, 1997).

FIGURE 2   Holy Jewelry (Uzbekistan, 1997).

FIGURE 3   Börk (Uzbekistan, 1997).

FIGURE 4   Pendants (Uzbekistan, 1997).

FIGURE 5 Silver Belt (Uzbekistan, 1997).

FIGURE 6 Amulet (Uzbekistan, 1997).

FIGURE 7   Arm Talisman (Uzbekistan, 1997).

FIGURE 8   Boots (Uzbekistan, 1997).

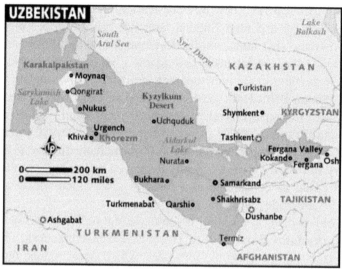

FIGURE 9   Map of Uzbekistan (www.orsam.org.tr).

HISTORICAL BACKGROUND

The history of Bukhara dates back to 50,000 to 10,000 years. There are 530 historic monuments in the city, 130 of which are in the World Heritage List by UNESCO. Palaces, bazaars, madrasahs, and mosques are some of the examples to these monuments, which were built during the 5th and the twentieth centuries B.C. by different states. The historic buildings in Bukhara are the most beautiful examples from the medieval times. Moreover, Bukhara is listed as a World Heritage Site not only because of its historic buildings but also because it was the center of handcrafts, religion, trade, and science (Babaev, 2008).

A triangle tablet and some other archeological remains found by Akhrorov proved that in ancient times, 50,000–10,000 years ago, while Bukhara was a desolate steppe, the region was inhabited by people who could farm and use natural resources and materials such as stones (Tashkenbayev, 1997).

Around 4500–4000 B.C., the steppes of Bukhara were fertilized by digging ditches. Around 3500–2500 B.C., the first city civilizations were founded in the Mawarannahr region also known as "Lapis Lazuli Road" (Gorshenina and Rapin, 2008).

About 188–550 B.C. new city civilizations were established and Samarkand became a central Sogdian and Kengeres (Turkic) city (Esin, 1978). Bukhara, also, had a similar development. In the 1950s and 1960s, archeologists like Obelchenko, Gulyamov, Zhukov, and Shishkin made several excavations in the sites such as Kuyu-Mezar, Liyavandak, Makhan –Darya, Zaman-Baba, Bash-Tepe, Ayak-Tepe ve Varakhsha. In these excavations, various pottery, jewelry, glass beads, and small golden sculpture were found (Frumkin, 1970). Some of the diggings were 20 meters deep and the findings were dated as 500 B.C. (Mukhamedjanov, 1997). The discovery of the city walls by Shishkin showed that as early as 500 B.C., Bukhara could be considered as a fortified city, which was a center of handcrafts and trade (Frumkin, 1970).

The oldest historic building in Bukhara, dating back to 500 B.C., is the **Buharhudatov Fortress** (Fig. 10). It is also called the **Ark**. The name "ark" was usually given to the fortresses, which encompassed the palace of the khans in Central Asia (Esin, 1997). In fact, if we redepict Bukhara as a young maiden, this fortress is a golden necklace with a turquoise stone hanging round her beautiful neck. This necklace has a vital importance for Princess Bukhara.

FIGURE 10   Buharhudatov Fortress (500 B.C.) (www.bura.org.tr).

Bukhara was a beauty who was desired by many tyrants from the very first day it was founded. Much blood was shed in several sieges in history. Finally, in the seventh century, the wise men of the city offered a charm to protect Bukhara forever. They suggested building large city walls with seven gates and towers (Fig. 11). In Turkish cosmology, Tengri is believed to dwell in the North Star which has seven points. This new monument, the shadow of the North Star on Earth, would give Bukhara the blessings of Tengri. This holy city would be under the protection of Tengri. Even today, when you visit Bukhara, you can see this invaluable necklace, with its seven gates, seven towers, and monumental entrance. In his book *History of Bukhara*, Narshakhi points out that the ruler Bidun, who gifted this necklace to Bukhara, was a descendant of the Bukhar-khudat Dynasty, which ruled Bukhara for 22 generations (Narshakhi, 1954). During the same period (500 B.C.), Bukhara was beginning to establish the basis for the historical trade route "Silk Road"; besides, it was becoming involved with the second religion after Tengriism in its history, Zoroastrianism.

FIGURE 11   Ancient City of Bukhara "Ark" (www.bura.org.tr).

Bukhara got acquainted with the Achaemenid culture in 550–330 B.C. and later with Hellenistic culture in 330 B.C.–10 A.D. under the rule of Alexander the Great and his successors. During the reign of Kushan ruler Kanishka (78–101 A.D.), Buddhism had its most influential period in Bukhara (Frumkin, 1970; Gorshenina and Rapin, 2008). Bukharan merchants and governors trading with Kushans protected their city and lands against Kushans by paying taxes; moreover, they improved the cultural bonds, which was a Bukharan sociopolitical tradition.

Between the years 230- 350, Bukhara was under the rule of the Kushan Empire. However, after a long period of conflicts between Sassanids and Hephtalites (White Huns), Bukhara fell into the power of Hephtalites between 375 and 557 (Akbulut, 2002).

İstami Qaghan (552–576), the ruler of the Western part of the Göktürk Khaganate, defeated the Hephtalites in 557. Between the sixth and the eighth centuries, Göktürks, who were long in a trade with the Sogdians and lived with them in many regions along the Silk Road, dominated the whole Turkestan (Taşağıl, 2003). Aside from several monuments, the most significant gift the Göktürk Qaghans presented to Princess Bukhara was free trade. Bukhara, for the first time eliminated the intervention of Persia; thus, developed its trade by offering one hand to the Byzantine Empire, and the other hand to China. This free trade without paying any taxes to Persia resulted in great wealth for Bukhara. On account of becoming rich under the protection of Göktürks, merchants built several palaces the walls of which were covered with pictures, stucco work, and wooden panels. Princess Bukhara wore these works of art like a silken ikat. Today, it is possible to see most of these works in the Hermitage Museum in St. Petersburg and this breaks the heart of Princess Bukhara.

One of the masterpieces built between the fourth and eighth centuries and still an interest for art historians today is the **Varakhsha Palace**, which is located 30 kilometers north-west of the city Bukhara. Varakhsha Palace excavated by Shishkin in 1937 was most probably built by a Göktürk Qaghan (Esin, 1987). During these excavations several hills were found. The hills are an indicator of the existence of a medieval palace with gofras on its walls between the fifth and the eleventh centuries. The figurative drawing of the palace by A. Nil'sen (Fig. 12) and the depiction of a medieval palace on a silver plate found in excavations in Mawarannahr region (Fig. 13) have major similarities. The wall paintings in Varakhsha Palace were found in four separate rooms. Extensive digs were carried out mainly in the big hall, the red room, the eastern room, and the western room. Paintings on the walls of these rooms are 1.80–2.00 meters high (Belenitsky, 1968). Some of the wall paintings are not very well-preserved. The wall paintings depict a hunting scene (a horseback archer shooting an arrow backwards is a typical scene in Turkic art), a scene where monsters (winged tiger, tiger, and leopard) attacking heroes riding on elephants (a scene thought to be mythological) (Fig. 14), and a ceremony scene of celebration (Belenitsky, 1968; Frumkin, 1970). The motifs on the clothes of the people in the wall paintings are parallel to the wall paintings found in trade centers on Silk Road such as Balalık-Tepe, Panjikent, Afrasiab, and Kızıl ve Eastern Turkestan. Moreover, even though wall paintings in Panjikent, Afrasiab, Balalık-Tepe ve Varakhsha are reminiscent of Buddhist paintings in India, they are secular paintings not including Buddhist characters. In Varakhsha Palace, glorious stucco work ornaments made in the Islamic era can be seen. Some of these ornaments belonging to the early Islamic era are figures of animal and human heads (Frumkin, 1970).

FIGURE 12   Varakhsha Palace (Shishkin, 1963).

FIGURE 13   Silver Plate (Pugachenkova, 1958).

FIGURE 14   Varakhsha Palace Mural Painting (Belenitsky, 1968).

Until the Arab invasion in the early eighth century, in the center of Bukhara, there was a bazaar (Babaev, 2008; Frumkin, 1970). This bazaar, in which there were markets and shops, was covered in time. A bigger part of the covered bazaar was destroyed during the Mongol invasion in 1220. The remaining part of the bazaar took its final form in the sixteenth century (Fig. 15). One of the major factors leading Bukhara to be a center of trade throughout history is that money was widely used in Bukhara since early second century B.C. (Frumkin, 1970). Central Asian rulers knowing that money was a sure sign of power and prestige, minted coins bearing their names. A variety of symbols depicted on the coins are noteworthy. *Bugra* (Male camels), crescent and star, the portraits of the qaghans and khatuns are the most common symbols (Simirnova, 1981).

FIGURE 15   Grand Pazar (www.trekearth.com).

When Arab forces threatened Bukhara in 673 by crossing the river Amu Darya, Kabaç Khatun, the ruler of Bukhara, kept the Arabs away until 709 by paying taxes. However, in 709 Bukhara was completely conquered by the Arab commander Kuteybe b. Muslim (Kutabi). During the next 150 years, Sogdians and Turks who settled in Bukhara rebelled against the Islamic forces. Nevertheless, none of the rebellions could prevent the spread of Islam in the region (Uydu, 1995).

From the middle of the ninth century to the late tenth century, Bukhara was the capital of the Samanid Empire (875–999). During this period, the city was fortified by two city walls. Most of the inhabitants of the city became Muslims during the Samanid era. Tomb of Ismail Samani is a historic monument in Bukhara remaining from the same period.

After the decline of the Samanid Empire, Bukhara passed under the rule of Karakhanid Dynasty (999–1141), when it lived its golden age. The above-mentioned saying, "In all other parts of world light descends upon earth; from holy Bukhara it ascends," clearly expresses the importance of Bukhara in the world as a glorious center of science, religion and art (Blunt, 1973).

Two of the most prominent scholars who were educated in the library of the emperor's palace were Muhammad al-Bukhari (810–870) and Ibn-i Sina (Avicenna) (980–1037). Ibn-I Sina wrote his world famous book on medicine *"al-Qannun fi-tibb,"* known as *"Canon Avicenna"* in the western world, in the library of the emperor. This book was the most significant medical textbook throughout the world in the seventeenth century. Another very important book *"History of Bukhara"* by Narshakhi (899–960) was also written in 933 in Bukhara (Esin, 1983).

According to Arab resources, especially during the times of I. İbrahim bin Nasr I. İbrahim (Tamgach Bugra Khan) (1052–1068), Shems el-Mulk Nasr bin İbrahim (1068- 1080), and Muhammed bin Süleyman Arslan Khan (1102–1130), due to the emphasis given to scholarship and art, Bukhara and Samarkand developed extensively and lived their golden days in the field of architecture. During the Karakhanid era, monuments such as **Kalya Minaret and Ulug Mosque**, **Magok-I Attari Mosque** and **Ribat'ül Melik Caravanserai** were built and they still remain well-preserved today. The tradition of stone carving and reliefs, ornament with green and turquaz glazed tiles, which the Karakhanids carried on from their pre-Islamic capital Kashgar, can be seen in several turquoise and green shiny domes and minarets in Bukhara and Samarkand. These monuments A'mak describes as "golden oil lamps lit in front of emerald shrines" are the symbols of Central Asia Islamic architecture (Esin, 1986).

HISTORICAL MONUMENTS

KALYAN MOSQUE AND KALYAN MINARET (1127)

It was built in 1127 by the Karakhanid Qakhan, Arslan-khan (1087–1130). Although the mosque remaining today took its last form in 1574 during the time of Shaybani Uzbek Khan, the 74 meters high Kalan Minaret (Fig. 16), which is a glorifying example of stone carving, belongs to the Karakhanid period. As told by Narshakhi in his book *History of Bukhara* written in 933, minarets built in Samanid era were wooden; hence, they were completely destroyed by fires. On the other hand, Karakhanids erected monuments constructed of stone and brick (Narshakhi, 1954). As a result of this, the oldest minarets remaining today in Turkestan are from Karakhanid era. Another significant minaret in Bukhara is Vabkent Minaret, which was built in 1196–1197 and which has simpler motifs. Kalyan Minaret, as a major Karakhanid architectural form, was an archetype to many Timurid and Seljuk minarets, and especially the Bibi Khatun Mosque in Samarkand (Aslanapa, 2007). If Princess Bukhara had had a seal, it certainly would have been Kalyan Mosque. On account of the symbols the mosque and its minaret represent, it is not wrong to describe these two as a signet ring, worn on the right hand finger of Princess Bukhara. Considering the fact that almost all minarets in Central Asia took Kalyan Minaret as a model, the Princess can be assumed to have stamped her seal on the whole Turkestan land, as if she registered the spread of Islam in Central Asia.

FIGURE 16   Kalyan Minaret (1127) (www.bura.org.tr).

MAGOK-I ATTARI MOSQUE

Hsuang-Tang, a Chinese Buddhist monk and a traveler, recorded during his travel from China to the west in 629 that there were various temples in Bukhara for Nestorians, Buddhists, Manichaeists ve Zoroastrianists. One of these temples, Mug temple in central Bukhara, was an important center (Blunt, 1973). This temple was converted to a mosque in the twelfth century by Karakhanids. The mosque, Magok-I Attari (Fig. 17), was named after the former temple and the bazaar of Bukhara, around which there were several attars (herb sellers). The portal of the mosque, which is ornamented with geometrical and plant figured stone carvings, is one of the masterpieces of Bukhara (Aslanapa, 2007). Although this monument, buried in the heart of Princess Bukhara, changed its form several times, it always had the same meaning: a meaning all the religions are craving for, which is eternal love.

FIGURE 17   Magok-I Attari Mosque (thirteenth century) (www.bura.org.tr).

RABATI MALIK CARAVANSERAI (1078–1079)

Karakhanids built monumental mosques and minarets, hospitals, madrasahs, mausoleums, khans along trade routes, and külliyes called "ribat" or "munyalık" as an act of charity by means of Islamic foundations. Karakhanids constructed Islamic monuments by using the architectural techniques developed in Buddhist temples in eastern Turkestan for centuries.

Therefore, there is an exceptionally rich architectural heritage (Esin, 1978). Rabati Malik, which was built by Karakhanid Khan Shams-al-Mulk Nasr as a caravanserai on the route between Bukhara and Samarkand (Fig. 18), is the most important monument of this heritage. This monument dating as 1078–1079 resembles a fortress by its 54/56-meter-high walls. Building a very wide entrance portal, erecting towers on each corner of a square floor, and covering the square floor with a central large dome surrounded by smaller domes became a well-established architectural tradition. This tradition continued in later Timurid, Seljuk, and Ottoman structures, Mimar Sinan being the most prominent architect applying this style of architecture. Rabati Malik Caravanserai and the other architectural structures of Karakhanids are especially significant in being original models for later Turkic-Islamic and Islamic constructions (Aslanapa, 2007).

FIGURE 18   Ribat-ul Malik Caravanserai (eleventh century) (www.bura.org.tr).

In 1220, during the Mongolian invasion, Bukhara was destroyed and many scholars died under the wrath of Genghis Khan. Rashid ad-Din recorded that about 30,000 people were killed, and the whole city was burned down except Kalya Mosque and some palaces (Özdemir, 2002).

After the invasion of the Mongols, Bukhara was revived during the reign of the Timurid Dynasty (1370–1405). The founder of the Timurid Dynasty, Tamerlane, who held Samarkand so dearly, visited the most respected scholars of Islam in Bukhara.

THE TOMB OF HAZRAT NAQSHBAND (FIFTEENTH CENTURY)

Baha-ud-Din Naqshband Bukhari (1318–1389) was the great master of one of the 12 spiritual orders of Islam, the Naqshbandi order, which was named after him. Traveler Clavjio reported the deep respect of Timur for Baha-ud-Din Naqshband Bukhari, both of whom lived during the same age. The tomb of Hazrat Naqshband is the divine radiance and the sheer joy on Princess Bukhara's face. The tomb is like an elixir of immortality for the Princess. Its existence enhanced the spirituality of Bukhara (Fig. 19).

FIGURE 19   Tomb of Baha-ud-Din Naqshband Bukhari (www.bura.org.tr).

THE ULUGH BEG MADRASAH (1417)

The Ulugh Beg Madrasah was constructed in 1417 by the Timurid ruler Ulugh Beg, the grandson of Timur. Ulugh Beg was a mathematician and an astronomy genius as well. On the portal of the Ulugh Beg madrasah (Fig. 20), there is an epigraph: "Scholarship is a religious duty ordained for all men and women." This epigraph is quite notable that it reveals the importance given to women as scholars. The sides of the entrance portal are tiled with blue ceramics symbolizing the "Rivers of Paradise" flowing down. It is the oldest madrasah existing today in Central Asia (Pander, 2002). This beautiful madrasah is the silk embroidered cap on Princess Bukhara's head. It is not possible to talk about any civilization where there is no logic or knowledge. The most valuable virtue of civilized people, and especially a princess is the respect for knowledge and scholars. The caps with silk ornaments that women were wearing in Turkestan were precious tiaras deserving the respect of others because of their elegance. Ulugh Beg madrasah is such a gorgeous tiara of scholarship. One cannot think of Princess Bukhara without it.

FIGURE 20 Ulugh Beg Madrasah (1417) (www.bura.org.tr).

After the invasion of the Mongols, the complete revival of Bukhara was not until the sixteenth century. Some nomadic tribes who called themselves the Uzbeks and who claimed to be the descendants of Uzbek Khan, one of the grandsons of Genghis Khan, ended the Timurid sovereignty in Bukhara and Samarkand under the leadership of Shaybani Khan. Shaybani Khan moved the capital from Samarkand to Bukhara. Mir-I Arab Mosque (Fig. 21), remaining from this period, was the only mosque used as an educational center even in the soviet Socialist Republic. The mosque and its madrasah were built by Sayyid Mir Abdullah as-Sairami in the years 1535–1536. Mir-I Arab Mosque has an entrance portal tiled with turquoise ceramics (Uzbekistan, 1997). It is situated just across from the Kalyan Mosque. Building two monumental structures across each other as if being reflected in a mirror was a tradition that belonged to Samarkand and Bukhara.

FIGURE 21 Mir-i Arab Mosque (1535) (www.bura.org.tr).

Bukhara was independent from the sixteenth century until 1868. Between 1868 and 1920 it was semi-independent under the control of Russia. During these periods, the Khanate of Bukhara was ruled by three khanates: Shaybanids (1500–1599), Canogulları (1599–1785), and the Manghit Dynasty (1785–1920). Khanate of Bukhara lasted until the Bolshevik Revolution (Alpargu, 2001). Then it was integrated in the Uzbek Soviet Socialist Republic between 1924–1936; finally, in 1992 it declared its independence as the Republic of Uzbekistan (Gömeç, 1999).

CONCLUSION

Presently, Princess Bukhara might not have the prominence it deserves, yet this does not lower her value. She might not thoroughly express her notable role in history despite her glorious belongings still shining today. She might even be shedding tears for all the masterpieces grabbed from her arms. However, she has always been the Princess Bukhara. Her worth is esteemed by anyone who looks for the ray of truth through the pages of history. Her value might not be well comprehended in this world but it is definitely appreciated by Tengri over the sky. Since she is the sun on earth, Bukhara will continue to ascend its light eternally. We might not see her blinded by the darkness of our age; still she keeps shining somewhere else.

BUKHARA TODAY

TRADITIONAL HANDCRAFTS IN BUKHARA

Bukhara has been the best-known center for handicrafts in Turkestan. Handicrafts such as metal work, making weapons and armors, ceramics, glass work, designing jewelry, working with gemstones, especially turquoise, embroidery, Suzani (Fig. 22), silk embroidered caps, and ikat still continue to date from ancient times. The patterns and the colors of the traditional clothes in Bukhara differ according to different families or tribes. Although fashion changes in the world, kaftans made from ikat, cashmere, woolen or cotton fabrics have been worn in Bukhara for centuries. One of the major parts of these kaftans is the belts, which bear the sign of nobility.

Traditional jewelry making, designed in Bukhara for centuries and exhibited in the Treasury of the Museum in the Ark, was also carried on in regions such as Herat, Khrozem, and Khiva.

FIGURE 22   Suzani (Uzbekistan, 1997).

Jewelry: Caps, earrings, pendants, or temple jewelry were ornamented with pearls, malachite, jades and topaz designed specifically for Bukhara. Cylindrical or rectangular amulets, ornamented by turquoises, are the symbols of Bukhara. Amulets worn by men around the upper part of the arm to protect them against the evil and to give them power is a very old Turkic tradition. After Islam, this tradition continued as writing verses of the Koran on them.

Metal Work: The most interesting metal work of copper or silver pieces is the "alms-bowl of dervish" (Fig. 23). Differing from other metal works, the motifs on these bowls depict animal fights. Scenes of animal fights are a Turkic art scene, which is significant in showing the continuity of Turkic art in Turkestan. On the copper bowl in Fig. 24, there is a figure of a man playing a musical instrument. On the both sides of this figure, there are Buddhist knots, which symbolize eternity in Buddhism. This motif shows that Bukhara was a center of religions and there was a religious transition in art.

FIGURE 23   Alms-bowl of Dervish (seventeenth century) (Uzbekistan, 1997).

FIGURE 24   Copper Bowl (Uzbekistan, 1997).

MUSEUMS

The most important historical museum in Bukhara is the Treasury of the Museum in the Ark. A lot of historical findings found during the archeological excavations carried on by Rempel in 1900 s are exhibited in this museum. Jewelry and coins are significant findings to understand the history of Bukhara. Some of the other museums in Bukhara are Feyzulla Khodjaev Museum, Bukhara State Museum, and Baha-ud-Din Naqshband Museum.

KEYWORDS

- Bukhara
- Alp-Er-Tunga
- Varakhsha
- Baha-ud-Din Naqshband Bukhari
- Timur

REFERENCES

Akbulut, D. A. (2002). Akhunlar (Kionit/Hyon) ve Eftalitler Çağında Maveraünnehir ve Horasan'da Türkler. In H. C. Güzel, K. Çiçek, & S. Koca (Eds.). *Türkler Ansiklopedisi* (Volume 1, pp. 831–843) Ankara: Yeni Türkiye Yayınları.

Alpargu, M. (2002). Türkistan Hanlıkları. In H. C. Güzel, K. Çiçek, & S. Koca (Eds.). *Türkler Ansiklopedisi* (Volume 8, pp. 557–605) Ankara: Yeni Türkiye Yayınları.

Arapov, A. (2006). *Historical Monuments of Uzbekistan Samarkand Bukhara Khiva*. Tashkent: San'at.

Aslanapa, O. (2007). *Türk Sanatı* (8th edition). İstanbul: Remzi Kitapevi.

Kalter, J., Pavaloi, M. (Eds.). (1997). *Heirs to the Silk Road Uzbekistan*. London: Thames and Hudson.

Babaev, T. (2008). Historic Center of Bukhara. *Proceedings of The Workshop on Conservation and Management of Temurids Architecture: 21 April-2 May 2008* (pp. 25–31). Uzbekistan: Republic of Uzbekistan Tashkent, Samarkand, Shakhrisyabz, Bukhara, Khiva, UNESCO &International Institute for Central Asian Studies (IICAS).

Baratova, L. S. (2002). Orta Asya'daki Türk Kağanlığı (M.S. 600–800). In H. C. Güzel, K. Çiçek & S. Koca (Eds.). *Türkler Ansiklopedisi* (Volume 2, pp.89–96) Ankara: T.C. Kültür Bakanlığı.

Belenitsky, A. (1968). *Archaeologia Mvndi Central Asia*. (Hogarth, J. Trans.) Geneva: Nagel Publishing.

Blunt, W. (1973). *The Golden Road to Samarkand*. London: Hamish Hamilton.

Chavannes, E. (2007). Çin *Kaynaklarına Göre Batı Türkleri* (Koç, M. Trans.). İstanbul: Selenge Yayınları.(Original work published 1903).

Çeşmeli, İ. (2007). Antik Çağ'dan XIII. Yüzyıla Kadar Orta Asya ve Karahanlı Dönemi Mimarisi. İstanbul: Arkeoloji ve Sanat Yayınları.

İBN BATTUTA TANCİ. (2000). İbn *Battuta Seyahatnamesi I* (Aykut, S.A. Trans.) (4th edition). İstanbul: Yapı Kredi Yayınları. (Original Work Published fifteenth century).

Esin, E. (1973). Türk Ul-Acem'lerin Eseri Samarrada Cavsak Ul- Hakani'nin Dıvar Resimleri. *Sanat Tarihi Yıllığı*, 5, 309–358.

Esin, E. (1978). *İslamiyet'ten Önceki Türk Kültür Tarihi Ve İslam'a Giriş*. İstanbul: İstanbul Üniversitesi Edebiyat Fakültesi Yayınları.

Esin, E. (1983). İbni Sina Çevresinde Türk Kültürü. *Uluslararası İbni Sina Sempozyumu Bildirileri 17–20 Ağustos 1983.*

Esin, E. (1986, Mayıs). Ribat-i Melik, Hakani Sülalesinden İbrahim-Oğlu Çu Tigin İkinci Naşr Şemsü'l- Mülk ve Harcang'de H. 471/1078'de Yaptırdığı Külliye. *ERDEM,* 2 (5), 405–425.

Esin, E. (1997). *Türkistan Seyahatnamesi* (2nd edition). Ankara: Türk Tarih Kurumu.

Esin, E. (1987). Türkistan Türk Devlet ve Beylikleri *Tarihte Türk Devletleri.* Ankara: Üniversitesi Yayınları.

Frumkin, G. (1970). *Archaeology In Sovıet Central Asi.* Leigen/ Köln: E.J. Brill.

Gorshenina, S., Rapin, C. (2008). *Kabil'den Semerkand'a Arkeologlar Orta Asya'da* (2nd edition). İstanbul: Yapı Kredi Yayınları.

Gömeç, S. (1999). *Türk Cumhuriyetleri ve Toplulukları Tarihi.* Ankara: Akçağ Yayınları.

Mukahamedjannov, A. R., Mukahamedjannov. (1997, October). The City of Bukhara—2500 Years Old. *Scientific and Cultural Heritage of Mankind—To the Third Millennium* (pp. 9–10) Tashkent: UNESCO.

Narsharhi. (1954). *The History of Bukhara* (Frye, R.N. Trans.) Massachusetts: The Mediaeval Academy of America Cambridge. (Original work published 933)

Özdemir, A. H. (2002). Cengiz İstilası. In H. C. Güzel, K. Çiçek & S. Koca (Eds.). *Türkler Ansiklopedisi* (Volume 8, pp. 312–320) Ankara: Yeni Türkiye Yayınları.

Pander, K. (2002). Timuroğullarının Orta Asya Mimari Sanatına Kattıkları. In H. C. Güzel, K. Çiçek & S. Koca (Eds.). *Türkler Ansiklopedisi* (Volume 8, pp. 852–861) Ankara: Yeni Türkiye Yayınları.

Pope, A. U. (Eds.) (1938–39). *A Survey of Persian Art.* Japan: Sopa, Ashiya.

Pugackenkova, G. A. (1958). *Puti Ravzitiva Arhitektury Yuznogo Turkmenistana Pory Rabovladeniya i Feodalisma.* Moskova.

Pugachenkova, G. A. (1960). *Vidayushchiesya pamyatniki izobrazitelnogo iskusstva Uzbekistana* Gosudarstvennoe Izdatelstvo Kh. Tashkent.

Smirnova, O. I. (1963). *Katalog Monet s Gorodişçe Pencikent.* Moskova.

Smirnova, O. I. (1981). *Svodniy Katalog Sogdiyskikh Monet, Izdatelstvo Nauka Glavnaya Redakthiya Votoçnoy Litaroturi.* Moskova.

Staff, J. K. (2002). VI-VIII Asırlarda Türkistan Vahalarında Batı Türk Hâkimiyeti. In H. C. Güzel, K. Çiçek and S. Koca (Eds.). *Türkler Ansiklopedisi* (Volume 2, pp. 97–106) Ankara: Yeni Türkiye Yayınları.

Şeşen, R. (2001). İslam *Coğrafyacılarına Göre Türkler ve Türk* Ülkeleri (2nd edition). Ankara: Türk Tarih Kurumu.

Tashkenbayev, N. (1997). From The History of The Ancient Period of Bukhara. *Scientific and Cultural Heritage of Mankind-To The Third Millennium* (pp. 11–12) Tashkent: UNESCO.

Taşağıl, A. (2001). *Gök-Türkler I.* Ankara: Türk Tarih Kurumu.

Uydu, M. (1995). *Türk-İslam Bütünleşmesi.* İstanbul: Hamle Basın-Yayın Organizasyon ve Dış Tic. Ltd. Şti.

www.bura.org.tr/13.11.2013.

www.trekearth.com/13.11.2013.

CHAPTER 5

KHIVA: A CONSERVED HERITAGE WITHIN THE SANDS

İSMAIL MANGALTEPE

CONTENTS

INTRODUCTION

In Central Asia, after covering hundreds of kilometers along the steps alongside an endless desert, one can imagine that, oasis settlements, flourished near the rivers and gave life to deserts, have been here for thousands of years. However, as seen in the Amu Darya (Oxus) river example, rivers can sometimes change their beds or even flood, resulting in the destruction of the old civilizations, that themselves had nurtured, and then creating new ones along their new routes. The biggest challenge of archaeologists digging this vast region is not to work in the most difficult environment of the world, fighting with sandstorms and burning sun, but to decide where to start excavating to bring out thousands of years-old cities lying under the sands, without a trace. Some settlements came alive thanks to manmade irrigation channels, but later disappeared when these channels dried and dams were destroyed due to invasions. Then, they laid silently under the thick sand layer until a new tribe discovered them and adopted the land as their homeland. The story of Khiva is a result of these two Central Asian facts.

Khiva is a historic city in the Khorezm province of Uzbekistan, situated south of the Aral Sea and the lower parts of Amu Darya. It is one of the oldest agricultural centers in Central Asia. Fishing, and water transportation done for commercial and military purposes on Amu Darya irrigation channels, were always important for this wetland and woody region. By Islam geographers, Khorezm is defined as being surrounded by the Usty-urt plateau in west, the Turk territories which refer to the Kirghiz steps in north, Khorasan in the south and Mawarannahr (Transoxiana) in the east (Özaydin, 1997) (Fig. 1).

Its importance for Silk Road trade comes from connecting roads from the East to the North towards Russia, the Black Sea and the Scandinavian countries. Khiva, connected from the South with the Karakum Desert and the Kizilkum Desert from the east, has very cold winters and very dry, hot summers. Additionally, the fact that the Aral Sea is drying more each day due to the wrong irrigation policies conducted during the Soviet period, is a very important problem for the region's future and makes the continental climate even heavier every day.

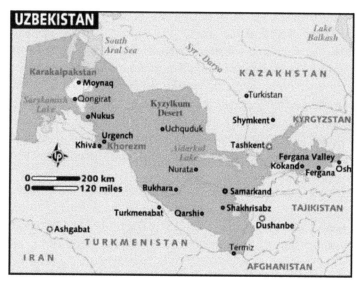

FIGURE 1   Uzbekistan Map and Khiva (www.orsam.org.tr).
Retrieved   November   15,   2013   from   http://www.orsam.org.tr/tr/haritaGaleri.
aspx?HaritaID=45.

HISTORICAL BACKGROUND

According to one legend, in the days when the Khorezm territory was not occupied by any settlement, people escaping from the cruel Persian ruler Zahhak started to live near the small river streaming in these lands and almost transformed this red desert into a forest. Years later, when found by the Persian ruler Feridun, who intended to take them back to their country, they didn't want to leave these lands where "even a gold coin gets green when seeded." But they asked the ruler to open a channel for the river loosing its water in August. A big riverbed was dug and the river was given the name *Belkendi Peridun*. Getting the name *Amu Darya* over time, the river streams anywhere it likes since its bed is not cleaned out of its sands every year (Galima and Corayeff, 2001). Another legend about the exiled people mentions that the ruler's soldiers witnessed the Khorezm people fishing and cooking what they caught in fire. As meat is *Hâr* (pronouns as "Khar") and wood is *rizm/rezm* in the old Khorezmian language, they started calling this land *Khwarezm* (Özaydin, 1997). The meaning of Khorezm is also explained as "Eastern Lands", "Sunrise Lands," and "Fertile Lands" in different sources.

Another legend about Khorezm is dated to the Prophet Suleyman (Soliman) period. Hz. Suleyman sent a fairy into exile with a giant companionship. In their flight, when they noticed Khorezm, they decided to live there and got married and had many children., the Khorezmians (Galima and Corayeff, 2001).

According to the historians' narratives, Khorezm was established by the famous legendary Persian ruler Siyavush and served as his homeland. Al-Makdisi reports that the ancient people of Khorezm were the children of Persian men and Turkic women (Esin, 1997). It is widely believed that Khorezmians were a Persian tribe exiled from the Balkhan Mountains by their Persian or Turkic ruler in 1292 B.C. (Togan, 1951). In Islamic sources, it is written that Khorezmians, whose mothers were Turks, had good morals and beautiful faces as Turks. Whatever legend is closest to reality, Khorezm is the only place in Central Asia, which kept its name from the beginning and its rulers' title until the 19th century (Munîs and Agahî, 1999).

Well-known Russian archaeologist and ethnologist Tolstov, who worked extensively in Khorezm, Kazakhistan, and Turkmenistan, unearthed many old cities dating back to 3000 B.C. in Khorezm. Interestingly, he discovered a large irrigation channel network making the researchers think of an industrial revolution and dated it nearly to the middle of the first thousand years B.C. (Frumkin, 1970). According to Herodotos, Hecataeus from Miletus and Avestian texts, Khorezmians have established a developed confederation well before Achaemenids ruled this region (Gorshenina and Rapin, 2008). Particularly, Herodotos reports that Khorezmians were the leading of the five tribes whose lands were irrigated by the five channels taken from the Grand Axes (Amu Darya) where agriculture was made (Togan, 1951).

Available heritage from the Kelteminar culture, created by fishers and hunters at the end of 3rd–4th thousands B.C., corresponds to the Neolithic period of Khorezm. Its most important example is Janbazkala IV. The Bronze age, between mid of second thousand years B.C. and beginning of first thousand B.C., is called Tazabagyab and presents many similarities with the Andronovo Culture of Kazakhstan and South Siberia. That is why Tolstov proposed that a considerable migration happened from Central Asian steps to the south, towards Khorezm, Turkmenistan, Iran and

Afghanistan in the second half of second thousand years B.C. (Frumkin, 1970).

As for religions in Khorezm, old Khorezmians have adopted Zoroastrianism, Christianity (Melchites denomination) and Judaism before Islam (Togan, 1951). Tolstov reports that even Khazar Turks adopted Judaism due to their good relations with Khorezmians (Esin, 1997).

Khorezmians regained their independence after Achaemenids, before Alexander the Great (336–323 B.C.)'s army arrival. While Alexander was in Bactria, Khorezmian king Pharasman visited him with his 1500 person court, and proposed to guide him in his conquests, as his lands spread to the Blacksea shores. But they only signed a friendship agreement when Alexander replied that he was not planning to go north. (Togan, 1951). Tolstov attributes the post-Achaemenid and pre-Kushan period (4th century B.C.–1st century A.D.) to the "Kangha (or Kanghui)" tribe whose country was lying between the Tien-shan Mountains and the Caspian Sea. This period shows a high progress in Khorezm city settlements (new cities like Kalaly Gyr, Janbazkala and Koy-Kyrylgan-Kala), handcrafts, and irrigation. The Kangha people mentioned by Tolstov was a Turkic tribe corresponding to the *Kangar* in Turkish. In the period between 1st–3rd century A.D., Kushan sovereignty was put on display in cities like Koy-Kyrylgan-Kala and Toprak-Kala (Frumkin, 1970).

According to Khorezm narratives reported by Al-Biruni (?–1048), the local dynasty Afrighids ruled Khorezm starting from the 3rd century A.D. The 6th century was the start of the Turkic sovereignty period, beginning with the Ephtalites ("White Huns") and followed by the Western Turks. It lasted until the Arabic invasion, but Turks kept the local Khorezm dynasty in administration. When Khorezm was conquered by Arabs in 717, they left only one of the two titles of the Khorezm rulers, which is "Khorezm-shah" (Togan, 1951). Muhammed ibn Musa Al-Kharezmi (?–850), the founder of algebra, was born and got his first education in Khorezm. He wrote his important books on mathematics, astronomy and geography when he was working in the famous Beytu'l-Hikme (House of wisdom) in Bagdad under Abbasid Caliph Al-Ma'mun (813–833) patronage. Ibn Fadlan, who was sent to Volga Bulgar Turks as an ambassador of Abbasid Caliph Al-Muqtadir (908–932), reports in his travel book from the 10th century that Khorezmshah Muhammed ibn Irak was a vassal of Samanids and was helping them to propagate Islam especially among Khazar Turks (Şeşen, 2010).

Samanids gave up the administration of Left Khorezm (Gurganch), with high commercial importance, to a governor who was directly connected to them, called Ma'mun ibn Muhammed. The descendants of this governor, named Mamunids, defeated the Afrighids ruling Right Khorezm in 996 and united Khorezm. They patronized important scholars such as Al-Biruni and İbn Sina, known as Avicenna (?–1037) in the Ma'mun Academy that they established in Gurganch (today Urgench). Ghaznevids took over Khorezm sovereignty in 1017, resulting in the start of the Turkization period of Khorezm (Togan, 1951).

Ghaznevid Mahmud (998–1030) gave Khorezm's administration to governor Altuntash (1017–1032). Then Seljuks conquered Khorezm with the leadership of Chagri Bey (died 1059). Although they kept local governors at the beginning, Sultan Malik Shah I (1072–1092) handed over the governance to Anush Tigin (1077–1097). During the Anush Tigin's son Qutbuddin Muhammad (1097–1128) period, the greatest state which chose Khorezm as its center and reached its largest borders from Syr Darya to Iraq at the beginning of the 13th century, the Turkic Khwarezmid (or Khwarezm-Shah) State, was established (Kafesoğlu, 2000). In their sovereignty, Kunya Urgench became the capital and caught the high level of Khorasan cities. Many scholars like Al-Zamakhshari, Fahraddin Al-Razi, Najmuddin Kubra were active in this period (Taneri, 1997).

In 1221, Mongols conquered Kunya Urgench, destroyed it and put an end to the Khwarezm-Shah State. When Genghis Khan was partitioning his conquered lands among his sons, the Eastern Dasht-e Kipchak (the Kipchak plain on the Volga River sides) and Khorezm were left to Cudji Khan (1206–1227). But as Cudji died before his father in 1227, Khorezm was given to the founder of the Golden Horde State, Batu Khan (1240–1255). In the second land partitioning after the Ilhanid State establishment, Northern and Western Khorezm were decided to be governed by the Golden Horde, and Khiva and Kath by the Chagatai Hanate. The Qungrads, one of the most important tribes of Golden Horde, came to govern Khorezm in the 15th century by establishing the Sufi Dynasty (Kafali, 1976). Timur (1370–1405), the founder of the Timurid State, not only conquered Khorezm in 1388, but destroyed Kunya-Urgench worse than the Mongols had. The Timurid period was closed by the Uzbek Sheybani Han (1500–1510), when he took over Khorezm in 1502 (Özaydin, 1997).

Khorezm Uzbeks, defeated by the Persian ruler Shah İsmail (1501–1524) at Merv in 1510, rebelled against the Persians in 1511 and declared the son of Yadigar Khan İlbars (1515–1525) as their khan. This dynasty, known in the history as the Arapshahid or Yadigarids, ruled Khorezm until 1740 (Özaydin, 1997; Saray, 1997). In this way, with the participation of the Uzbeks and the Yomud Turks, the Khorezm Khanate, known especially in Russia and Western Europe in the 18th century as the Khiva Khanate, was established. In the beginning of the 17th century, this khanate's homeland was extending from the Amu Darya lowers to Khorasan and Mangishlak. In the Arap Muhammed Khan period (1602–1623), Khiva became the capital of Khorezm. After the strong governance of Abu Al-Gazi Bahadir Khan (1643–1663) and his son Anusha Khan, Sheybanids of Bukhara captured Khorezm in 1687 for a short period. Due to the internal conflicts and the attacks led by Kalmyks and Dzungars, the domination of Iranian ruler Nadir Shah (1736–1747) was accepted between 1740 and 1747.

The fights between the Khiva Khanate and Iran, especially for the Khorasan region, continued until the second quarter of the 19th century. In this difficult period, the Khiva Khanate, who was in rivalry with the Buhkara Emirate, also had a hostile relationship and underwent destructive attacks (Saray, 1993). Khorezm was taken back by Gaib Han (1747–1758) in 1747, but again, the sovereignty disputes started and resulted in the change of the ruling dynasty in favor of the Qungrads. This dynasty ruled Khorezm independently until 1873 and under Russian occupancy between 1873–1920 (Hayit, 1995). After the political regime change in Russia, Khorezm People's Soviet Republic was established and survived between 1920–1924. In 1924, the eastern lands of the Khiva Khanate were given to the Uzbekistan Soviet Socialist Republic while western lands were left to the Turkmenistan Soviet Socialist Republic. The ethnic groups in the Khiva Khanate were Uzbeks, Manghits, Qungrads, Turkmens and Karakalpaks. Today, the historical Khorezm region is shared by Uzbekistan, Turkmenistan and the Karakalpak Autonomous Republic of Uzbekistan.

Due to its crossroards position, both import trade (watermelon, dried melon, grapes, rice, dried fish, honey, cheese, silk and cotton fabrics) and transit trade between Siberia, China, Iran, India, Russia and the Scandinavian countries (leather, paraffin, cloths, armor, sword, livestock) were very colorful in Khorezm. All these products were sold in the Khorezm bazaars. It is argued that the main reason for the Mongol invasion of Khorezm and the eastern Islam lands in the 13th century was this lively trade environment (Özaydin, 1997).

Today, Khorezm still has 400 historical monuments, among which 124, have national significance and are protected by the state, 240 have regional signifance and the remaining 136 are protected by the municipality and local government. Furthermore, Khorezm has an attractive natural heritage with Amu Darya and a lot of lakes. It is also very convenient for ecology and adventure tourism, as it presents both desert and forest features. Khorezm is also an important handcrafts and applied arts center since the very ancient times, and the best examples are exhibited in local museums (Babadjanov, 1999).

Coming to Khiva, there are two narratives related to the son Sam of prophet Noah about Khiva's first settlement. In one of them, Sam landed his boat on a hill where Amu Darya waters could not reach. Then, in his dream, he saw that there were thousands of candles lit around this hill. Telling his dream to his father, he was advised to setup a castle with high walls, which is referred to as Ichan Kala (Fig. 2) today, and they settled there. The other narrative reports that Sam dug a well on the hill he saw in his dream and named this place "Hiyvak" which meant "well" in old Khorezmian language. This legendary well is still identified with the well situated in the north-west direction of Ichan Kala (Galima and Corayeff, 2001).

FIGURE 2   Khiva Ichan Kala (commons.wikimedia.org, Photo by Patrickringgenberg / CC BY-SA 3.0).
Retrieved November 15, 2013 from http://commons.wikimedia.org/wiki/File:Khiva_Itchan_Kala.JPG

The oldest studies relating to the age of Khiva are found in the 10th century written sources (Al-Istakhri, Al-Makdisi, Abd al-Razzak Samarkandi, Abu Al-Gazi Bahadir Khan, etc.). Gulyamov mentions that Khiva was a settlement developed on top of the old Khaykonik (modern Palvanyab) channel in the archaic period. Starting from the 10th, historical records state Khiva's names as Khivak, Khiva, Khayvanik, Khaykonik and Raml. "Khaykonik" among them means "big river/channel" and gives its name to the mentioned channel (Mukhamedjanov, 1997). During the 16th century, when Amu Darya changed its bed and flowed into the Aral Sea instead of the Caspian Sea, Urgench (today Kunya-Urgench) lost all its water and Khiva became the capital of North Khorezm for the first time, and later of all the Khorezm region.

In order to reveal the age of Khiva, six excavations were made on a 1200 square meter area of Ichan Kale, the inner city of Khiva. The oldest city has been discovered at a 7 meters depth, and with 10 historical layers, the 2,500-year old city history was recovered. This also proved that Ichan Kale is the oldest settlement of the city. The oldest ceramics findings and wall ruins date back to the Viet–4th centuries B.C. In the second layer corresponding to the 3rd–4th centuries B.C., the old city walls were fortified with two additional brick layers and defense towers. It is observed that Khiva was an agriculture center thanks to the Khaykonik channel waters, and also a crafts center in this period. Due to unknown reasons, the city suffered a decline starting from the 1st century B.C., was covered by sands and the city walls wore down. However, the city was reborn in the next layer and started to become a trade center from the 1st century A.D. onwards and a palace was built on its west side. The second decline of Khiva corresponds to the end of the 4th century until the end of the 5th century, being covered by the sands again. In the 6th century, the city was restored and Dishpan Kala (the outer city) developed as the city expanded. According to fifth layer findings, dating from the period between the 6th and the beginning of the 12th century, Khiva was involved in Silk Road trade besides its arts center status. Dishpan Kala was shaped by the settling of craftsmen quarters. This prosperous period ended with the Mongol invasion in 1220–1221, however, the city was reborn again. The last layer represents the period when city culture grew most, dated to the 16th–19th centuries. The unique architectural integrity is a result of these centuries.

Khiva Khans cared much about historiography and used the Chagatai language, one of the Turkish dialects, unlike the other Turkish khanates, which promoted Persian instead. Important chroniclers such as Munis and Agahi also served as a statement, some Khans like Abu al-Gazi Bahadir and his son Anush wrote about Turkic history and the khanate themselves. So, Khorezm was the castle of Turkish language and literature from the Mongol invasion until the 20th century (Munîs and Agahî, 1999).

TOURIST ATTRACTIONS IN KHIVA

The most important feature of Khiva, which is recognized as a "museum city" since 1967 and has been under UNESCO protection since 1990, is its architectural integrity reflecting the past despite the fact that most of the monuments are inherited from the 19th century. Most monuments are of adobe-based architectural heritage and Islamic civilization monuments like mosques, minarets, madrassahh, and caravanserais are present. The high walls encircling "shahristan" (the inner city), palaces, narrow streets, houses with a single wooden column in front of their eiwans and fantastic wooden doors are also characteristics of Khiva.. Unlike Samarkand and Bukhara, where modern life surrounds historical buildings, Khiva presents a film studio atmosphere that takes the tourists back to the Khiva Khanate period. Unfortunately, due to human factors (i.e. historical monuments used for different functions) and natural factors like water level, earthquakes, material aging, these world heritage architectural sites have been degrading. Currently, the Khorezm Ma'mun Academy, established by Islam Karimov with the same name as the historic sciences academy of the 10th century, does research on how to conserve historical monuments in Khorezm.

The most important elements of Khiva's local architecture are the techniques used on its buildings, the artistic style resulting from the synthesis of the Islamic civilization with different cultures from the old ages and the continuity of tradition of these two features from the Middle Ages. During the whole Khiva Khanate period, traditional building techniques and architecture thrived in a country closed to the outside world. Under Soviet ruling, religious monuments' functioning were forbidden and the city was emptied, loosing its soul. However, local masters continued to build new houses based on old tradition (Prochazka, 1990). Although most buildings are only 100-years old, they include very old materials taken from old buildings dating back to the 10th century. As an example, it is said that some of the oldest wooden columns in the Friday Mosque were brought from the old capital Kath. To really show Khiva's atmosphere, we need to present a list of must-see monuments for a tourist walking around Ichan Kala within this dense city (Fig. 3).

FIGURE 3 Ichan Kala plan and monuments (Pugachenkova, 1976): 1. Sayid Bay Madrassah; 2. Allah Kuli Khan Madrassah; 3. Kutluk Murad Madrassah; 4. Baths of Anush Khan; 5. Allah Kuli Khan Caravanserai and Tim; 6. Tash Hauli Palace; 7. White Masdjid; 8. Friday Mosque; 9. Sayid Alauddin Mausoleum; 10. Mohammed Amin Khan Madrassah and Kalta Minar; 11. Kunya Ark; 12. Mohammed Rakhim Khan Madrassah; 13. Shir Gazi Khan Madrassah; 14. Arab Khan Madrassah; 15. Pakhlivan Mahmud Mausoleum Complex; 16. Bagbaniy Mosque; 17. Islam Hodja Mosque and Minaret; 18-Kheivan Well; 19. Bagcha Darvaza; 20. Palvan Darvaza; 21. Tash Darvaza.

ICHAN KALA

This is the *shahristan* (inner city) covering a 26 hectares area and holding the oldest administrative, political, social and economical buildings. The walls encircling Ichan Kala, of which the oldest parts date from the 5th century, are 2200 meters long and 6–8 meters high (Gombos, 1976).

They are strengthened with semicircle towers within a defined interval (Fig. 4). Part of these walls, very effective in city defense, was destroyed by the Iranian ruler Nadir Shah in the 18th century. Ichan Kala, honored as a member of UNESCO's World Heritage List, includes 2 royal palaces, 60 madrassahs, one great-size mosque (the Friday Mosque), many smaller mosques, minarets, mausoleums, a covered bazaar, a caravanserai, a hammam, and administrators' and traders' dwellings.

FIGURE 4   Ichan Kala city walls (commons.wikimedia.org, Photo by Patrickringenberg/ CC BY-SA 3.0).
Retrieved November 15, 2013 from http://commons.wikimedia.org/wiki/File:Khiva_ Itchan_Kala_walls.JPG

Ichan Kala has four gates called *darvaza*. The western gate, Ata Darvaza, is the youngest, being 50-years old, as the previous gate was canceled while opening the city to motor traffic and is located near Kunya Ark. The northern gate, Bagcha Darvaza, opens up towards Urgench, the eastern gate, Palvan Darvaza, opens towards Hazarasp and the Amu Darya river, and the southern gate, Tash Darvaza, opens towards the Karakum Desert. Ichan Kala, emptied during Soviet Russia, is now populated by only a small portion of the local city population, especially by the families of craftsmen (Macleod and Mayhew, 2004).

The eastern and oldest city gate, Palvan Darvaza, hosted a prison in the 17th century. This strongest gate was an important place, where the khan's edicts were announced to the Khiva people, and where runaway slaves were nailed on their ears, after being killed in the bazaar square (Khiva,

1993). Today, as a 60 meter tunnel-like passage, it is a small indoors shopping center. Palvan Darvaza draws attention with its six cupolas, eiwan, niches next to the gate, attractive blue tiles on its arc and towers (Figure 5).

FIGURE 5   Palvan Darvaza Gate (commons.wikimedia.org, Photo by Faqscl / CC BY-SA 3.0).
Retrieved November 15, 2013 from http://commons.wikimedia.org/wiki/File:Palvan_Darvoza_Porte_Est_East_gate_Khiva.JPG

KUNYA ARK

Next to the western gate Ata Darvaza, one can visit Kunya Ark (means "old castle") whose different parts were built in various times throughout 13th, 14th, 17th and 19th centuries (Fig. 6).

FIGURE 6   Kunya Ark and Ak Sheikh Baba Bastion (commons.wikimedia.org, Photo by upyernoz / CC-BY 2.0).
Retrieved November 15, 2013 from http://commons.wikimedia.org/wiki/File:Kukhna_ark,_khiva_(472547).jpg

The first palace of Khiva khans, dated back to the 17th century, is located inside this oldest city center. Its called as "old" after Tash Hauli Palace was built in the 19th century. The castle is separated from the city with its high walls, connecting to Ichan kala walls with Ata Darvaza. It includes harem, the working place of khans, throne room, reception room (*arz hauli*), arsenal, mint, summer mosque and meeting hall (Khiva, 1993).

It is exciting to trace the reflections of rural and urban architecture traditions to royal architecture in Khiva. In palace architecture, there are many rectangular courtyards used for different purposes. The palace courtyard, where administration tasks and celebration ceremonies take place, is called *kurinishhana, mehmonhana* or *ishrathauli*. The most important part in this division is the throne room with its magnificent decorations, especially in its iwan. Khan would accept the people in the open iwan in summer, and in the *yurt* (tent) built on top of the brick platform (Fig. 7) in winter (Mankovskaya, 1982).

This is the area where the *cülus* ceremony takes place, in which the khan is given his sword and crown turban (Esin, 1997). The court building where state affairs are conducted is a called *arz-hauli*, which carries similar architectural characteristics as the kurinishana. *Ichan-hauli* or *harem*, located at the north, is a long courtyard where the sultans wives reside.

The largest area is for the khan, and there are two story buildings for the concubines and the servants (Mankovskaya, 1982).

FIGURE 7   The oval platform where khan's yurt is placed (Pugachenkova, 1976).

Ak Sheikh Baba Bastion, being the oldest building in the city, is at the highest point in Kunya Ark. It is named after a sufi who is claimed to lead a life of seclusion here in the 14th century. The two story building, which survived until today, has served as a watch tower and gun-powder arsenal. The blue-white tiles, decorating the inner side of the summer mosque (1838) in Kunya Ark, were made by the local tile makers, Ibadullah and Abdullah Jin, whose tiles also decorated the Tash Hauli and Pakhlavan Mahmoud tomb.

TASH HAULI PALACE

In this new center, of which its construction was initiated by Abdullah Kulu Han (1825–1842) in 1830 as the city center was being moved towards east and of which construction has lasted for 8 years, a big palace was built with 163 rooms and 3 large courtyards. It has the appearance of a fortress with its loopholes, towers and gates. Tash Hauli consists of three main parts, all constructed in different periods, laying around the large courtyard and made up of the windowless iwans with tiles, being carried by thin wooden columns. In the northern section lies the Harem, built between 1830–1834, with high walls, and in the southern section are the reception and meeting rooms (Gombos, 1976). As you move from the dark tunnels of the palace towards the rooms among the iwans, covered all around with tiles, the darkness yields itself gradually to a sweet tranquility and coolness. The circular platform seen in Kunya Ark, where the royal tent of the khan is set-up, also exists in this palace (Esin, 1997).

To the south of the harem, where the khan family, relatives and concubines live, there exists five rooms for the khan and his four wives. The harem, with the blue-white tile panels decorating the walls in the iwans, the ceiling decorations where red color is extensively used, and thin wooden Khiva columns, present a unique architecture (Fig. 8).

FIGURE 8   Tash Hauli Palace Courtyard (commons.wikimedia.org, Photo by upyernoz / CC-BY 2.0).
Retrieved November 15, 2013 from http://commons.wikimedia.org/wiki/File:Tash_Hauli_Palace,_Khiva_(481385).jpg

DISHPAN KALA

The walls of Dishpan Kala were built in 1842 to be protected from Turkmen attacks. The walls being 6 km long, were said to be finished in 6 weeks by making one fourth of the population of the city participate in its construction. All the crafts workshops and bazaar units are located behind the walls. Although 10 gates existed in the construction of Dishpan Kala, today only three gates are in use. In the eastern most gate Koy-Darvaza, the upper floor is used for looking out, and the lower floor is composed of guard rooms. Since this gate, with a length of more than 12 m leads to Hazerasp, it is also called Hazerasp-Darvaz (Khiva, 1993). The northern gate, Koy Darvaza, (Fig. 9) on the other hand, leading to Urganch, with the four domes, two belts, three cylindrical towers decorated with blue tiles on top and mosaic bricks on the body, presents itself as a magnificent gateway (Mankovskaya, 1982).

FIGURE 9 Dishpan Kala Koy Darvaza Gate (sambuh.com).
Retrieved November 15, 2013 from http://sambuh.com/en/uzbekistan/cities/khiva/dishan-kala.html

FRIDAY MOSQUE

Friday mosque, depicted the first time by Arab geographer Al-Makdisi, with its 55 × 45 m. inscription dated 1789, is the biggest mosque of Khiva and was constructed at a very central locale, at the crossroads of the two main streets connecting the gates of Ichan Kala. Unlike the other mosques, it lacks a courtyard and is fully enclosed, which suggests early Islamic traditions with a single story and multicolumn architecture (Fig. 10) (Prochazka, 1990). Its minaret, with upwardly tapering body and turquoise blue tiles, is quite impressive. The big entrance next to the minaret opens up to a wide hole with 212 wooden columns, each of which is 3.15 m. tall, all parts of the bodies having been covered with local motifs (Aslanapa, 1996). The area, which is covered with a flat ceiling with no ornaments, is lit up by two light holes through which the blue Khiva sky is seen, and leaves an ethereal effect on people. Some of these columns are from the 10th, 12th, 15th and 16th centuries (Mankovskaya, 1982).

FIGURE 10   Friday Mosque inner view (commons.wikimedia.org, Photo by dalbera / CC-BY 2.0).
Retrieved November 15, 2013 from http://commons.wikimedia.org/wiki/File:La_ mosquée_Juma_Masjid_(Khiva,_Ouzbékistan)_(5587004464).jpg

Khiva, like Bukhara, has been the center of Islamic science since the Middle Ages. The most important sign of this is that, the buildings which shape the city panorama the most, are madrassahs some of which have capacities reaching 250 students and contain large libraries. Generally, among the madrassahs which are recognized by the name of the statesman by whom they were built, the ones that should be seen are Mohammed Rakhim Khan, Mat-Niyaz-Divanbeyi, Allah Kuli Khan, Kutluq Murad Inaq, Muhammad Amin Khan and Shir Gazi Khan madrassahs. Madrassahs form squares by lining up opposite each other with their high tiled portals (also called *pishtak*).

SHIR GAZI KHAN MADRASSAH

Shir Gazi Khan is the oldest madrassah in Khiva, and was built by 5000 Iranian slaves between 1718–1720, who were taken over by Shir Gazi Han (1715–1728) after a campaign to Mashad. When the khan, who promised to release the slaves once the construction was completed, was not content with the building and asked for new work, he was lynched by the slaves before the construction was over. The building is comprised of two-story rooms on the entrance wing, and single-story rooms around the courtyard. The reading room rests behind the big portal of the entrance wing. This madrassah has been the center of Islamic science of the Khiva Khanate and was named "House of Scholars" in local language. Today it is used as an area for exhibitions of poetry (for example the famous Turkmen poet Mahtum Kulu, who graduated from here) and medicine (Gombos, 1976; Macleod and Mayhew, 2004).

MUHAMMAD RAKHIM KHAN MADRASSAH

This madrassah was built in 1871 by Muhammad Rakhim Bahadir Khan (1864–1910), who wrote under the nickname Feruz and recognized the domination of Khiva by Russians during his reign. It is known by the blue tiled pishtak and facade, and the little domed towers placed at the corners of the building. (Fig. 11) New functions have been assigned to the madrassah; initially as Khiva Handcrafts Center in 1998, and nowadays as a museum which reflects the last periods of Khiva with local clothes and arms, flags, and photos of Feruz and Isfendiyar Khan (Macleod and Mayhew, 2004).

FIGURE 11 Muhammad Rakhim Khan Madrassah (flickr.com, Photo by dalbera / CC-BY 2.0).
Retrieved November 15, 2013 from http://www.flickr.com/photos/dalbera/5606468162/sizes/m/in/photostream/

KUTLUQ MURAD INAQ MADRASSAH

This madrassah consists of 81 cells (1804–1812), that house the tomb of Allah Kuli drew Khan's (1825–1842) uncle, Kutluk Murad Inak's, attention with its two stories and by being the only madrassah with unglazed earth reliefs on its corner towers (Fig. 12). Since somebody who died outside the city walls cannot be taken inside the walls according to the Khiva law, when Kutluk Murad Inak died outside, some parts of the city walls had to be destroyed to bury him here. In the courtyard there exists a *sardoba* (cistern) located at the bottom of stairs. The higher platform, on which the bazaar used to be set-up, today hosts dance and song performances (Macleod and Mayhew, 2004).

FIGURE 12 Kutluq Murad Inaq Madrassah (commons.wikimedia.org, Photo by Hylgeriak /Wikipedia/ CC BY-SA 3.0).
Retrieved November 15, 2013 from http://commons.wikimedia.org/wiki/File:Kutlug_Murad_Inak_Madrassah_Khiva.jpg

ALLAH KULI HAN MADRASSAH

This second biggest madrassah of Khiva, dated 1835, sits across from the Kutluk Murad Inak madrassah, has plenty of decorations, and has a courtyard surrounded by 99 cells on all four sides. Entrance portal has a single iwan, and the side wings consist of two stories with three iwans on each

(Aslanapa, 1996). The madrassah, which had a library built inside that did not survive to present day, is now being used as a museum presenting the theme "Health in Khorezm" (Prochazka, 1990).

MUHAMMAD AMIN KHAN MADRASSAH

Built in the second half of the XIXth century by Muhammad Amin Khan (1845–1855), this madrassah consists of four iwans, 38x38 m in size. The courtyard is surrounded by 99 cells, and a high portal (Fig. 13). With its capacity of 250 students and a covered area of 72x60 m, it is the biggest madrassah in the city, housing one summer and winter mosques, thought to be used for education purposes. Unfortunately, despite the warnings from UNESCO, it is being used as a hotel today.

FIGURE 13 Muhammad Amin Khan Madrasah (commons.wikimedia.org, Photo by upyernoz / CC BY-2.0).
Retrieved November 15, 2013 from http://commons.wikimedia.org/wiki/File:Mohammed_amin_khan_madrassah,_khiva_(463810).jpg

KALTA-MINAR (KOK-MINAR)

This minaret, outside of which is covered with colorful glazed bricks (Fig. 14) sits in front of the main entrance of Muhammad Amin Khan madrassah. Kalta Minar, whose construction was started in 1852 by Muhammad Amin Khan, became the widest and tallest minaret of Islam world with a 14.2 m. base diameter and height reaching 70 m., with the intention of "watching over Bukhara from the top," was not completed after the death of the khan in 1885, and with a final height of 26 m was named the "short minaret."

There is a story, which states that because the architect agreed to make a taller minaret for the Emir of Buhara, he was taken down from the top of Kalta Minar and killed. The most spectacular view of the city can be experienced from the top, which is reached by 64 feet spiral stairs (corkscrew) (Macleod and Mayhew, 2004).

FIGURE 14   Kalta Minar (commons.wikimedia.org, Photo by pastaitaken / CC-BY 3.0). Retrieved November 15, 2013 from http://commons.wikimedia.org/wiki/File:Kalta_Minar.jpg

ISLAM HODJA COMPLEX

This mosque complex was built in 1910 as the last monument of Ichan Kala by Islam Hodja in 1910, who was the vizier of Isfendiyar Khan (1910–1918), and was killed despite his various reforms in education, transportation and health care. With its decorated facade, Islam Hoca madrassah has a traditional structure. Its minaret, being the tallest in Khiva with a length of 44.5 m and a base diameter of 9.5 m, resembles a lighthouse (Fig. 15), and has served as a Watch Tower for Turkmen attacks. It can be seen from all sides of the city and with its rich ornaments of blue and green tiles, creates the impression of the Timur period (Aslanapa, 1996). Today, the 42-room madrassah is serving as an applied local handcrafts museum, with pieces ranging from local women's clothing to architectural pieces (Macleod and Mayhew, 2004).

FIGURE 15 Islam Hodja Minaret (flickr.com, Photo by dalbera, CC BY 2.0).
Retrieved November 15, 2013 from http://www.flickr.com/photos/dalbera/5586414709/sizes/m/in/photolist

In Khiva, mausoleums built for religious leaders, khans or respected people are usually covered with small domes. In or around the courtyards of tombs, people frequently see graves with no tombstones, made in the form of stone sarcophagi only with brick.

PAKHLAVAN MAHMOUD MAUSOLEUM COMPLEX

To the south of the Friday Mosque stands the most important mausoleum of Khiva, built for Pakhlavan Mahmoud (1247–1325), an important poet named "Hayyam of Khorezm" and was said to be an unbeatable wrestler and has grown to be a legend with his healing powers. This tomb defined by Vambery who traveled to Khiva as a "four hundred year old structure" is comprised of parts constructed in different periods (Gombos, 1976). Its current plan was arranged in 1816 by Mohammed Rakhim Khan (1806–1825). Pakhlavan Mahmoud, who at the same time was doing furriery, is known as a poet and philosopher in Khorezm and India, and as the "protector of Khiva" in Khiva (Mankovskaya, 1976). Another important thing about this site is that it houses the graves of important Khiva khans such as Abu Al-Gazi Khan, Anush Khan, Mohammed Rakhim Khan, Allah Kuli Han, and the tomb of the mother of the last Khiva khan, Isfendiyar Han. In the mausoleum complex, besides the tomb rooms, there exists an open summer mosque and a *tekke* (dervish lodge) (Macleod and Mayhew, 2004). In the adjacent cemetery, besides the stone sarcophagus shaped mud and brick tombs unique to Turkestan, there also exist small tombs with domes (Fig. 16).

The mausoleum has a turquoise-blue tiled dome visible from all around Ichan Kala, and again has a blue tile decorated facade. The inner side is famous for its blue-white, indigo and violet tiles with plant decorations covering all walls and also having Pakhlavan Mahmoud *rubai*s on (Esin, 1997).

FIGURE 16   Pakhlavan Mahmoud Mausoleum and tombs around (flickr.com, Photo by dalbera / CC BY 2.0).
Retrieved November 15, 2013 from http://www.flickr.com/photos/dalbera/5596932909/in/photolist

SAYID ALAUDDIN MAUSOLEUM

Sayid Alauddin (d. 1302) was a local Naqshibandi sheik and sufi in the time of Pakhlavan Mahmoud. Sayid Alauddin Mausoleum is the oldest structure in Khiva, and was built by his successor, Emir Kulyal (d. 1370) as a tomb room and adjacent mosque (Fig. 17). The mausoleum consists of two chambers, one being a *ziyarethane* where people can visit and "guest-room" for the visitors, and the other being *gurhane* where the grave is located The feature in the plan of the structure is intended to draw attention and light towards the burial chamber (Prochazka, 1990). Being a 14th century Mogol era building, it was built again by Allah Kuli Han. The sarcophagus in the very plain looking tomb is especially worth seeing with its light-blue, dark-blue and white floral-patterned tiles (Gombos, 1976).

FIGURE 17   Sayid Alauddin Mausoleum (flickr.com, Photo by dalbera/ CC BY 2.0). Retrieved November 15, 2013 from http://www.flickr.com/photos/dalbera/5596918457/in/photolist.

In Khiva, the bazaars with shops, the caravanserais, the covered bazaar called *tim*, and hamams are located close to the city gates. The bazaar area, which is primarily located at the east gate, moved out of Ichan Kala in the 19th century, when Tash Hauli and Kutluk Murad Inak madrassahs were built and the area got smaller. The bazaar, which started immediately behind Palvan Darvaza used to extend to the slave market, but still remained within Dishpan Kala (Mankovskaya, 1982). According to Khudaiberdy bin Kushmuhammed Khivaki, Allah Kuli Khan bazaar was created in 1832 by filling the lake to the east of the city in 45 days (Akhmedov, 1997). This bazaar, also known as the "palace bazaar," connects the city to the great bazaar and to Allah Kuli Han Cervanserai, again dated 1832.

It is possible to see the wooden columns, which are named after the city and present a high wood craftsmanship, in the dwellings, the palaces and the mosques in Khiva. The Khiva column (Fig. 18), one of the most striking features of local architecture, with its unique color and decorations all around, gets thinner as it goes down, and appears ready to snap lands on its wooden, stone or marble base. Despite the waist, which bends carrying the whole weight of the building, it dazzles the watchers with the charm of an old lady aware of her beauty, defying the years that have passed. The same kind of craftsmanship is observed on the wooden doors, which with their complex decorations turn the entrance of even the simplest homes into palaces (Fig. 19). When it comes to tile crafting, the color and design of the high quality tiles maintain the tradition of the Timur period (Uzbekistan, 1997). The 18th century tiles are especially elegant with a common appearance of blue-white floral. On the glazed bricks which decorate the facades of minarets and buildings one can see small amounts of Kufic writing, which when in sequence result in decorative shapes (Esin, 1997).

FIGURE 18   Typical Khiva Column (flickr.com, Photo by dalbera / CC BY 2.0). Retrieved November 15, 2013 from http://www.flickr.com/photos/dalbera/5597503122/sizes/m/in/photostream/

FIGURE 19   A Khiva wooden door with colorful floral motives (Pugachenkova, 1976).

HANDCRAFTS AND APPLIED ARTS IN KHIVA

In Khiva, just like in Khorezm area, one of the most important traditional handcrafts is jewelry making (Figs. 20 and 21). In the Khorezm jewelry, made by Karalpak Turks and Turkmens, the materials used are silver, coral, turqoise and colored glass; and the figures used are stylized double-headed eagle and human figures, diamond shaped leaves and keys symbolizing the doors opening to heaven (Uzbekistan, 1997).

FIGURE 20   Temporal pendant, Khiva, end of 19th century (Uzbekistan: Heirs to Silk Road, 1997).

FIGURE 21   Forehead pendant, Khiva, end of 19th century (Uzbekistan: Heirs to Silk Road, 1997).

Khiva today is the center of music, poetry and fine arts. Khorezm is famous for the black sheep fur hats that men have been wearing since ancient times. Besides cotton production, carpentry, cloth, and wood and stone carvings are still alive in Khiva. In Ichan Kala, it is possible to watch various shows about traditional Khiva folklore with music and dance, to purchase various handcrafts like traditional clothes (Fig. 22), fur hats (*karakul tilpak*), carpets, textile products (*suzani, ikat*), and jewelry. Khorezm History Museum, which previously used to exist in Tash Hauli palace, now resides in a stand-alone building. One section of the museum exhibits archeological and ethnographical findings found in the excavations done in Koy-Kyrylgan Kala and Toprak Kala by Tolstov. Other museums are found in palaces and madrassahs. Khorezm Life and Applied Arts Museum is located in Kazi Kalyan Madrassah and presents samples from wood, stone and metal craftsmanship, jewelry, carpet, and ceramics made by Khiva artists since the 13th century. Handcrafts Museum, which exhibits tools of Khorezm craftsmen (blacksmiths, silversmiths, weavers, gunners), is located in Matpana Bay Madrassah.

FIGURE 22   Khorezm female dress, silk-cotton mix, ikat, beginning of 20th century (Uzbekistan: Heirs to the Silk Road, 1997).

CONCLUSION

Khiva, pearl of Khorezm in its heydays and the open-air museum today, is worth visiting because of its ancient city atmosphere where time is felt frozen. You can still take refuge of the burning sun to the shadows of the old city walls, stride through Khiva hans' palace courtyards, feel as a middle age student studying in the madrasahs, pray in ancient mosques among wooden columns and on top of blue-tiled minars.

KEYWORDS

- Ichan Kala
- Kalta Minar
- Khiva
- Khorezm
- Tourism
- Uzbekistan

REFERENCES

Akhmedov, A. (1997, October). Valuable Sources on the History of Khiva, *Scientific and Cultural Heritage of Mankind—To the third millenium / Theses of Reports of the International Symposium Dedicated to the 2500 Anniversary of Bukhara and Khiva October 18–20 1997* (pp. 142–145). Tashkent: UNESCO.

Arapov, A. (2006). *Historical monuments of Uzbekistan: Samarkand, Bukhara, Khiva* (E. Soldatova, & K. Kuzmin Trans.). Tashkent: San'at Press.

Aslanapa, O. (1996). *Türk Cumhuriyetleri Mimarlik Abideleri*, Ankara: Türksoy Yayinlari.

Askarov, A. (1997, October). The formation and the main stages of the development of the city culture of Khiva, *Scientific and Cultural Heritage of Mankind—To the third millenium / Theses of Reports of the International Symposium Dedicated to the 2500 Anniversary of Bukhara and Khiva October 18–20 1997* (pp. 137–139). Tashkent: UNESCO.

Babadjanov, İ. (1999, April). How To Involve Local Communities In Presenting Their Cultural Heritage. *WTO/UNESCO Seminar on Tourism and Culture: Samarkand/Khiva, Republic of Uzbekistan, 20–21 April 1999* (pp. 61–62). Madrid: World Tourism Organization.

Chuvin, P., Degorge, G. (2003). *Samarkand, Bukhara, Khiva*, Paris: Flammarion, London: Thames & Hudson.

Durdiyeva, G. (2008). Research and Analysis of Cultural Monuments of Ichan-Kala of Khiva. *Proceedings of The Workshop on Conservation and Management of Temurids Architecture: 21 April-2 May 2008, Republic of Uzbekistan Tashkent, Samarkand, Shakhrisyabz, Bukhara,*

Khiva (pp. 51–54). Uzbekistan: United Nations Educational, Scientific and Cultural Organization (UNESCO) & International Institute for Central Asian Studies (IICAS).

Esin, E. (1997). *Türkistan Seyahatnamesi* (2nd edition), Ankara: Türk Tarih Kurumu.

Frumkin, G. (1970). *Archeology in Soviet Central Asia*. Leiden/Köln: E.J. Brill.

Galima, M. *Turan'in Alp Kizlari*; Corayeff, M. *İpekyolu Efsaneleri* (2001) (D. A. Batur, Trans.). İstanbul: Şa-To Türkiyat.

Gombos, K. (1976) *The Pearls of Uzbekistan* (I. Kimenez, Trans.). Budapest: Corvina Press.

Gorshenina, S., Rapin, C. (2008). *Kabil'den Semerkand'a Arkeologlar Orta Asya'da* (S. Özen. Trans., 2nd Edition.). İstanbul: Yapi Kredi Yayinlari.

Hayit, B. (1995). *Türkistan Devletlerinin Milli Mücadeleleri Tarihi*, Ankara: Türk Tarih Kurumu.

Kafali, M. (1976). *Altin Orda Hanliğinin Kuruluş ve Yükseliş Devirleri*. İstanbul: İstanbul Üniversitesi Edebiyat Fakültesi Matbaasi.

Kafesoğlu, İ. (2000). *Harezmşahlar Devleti Tarihi (485–618/1092–1221)* (4th edition). Ankara: Türk Tarih Kurumu.

Kalter, J., Pavaloi, M. (Eds.) *Uzbekistan: Heirs to the Silk Road*, London: Thames and Hudson.

Nedvetsky, A. G. (Ed.) (1993). *Khiva. Caught in time: great photographic archives*. Reading: Garnet Publishing.

Mankovskaya, L. (1982). *Khiva: A reserve of Khorezm architecture*. Tashkent: Izdatelstvo Literaturi i Iskusstva.

MacLeod, C., Mayhew, B. (2004). *Uzbekistan The Golden Road to Samarkand*. Hong Kong: Airphoto International Ltd.

Mukhamedjanov, A. (1997, October). "On The Etymology of The Toponym "Khiva" and Hydronym "Palvanyab"," *Scientific and Cultural Heritage of Mankind-to the Third Millennium: theses of reports of the international symposium dedicated to the 2500 anniversary of Bukhara and Khiva October 18–20 1997* (pp. 140–141). Tashkent: UNESCO.

Munîs, S. M. M., Agahî, M. R. M. (1999). *Firdaws al-iqbal /History of Khorezm* (Y. Bregel, Trans.), Leiden, Boston; Köln: Brill.

Ochilov, E. (1997, October). Omar Khayyam's Traditions In the Works by Pakhlavan Mahmud. *Scientific and Cultural Heritage of Mankind-to the Third Millennium: theses of reports of the international symposium dedicated to the 2500 anniversary of Bukhara and Khiva October 18–20 1997* (pp. 68–69). Tashkent: UNESCO.

Özaydin, A. (1997). Hârizm. *Türkiye Diyanet Vakfi İslam Ansiklopedisi* (XVI, pp. 217–220). İstanbul: Türkiye Diyanet Vakfi.

Prochazka, A. B. (1990). *Khawarizm.*Prague: Muslim Architecture Research Program. Zurich: Muslim Architecture Research Program. Jeddah: Organization of Islamic Capitals and Cities.

Pugachenkova, G. A. (1976). *Termez Shahr Siabz Khiva,* Moscou: Iskousstvo.

Saray, M. (1993). *Özbek Türkleri Tarihi*. İstanbul: Nesil Yayinlari.

Saray, M. (1997). Hive Hanliği. *Türkiye Diyanet Vakfi İslam Ansiklopedisi* (XVII, pp. 167–170). İstanbul: Türkiye Diyanet Vakfi.

Şeşen, R. (2010). *İbn Fadlan Seyahatnamesi ve Ekleri*. İstanbul: Yeditepe Yayinlari.

Taneri, A. (1997). Hârizmşahlar. *Türkiye Diyanet Vakfi İslam Ansiklopedisi* (XVI, pp. 228–231). İstanbul: Türkiye Diyanet Vakfi.

Tolstov, S. P., İrina, M. A. (Eds.) (1960). *Polevie İssledovaniya Khoresmskoy Expeditsii v 1957 godu*, Volume IV. Moskva: İzdatelstvo Akademii Nauk SSR.

Pulmanzo, J. (Ed.) (1996). *The Art of Central Asia,* England: Parkstone Press.

Togan, Z. V. (1951). *Horezm Kültürü Vesikalari I : Horezmce Tercümeli Mukaddimat Al-Adab / Documents on the Khorezmian Culture I: Muqaddimat Al-Adab with the Translation in Khorezmian.* İstanbul: İ.Ü. Edebiyat Fakültesi Umumi Türk Tarihi Enstitüsü.

CHAPTER 6

MERV: AN OASIS CAPITAL IN THE ANCIENT PARADISE

M. EBRU ZEREN

CONTENTS

INTRODUCTION

A thousand years ago, in the days when Muslim geographers roamed over Asia, imagine yourself in a caravan, on a camel, on the legendary east-west road from Nishapur to Bukhara... After fighting with sand storms in the Karakum Desert and just when your food is about to expire, you arrive at an oasis, which you thought was just a mirage. Such a city that when you go inside the castle walls; once you have inhaled the sweet smell of melons rising from the bazaar and feasted your eyes with colorful silk fabrics and carpets, all you want to do is to see the city's palaces and mosques, and run to the libraries for the unique books and manuscripts that you can find only in this city. Because, the place that you arrived is none other than Merv, at those times the eastern capital of Islam and the next most important Muslim city after Baghdad; of whose observatories were visited by the likes of Omer Hayyam, of whose libraries had welcomed scientists like Yakut Al-Hamawi, and who had deserved to be named "Marvelousness."

Today Merv, located in the Mary province of Turkmenistan, is an oasis city established on the delta of the Murgab river, which takes its roots from the Afghan mountains and vanishes up north in the Karakum desert (Fig. 1). Being surrounded by the Karakum desert has provided a natural isolation for Merv, and also made it an important stop for obtaining food on the Silk Road.

FIGURE 1   Turkmenistan Map and Mary province (www.orsam.org.tr).
Retrieved November 15, 2013 from http://www.orsam.org.tr/tr/haritaGaleri.aspx?HaritaID=38

Merv oasis, at 200 meters above sea level and an 85 km × 74 km flat area, exhibits continental climate. Because of its location, irrigation has always been very important for Merv and the first settlements (in Merv) appeared in the Bronze Age (2500–1200 B.C.) in the northern regions where the surfacing of the waters of the Murghab river had made it easier to use. Later, with the advent of irrigation techniques, settlements were established in the south and Early Iron Age sites (1200–300 B.C.) were created.

Merv is one of the most important crossroads on the Silk Road because this important trade and culture road coming from the East through Amul (Chardjzou) splits into many roads here: the north road leading to Khwarezm, the east road leading to Termez, Balkh and Herat, the south-east road leading to Serakhs and Nishapur, and the west road leading to Nisa (Tucker, 2003). In the Middle Ages, the most significant sources of income for Merv people were cotton, sesame, cotton oil, silk and cloth making, copper crafting, animal breeding and trade (Puschning, 2006). Besides, the old documents seldom mention the tastes of fruits like pears, raisins and melons grown in Merv, "a flower blossoming in the desert."

Due to its unique geographical position, Merv also served as a home and passage for different religions. During the Parthian period, the main religion was Zoroastrianism (also called Mazdaism). This religion was significantly observed under the reign of Sassanids.

In addition, a Christian Bishop was noticed in Merv in 323 (Güngör, 2002), and it is also known that the Merv Nestorian Bishop was exceptionally active in the 6th century and 7th century.

As far as Buddhism is concerned, the analyzes of Buddhist artifacts found in the city suggest that Buddhism probably came in through Kushan centers in Balh, which carry the Gandhara culture, and then later traveled to China. A 5th A.D. century vessel, which was initially used to preserve bones and later Buddhist manuscripts, was found in the Buddhist stupa in Gyaur Kala (Fig. 2). In a style similar to Afrasiab, Penjikent and Varakhsha wall paintings, the life phases of a ruler are pictured on it (Esin, 1978; Tucker, 2003). Because Merv also serves as a passage to the north, it is possible to argue that Judaism traveled to the Caspian Sea region and Eastern Europe through here (Durduyev, 1998). İbn al-Faqih on the other hand reported that a Manichaean temple, named Key-Merzûban, existed in Merv (Sayan, 1999). But the place and importance of Islam religion is undisputable in the history of Merv. Being one of the bases of Islamic science and technology, Merv has witnessed the Islam civilization in all its glory starting from the 7th century with the reign of Arabs, but especially during the Seljuk Turks period.

FIGURE 2   Painted Clay Vessel representing the life of a ruler, 5th century, Turkmenistan National Museum, Ashkhabad (Pugachenkova, 1967).

HISTORICAL BACKGROUND

According to a narrative communicated to us by Mahmud Kashgari, Merv was established by Turkish ruler Alp-Er-Tunga. However, the famous Persian epic Shahnameh written by Firdawsi argued that the third Persian ruler Tahmures is the one who established the city. According to Avesta, the holy writing of Zoroastrians, Merv, along with Balkh, was one of the most fertile lands created by the god Ahuramazda.

On the other hand, the Khorasan province, where Merv is located, being on the border, has for thousands of years witnessed fights for domination between the Turk and Persian nations. The wars between Turks and Persians in West Turkestan are vividly told in Avesta and Shahnameh. In Avesta, the city of Tura (Turk) tribe is named Kanha, and the Turkish ruler Franrasyan. Kanha in Avesta is described as "Kang-kü/Kang-ki" in Chinese sources, and as "Kangar/Kangli" tribe in Turkish and lately as the "Kengeres family," who has grown from this tribe to become the ruler family of Turkestan cities. The Turkish ruler Franrasyan was named as Frasyab or Afrasyab by the 9th century Muslim writers, and as Alp-Er-Tunga in Turkish epics and documents (Esin, 1978). The Turkish epic of Alp-Er-Tunga tells about this great ruler of Turks. It is the common opinion of old Muslim and Persian writers who tell about the old Persian legends (Bal'ami, Tha'alibi, Narshahi, Zamakhshari) that Merv with some other cities like Semerkand and Bukhara was established by Turks (Togan, 1981).

The legend that Merv was established by Afrasyab relies on a verbal history, which maybe tells more than the written history and the evidence put forth by many thousand years old archeological sites. Merv is called "Moura" in Avesta, and as "Margush" in the Behistun inscription of the Darius the 1st century (522–486 B.C.) (Esin, 1976). While it was called "Margiana" during the Greek period and "Antiochia Margiana" during the Seleucid period, it was named "Merv" during the Islamic period. It was named "Merv eş-şâhicân" by the travelers in Middle Ages, to emphasize its importance and to distinguish it from the small southern city of Merv er-rûz (Sayan, 1997).

During the 5th–6th centuries B.C., Achaemenids came to Merv and established the Erk Kala as the first residential site. During the first quarter of the 4th century B.C., one of Alexander the Great's commanders conquered Merv and started the Hellenistic era. This continued with the Seleucids, and Antiochos the 1st century (281–261 B.C.) created the Gyaur Kala residence by surrounding the region to the south of Erk Kala by thick city walls in square form, with moats around. The seminomad Parthians who conquered Merv in the 2nd century B.C. extended the city and had the Erk Kala walls enlarged by captive Roman soldiers. During these times, as Strabon and Pliny mention, Merv became one of the most important cities of Central Asia. The recovered old coins even suggest that, during the reign of Parthian King Phraates (138–128 B.C.) a mint operated in Merv. The Sassanids, who established a powerful nation in Persia, came to Merv in the 3rd century A.C. and Merv became the most important commercial center of the Persian Empire in Central Asia. The Huns and Turk tribes from the banks of Syr Derya and around the Aral Sea came to Merv around the 5th century A.C. It is known that the Hephthalites, who were a branch of the Huns, fought with the Sassanids for the domination of Khorasan and Mawarannahr (Transoxiana) and have ruled this region for a period. They were succeeded by The Western Turk Khanate, who has ruled in the Khorasan and Mawaraunnahr regions starting from the second half of the 6th century until the Arab conquest. Islamic sources report that Yazdigerd the 3rd (632–651), who fled the Arabic army in the middle of the 7th century, also sought refuge under a Turkish ruler.

In the early Islam period, after the victory against the Sassanids, Arabic forces came to Merv in 651. Probably due to its strategic position and economical importance, Merv, which is one of the first cities who accepted Islam, was made the capital of Khorasan, the most eastern Islamic province, and the base for conquest of Central Asia. Another importance of Merv to the Muslims is that the caliphate passed from Umayyads to Abbasids as a result of the movement initiated against Umayyads in Merv in 749 by the ruler of Khorasan, Abu Muslim.

During his short reign, Abu Muslim established a new city named Sultan Kala (Fig. 3) to the west of Erk Kala and around the Madjan channel. The Arab reign, which started in the second half of the 7th century with the Islam conquests, lasted for two centuries during the Umayyad and Abbasid dynasties being governed by the caliphate centers in Syria and Persia, and resulted in the diffusion of the Islam civilization to Merv. In the first years of conquest, Arabs took advantage of the Sassanid bureaucracy and tried to increase the Arab population by bringing their soldiers' families from Kufa and Basra (Özgüdenli, 2006).

FIGURE 3   Sultan Kala City Walls, 8th century (Sayan, 1999).

Caliph Al-Ma'mun named Merv the capital of Abbasids for a short period. Later, during the caliphate wars, because he defeated his brother Emin with the help of Persians, he left the governance of eastern provinces to Persian rulers. In the reign of the Persian family of the Tahirids the capital was moved to Nishapur. Then, governance of Merv was taken over by Saffarids from Sistan for a short period. Samanids, who had the capital in Bukhara, came out as the rulers as a result of the upheaval in Khorasan in the last quarter of the 9th century. But after the partitioning of the

Samanids' land by the Turkish states of Ghaznavids and Karakhanids in 999, Ghaznavids started the Turkish reign in Merv, which lasts till today.

When we reached the 10th century, the Oghuz Turks, which are the ancestors of Turkmens who form today's Merv people, were living in the region from Syr Derya to the Caspian Sea and from the Aral Sea to Khorasan. Al-Biruni, the famous Kharezm scientist who lived in the 10th–11th centuries, when talking about the Khorasan and Mawaraunnahr regions, named the Karakum deserts as "Oghuz deserts" (Mufazat el-Guziyye) and "Oghuz realm," and the Kızılkum deserts as "Turkmen country" (Ard el-Turkmaniya) (Togan, 1960). According to the Muslim writers of the time, the Turkmen name was given by the non-Muslim Oghuz people to the Muslim Oghuz people. Indeed, the acceptance of Islam by the Oghuz people had commenced in the second half of the 9th century (Saray, 1993).

After the establishment of the Great Seljuk Empire by an Oghuz tribe, which followed the defeat of Ghaznavids by Chagri Bey (died 1059) and Tugrul Bey (1016–1063) in the Dandanakan War of 1040 around Merv, governance of Merv was given to Chagri Bey. Merv, then, served as the capital of this great state, which extended from Amu Darya to the Mediterranean, and lived its brightest times during the reign of Sultan Sanjar (1119–1157). The dam (Sultanbend) which Sultan Sanjar had built on Mugrab played a significant role in the prosperity of Merv.

With his death, the governance was taken over by Turkish Khwarezmids. Merv, which in 1153 was plundered by the rebelling Oghuzs against Seljuks, was reconstructed during the Khwarezmid period. But the Mongol invasion in 1221 with the leadership of Tuli Han, the son of Genghis Han, completely demolished the city and as the Murgab bend, the main life stream was destroyed, and for about two hundred years there was no significant residence in the city. It is so significant that the city's population before the Mongol invasion could only be reached very recently. After the Mongol invasion, with the establishment of the Ilhanids State (1256–1336) in Persia by Hulagu (1256–1265), Merv got located in this nation. The coins produced in Merv show that Merv was governed by the Chagatai Khanate during the final periods of Ilhanids and by the Golden Horde State for a brief amount of time. Ibn Batuta, who visited Merv in the beginning of the 14th century mentions that, among the four biggest cities, Merv and Balkh were ruined whereas Herat and Nishapur were flourishing (Ibn Battuta Tanci, 2000).

At the end of the 14th century, Merv accepted the dominance of the famous Turkish ruler Timur. Only in the beginning of the 15th century, with the order of the Timurid ruler Shahruh (1405/6–1447), were some of the buildings and water bend fixed, and the city reconstructed and inhabited by people brought in from different places. The new city was built between 1407 and 1409 in the south of old city, with the name Abdullah Han Kala (Fig. 4) (Sayan, 1999).

FIGURE 4   Abdullah Han Kala City Walls, 15th century (Sayan, 1999).

The Turkmens in Khorasan and Mawarannahr lived with other Turk tribes like Uzbeks, Khazaks, Kirghiz and Karakalpaks, and lived under the reign of Mongols first, and then Timurids. In the 16th and 17th centuries, Merv was first ruled by Uzbek Sheybanids and later for a short while by Safavids. After the Sheybanids took charge again, the Bukhara Emirate and Khiva Khanate fought for power to rule Merv in the 18th and 19th centuries. The Turkmens who lived in Mangishlak went to the Kopet mountains after the 17th century and got stronger there. Being disturbed by this, the Khiva khan and Persian shah, backed by the Uzbek-Turkmen coalition, started their Turkmen attacks and invaded Merv. The Turkmens who successfully fought for their freedom in 1830–1860, this time were faced by the attacks of tsarist Russia, who wanted to invade their lands. After bloody wars, in 1884, the Khiva Khanate decided to recognize the ruling of Russia, and became a colony of Russia. In 1924, after the Russian Bolshevik Revolution, the Soviet Socialist Republic of Turkmenistan was declared as one of the six socialist republics of Russia, and after the disintegration of the Soviet Union in 1991, achieved independence as the Republic of Turkmenistan (Saray, 1993).

Bayramali Khan Kala, built adjacent to Abdullah Khan Kala, was the last castle built in the city. It was built by a Turkish ruler who had recognized Persian management in the 18th century. Merv and its life-giving Sultanbend, especially in the 18th century, was destroyed by the khans of Bukhara. Revived after the opening of the Niyazov (Karakum) canal by Russia in 1950s, Merv has continued to grow in the southern direction, and Bayramali today has become one of the important counties of Turkmenistan.

TOURIST ATTRACTIONS IN MERV

In 1999, UNESCO nominated Merv as a World Heritage Center, with status of Historical City and Cultural Park. Merv is one of the rare archeological parks where the civilizations built during the five thousand year period are not in the form of layers on top of each other. In other words, a palace compound, which is over four thousand years old is not located under a Seljuk palace which was built 3000 years later, but a few kilometers away; just this way, one fire temple, the Buddhist stupa artifacts, and Prophet Muhammad's companions' (called *askhab)* tombs are separated by similar distances. To visit this park is like taking on a walk in a kind of time tunnel. Unfortunately, the main building material of most monuments in Merv is mudbrick, which makes them open to weather, water, human, plants, animals and other threats. That is why ancient Merv was included in the list of world heritage sites in danger by UNESCO. "The Ancient Merv Project" is run seriously, led by the University College of London Institute of Archeology and collaborating with other institutions like the World Monuments Foundation for its conservation. An interpretation center is aimed at educating local people on conservation and informing all tourists in detail about Merv (University College of London, n.d.).

As far as the museums of Merv are concerned, the most important one is the Mary Region Museum, which happens to be the best Museum of Turkmenistan outside of Ashkabat. Here, besides the archeological artifacts of Old Merv and Bronze Age settlements, entnographic objects and masterpieces of Turkmen people are displayed. Secondly, in Merv, which was chosen as "Historic City and Cultural Park" by UNESCO, to the north of the oasis there is the Margush Archeological Museum, which exhibits the works belonging to Bronze Age settlements. In Bayramali, on the other hand, for the interested, there is the Factory Museum of Cotton seeds, next to the cotton oil factory. It is also possible to buy handcrafts like jewelry and rugs from the central bazaar in Bayramali (Brummel, 2005).

Merv settlements must be studied in two main categories. The first one of these is the northern Bronze Age and Iron Age settlements, dated back to 2500 B.C., and the second is the settlement called "the old Merv" (Fig. 5), which reaches the present day from the 6th and 5th centuries B.C., covering the settlements of Erk Kala, Gyaur Kala, Sultan Kala, Abdullah Khan Kala and Bayramali Khan Kala.

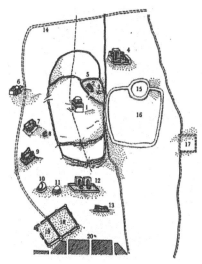

FIGURE 5   Old Merv Monuments from Atagarriev: 1 – Sultan Sanjar Mausoleum 2 – Divanhane 3 – Palace 4 – Yusuf Hamadani Mausoleum 5 – Shahriyar Ark 6 – Muhammed Ibn Zayd Mausoleum 7 – Lesser Kyz Kala 9 – Greater Kyz Kala 10,11 – Icehouses 12 – Mausolea of Two Askhabs 14 – City walls, 15 – Erk Kala, 16 – Gyaur Kala, 18 – Abdullah Han Kala, 19 – Bayramali Khan Kala, 20 – Modern Bayramali (Aslanapa, 1996).

The archeological excavations initiated by Russians in Merv and Turkmenistan are being continued heavily at present by Russian, English, American and Italian excavation teams and research institutes, with the big support of the government (Durduyev, 1998). In the excavations done around Merv during approximately the past 40 years, many settlements were unearthed which are thought to belong to the Margush country mentioned in the Behistun inscriptions (Sarianidi, 1986), and 1000 archeological sites were unearthed in the 80,000 km^2 region in the Murgab delta. The most important Bronze Age sites are Gonur Depe, Togolok Depe, Kelleli, Adji Kui, Taip; Iron Age sites are Yaz Depe, Gobekli Depe and Tahirbash Tepe (UNESCO WHC Document, 1998).

GONUR DEPE AND TOGOLOK DEPE 21

Gonur Depe, approximately 100 km away from Bayramali city, is found at the old fork in the mouth of the Murgab river (Fig. 6). Margush, with its history dating back to 3000–2000 B.C. Bronze Age, is thought to be the first Merv settlement, and points to a rising civilization of its time, with living and crafting areas, monarch castles, king necropoli, temples for fire altars and complex city fabric (Sarianidi, 2005).

FIGURE 6 Gonur Depe Margush settlement, 3000–2000 B.C. (http://countryturkmenistan. tripod.com).
Retrieved November 15, 2013 from http://countryturkmenistan.tripod.com/index. blog?start=1118049427&topic_id=1016195.

Another settlement belonging to the Late Bronz Age, known as To-goloktepe 21 and Togolok 21 was found to the south-west of Gonur Depe. Out of the excavated mound, a square shaped building which was fortified and is believed to be a fire temple was unearthed.

ERK KALA

This city, dating back to the 6th century B.C., was built during the Ahame-nids period and houses a palace, a temple, and civil architectural samples inside its oval shaped high walls.

GYAUR KALA

This is a settlement built in the Seleucids period around Erk-Kala, with an irregular rectangular plan, surrounded by adobe walls and with government buildings in the middle. Gyaur Kala was inhabited for approximately one thousand years during the Parthian, Sassanid and early Islam periods. This settlement is approximately 360 hectares with all places within walking distance. It is thought that during the Abbassid period Gyaur Kala was used as a region for craftsmen and iron and steel workshops (Fig. 7).

FIGURE 7   Erk Kala and Gyaur Kala (Wikipedia, Photo by Mark and Delwen / CC BY 2.0).
Retrieved November 15, 2013 from http://en.wikipedia.org/wiki/File:Mervturkmenistan. jpg

As an example of medieval civil architecture, the *koshks* (kind of castle-mansions) occupying a square land, built by landowners called *dihkan*, are also seen in and around Merv. These are buildings totally special to Central Asia, with the most beautiful and best-preserved samples in Merv. Their high, thick, adobe walls are decorated with corrugations. The Greater and Lesser Kyz Kalas (meaning *girl castles*) to the south of the Sultan Kala are considered among the oldest examples of koshks in Merv due to their building techniques. (Fig. 8). Although exact dating is not possible, it is argued that these belong to the 6th–7th century Parthian – Sassanid period or the 8th–9th century Abbassid period. Of these two koshks 100 m apart from each other, the Greater Kyz Kala occupies an area of 42.2 m × 37.2 m, and the Lesser Kyz Kala 22.50 m × 22.10 m, and remains of the rooms leading to the space in the middle are observable. There are many stories regarding these koshks but the most interesting refers to the Greater Kyz Kala as the castle for girls and the Lesser Kyz Kala as the boys' castle and reports that a boy wishing to marry a girl in the other castle should fire a projectile to land in the greater castle (Brummel, 2005). In addition to these, the Greater and Lesser Nagm Kalas to the north of Merv, Haram Koshk to the north of Sultan Kala, Garam Koshk, Byash Parmak Koshk, and Suli Koshk are other architectural monuments of this kind around Merv (Herrmann, 1999).

FIGURE 8   Greater Kyz Kala with camels (www.flickr.com, Photo by David Stanley / CCBY 2.0).
Retrieved   November   15,   2013   from   http://www.flickr.com/photos/davidstanleytravel/5731116064/

It is known that the Arabs called these castle-mansions *kal'a* and established quarters around them. But, despite the protective nature of these mansions, it is identified that the nobles had two-story dwellings, with the lower floor serving as the pantry and upper floor as the living space. Narrow and multistory buildings, called *ding* in local terminology, used as watch towers, are also found in Merv as in some other places in Central Asia.

Al-Istahri, who in the 10th century praises Merv, shaped as an Islamic city preserving the religious, social and commercial buildings in *shahristan* (inner city), inside the walls, under Arab domination, mentions three great mosques in the city. In the time of Caliph Al-Ma'mun (813–833 A.D.), a palace and a military garrison was also established (Sayan, 1999). Madrassahs, established to study science and religion for higher education, were decorated with libraries with very special collections; the tombs where sultans and religious elders are buried, took their places in the city architecture with domes and their elaborate stonework.

The Islamic city of Merv continued to live during the periods of Tahirids, Saffarids, Samanids and Ghaznavids, and new institutions were built in different places. However, since the capital of the region and center of gravity were then made Nishapur, and briefly Bukhara, the progress that Merv showed was interrupted. The dynasty, which was to awaken the city from this slumber was the Seljuks, who settled in Khorasan beating the Ghaznavids and made Merv the capital again.

SULTAN KALA

It was built during the Seljuks period by Sultan Malik-Shah I (1072–1092) between the years 1080–1090 to the west of Gyaur Kala, on a rectangular land approximately 1700 m × 2200 m. The walls, quite devastated today, used to surround the Seljuk city. The towers, known to be located on the corners and the doors, were appropriate to the Turkish city customs. The castle walls were surrounded by moats for security and by water channels in two directions. Shahriyar Ark, built to the Turkish architectural traditions on the north-west of the city, is an inner city (where the ruler with his army and statesman reside) containing a Seljuk palace and government buildings.

The north-west remains were identified as the shelter of guards, the middle ones as the sultan's palace (Fig. 9) and *divanhane* (statesman meeting place) (Fig. 10). The palace plan was identified by Pugatchenkova having two-stories and four courts with iwans, and more than 50 rooms (Hermann, 1999). It has been suggested that the Divanhane was the meeting hall used to discuss state affairs, being identified as rectangular shaped, with outside grooved walls, vault covered and single-story structure (Sayan, 1999). Other views are that the building with this architectural form is a *keboterhane* (noted as *kepterkhana* by Herrmann, meaning *pigeon house*) with samples in the city or the high and windowless walls suggesting that it had been used as the state archives or treasury (Herrmann, 1999).

FIGURE 9 Shahriyar Ark -Palace, 11th century (Sayan, 1999).

FIGURE 10 Shahriyar Ark-*Divanhane /keboterhane*, 11th century (Sayan, 1999).

SULTAN SANJAR MAUSOLEUM

The most important monument in Merv is the mausoleum that the Great Seljuk Sultan, Sultan Sanjar (1118–1157), had built for himself in the 12th century by the Serakhsian architect Muhammed bin Atsız, and had named *"dârû'l-âhire"* (Sayan, 1999). This building, which satisfied one of the criteria that enabled Merv to be listed among the UNESCO World Heritage Sites, contains all the improvements and innovations of its time in tomb architecture, and with the 17 m diameter inner dome happens to be the biggest tomb with dome, earning a unique place in world's art history (Fig. 11). As mentioned in the historical sources, the existence of the tomb within a complex is backed by the mosque built adjacent to the tomb, a well, and the several building ruins, which were unearthed in various excavations.

FIGURE 11   Sultan Sanjar Mausoleum, 12th century (www.fickr.com, Photo by Peretz Partensky / CC BY 2.0).
Retrieved November 15, 2013 from http://www.flickr.com/photos/ifl/3892634354/sizes/m/in/photostream/

The mausoleum's dome sits on a cubical body, which is in the form of a square and rises shaped as galleries. The opinion that the tomb's high cubical body was affected from Buddhist stupas also exists. Arched galleries exist on the dome tambour and on the upper part of the body. The brick ornament on the outer facade is composed of both kufic arabic writings and geometrical-plant motives. Golden plates unearthed in the excavations were discovered to be decorating the arch pediments. The inner surface of the dome is decorated with geometrical motives, forming an eight-armed star motive in the middle. Yakuti writes that, the blue tiles covering the outer dome, which couldn't make it to today, could have been seen at a one-day distance (Esin, 1976). The tomb, which was plundered and burned by the Mongols in 1221 still survived; however, reaching today it went through a number of renovations, the latter sponsored by the Turkish government.

MOHAMMED IBN ZAYD MAUSOLEUM

Mohammed Ibn Zayd lived at the end of the 7th and beginning of the 8th centuries and was the leader Shias that rebelled against the Umayyad. His mausoleum was built by the governor of Khorasan and vizier of Sultan Sanjar, Sherafeddin Abu Tahir, in 1112–1113, on his own estate where he died and was buried. The tomb, which is located about 1 km to the west of Sultan Kala, is an 8.5 m × 8.5 m square building on the outside having a single dome. In the later period it was turned into a building complex, through the addition of another grave to the north-east and the addition of a two-domed mosque to the west (Fig. 12). Inside the dome, whose facade is decorated with brick and terracotta pieces, the walls on four sides at the top are surrounded by a kufic inscription together with floral motives (Sayan, 1999).

FIGURE 12   Mohammed Ibn Zayd Mausoleum, 12th century (www.culture.gov.tm). Retrieved November 15, 2013 from http://www.culture.gov.tm/Merw/Merw_eng.html

TALHATAN BABA MOSQUE

The Talhatan Baba Mosque, remaining from the end of the 11th and beginning of the 12th centuries and located in the Yolöten region approximately 30 km from Merv, is completely made of brick and is an important work due to its architecture and plan (Fig. 13). The rectangular shaped 18 m × 10 m mosque, being a single domed plan extended to the sides by small crossed vaults, led the way of single domed 16th century mosques of Mimar Sinan, the greatest Ottoman architect (Aslanapa, 1996).

FIGURE 13   Talhatan Baba Mosque, 9th–12th centuries (www.culture.gov.tm).
Retrieved November 15, 2013 from http://www.culture.gov.tm/Merw/Merw_eng.html

MAUSOLEA OF TWO ASKHABS

The Mausolea complex located to the east of Sultan Kala, is comprised of
two askhabs' tombs next to each other, two iwans to the back added during
the Timurid era, and a mosque to the west. Recounted by Yakut, Prophet
Mohammed describes Merv as a fertile city, which will fight evil until
doomsday, and has willed his askhab Buraidah Ibn Al-Huseib Al-Aslami
to go to Merv (Esin, 1976). The tombs of Buraidah Al-Islami and Al-Ha-
kim Ibn Amr Al-Gifâr are located in the mentioned mausolea complex
(Fig. 14). Although the exact construction date is unclear, it is estimated
that they were constructed in the Seljuk period (9th–12th centuries), and
destroyed during the Mongol period. Iwans are decorated by blue, dark-
blue glazed bricks, arabic writings and geometrical motives on the inside
(Sayan, 1999). In the middle of square shaped and low tombs, there are
marble sarcophaguses each filled with inscriptions on their surfaces.

FIGURE 14   Mausolea of Two Askhabs, Timurid period (Sayan, 1999).

YUSUF HAMADANI MAUSOLEUM COMPLEX

The mausoleum complex at the north-east of Sultan Kala is composed of the square shaped tomb of Hodja Yusuf Hamadani, who was among the important religious and scientific persons of his era, and two mosques, the first one being built in the 16th century by Timurids, and the second by Guljamal Khan in 1890 (Fig. 15). The body of Hodja Yusuf Hamadani, who died in a place called Balin, was transferred to this tomb built during the Seljuk period. The tomb, which was thought destroyed during the Mongol invasion, was completely renovated in 1990. However, the two mosques retain their authenticities (Sayan, 1999). The other tombs that can be visited around Merv are the tombs of Turkan Khatun (Sultan Sanjar's wife), which is known as Kyz Bibi, Imam Bekr, Hudayi Nazar Evliya, Imam Shaafi, Abdullah İbn Buraidah, and Kok Gumbaz.

FIGURE 15   Yusuf Hamadani Mausoleum Complex, Timurid period and later (Sayan, 1999).

ICE HOUSES

The remains of three structures exist between Sultan Kala and Abdullah Khan Kala, which the locals call the "tandoor of Hacı Melik" due to their resemblance to the specific oven built under the earth (Fig. 16). Made out of adobe and conic shaped, the biggest of these was built in the 12th–13th centuries, and others in the 15th century, and they were used to store snow (Sayan, 1999).

FIGURE 16   Ice House (www.flickr.com, Photo by Peretz Partensky / CC BY 2.0).
Retrieved November 15, 2013 from http://www.flickr.com/photos/ifl/3891851361/

Another architectural structure often seen in Merv is the keboterhane (or kepterkhana) already mentioned. These units found in farm structures are long, narrow, corridor like and rectangular structures (Cezar, 1977). Although they were first thought to have been built for pigeons, often no animal traces were encountered, and with the small niches inside, it is believed that they were serving as cellars.

HANDCRAFTS AND APPLIED ARTS IN MERV

Merv in the Middle Ages, had been one of the world's most advanced centers of silk and cotton weaving. According to Arab historian Al-Sâlibi, the Arabs called these fine fabrics brought from Khorasan "Al-Shahijan," and only the rich could own these. Thin yellow silk fabric still woven in Turkmen villages is called "Shahijan" or "Shahi." Due to the interest of caliphs and sultans in Merv clothes, state controlled fabric weaving shops were opened in Merv, and scientific studies were conducted in the academy of silk fabric called "Dyvekush" to increase the quality of Merv fabric (Bayram, 1996).

Merv became one of the most important centers of Turkmen jewelry, especially in the area of silver making, with their diversity, content, the precious metals and stones they are made of, and the incredibly esthetic embroidery which is used to process the original motives (Dinç and Çakir,

2010). The various forms and motives of Turkmen jewelry are closely related to the time and space concepts, mountain, tree, cult of ancestors, religious and cosmological beliefs they adopted, which have prevailed in Central Asia (Schletzer and Schletzer, 1983).

For example, especially the children, young girls and women use amulets and talismans of various kinds to guard against evil eyes. These can be worn in front or behind dresses, in the hair, on headpieces, or around the neck. Jewelry, clothes and headwear vary according to age groups and marital status. Jewelry is made by silversmiths by using primarily silver, but also gold, copper, agate, turqoise, half-precious stones and glass beads. Other types of jewelry include various necklaces, back ornaments (*asık*), head bands and ornaments, bridal head wear (*egme*), head wear worn until marriage, forehead pendant jewelry, bracelets, rings and ear rings (Figs. 17–19). (Schletzer and Schletzer, 1983).

FIGURE 17   Merv oasis Teke tribe made necklace "*bukov*," 19th century (Schletzer and Schletzer, 1983).

FIGURE 18   Turkmen headgear (Schletzer and Schletzer, 1983).

FIGURE 19   Turkmen bracelets (Schletzer and Schletzer, 1983).

Merv has been the center for ceramics from the beginning and became a tile production center since the 9th century. In the Seljuk period, the jugs made from mold, decorated with human, bird, legendary animal and plant patterns, have taken their place among Merv ceramics (Figs. 20 and 21). In addition, the metal work, especially gold and sliver, reached very advanced levels (Esin, 1976).

FIGURE 20   Merv ceramic vessels, 12th–13th centuries (Pugachenkova, 1967).

FIGURE 21   Merv ceramic vessels, 12th–13th centuries (Pugachenkova, 1967).

Turkmenistan is one of the countries where carpet art started, and the only country with a carpet symbol on its flag. In the Syberia collection of the Saint Petersburg Hermitage State Museum, in the section where the oldest carpet, coming out of the Pazırık Kurgan and woven with Turkish knots in the 4th–5th centuries B.C. is displayed, bronze carpet knife blades, which have been recovered in the excavations in Turkmenistan Sumbar Kurgan and dated to the 14th century B.C., are exhibited. The experts claim that motives similar to Turkmen carpet design exist on the Pazırık carpet and ceramic pottery recovered in Turkmenistan excavations.

Turkmen carpets and rugs exhibit different motives and interpretations depending on the tribes who had woven them (Fig. 22). These characteristic motives show themselves in all kinds of fabric. The main Turkmen weaving products are comprised of rugs, sacks, saddle bags, bags, clothes put on the chests of camels during marriage ceremonies, tent bands, tent door bands, and prayer rugs (Eiland and Eiland, 2008). In the Turkmen weaving, where different shades of red are widely used, the most common motif is the *lake*. This motif, usually woven in as an octagon, takes different shapes depending on the tribe. Starting with Teke, the main Turkmen tribes around Merv, who had a reputation for carpet weaving, are Yomut, Salur and Sarik. Unfortunately, carpet weaving has lost its former importance in the industrialization of Merv and has reached today with only small-scale productions.

FIGURE 22   Turcoman Yomud Rug (Turcoman Rugs, 1966).

CONCLUSION

Merv, the prosperous capital of the ancient paradise, is ready to offer its political, religious, cultural and art history readable through its state-of-art monuments, settlements and artifacts, with many details hidden either on a carpet motive or a trace on the sands to be discovered by careful eyes.

KEYWORDS

- Archaeology
- History
- Khorasan
- Margush
- Merv
- Sultan Sanjar
- Tourism
- Turkmenistan

REFERENCES

Aslanapa, O. (1996). *Türk Cumhuriyetleri Mimarlık Abideleri*. Ankara: Türksoy Yayınları.

Bayram, K. (1998). Türkmenlerde Kumaş Dokumacılık Sanatı. In A.Aktaş Yasa, S. Leloğlu Ünal, Ş. Ercebeci, E. Kalender (Eds.). *Türk Soylu Halkların Halı, Kilim ve Cicim Sanatı Uluslararası Bilgi Şöleni Bildirileri 27–31 Mayıs 1996 Kayzeri* (pp.57–64). Ankara: Atatürk Kültür Merkezi Başkanlığı Yayınları.

Beresneva, L. (Ed.) (1976). The Decorative and Applied Art of Turkmenia (V. Dereviagin, Trans.), Leningrad: Aurora Art Publishers.

Brummell, P. (2005). *Turkmenistan The Bradt Travel Guide*. UK:Bradt Travel Guides, USA: The Globe Pequest.

Cezar, M. (1977). *Anadolu Öncesi Türklerde Şehir ve Mimarlık*. İstanbul: Türkiye İş Bankası Kültür Yayınları.

Dinç, A., Çakır, R. (2010). Türkmenlerde Kuyumculuk Sanatının ve Takıların Tarihi Gelişimi ve Türkmen Kadını. *Türk Dünyası İncelemeleri Dergisi / Journal of Turkish World Studies, X* (1), 23–34. Retrieved March, 13, 2012, from http://tdid.ege.edu.tr/files/ahmetdinc-ramazan-cakir-10-1.pdf.

Durduyev, M. (1998). Türkmenistan'ın Arkeoloji Abideleri (A.Allahnazarov, Trans.), In B. Ersanlı & Orazpolat Ekaev (Eds.). *Türkmenistan'da Toplum ve Kültür* (pp. 1–19). Ankara: T.C. Kültür Bakanlığı.

Eiland Jr, M. L., Eiland III, M (2008). *Oriental Rugs A Complete Guide*. London: Laurence King Publishing.

Esin, E. (1972). Orduğ (Başlangıçtan Selçuklulara Kadar Türk Hakan Şehri). Ankara Üniversitesi Dil ve Tarih-Coğrafya Fakültesi Tarih Araştırmaları Dergisi. VI (10–11). Ankara: Ankara Üniversitesi Dil ve Tarih-Coğrafya Fakültesi. 135–215.

Esin, E. (1976). Merv, *Türk Ansiklopedisi* (XXIV, pp. 18–21). Ankara: Milli Eğitim Basımevi.

Esin, E. (1978). *İslamiyetten Önceki Türk Kültür Tarihi ve İslama Giriş (Türk Kültürü El Kitabı, II, Cilt I/b'den Ayrı Basım)*. İstanbul: Edebiyat Fakültesi Matbaası.

Fihl, E. (2010). *Exploring Central Asia From the Steppes to the High Pamirs 1896–1899*. Volume II. Washington D.C.: University of Washington Press.

Frumkin, G. (1970). *Archeology in Soviet Central Asia*. Leiden/Köln: E.J. Brill.

Gorshenina, S., Rapin, C. (2008). *Kabil'den Semerkand'a Arkeologlar Orta Asya'da* (S. Özen. Trans., 2nd Edition.). İstanbul: Yapı Kredi Yayınları.

Hayit, B. (1995). *Türkistan Devletlerinin Milli Mücadeleleri Tarihi*, Ankara: Türk Tarih Kurumu.

İbn Battuta Tanci. (2000). In A.S. Aykut (Ed. Trans.) *İbn Battuta Seyahatnamesi*. Volume I (4th edition). İstanbul: Yapı Kredi Yayınları. (Original work published in 1356).

Güngör, H. (2002). Eski Türklerde Din ve Düşünce. In H.C. Güzel & A. Birinci (Eds.). *Genel Türk Tarihi Ansiklopedisi* (II, pp.387–424). Ankara: Yeni Türkiye Yayınları.

Herrman, G. (1999). *Monuments of Merv: Traditional Buildings of the Karakum*. London: Society of Antiquaries of London.

Özgüdenli, O. G. (2006), Yok Olan Bir Ortaçağ Şehri:Merv. In Y. Çoruhlu, N. Türkmen, N. Seçgin, A. Yılmaz (Eds.). *Orta Asya'dan Anadolu'ya Türk Sanatı ve Kültürü Prof Dr. Nejat Diyarbekirli'ye Armağan* (pp. 239–251). İstanbul: Yeni Türkiye Yayınları.

Pugachenkova, G. A. (1967). *Iskusstvo Turkmenistana:ocherk s drevneyshih vremyon do 1917 g.*, Moskva: Izdatelstvo Iskusstvo.

Puschning, G. (2006). *Ceramics of the Merv Oasis / Recycling The City*. Walnut Creek, California:Left Coast Press.

Saray, M. (1993). *Türkmen Tarihi*. İstanbul: Nesil Matbaacılık ve Yayıncılık.

Sayan, Y. (1997). Merv, *Türkiye Diyanet Vakfı İslam Ansiklopedisi* (XXIX, pp. 221–225). İstanbul: Türkiye Diyanet Vakfı.

Sayan, Y. (1999). *Türkmenistan'daki Mimari Eserler (XI.-XVI. Yüzyıl)*. Ankara: Türk Tarih Kurumu Basımevi.

Sarianidi, V. I. Victor Ivanovi (2005), *Gonur-Depe City of Kings and Gods,* Retrieved March, 13, 2012, http://www.margiana.su/publication/book/Gonur-Depe_City_of_Kings_and_Gods_2005.pdf.

Sarianidi, V. I. (1986). Le complexe cultuel de Togolok 21 en Margiane. *Arts Asiatiques*. 41. 5–21.

Schletzer, D., Scletzer, R. (1983). *Old Silver Jewelry of The Turcoman An Essay on Symbols in the Culture of Inner asian Nomads* (P. Knight, Trans.). Berlin: Dietrich Reimer Verlag.

Togan, Z. V. (1960). *Türk Türkistan*. İstanbul: Toprak Yayınları.

Togan, Z. V. (1981). *Umumi Türk Tarihine Giriş Cild I En Eski Devirlerden 16. Asra Kadar* (3rd edition). İstanbul: Enderun Kitabevi.

Tucker, J. (2003). *The Silk Road: Art and History*. London: Philip Wilson.

*Turcoman Rug*s, Fogg Art Museum—Harvard University, Cambridge, Massachussets 1966.

UNESCO World Heritage Center. *UNESCO WHC Nomination Document.* (n.d.) Retrieved March, 13, 2012, from http://whc.UNESCO.org/uploads/nominations/886.pdf.

University College of London. *UCL Institute of Archeoleogy Ancient Merv Project.* (n.d.). Retrieved March, 13, 2012, from http://www.ucl.ac.uk/merv/.

CHAPTER 7

SAMARKAND: QUEEN OF ALL CITIES

MUALLA UYDU YÜCEL

CONTENTS

INTRODUCTION

A glance at the map of Asia, one could not have a thorough idea about how gigantic this continent is. In order to have a real impression about the size of Asia, you must go back hundreds of years and travel between China and Anatolia on a trade caravan. To walk with camels along this long route would be in a sense to stroll through the pages of human experience and its civilizations. Starting at Anatolia on the west, covering the area of the *Fırat* and *Dicle* passing south of the Caspian sea and the caucuses, looking ahead to the east, thinking thousands of kilometers you've already left behind is only the beginning of the journey, may give you an awful feeling of tiredness.' But you would walk on and arrive in Samarkand. No matter who you are or where you come from she would embrace you with a maternal love. There you would witness the east and the west, the north and the south all in one city. Despite wanting to stay you would continue. The Silk Road would finally take you to Beijing hence you would then know that the size of Asia is as vast as the human history itself. Dating back as far as 1500 B.C. to Early Iron Age, Samarkand and its faithful sister Bukhara have been called "The Gateway to the East" because of their unique location in the middle of ancient Silk Road, which stretches between Europe and China passing through Turkey, Iran, Afghanistan and India. Especially Samarkand has always been a sanctuary in the middle of the steppes with stunning vineyards and fabulous gardens. The best way to describe these cities is to portray them as two sisters. Standing hand-in-hand, here in the heart of Asia. Standing tall and proud all throughout the ages, yet still standing today welcoming every stranger that passes by with the same graceful beauty.

The trade caravans that are traveling from east to west encounter Samarkand and hail it first. Bukhara may be the younger sister of Samarkand but nevertheless she is an inseparable part of her. They were born together and their faith has brought them to this age without untying their devotion to each other. The best way to describe these two cities is to envision them as two beautiful women as they are indeed.

HISTORICAL BACKGROUND

First Samarkand; She was born ages ago as a Turkic baby. Her Father *Alper Tunga*, as described in the legends, laid the foundations of the city with sacred aspirations accordance with the Turkish etiquette at today's archaeological site known as *Afrasiyap* Hill (Fig. 1). Samarkand is located in the area called *Mawarannahr* (Transoxiana), between the rivers of *Amu Darya* (ancient Oxus) and *Syr Darya* (ancient Jaxartes), in the oasis of *Zarafshan* watered by Zarafshan river. Besides the beauty of this location Samarkand was also blessed with a gift of fertility. With six hundred thousand inhabitants, she still stands as the agricultural core of Central Asia, as a testimony to the fertility of this land that has been abiding right through the ages (Fig. 2).

FIGURE 1   City of Afrasiab Illustration (Arapov, 2006).

FIGURE 2   Map of Uzbekistan (www.orsam.org.tr).

Samarkand is situated in the central part of the Zarafshan valley at Mawarannahr with moderate climate and altitude of ideal range with an average height of 695 meters above sea level. Her climate is dry and terrestrial. January is the coldest month with −5 to 5°C and July is the hottest with 29–30°C.

According to legend, Timur who was the dominant of Turkistan, applied an ancient Turkish tradition to determine the location of the city that was to be made the capital. He would have his servants kill and flay sheep to be hung on poles at chosen locations under his rule including his birth town of Shehri-Sebz. Then the meat would be checked to determine rotting every day. The city where the meat doesn't rot for the longest would be Samarkand. So Samarkand once again proving why she was called the "Haven on Earth" for centuries becomes the capital of Timurs' State.

Long before Timur, another legend recounts when Samarkand was just a young, attractive girl, after looting all the surrounding cities, the cruelest of many who wanted to possess her suddenly attacked her gates at the Afrasiab Hill. People of Samarkand resist the enemy who were as many as the grains of sand and a lot of blood was spilled. A miracle happens just when the enemy was about to capture the city. A colossal sand hill and a shepherd who dwells on top of it come down on to the enemy high up above from the sky. That mound still exists today and is called the *Kuhak* hill, also known as the "Father Shepherd" (Esin, 1997). Due to this miracle people think of this site to be a sacred place. They dig for gold and silver with extreme gratitude towards this holy place. They cannot find any gold or silver but they find flint, marble and excellent sand which makes Samarkand the pottery center of the world. Ever since, Samarkand has been the pottery hub of the world for centuries and these fine arts' masters have always been the *Oghuz* tribe of Turks. Ceramics that were produced had red or a pink surface and decorated with black and red drawings (Rice, 1997). Today many of these works are exhibited in the Museum of History and Culture of Uzbeks in Registan (Fig. 3).

Even though having the Turan King as a father, Samarkand could not have achieved its prosperity without her loyal Sogdian bureaucrats and merchants. Sogdians, who had been living side by side with the Turks since 1000 B.C. in the Mawarannahr region, always achieved to make their skills sought-after no matter who ever was the ruler and never mixing in politics. Chinese chronicles record Yueh-chis as the forefathers of Sogdians and the K'ang-chus as the forefathers of Turks (Esin 1978). Achaemenids annexed the Mawarannahr region after the collapse Assyrians in 606 B.C. (559–330 B.C.). Achaemenid king Darius (552–485 B.C.) built a palace for himself at the top of the city center Afrasiab Hill (Fig. 4), (Pope, 1939). In Mawarannahr there existed a system of governance where Samarkand was the center for the surrounding city principalities. During their rule Achaemenids only controlled Samarkand and allowed the city principalities to continue their trade with China and the West freely and the so-called Turk Yagbus, K'ang-chus continued to be dominant of their region (Togan, 1981).

FIGURE 3   Ceramic Plate (Uzbekistan, 1997).

FIGURE 4   Darius Palace Plan (Pope, 1939).

After Achaemenids, Alexander the Great (336–323 B.C.) conquers the region. He was met with stiff resistance of the Turks and the Sogdians. Upon the death Alexander his successor Seleucid (312–65 B.C.) was to be the reign of the region. Between 250–50 B.C. Seleucid and his successors sustained their dominance to the south of the area as the Greek-Bactrian rule (Compareti, 2001). During this period Mawarannahr' city principalities governance system persisted.

In the second century B.C. Huns defeated Yueh-chis, and forced them to shift starting a huge migration of nations towards Central Asia, West Turkestan, Afghanistan and Northern India. This pushed out the Greco Bactrian colonies of the region. Herodotus, and Strabo give some information about the ethnicity and the mass migrations in this geography. In addition, Persian, Indian and Chinese sources are the main root of the chronicles in the region.

Kushans who were the dominants of the region during the 1st–3rd Century A.D., eliminated the rule of Alexander's residual the Greco Bactrian state and came to Bukhara from north of Kabul. Buddhist ruler Kanishka (78–101) achieved the dream of Chi-Chi the Qaghan of Huns and dominated the whole of India and Turkistan. Kushans took control of trade over by removing Iran out of the land and the sea routes between India and Rome. A further fight to dominate the Kushan territory began during the year 240 between the Sassanid Ruler Shapur (241–272) and a branch of the Huns the Hephthalites; especially after 438, resulted in Mawarannahr, Afghanistan, Northern India falling into the hands of Hephthalites. Kushan ruler Kanishkas' purpose of spreading Buddhism to the world was well known. A unique Kushan-Hindu art form was shaped during this period, also having an influence on the near trade partners the Sogdians. Some of the later palace paintings of Göktürk (Turkic Khaganate) period in Samarkand illustrate this effect. In fact, according to Esin this is why the westerners identified Afrasiab, Panjikent palace wall paintings as simply Sogdian instead of Göktürk. Yet Turkic military uniforms appear in Kushan sculptures, a Turkish word "kucula" which means beautiful is engraved on their coins. This clearly exhibits the interaction of Turkish and Kushan cultures.

Huns moved towards Europe in 375. Hephthalites on the other hand grew their military, political and cultural mark on Mawarannahr as a strong state during 375–479. The Hephthalites were finally destroyed by the Qaghan of Western Göktürks, Istemi in 557. The Göktürks' dominance of Mawarannahr resulted in Istemi Qaghan taking full control of the Silk Road trade and the formation of first Turkish–Byzantium direct relations in 567, due to the ambassadorship of the Turkish prince Maniakh of Samarkand. Maniakh recommended removing the Persians out of the silk trade. Consequently the region enjoyed its most prosperous times during 6th and 7th century. The mural paintings of this period in Afrsiab and Panjikent palaces reflect a perfect synthesis of Turkic-Sogdian art (Figs. 5–8).

FIGURE 5   Mural Painting of Afrasiab Palace (Cezar, 1977).

FIGURE 6   Afrasiab Palace Mural Painting (Cezar, 1977).

FIGURE 7   Afrasiab Palace Mural Painting (Cezar, 1977).

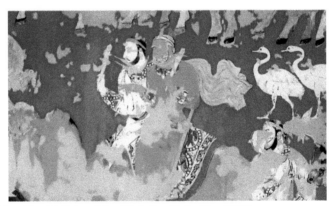

FIGURE 8   Afrasiab Palace Mural Painting (Belenitky, 1968).

If we go back to describing Samarkand as a beautiful princess, we may portray these paintings as the silk garments she wore so proudly. As it is well known silk is actually the pinnacle of the Eastern artwork. Hence these paintings were also meticulously made with attentive skills as silk is weaved and vested on the queen. A bridal procession is observed in the paintings dating 6th–7th centuries. Western Göktürks Qaghan "T'ung Yagbu" married the daughter of Sogdian *ihshid* (Sogd land owner) named "Sogdu" in 605–616. The Sogdians seen in Fig. 5 appear to be waiting to welcome the bridal procession. Horsemen in Fig. 6 are the Turkish delegation with their characteristic hair fringe. In Fig. 7 bride "Sogdu" is on a white elephant but cannot be seen clearly because of extensive damage. In Fig. 8, Sogdian ambassadors riding camels carrying scepters of ambassadorship are seen. The sacred swans seen in the background are an indication of a royal wedding. The name of Alp-er Tungas' daughter was "korday" which means swan in Turkish. Korday symbolizes long life and divinity. When Turkish qaghans ascended to the throne, they were given gifts such as birds (Esin, 1973; Pugackenkova, 1968). These mural paintings are now exhibited in the Afrasiab Museum of History. On the other hand, all the colors that are used in these paintings and particularly the "lapis" blue (Fig. 8) with mesmerizing stamina have an impressive effect on viewers. This type of blue is produced only by Samarkand's' lapis powder. Lapis powder naturally contains a small amount of gold dust, which gives its distinctive vividness. Being so expensive it was only used by the very rich. Many frescoes by Michelangelo in Florence and Rome is known to contain Samarkand's' lapis powder.

More mural paintings relating to the 6th–7th centuries were found 60 km east of Samarkand in Panjikent (Fig. 9). These paintings probably belong to a Turkish Qaghan of Penc from the tribe of Khalaj. This could be understood by the writing of the *Khalaj Army* in Turkish that is engraved on the coins of the same region (Esin, 1973). According to Russian archaeologist Belenitsky, the Panjikent palace was a building with domes and vaults. He had excavated many wooden artifices, clay sculptures, and ceramic household items. In the east of Panjikent at Mug Castle an archive of written texts was found. Most of these texts are in the Sogdian language. More than 50 pieces of mural paintings were found in Panjikent. Although extraordinarily varied in subjects, these paintings are all produced in very rich colors and contain the Samarkand's' unique lapis blue. Legends, daily life, religious ceremonies, hunting scenes, feasts and competitions are among the subjects of these paintings which evidently summarize the wide cultural and spiritual diversity of the region since the foundation of Samarkand (Marshak, 2002). This cultural diversity had its most valuable times during the 5th–8th centuries in the Turkic Yagbu period before Islam (Cezar, 1977). Today some of the Panjikent mural paintings are exhibited in the Uzbek History and Culture Museum at Registan, and a number of them are in Hermitage Museum in St. Petersburg.

FIGURE 9   Panjikent Palace Mural Painting (Belenitky, 1968).

In the middle of the eighth century the Göktürk state started to weaken, resulting in Arab dominance of Mawarannahr. Arabs first took over Balkh and later Bukhara and Samarkand. Under the command of Qutayba Ibn Muslim, Arabs annexed the whole of Mawarannahr between 710 and 716 (Togan, 1981). Later in 751 in the Abbasid age the defeat of the Chinese at Talas, resulted in extensive spread of Islam all around the Western Turkestan. Throughout the hundred years of Arab dominance they ruled the land by appointing Turks and Persians as governors. Arab sources like the Al-Tabari, Al-Isfahari, Al-Ya'kubi describe in detail all governors and tribes in the region. After the Talas war many Chinese prisoners were brought to Samarkand who were said to have established the paper industry. Consequently Islamic scholars found a chance to translate many ancient Greek inscriptions and replicate them therefore the west had the opportunity to learn about its past.

Samarkand had a bright period between the 9th–13th centuries under the rule of Samanids (874–999) and the Karakhanids (99–1120), respectively, and became the capital of the state of Khorezm. During this period there were many madrasahs, baths and caravanserais in the old city center at the Afrasiab Hill. In the year 1220, the beautiful queen Samarkand had undergone an invasion by the Mongol ruler Genghis Khan. Genghis was very crude towards the queen as no one had been before. The deep scars on queen's delicate skin that were left by Genghis can still be seen today. He literally destroyed her. Fortunately the queen covered up the traces of this unfair treatment with wonderful jewels that were given to her by her next ruler Timur (Tamerlane).

Samarkand became the capital city of the Timur State in 1369 after the Mongol invasion (Aka, 2000). The Timur (1370–1405) period was to become the most brilliant period of Samarkand that were to last for three hundred years. He gathered all the best architects and artists to the city making it the science and the art center of the world. Timur erected magnificent architectural monuments (madrasahs, palaces, tombs, complexes etc.) so as to redefine the appearance of the city. Spanish voyager Clavijo has seen these works of art being built. This is what he wrote about Samarkand: "The soil is very fertile and cotton is well-grown. There are gardens, fruit trees and vineyards that exist between all the houses in the city. Timur's shield is a triangle that is formed by three small circles, meaning he possess three-fourths of the world. This shield is stamped on the coins and on every building commissioned by him. In all cities under his domination palaces, madrasahs are being built. Most of these palaces are huge; decorated with blue and gold colored tiles, marble floors, fitted with courtyards and pools."

Clavijo continues: "Six elephants welcomed us at Timur's palace in Samarkand. The riders were sitting in wooden castles on the top of the elephants. There was a fountain in Timur's court with apples in it. Timur was wearing a silk robe, and a crown decorated with pearls and rubies. Inside the palace towards the way to the bedrooms there stood two golden tables with seven golden wine jugs inlaid with pearls and emeralds and golden glasses."(Clavijo, 2007) Clavijo is talking about Timur's Dilkusha palace, which did not survive, to our times. Clavijo being in Samarkand as an envoy, visited the army camp system applied and the marquee of the khan installed outside the city, which is a Turkish military tradition of hundreds of years. The marquee and all of the tents along with surrounding high walls and towers were made out of colorful silk fabrics. Each tent had an owner's totem on top. Clavijo describes the wealth of Samarkand as astonishing and claims that two Turkish words "semiz" and "kand" meaning "fat" or "wealthy" and "city" comes together to give Samarkand its name "Wealthy city." The true wealth of Samarkand was the beauty of the silk and gold brocade fabrics woven, gold and blue tiled structures and the most talented artists and scholars that were brought to the city from the conquered countries.

HISTORICAL MONUMENTS

The most important Samarkand's architectural works of the period of Timur is as follows:

SHAH-I ZINDEH MAUSOLEUM COMPLEX (10TH–19TH CENTURY)

Beautiful queen Samarkand carries—Islam's precious gift to her—the Tomb of Shah-I Zindeh, like a brooch that she wears right on top of her heart. This shrine would be the most valuable of all the spiritual possessions of the city. During Imam Osman's period Kussam Ibn Abbas had come to Samarkand upon his uncle Profit Muhammad's wish to spread Islam in Mawarannahr. Martyred on an "eid ul-adha," (feast of sacrifice) Kussam Ibn Abbas is given the name "Shah-i Zinde" (King of the Living) in accordance with the verse that says martyrs never die. The historic cemetery on the way to Arasiab hill is dated as far back as the tenth century (Fig. 10). Oldest graves are aligned with the narrow road leading down from the tomb of Shah-I Zinde. During and after the Timur period, the shrines for members of the dynasty, important statesmen and scholars continued to be made on this sacred hill. The structure of the tomb gate is made with great mastery of ivory ornament. The most important architectural feature of the structure is the polished, baked earth and blue colored different sized ceramics. Some of its rooms include colorful ceramic panels (Pander, 2001). The section that belongs to the ladies of Timur's family had a portal entrance that contained literally the most beautiful lace like lapis-colored pottery of Samarkand. Here stands so devoted the tomb of beloved first wife of Timur, Olcay Turkan (Fig. 11).

FIGURE 10   Shah-I Zindeh Necropolis (danzon2008.blogspot.com).

FIGURE 11   Timurid Female Necropolis (danzon2008.blogspot.com).

MADRASAH AND MAUSOLEUM OF BIBI KHATUN (1399–1405)

One of the most delicate and glorious works of its times the Bibi Khatun complex was built for one of Timur's wife's Lady Bibi. The structure consists of a Friday mosque, madrasah and the tomb of Lady Bibi, both of which are decorated with turquoise glazed tiles and magnificent doors that rise tall as if reaching out to the sky. Verses are written with tiles on top the entrance gates of the shrine. Esin visited the complex when she was in Samarkand and describes it: "while one enters through the monumental gates to the courtyard, a yellow rose garden and nightingales welcomes you as if you have arrived into a lady's house" (Esin, 1997). Commissioned by a woman, having an extremely feminine texture, this fine piece of art could be, if needed, depicted as a lapis ring. Queen Samarkand wears this treasure with honor on her left hand like a wedding ring (Fig. 12).

FIGURE 12   Bibi Khatun Madrasah (sonnurozcan.blogspot.com).

GUR EMIR MAUSOLEUM (15TH CENTURY)

The structure embraces the tomb and the madrahsa of Timur, which guided the Central Asian, Persian and Afghan architectural movement for two centuries. The most important feature of the Gur Emir is its 34 meters high melon shaped dome covered with fluted and superbly colorful mosaic tiles. The sunlight reflected from the ribbed dome during different times of the day, transforms these ceramics and creates the allusion of birds flying briskly above the city. Double dome of the tomb has later been a model for many Islamic buildings. Inside the tomb Timur's family tree and story of his life are engraved upon an agate gravestone. Along with him his sons, grandson Ulugh Beg and his Sheikh also lay here (Pander, 2001). It wouldn't be correct to portray this shrine as a jewel that Samarkand wears. Queen had buried his most loyal son Timur, deep inside of her heart. In this sense today, Timur's tomb (Fig. 13) stands with its battered beauty as a monument to all of the pain and suffering on one hand, happiness and good fortune on the other; that the city has witnessed all throughout history. Undoubtedly Timur has given Samarkand its most beautiful architectural gifts and indeed, he lies comfortably in her heart never to be forgotten.

FIGURE 13   Gur Emir Tomb (www.edebi.net).

REGISTAN SQUARE

Registan Square is the royal crown queen Samarkand wears with conceit. Those who see this square feel themselves to be very small as if in presence of a magnificent queen. Buildings encircling the square look like embroidered jewelry. Tons of gold and gorgeous ceramics were used to embellish these structures and further more the design that is beyond their time bewilders the onlookers (Fig. 14).

FIGURE 14   Registan Square (tr.wikipedia.org).

Registan square is actually the city's oldest market place. Throughout the history this open place has seen many invasions, celebrations and victory parades. Timur's grandson Ulugh Beg (1393–1449) built a madrasah here. Ulugh Beg himself was a great scholar in astronomy and mathematics. His pursuit for higher science pushed this structure to be artistically, technically and scientifically the best example, thus making it a guide for his successors to come. The most important and amazing feature of Ulugh Beg madrasah is its mosaics that are cut so accurately with fine patterns, bright colors and excellent polish (Pander, 2001).

When one looks straight to Registan Square, he would see the Ulugh Beg Madrasah on the right, Tilla-Kari Madrasah further back in the middle and Sher-Dor Madrasah on the left. Tilla-Kari Madrasah (1646–1660) may be the smallest of all, nevertheless its marbles gilded with gold leafs highlight its beauty and carries it forward (Esin, 1997).

Sher-Dor Madrasah (1619–1635/36) was the last one to be built out of the tree. It gets its name from the lion figures made of mosaics above the main portal. Structure adds color to Registan Square with its fluted dome's bright mosaics. All tree madrasahs at this square still stand today with their exceptionally striking colors, astonishing mosaics and monumental portals, still waiting to serve science and humanity (Esin, 1997).

ULUGH BEG OBSERVATORY (1421)

Ulugh Beg Observatory was built in 1421 at the top of the Afrasiab Hill by Ulugh Beg who was an astrologer himself. Being the most advanced astronomical observatory of the era, its' protractor and other instruments were built into a massive rock. Considering the astrological calculations were made without using any telescopes or binoculars, one should appreciate how sophisticated Ulugh Beg observatory was even by today's standards (Pander, 2001). Renowned scientists of the period such as Kadızade Rumi from Bursa, Ali Kuscu, and Cemsid gathered all the research and work done in two books called "Zeych Kurkani" and "Zeych Cedit Sultani" which were used as source books both in the west and east. Grandson of Timur, Ulugh Beg's gift to queen Samarkand cannot be portrayed as jewelry to be worn, just as in Timur's tomb. But it would be rather more correct to imagine this observatory to be the light of inelegance in the mind of the city. In order to measure the true value of this center of science one must comprehend how ahead of its time it was. As Timur's tomb is buried in the heart of city, the observatory of Ulugh Beg finds its place in the superior mind of it.

In the 15th century the Uzbek Khan Shayabak (1500–1597) ended the dominance of the Timur's and moved the capital out of Samarkand to Bukhara. Later in 1868 Samarkand is tied to the general center for Turkestan when the Uzbeks are defeated by the Czar of Russia. She becomes the capital of Soviet Uzbekistan again between the years of 1924 and 1930.

CONCLUSION

If one day ever your road leads you to Samarkand the beautiful city of Uzbekistan, think of her as a summary of the human history. All along her adventures she had seen some good days and some dark times, never the less she still stands and will embrace all her visitors with her everlasting grace. Queen Samarkand might open up her secrets to you if you are able to find her spirit hidden in the works of art that she wears and bears on herself and if you are able to feel her spirit, you might also fall in love with her. But know that you won't be the first, for Queen Samarkand had many lovers throughout history. "Love" is in truth the story of Samarkand in a single word.

SAMARKAND TODAY

TRADITIONAL HANDICRAFTS OF SAMARKAND

Samarkand has been the most important city of the Silk Road for many centuries. Thus handmade crafts have very long roots planted deep in its history. Reaching back as far as before Christ; Mawarannahr's many tribes and nations have demonstrated their talents in different crafts making Samarkand the most precious center for arts and trade in the entire world. The Turkish tribe of Oghuz discovered and perfected the art of ceramics, Sogdians were masters of gold and silver works, Taciks were master of textiles. Many art works of the region are exhibited in prestigious museums all over the world. Today traditional handmade crafts still survive and are produced. A good example for crafts of our times would be "Suzanis" blankets. Suzanies are produced by colorful silk threads embroidered on cotton fabric. These works' value is judged by the amount of embroidery and colors and complexity of the motifs (Fig. 15).

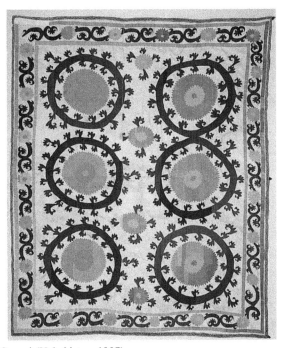

FIGURE 15   Suzani (Uzbekistan, 1997).

Doppi are the hats that people wear to mark their status and place in society. They have been used for centuries in the region. "Doppi"s motifs differ from city to city. They are produced by embroidery of silk motifs on single color cloth. The motif of "Kuskandı" is one of the oldest that is still used today. It means grace, happiness and sovereignty. Kids "Doppi"s are decorated with bird feathers, and women's are made with flower motifs (Fig. 16).

FIGURE 16   Doppis (New York Turkish House Exhibition, 2009).

"Ikat" dress robes were worn for centuries as a fundamental part of the Uzbek culture. These robes bear motifs and colors that are similar to the works of futurist painters. Colors used are very vibrant. In this respect "Ikat"s robes look like contemporary art made hundreds of years ago. They have been the choice of executives and the wealthy elite. Due to their high value they were used as the most prestigious gift. Also they were used to pay for taxes or services of great importance. In some instances "Ikad"s were valued higher than gold (Çetinkaya, 2007), (Fig. 17).

FIGURE 17   Ikats (Çetinkaya, 2007).

The metal works have always been a craft of Samarkand since ancient times. Jewelry was produced with incredible detail. Superior craftsmanship is world famous. Brides wear such ornaments as seen in the picture (Fig. 18).

FIGURE 18   Uzbek Female Crown (Uzbekistan, 1997).

CITY MUSEUMS OF SAMARKAND

Samarkand bears the most beautiful examples of Islamic architecture. For this reason, the city is under protection of the UNESCO World Heritage List. Although the city is like an open-air museum, there are of course many museums to be seen in Samarkand. Some of them are as follows:

Afrsiyap History Museum: The museum is established very close to the excavation site of ancient Afrasiab Hill that was the center of the Samarkand at sixth century B.C. Wall-paintings of Afrasiab palace and many artifacts that were unearthed are exhibited in this museum.

Sadriddin-Ayni Museum: A poet and a writer Sadreddin-Ayni also served as president of Tajikistan. The museum is in the Registan Square. It has been restored in accordance with the traditional architecture of its period.

Historic Museum of Uzbek Culture: Some of the exhibits are; Panjikent palace wall paintings of the seventh century, Mug Hill frescos, terracotta sculptures, ceramic plates with Arabic inscriptions of the early Islamic period, tile works and glasswork.

Alisher Navio Museum: Alisher Navoi is a scholar that lived during the Tamerlane period in the 15th century. He had written five Divans in Persian and in Chagatai Turkic. He proved the Chagatai language to be as effective as Persian in literature and gained the respect of his times' writers. He founded a miniature school that survived until the 19th century and his works were depicted in miniatures.

KEYWORDS

- Ahamenid
- Alp-Er-Tunga (Afrasiab)
- Semerkand
- Timur
- Turks

REFERENCES

Aka, İ. (2000). Timur ve Devleti. Ankara: Türk Tarih Kurumu.

Akbulut, D.A. (2002). Akhunlar (Kionit/Hyon) ve Eftalitler Çağında Maveraünnehir ve Horasan'da Türkler. In H. C. Güzel, K. Çiçek, S. Koca (Eds.). Türkler Ansiklopedisi (Volume 1, pp.831–843) Ankara: Yeni Türkiye Yayınları.

Arapov, A. (2006). Historical Monuments of Uzbekistan Samarkand Bukhara Khiva. Tashkent: San'at Press.

Aslanapa, O. (1996). Türk Cumhuriyetleri Mimarlık Abideleri, Ankara: Türksoy Yayınları.

Belenitsy, A. (1968). Archaeologia Mvndi Central Asia (Hogarth, J. Trans.). Geneva:Nagel Publishing.

Bulatova, V., Shishkina, G. (1986). Samarkand A museum In The Open. Tashkent:

Cezar, M. (1977). Anadolu Öncesi Türklerde Şehir ve Mimarlık. İstanbul: Türkiye İş Bankası Kültür Yayınları.

Clavijo, R. G. (2007). Timur Devrinde Kadis'ten Semerkand'a Seyahat. (Ö. R. Doğrul, Trans.). İstanbul: Kesit Yayınları.

Comparetti, M. C. (2002). Sogdiyana Tarihine Giriş. In H. C. Güzel, K. Çiçek, S. Koca (Eds.). Türkler Ansiklopedisi (Volume 2, pp.157–165) Ankara: Yeni Türkiye Yayınları.

Cöhce, S. (2002). Hindistan'da İlk Türk Hâkimiyeti: Kuşanlar Ve Akhunlar. In H. C. Güzel, K. Çiçek, S. Koca (Eds.). Türkler Ansiklopedisi (Volume 1, pp. 815–826) Ankara: Yeni Türkiye Yayınları.

Çetinkaya, M. (2007). 99 Ikats Chapans. İstanbul: Mas Matbacılık.

Ekrem, N. H. (2002). Chan-ch'ien'in Seyahat Raporuna Göre Hunlar Dönemindeki Orta Asya. In H. C. Güzel, K. Çiçek & S. Koca (Eds.). Türkler Ansiklopedisi (Volume 1, pp. 765–769) Ankara: Yeni Türkiye Yayınları.

Esin, E. (1973). Türk Ul-Acem'lerin Eseri Samarrada Cavsak Ul-Hakani'nin Dıvar Resimleri. Sanat Tarihi Yıllığı, 5, 309–358.

Esin, E. (1978). İslamiyet'ten Önceki Türk Kültür Tarihi Ve İslam'a Giriş. İstanbul: İstanbul Üniversitesi Edebiyat Fakültesi Yayınları.

Esin, E. (1983). İbni Sina Çevresinde Türk Kültürü. Uluslararası İbni Sina Sempozyumu Bildirileri 17–20 Ağustos 1983.

Esin, E. (1986, Mayıs). Ribat-i Melik, Hakani Sülalesinden İbrahim-Oğlu Çu Tigin İkinci Naşr Şemsü'l-Mülk ve Harcang'de H. 471/1078'de Yaptırdığı Külliye. ERDEM, 2 (5), 405–425.

Esin, E. (1997). Türkistan Seyahatnamesi (2nd edition). Ankara: Türk Tarih Kurumu.

Esin, E. (2002). İç Asya'da Milattan Önceki Bin Yılda Türklerin Atalarına Atfedilen Kültürler. In H. C. Güzel, K. Çiçek, S. Koca (Eds.). Türkler Ansiklopedisi (Volume 1, pp. 494–515) Ankara: Yeni Türkiye Yayınları.

Frye, R.N. (2009). Antik Çağlardan Türklerin Yayılmasına Orta Asya Mirası (2nd edition). Ankara: Arkadaş Yayınları.

Hmelnitskiyh, S. (2000). Mejdu Kuşanamai i Arabami. Berlin: Riga.

Gömeç, S. (2006). Türk Kültürünün Ana Hatları. Ankara: Akçağ Yayınları.

Kaşgarlı Mahmut. (1985). Divan-ı Lügati't-Türk. (B.Atalay Trans.). Volume 3. Ankara: Türk tarih Kurumu. (Original work published 1072–73).

Konukçu, E. (2001). Akhunlar, In H. C. Güzel, K. Çiçek & S. Koca (Eds.). Türkler Ansiklopedisi (Volume 1, pp. 827–830) Ankara: Yeni Türkiye Yayınları.

Marshak, B. (2002). Legends, Tales, and Fables In The Art of Sodiana. New York: Bibliothea Persica Press.

Mukahamedjannov, A. R., Mukahamedjannov. (1997, Octobar). The City of Bukhara-2500 Years Old. Scientific and Cultural Heritage of Mankind-To The Third Millennium (pp. 9–10) Tashkent: UNESCO.

Pander, K. (2001). Timuroğullarının Orta Asya Mimari Sanatına Katkıları. In H. C. Güzel, K. Çiçek, S. Koca (Eds.). Türkler Ansiklopedisi (Volume 8, pp. 852–861) Ankara: Yeni Türkiye Yayınları.

Pope, A. U. (Eds.) (1938–39). A Survey of Persian Art. Japan: Sopa, Ashiya.

Pugachenkova, G. A. (1958). Puti Ravzitia Arhitektury Yuznogo Turkmenistana Pory Rabovladeniya i Feodalisma. Moskova.

Pugachenkova, G. A. (1960). Vidayushchiesya pamyatniki izobrazitelnogo iskusstva Uzbekistana Gosudarstvennoe Izdatelstvo Kh. Tashkent.

Pugachenkova, G. A. (1987). Kangars in samarkand 1st B.C.-2nd c. A.D.Images of the Kangar (Ch Kangju) in Sogdian Art. Retrieved March 13, 2012, from http://s155239215.onlinehome. us/turkic/22KangarsRugachenkovaKangarsEn.htm.

Rice, D. T. (1971). Islamic Painting A Survey. Edinburg: Edinburg University Press.

Rice, D. T. (1977). Islamic Art. London: Thames and Hudson.

Rice, T. T. (1969). Some Reflections on the Subject of Arm Bands. Forschungen Zur Kunst Asiens In Memoriam Kurt Erdman (pp. 263–277). İstanbul: İstanbul Üniversitesi Edebiyat Fakültesi Türk ve İslam Sanatı Kürsüsü.

Şeşen, R. (2001). İslam Coğrafyacılarına Göre Türkler ve Türk Ülkeleri (2nd edition). Ankara: Türk Tarih Kurumu.

Togan, Z. V., (1981). Umumi Türk Tarihi'ne Giriş. İstanbul:Enderun Kitabevi.

Zasipkin, B. (1928). Arhitekturnie pamyatniki Srednii Azii:problemi issledovaniya i restavr Izdanie Tsentralnikh Gosudarst. Moskva.

www.danzon2008.blogspot.com

www.edebi.net/13.11.2013

www.sonnurozcan.blogspot.com/13.11.2013

www.tr.wikipedia.org/13.11.2013

CHAPTER 8

CINEMA AS BRANDING

SAULESH YESSENOVA

CONTENTS

INTRODUCTION

When the Soviet Union went into its death throes, no one thought of Kazakhstan, the last socialist republic to break away, as a state that would make a major breakthrough in economic development, outpacing Russia, its former boss, and the countries of Eastern Europe. Initially regarded as a soap bubble blown by global ambitions in the energy-rich Caspian Basin, its success has revealed sound economic and political strategies that paved the way for continued economic growth. Nevertheless, oil has been a major factor behind the country's 'miracle,' significantly informing public culture and identity of this newly emerged nation. And yet – neither the impressive transformation from a designated 'bread basket' within the Soviet division of labor into a player on the global oil market with a rizing economic profile, nor the earlier decision to dismantle the country's nuclear arsenal, or the contribution to greater regional cooperation and security – helped to shape Kazakhstan's global image, which remained, in an international view, an obscure place in Russia's backyard.

Such deficiency in the world's perception has not been overlooked by the Kazakhstan's savvy leadership striving to reposition the country within the global political economy. They embarked on the task of image-making in a comprehensive manner: trained Kazakh astronauts, dressed Olympic teams, sent troops to Iraq, and patronized global media networks that run front-page PR campaigns, introducing the country to the world. However, 'Nation branding' has proved to be a difficult task. Aware of the situation, President Nazarbaev, the mastermind of the Kazakhstan's economic recovery and its only leader since 1991, proposed something else, a public diplomacy project that he thought would instantly put a popular spotlight on his country: a 'blockbuster' cinema.

The subtext of this project has been somewhat similar to cultural activism films made by subaltern indigenous groups, trying to disseminate their views and assert control over their images distorted by colonialism (Ginsburg et al., 2002). But unlike, for example, Tibetan or Palestinian activists who use film to give international visibility to their causes, which has become a recognized esthetic strategy to attract public attention and gain sympathy in places otherwise removed and disconnected, Kazakhstan's project was driven by a different agenda. Packaged as a commercially attractive product, the film was to let the world know that Kazakhstan is no longer a resource frontier whose only value is extractable, nonrenewable *raw* materials – a position by itself comfortable and self-praised but maligned and demeaning within the international division of labor and power relations. The film was to promote Kazakhstan's image as a creative economy, conducive of innovation and new ideas. In sum, the function of the future film was to liberate the country from anonymity, moving it up within the global hierarchies at the same time.

A heroic motion picture, *Nomad the Warrior* was released at home in 2005.[1] Styled as a 'sword 'n' sandal' epic (e.g., *Gladiator, Troy*), it is Kazakhstan's second most grandiose cultural endeavor (US$40 million) after the relocation of the capital from Almaty to Astana in the late-1990 s. Its story revolves around the events that took place in the 18th century in present-day south-eastern Kazakhstan. Shot in original location, the film features breath-taking landscapes, scaled battle scenes cast by real people, impressive stunt sequences with warriors on horseback, and splendorous 'period' costumes and decorations. Depicting action in a location hitherto unseen on global screen, its narrative addresses universal matters of courage, loyalty, and humanity, a recipe for popular appeal.

Nomad is a coproduction of Kazakhfilm, a national studio, and Wild Bunch, a French company, which casted actors from popular American TV shows for major roles in the film. Cinematography has been one of the most successful arts in Kazakhstan; foreign participation was solicited to harmonize local skills and cultural tastes with those of Hollywood.[2] A scriptwriter, Rustam Ibragimbekov, known for internationally acclaimed pictures *Burnt by the Sun* and *The Barber of Siberia*, was hand-picked, fitting in with codirectors, Ivan Passer, Sergey Bodrov, and Talgat Temenov on the Kazakh side, as well as Milos Forman and Sergey Azimov, as executive producers. Even before it was made, *Nomad* was presented to the

---

[1] In the version distributed in Kazakhstan, the film has been titled as *Köshpendiler* (*Nomads*).

[2] Kazakh cinematography traces its history to the WWII when Mosfilm, a major Russian studio was evacuated to Alma-Ata. The presence of Mosfilm film crew shaped local talents and aspirations, so that after the Russian studio returned home after the war was over, Kazakhstan's filmmaking picked up. Kazakhfilm studio is now named after Shaken Aimanov (1914–1970), one of the most renowned Kazakh directors who defined a Kazakh cinematic tradition with his films about the lives of individual Kazakh women and men, their encounters with Russians, and their responses to the Soviet rule (*Poema o luybvi* 1954; *Doch stepei* 1955; *Myzdes' zhivem* 1956; *Nash milyi doktor* 1957; *Konets atamana* 1970; *Zemlya otsov* 1966). Later major films made during the Soviet period include: Abdulla Karsakpaev *Menya Zovut Kozha* 1963, *Pogonya v stepi* 1979; *Soleonaya reka detstva*, 1983; Sultan Khodzhikov *Kyz Zhibek* 1970, Mazhit Begalin *Ego vremya pridyet* 1957 (about Chokan Valikhanov), *Pesnya o Manshuk* 1969; Kuat Abuseitov *Doroga zhizni* 1959.

nation as their country's entry in the race for Best Foreign Language Film at the Academy Awards.

The film was delayed for technical reasons, rumored to include the misallocation of funds by local crew members, the national pastime. But when it finally came out and was sent to the Locarno Film Festival in anticipation of a worldwide release, Kazakhstan's entry in the world of ultimate glamor, scheduled for 2007, was unexpectedly hijacked – brutally – by another film that rose to fame in no time, *Borat: Cultural Learnings of America for Make Benefit Glorious Nation of Kazakhstan* (2006) by Sacha Baron Cohen and the Twentieth Century Fox. "A mind-blowing comedy classic," according to *Rolling Stone*, it features Sacha Cohen as his "truly original Kazakh character Borat Sagdiyev" from HBO's *Da Ali G Show*.[3] The film sparked a controversy on both sides of the Atlantic for mocking Kazakhstan depicted as a misogynist and anti-Semitic society and humiliating people in a Romanian village where the film was partially shot with the participation of local extras who had no idea about their actual roles in the film. But this critical publicity only increased the popularity of *Borat* that has been profiled in a whole range of media from *Glamour*, *BBC*, and *CNN*, to *Anthropology News*.[4] The film grossed US$250 million, collecting awards across the board, including Golden Globe's Best Actor and an Oscar nomination in 2007 as a final blow to Kazakhstan's own pursuit of fame.

Individual Kazakh politicians threatened to sue Mr. Cohen. In response, the U.S. State Department declared Sacha Cohen (or Borat Sagdiyev?) a "victim of censorship" in Kazakhstan, a "corrupt and undemocratic oil-rich country."[5] This news came up at the tail end of the publicity flood that soon lost steam. President Nazarbaev is said to have admitted to the Prime Minister Tony Blair that 'no publicity is bad publicity' (referring to *Borat*,

---

[3]From the cover of the DVD.

[4]In *Glamour*, Borat's phrase "I like you. I like sex. Is nice" has become one of the "five truths to stick to your fridge about love" (Feb. 2007: 167); *CNN* has provided the most extensive coverage and even sent a reporter to Almaty ('With Borat fever sweeping cinemas everywhere...' 30 Oct., 2006; Borat Invited to 'real' Kazakhstan 19 October, 2006; 'Borat' is the most excellent comedy, 6 Nov., 2006), followed by *BBC* ('How Borat hoaxed America,' 23 Oct. 2006), *The Sunday Times* ('Welcome to my World!' 15 Oct., 2006), and *USA Today* ('Finding the *Real* Kazakhstan' 17 Nov., 2006). In anthropology, Borat inspired several authors who compared his work with what anthropologists do: Adam Fish 'Mining Difference for the Culture Industry' *Anthropology News*, January 2007: 6–7; and Bruce Grindal 'Borat as Trickster' *Anthropology News*, March 2007: 4).

[5]'Borat seen as human rights victim by U.S. government' *Reuters*, March 7, 2007.

not to his country's human rights record), which formally ended the affair. This neat comment, however, was nothing more than an empty diplomatic gesture because people learned from *Borat* about Sacha Cohen and not about Kazakhstan that came to be known as the comedian's invention. Caught in crossfire with *Borat*, an international distributor of *Nomad* did not release the film in March 2007, as was announced earlier. It arrived in Blockbuster stores months later, creating no splash in public consciousness whatsoever.[6]

On Kazakhstan's side, people with vested interests in *Nomad* blamed poor timing for the failure of their country's project. But this opinion ignored the fact that *Nomad* was unsuccessful on two fronts, international and domestic, suggesting that other factors were also at work. The film was highly anticipated in Kazakhstan but once it was released it generated no spontaneous public response; it simply became a nonevent.[7] My personal snapshot of reaction to the film by the Almaty public is revealing: after watching *Nomad*, my local companions told me that I was trying to read the film too deeply looking for some meaning that does not exist. "This film wasn't made for us," they said, explaining their disinterest in discussing the film: "they just wanted to create a Hollywood-like picture, that's all."

Film is an important cultural medium in the process of "negotiating between the local and the global." It is also important "for reconstructing society and public spheres after social traumas of civil war, revolution, state collapse, earthquake, and other massive social disruptions" (Fischer, 2003). In other words, the magic of film is that it works across cultural boundaries, simultaneously contributing to the national loyalty and development, something that a young nation-state as Kazakhstan, not short of social disruptions in its history, might consider useful. What the aforementioned comments by the Almaty movie-goers indicate is that *Nomad* has had no such appeal to the national audience, admitting it as unauthentic and fraudulent.

---

[6]It is hard to say why exactly the international distributor of *Nomad* chose not to screen the film in movie theatres on the wave of the *Borat* buzz that, at least in theory, could actually help promoting it.

[7]Several formal reviews came out in Kazakhstan in which the authors praised the film in attempt to valorize the state and its leadership (Sergey Kudryavtsev 'Kogda hochet'sya byt' kazahom' *Baiterek*, 3/18, June 2006: 10–13).

In this chapter, I try to rescue what was shown and said in the film and to situate its story within the past and present cultural milieus searching for the answers to the questions: (a) why this costly effort failed to produce a plausible narrative for the national audience and (b) what went wrong with this project designed to introduce the country, its people and their history to the world. I end my discussion of *Nomad*, a film that was expected to produce a particular international image for Kazakhstan, referring to the concepts of *place branding* and *creative environment*, which guided the country's leadership attempts 'to put their country on the map.'

BACKGROUND, ORGANIZATION, AND METHODOLOGY

The film draws on two episodes in Kazakh history. One is a story of the aftermath of serious military attacks on Kazakhs by Jungars, Mongol tribes, who will be discussed later. The scale of the devastation inflicted upon Kazakh communities was documented in oral narratives from this period (1723–1726) defined as *Aktaban Shubirindy* or *the Time of the Great Calamity*.[8] A central narrative here is *Elim-ay*, a song, which is well-known among modern Kazakhs. Its lyrics evoke human loss, loss of homeland, and disintegration of the society since different communities had to take up separate paths on their way to safety.[9] Before they split, they swore to never forget their grief, to rejoin and reclaim their land from the enemy. As they went on, they heard a baby camel crying over separation with his mother. They added their voices to his cry and it became the *Elim-ay* song. The passionate desire to reunite as a people forms a background in the film-story.

The other episode centers on a historical figure, Ablai (1711–1781) who entered the steppe politics in the late 1730s and, towards the end of his life, became a khan. Ablai's political career was shaped by the hostility between Kazakhs and Jungars. Yet, a number of skilled and dedicated war-

---

[8]*Aktaban Shubirindy* is transcribed as "the time when the entire people is laying down [exhausted] with the soles worn away from running and having no strength" (Yessenberlin [1973] 1989: 241). This event has been documented in written historical sources because of the devastating impact of the "arrival of desperate and destitute Kazakhs" on Central Asian cities, Samarkand, Khiva and Bukhara (Khodarkovsky 2002: 150).

[9]*Elim-ay* is transcribed as "Oh, my devastated people." As one of its verses goes: "Nothing is harder than to say good bye // when you don't know if you meet ever again!" (cited in, including the complete text of the song, in Kudayberdy-Uly [1911] 1990: 50).

riors and leaders emerged among the Kazakhs in response to the tragedy of 1723, and Ablai (given name Abulmansur) was only one of them. What makes his story part of collective memory are his character and his political career, which unfolds within the historical context, which in addition to Jungars, involved other significant political actors: his home rivalries as well as China and Russia who started making inroads to the steppe in the 18th century. Traditionally, the warfare with Jungars and the story of Ablai have been different historical narratives in terms of genre and message amid periodic intersections. The film-makers, on the other hand, tainted this convention by synchronizing the two episodes in a single storyline. Ablai, in the cinematic rendering of the story, is a long-awaited Kazakh warrior who mobilizes his people for a successful counterattack. His character is used as a symbolic means to achieve a moral closure to the drama of *Aktaban Shubirindy* and convey the rebirth of the nation. What has come out of this transformation and reduction of both historical facts and oral tradition?

I have organized my discussion in a 'braided' fashion: the cinematic image of Ablai is just one strand, whereas the other two are my attempts to (a) tell his story from oral tradition and (b) locate it within a broader historical context by drawing on contemporary history literature.[10] I am aware that the mixing of a Western tradition of recording the past and an oral tradition giving retrospective significance to events and personalities is conducive of methodological flaws.[11] Toby Morantz reminds us, that the differences in philosophies and discursive conventions, the absence of a shared narrative in oral tradition privileging localized stories as well as cultural remoteness of researchers from oral sources handicap the possibilities for writing adequate "blended stories" (2002). This is why I have chosen to discuss the story of Ablai and the historical context within which it took place separately.

I should explain that unlike many ethnohistorians, I did not face a challenge of acting as a cultural translator of oral tradition. The exposure to the Western tradition via a Russian educational system of some Kazakhs in the 19th century, and the society as a whole during the Soviet period has generated a pool of bicultural and bilingual specialists who, in their

---

[10] I draw on Natalie Davis' notion of "braided history," specifying "that history must tell everyone's story on equal terms" (2001, cited from: Morantz 2002: 3).

[11]For an in-depth discussion of this issue see Cruickshank (1998, especially, p. 41) and Burt (1998: 97 – 118).

representations of the past, were able to reflect both perspectives. Their work helped to see the complexity of the historical situation on the Kazakh steppe from the standpoint of the Kazakh society, as I argue below.

One of the first known records of the story of Ablai belongs to Bukhar zhirau (1693–1787), a traditional Kazakh songwriter and storyteller and a long-term companion of Ablai. He supported Ablai as a member of his entourage, but at the same time he tried to exert "a pedagogical influence" on him (Winner, 1958). This blend of admiration and critique, so characteristic to Bukhar zhirau, shaped the grounds for a future genre of social critique within the Kazakh literature (ibid). His work also set the tone for subsequent interpretations of Ablai's life by Kazakh writers.[12] Two accounts stand out: an essay entitled *Ablai* by Chokan Valikhanov (1835–1865) and a novel entitled *Desperation* [*Zhastalas*] by Illias Yessenberlin (1973).[13] Grounded in ethnographic research, these are ample efforts of addressing oral sources from the vantage point of their time. Both works are my key sources.[14]

The proliferation of literacy within the Kazakh society did not erase possibilities for multiple interpretations of the story of Ablai. Even today the story is not singular. People keep it 'alive' by investing the old story with the new meanings. In this regard, who else, if not Ablai, would make a better candidate for a lead character in a national epic film? Being part of this process myself, I think that the Kazakh storytellers and writers have left promising leads for the story of Ablai to be attuned to the realities of the post-independent Kazakhstan and told through a visual medium in a new and exciting way.

ABLAI IN ORAL TRADITION

Narratives of Ablai embody historical assumptions of power and identity in the Kazakh society, a product of cultural interaction at a crossroad of

---

[12]Most of these works are cited further in the text.

[13]This novel is the second novel in his historical trilogy *Nomads* [*Köshpendiler*]. The name of this trilogy apparently lent itself to the title of the *Nomad* film in a version released in Kazakhstan.

[14]Bukhar zhirau's verses were often performed by traditional song-writers and story-tellers, which helped them to be recorded by Russian ethnographers (e.g., Sobolev 1940). Later, his verses went into a collection of Kazakh poetry (Dzharmagambetov et al., 1958: 65 – 89). Ablai's story has been a recurrent theme in a Kazakh literary and history research, perhaps since the time of his death. Apart from Valikhanov and Yessenberlin, there are accounts dated from the early 20th century till now (Bokeikhanov [1903] 1995; Kasymbaev (1991; 1999a; 1999b; 2003).

Central Eurasia. Amongst other historical actors, the herding communities of Turkic origin and a Mongol meritocracy descending from Genghis Khan (the Töre) made the biggest contribution to the future Kazakh society shaping its cultural fabric and political institutions.[15] The communities of Kazakh pastoral nomads were organized into three loosely integrated tribal confederations (Uly *jüz*, Orta *jüz*, and Qushi *jüz*) governed by the khans and sultans chosen among the Töre. Although their privileged status was beyond question the political influence of individual Töre was tailored to their personal credibility in the eyes of local communities whose taste for a diffused and community-centered authority controlled their reach.[16] This system of Mongol patronage remained in place for over six centuries until it was replaced by the Russian colonial administration, which was installed on the steppe in the mid-19th century.

Standing outside the Kazakh tribal structure, the Töre, at the same time were part of the society and, albeit their exclusive status, were the same as the commoners in terms of language, religion, and a way of life. This double-sided engagement of the ruling elite with the designated communities made their authority relevant in ordinary times and indispensable at the time of political instability and military threat. This was because most political leaders in Central Asia claimed blood affinity with Genghis Khan and the Töre were positioned to create alliances across political and cultural boundaries that divided the region.[17] The Kazakhs identified collectively with particular Mongol khans and sultans in addition to a genealogical treatment of their own origins (the *shejýre*), which guided social relations on the steppe.

The *shejýre,* an important cultural resource, informed Kazakh oral tradition by fostering a particular perception of history as a dynamic succession of individuals who shaped communities and events. Among those individuals, Ablai – a son of Vali and a grandson of Ablai – is a major figure. His life and his relations inspired traditional storytellers and with the spread of literacy writers of different veins. But it is not the sheer greatness of his accomplishments that attracted curious and creative minds

---

[15]Töre is a term approximating in Kazakh language a 'dignified position' (Sultanov 1999: 58).

[16]This capacity rarely extended beyond one *jüz*, oftentimes, not even beyond khan's *ulus*, a territorially defined unit made of communities that personally expressed their loyalty to the khan (Tolybekov 1971: 90, 344 – 345 and 354).

[17]This factor helps to explain the endurance of the Mongol supremacy among the Kazakhs and beyond (Thackston 2002: xxxvi–xxxix).

to his story. The following verse by Bukhar zhirau is a succinct description of Ablai in the eyes of his contemporaries: "Oh, Ablai, Ablai // Always victorious over the enemies // And still you are not satisfied // You have squeezed the people with extortions // ... // Must I tell you what kind of man you are?"[18] It is his transgressive qualities as a man of unrestrained ambition, political talent, and a Töre, a combination the most rewarding as well as the most troubling within the given historical context which has kept his story 'going' over the centuries.

Narratives of Ablai begin with his passage from the existential limbo as a child survivor, taking refuge in a common family, to political stardom.[19] As a young adult, he joins Kazakh warriors in a fight against Jungars that ends his humble and anonymous life. A novice to battlefield, Ablai displays courage and aptitude, winning in a sword duel with a more experienced Jungar warrior. With this victory Ablai overcomes his vulnerability, moving to the center stage of the steppe politics. The tribes of Orta *jüz*, his designated domain, praise him as a capable Töre. An important detail here is that because Ablai spent his youth in exile so his demeanor escapes the usual public scrutiny. The story provides clues, however, to his uneven character by inscribing instances of his disregard of ordinary people among whom he matured and his unexplainable blasts of viciousness. His true self is revealed when he discards his given name and picks Ablai, a choice that shocks the society. 'Ablai' was the name of his grandfather who wrestled his way to power and was remembered by his nickname – a Bloodsucker (Khan-Icher). Ablai will confirm the society's fear that by picking his name he intended to repeat his grandfather's life: he sets tribes against one another, wipes out entire communities as a punishment for disobeying his orders, and betrays his allies. His pain-inflicting actions generate anger and frustration among people; but he has grown too fast and too powerful based on their premature blessing.

Ablai excels in manipulating his friends and foes. The warrior whom young Ablai kills in the duel is Sharish, a son of Galdan Ceren, a mature leader of Jungars. Seeking vengeance, Galdan Ceren captures Ablai. His ingenuity and his noble status, however, earn Ablai a special treatment

---

[18]Bukhar zhirau, fragment from 'Obrasheniye poeta Bukhara k khanu Ablayu.' Cited in English in Winner (1958: 88 – 89). Full text is available in Sobolev (1940: 225).

[19]His father, Vali khan, was killed in 1723, according to the Uighur sources, by Jungars when Ablai was 12 years old (Benson and Svanberg 1998: 37). His father's slave named Oraz rescued the boy. Two of them found sanctuary with Tole bi, the biy of Uly *jüz* (Yessenberlin 1989: 242–243; Kasymbaev 1999b: 135; Valikhanov, 1985: 111–116).

that opens space for a strange friendship between the two men of merit standing in an antagonistic relationship.[20] Being an honorable prisoner of Galdan Ceren for two years (1741–1743), Ablai marries his daughter disrespecting a taboo prohibiting Kazakh men to marry Jungar women in order to avoid social obligations towards their families. In fact, Ablai acquires several Jungar wives over time, locating himself in a gray area outside the orbit of the society's moral order, which does not stop him, however, from raiding his in-laws' home bases, including that of Galdan Ceren himself. By double-crossing the line with the sworn enemy and forming suspicious alliances with the Russian Empress and the Chinese Emperor, Ablai eventually achieves a certain degree of independence from other power contestants on the steppe. His political maneuvers and meanness secure his position in power, but also isolate him from his compatriots alarmed with the concentration of power and his disrespect of political traditions of the steppe that ruled out the uncanny deals, including those with the infidels and the settled.

The story of Ablai is always told from the society's perspective describing thoughts and experiences of ordinary people that constitute its background. Yessenberlin has done justice to the historical narratives by writing in the voice of Bukhar zhirau, representing in his novel a watchful eye of the society. By moving between the khan and his people, the character of Bukhar zhirau links the foreground and background of the story in a single discursive space. In the spring of 1781, Ablai utters from his deathbed his last wish to Bukhar zhirau, saying that he does not want "people … use [his] name to scare children" ([1973] 1989). He also shares his secret plan that he has been nourishing over the past years but had no time to implement.

He wanted to stop the encroachment of powerful neighbors on the Kazakh lands. Yet, the old way of doing this, by relying on an amateur army drawn from dispersed pastoral communities that regularly changed locations following seasonal migration, shifting their political allegiances as they saw fit, had exhausted its potential.[21] Ablai wanted to institute a standing army that would be sustained by a settled society. So this was his

---

[20]Being questioned by Galdan Ceren why he murdered his son, Ablai answered: "the accusation fell on my, but your son was killed by the people; I was an instrument of their will" (Valikhanov 2006: 12).

[21]The pattern of political institutions among the Kazakhs was based on community personal allegiance to a specific ruler rather than to a political office. It is understood as a loan from Mongols (Rossabi 1994: 31).

unrealized plan: to have Kazakhs to adopt a sedentary way of life. Switching thoughts to himself, he adds: "there is nothing more bitter in life than to be a ruler of a tiny frail realm" (ibid).

At the time of Ablai, during the 18th century, mobile pastoralism was a major source of livelihood and identity among the Kazakhs who held it as a pledge of commitment to their ancestors. Bukhar zhirau takes Ablai's idea as a sign of his ultimate betrayal of the people he was sworn to protect. This episode completes the dramatic logic of the narrative ending with Bukhar zhirau's reflection on the generations of Töre who were bred on the Kazakh soil but nevertheless remained distant strangers. Ablai was one of them: he had the strength to overcome the great odds but respected his own wishes only, just like his notable Mongol forebear from whom he inherited his title.

In sum, revolving around his ambivalence, the story has drawn an intense imagery of Ablai as a gifted politician and a committed leader; and, on the other hand, a cruel and insecure man who uses his power and his sword against his enemy as much as against his own people. Ablai's political legacy dies with him, destroyed by his house rivals and Russian colonial encroachment; his predicament, however, has formed a screen for addressing timeless issues concerning the meaning of power, identity, and loyalty that helped to cover his very appearance in history with mystical glaze. In the 1860s, Valikhanov admitted his bewilderment with Ablai who during his lifetime "acted against freedom in a despotic manner;" and yet, "managed to wrap up his deeds in such a way that his descendants would regard him as a saint" (1985: 116).

In the 21st century, not many Kazakhs would attribute such spiritual quality to Ablai. At the same time, after centuries of continuous cultural and political change, his idea of sedentarization can also show his ability to visualize the pressure for historical change. The departure of the society from the experiences of pastoral nomadism in the early twentieth century as part of the colonial project was destructive as was the subsequent unbinding from socialism during the end of the century. Yet, the pain of sedentarization and post-Soviet transition speaks of the ways in which these processes were orchestrated from the outside and not of the change *per se*. "Change need not be devastating to a culture," Morantz argues, "particularly when [it] … is directed from within the culture" (2002: 23). But, where do we draw the line between power and political ambition, and, on the other hand, popular desire, culture, and identity by which the society defines itself? This kind of analysis, engaging the issues of power and culture and problematizing the relationship between the local and the global, lends contemporary relevance to the story of Ablai. Perhaps for some individuals in Kazakhstan including Imangali Tasmagambetov, one of the closest allies of President Nazarbaev who was involved in the film as a history advisor, it was dangerously relevant.

CINEMATIC VERSION OF ABLAI

The film starts with a bird's eyeshot of a seemingly boundless spring blooming steppe, a landscape inviting esthetic meditation. The camera slowly glides down towards an iconic herding encampment (*aul*) featuring tents, animals, and pen enclosures, until it fills the frame. "Nomadic Kazakhs," the voiceover plugs in the soundtrack, "have inhabited this vast space from the Altai Mountains to the Caspian Sea since the ancient times." Casual movement of people animates the *aul*'s life whose peaceful nature is intensified by the sound of *dombra*, a Kazakh string instrument. Suddenly a group of armed men on horseback burst into the camera's view, transforming the serene imagery into a war zone, and the voiceover says that, unfortunately, the Kazakh land was always a target for the enemy, including the Jungars. Shot in a camera-eye style, the following scene depicts what could be the same *aul* turned into ashes and bones, making a close-up to a wrecked Kazakh cradle without a baby to convey the scale of destruction and grief. This dramatic, dark-colored scene then dissolves exposing a cutaway with an assembly of men in regal garments engaged in a heated debate. The narrator's voice reenters, taping over an emotional dialog between Abulkhair khan (Ron Yuan) and Barak sultan (Erik Zholzhaksynov), explaining that the Kazakhs lacked leadership to fight back leaving ordinary people with a "dream of a warrior who would come and unite Kazakhs in one strong fist and push the enemy out." This comment completes the establishing shot shaping a narrative frame of the film.

The next sequence introduces main characters. "*I* was waiting for that warrior too," says the narrator when a lone horseback rider, Oraz (Jason Scott Lee), comes towards the camera. His fictional character, combining qualities of a fine swordfighter and a Sufi brother, as the film soon reveals it, is positioned to orchestrate the events by unifying dramatic and mystic elements in the film. Oraz's structural opposite, albeit weaker and 'incomplete,' is an eccentric shaman. When Oraz receives a message from god about a newborn baby-boy (the future Ablai), so does the shaman who then rushes to warn Galdan Ceren (Doskhan Zholzhaksynov). The Jungar leader instructs his son, Sharish (Mark Dacascos), to "rip his heart out" who almost does so, but, in the last moment, Oraz rescues the baby from a sure death. This newly created dramaturgy personifies an antagonistic schema of good and evil, driving action throughout the film, which makes this sequence, including a series of well-composed and well-acted individual scenes, part of the story and not just an overture.

The next episode opens with Oraz's arrival in the city of Turkestan. The camera follows him from a distance showing details of a lively bazaar as he passes through to enter the khan's quarters. Vali khan (Kuman Tasmagambekov) barely responds to the incoming guest: he is grieving over an alleged murder of his son. Oraz unfolds his coat, revealing the baby, and the khan's face shows a wave of subtle and ingenious emotions captured in a head-on shot. Feeling overwhelmed, the khan tells Oraz that he would give him "anything he desires" in appreciation of his service. Once Oraz voices his request, the khan's feelings shift from disbelief to outrage: "how dare you ask me to give up my son!" Oraz convinces the khan that his son would not be safe at home while the camera follows a suspiciously looking khan's helper, sneaking around in the background as a visual implication of his argument.

The khan's son, Abulmansur (shortened in the film to Mansur), grows up happily with Oraz and other children in a Kazakh *aul*. A key scene in this sequence features Vali khan coming to visit them. Each boy introduces himself to the khan, calling his given name and his *ruw,* i.e., the name of his tribe ("I'm Bolat, a Naiman!"). Mansur and his friend claim the Kazakh identity instead ("I'm Mansur, a Kazakh!"). The khan, not knowing which boy in the group is his son, raises his eyebrows. In the traditional Kazakh society built upon patriarchal principles one's ancestral attachment was a key to participation in social life: without his family, lineage, and tribe, a man was deemed to be worthless. The khan's reaction manifests his initial confusion but, then the camera shows Oraz in all his confidence, and he seems to read the clue: Mansur's identity as a Töre could not be exposed.

This scene, however, is not merely about identity disguise. For modern Kazakhs, it evokes a predicament of their cultural identity whereas ancestral attachments are treated as a mixed blessing. On the one hand they link the society to the past helping individual families to establish relations across space and time and on the other they present a historical blueprint for multiple cultural divides, potentially hurting the nation (Yessenova, 2005). But Mansur is Töre who, at the time of khans, never mingled with the Kazakhs to ensure the reproduction of their dominant status within the society. His claim of Kazakh identity thus collapses with the existing interpretive schemes: it positions him to transcend the meanings attached to the Kazakh identity and that of the Töre in order to reaffirm the nation through an unambiguous unity, which is a major narrative premise in the film. But it strips the future Ablai of agency: the effect of this dramaturgical turn is that his call for unity becomes an innate feature of his mind as opposed to being a matter of character development. In addition, it obliterates possibilities for the dramatic transformation of Mansur into a powerful Töre upon his reintegration in his 'natural' social environment after years of invisibility in displacement, which helped to inscribe Ablai in history.

In the film, Ablai (Kuno Becker) is a one-dimensional sympathetic hero, an icon of determination (and a not very successful imitation of William Wallace in *Braveheart*). His actions show courage and commitment to his predetermined mission to unite his people. The screenplay draws on existing Kazakh accounts reenacting specific events for example his duel with Sharish and his subsequent encounter with Galdan Ceren seeking retribution for his son's death. Yet, those events have been adjusted to Ablai's new character altering their original meaning making the story flat and historically implausible. Thus, as Galdan Ceren's prisoner, Ablai declines a secret marriage proposal from his beautiful daughter (Dilnaz Akhmadieva), choosing an arranged sword duel under condition of freedom or death instead. He is not aware that his opponent, wearing an armor mask, is his best friend (Jay Hernandez) who sacrifices his life in a scene of *Gladiator* variety in order to set Ablai free. Galdan Ceren does not keep his word and throws Ablai back in the cage; but a Kazakh woman (Ayana Yesmagambetova), from his past whom Ablai loves, rescues him. Once free, Ablai, a young leader guided by Oraz and his father, mobilizes the people for a victorious counterattack. In the aftermath of the battle, Abulkhair khan presents Ablai with his grandfather's sword in lieu of recognition of his fine deeds.

In this scene, Ablai completes his altruistic mission and is declared a praiseworthy successor of his grandfather whose name he has chosen to bear. Ablai-the-grandfather (otherwise known as Bloodsucker) is presented on this occasion as a "great supporter of the Kazakh Khanate," which is difficult to imagine but it is the only way his odd persona can fit in the streamlined cinematic narrative drained of morally ambiguous characters. The film ends with Ablai's voiceover comment, addressing to his people and in a version distributed in Kazakhstan is followed by a written post-script from President Nazarbaev, urging the nation to cherish the past and "stay united." Oral tradition, however, has always drawn a line between a will to power and public commitment. In a message that Ablai is believed to have passed on his sons he advises them never to "solve intertribal problems because it is the squabbles and enmities that are the most reliable sources of khan's power" (Valikhanov, 1985).

The filmmakers thus reworked the story, creating a narrative serving the purpose of the newly created personality – Ablai the hero. But as David Edwards has summarized the insights from the study of Greek mythology, "a praiseworthy as heroes might be, they are also dangerous." "Noble and memorable indeed," he continues, "they also stand outside the normal orbit of human interaction and are never entirely fit for the ordinary society" (1996). Kazakh storytellers and writers understood this well. The original story of Ablai shows that it is precisely this ambivalence that makes characters *noble* and their stories *memorable*. After watching *Nomad*, on the other hand, one may wonder what this unsophisticated colorful video drama featuring the exotic hero and his enemy who look just the same was all about.

The filmmakers faced tough choices: on the one hand, the film they were commissioned to make was to project a positive and coherent image of the country. On the other, they were supposed to have Ablai as a protagonist. But, as told by the Kazakh authors, his story, which revolved around ruthless and fraudulent actions of local lords, was deemed to be unsuitable for such purpose unless they altered it. The Kazakh historical society had a strong appreciation of oral literature of which they had, as Winner said, an "almost inexhaustible reservoir" (1958). This is how the idea of synchronization of the story of Ablai and the Kazakh heroic epos came into being.

In some instances, Ablai was indeed attributed the prescribed qualities of a legendary hero in oral tradition. One example is his victory in the duel with Sharish, a powerful opponent who had never been defeated before. This is a common strategy in Turkic oral tradition to articulate the hero's "unusual strength" (ibid: 73).[22] In fact, Galdan Ceren did not have a son

---

[22]The episode, which has not been discussed in this study, when Ablai, already a mature man, is rescued from being assassinated by a camel is also usual for the epos where the unexpected interference of an animal, a woman, or some supernatural creature is a sign of a special status of the warrior (ibid; Yessenberlin [1973] 1989: 407–408).

named Sharish: his character was invented to convey Ablai's extraordinary stamina.[23] Yet, apart from these individual occurrences, Ablai's transgressive personality made him an odd fit for the heroic epos: this genre functioned to symbolize the "wished-for strength of the group in the face of the enemy" and "idealized virtues of bravery [and] military prowess" and was reserved for *batyrs*, the heroic warriors drawn from common people (ibid: 61, 71). The Kazakh writers approached the allegoric expressions in the story of Ablai carefully: Valikhanov marveled at why people decided to ascribe such high qualities to Ablai and Yessenberlin used the mythical lore as a narrative strategy to highlight his controversial character.

The filmmakers, on the other hand, matched the story of Ablai with the logic of the Kazakh epos. This is how, in the film, Ablai was born endowed with unusual qualities. He does not take favors from women from the hostile camp, showing his integrity. He is invincible but, at one point, a woman helps him to escape from a deadly threat. His life is followed from his birth to the apex of his heroic career, which is remarkably consistent in itself (ibid: 29). This uncritical drawing on historical epos made the film-story obsolete. It also confused the Almaty movie-goers who did not recognize the historical genre because of the obvious mismatch that led them to assume that what they saw on the screen was a deliberate attempt to simplify the story for the foreign audience.

Nor were the local viewers impressed with a moral closure of the drama of *Aktaban Shubirindy*. The Kazakh society experienced a series of social disasters in a more recent history including the revolution, Stalin's purges, collectivization, forced sedentarization, famine and in half a century later, shock therapy and decollectivization. Each of these generated dispossession, displacement, and suffering comparable to that of the *Aktaban Shubirindy*. The *Elim-ai* song, which narrates the loss and anxiety at the time of the warfare with Jungars, is part of today's collective memory because it has been used to underscore the impact of these modern disasters in contemporary documentaries and other commentaries on the history of Kazakhstan.

This is not the only problem with the film. In the following section, I will argue that the synchronization of different historical narratives and genres has not only disrespected the Kazakh oral tradition but it also re-

---

[23] Ablai was indeed a prisoner of Galdan Ceren; however, he was captured in the battlefield along with other Kazakh warriors and not after his duel. Yet, Ablai indeed won a duel with one of the Jungar nobles (Suleymenov and Moiseev 2006: 174–178).

duced the film-story to an ungrounded fiction that does little justice to the historical period within which it unfolded.

HISTORICAL PERIOD

Genghis khan's military projects in the 13th century created new political dynamics across Eurasia. "The hooves of the Mongol's warriors' horses," as Jack Weatherford described the stretch of his Empire, "splashed in the waters of every river and lake from the Pacific Ocean to the Mediterranean Sea" (2004). China and Persia broke away from his polity not long after, in 1335 and 1368, respectively. Russia paid tribute to Mongol khans until 1480 (ibid: 250). In Central Asia, the legacy of his Empire was more enduring. Even after the centralized power of Genghis khan had faded his descendants continued to form strong dynasties. As was noted earlier, individual rulers and princes maintained no ties with Mongolia and spoke no Mongolian language while being firmly grounded in local environment. In the early 16th century, they faced Jungars, the tribes that arrived from Mongolia proper. Jungar leaders also claimed a relationship with Genghis khan, not through blood affinity, but the one based on cultural proximity and almost vicious adherence to his military and political traditions.

The name Jungars was used as an umbrella term for the four western Mongolian tribes: Choros, Dörböt, Torghut, and Khoshot.[24] During the late 15th century, they moved to the passes of the Tarbagatai Mountains that lie across the border between present-day Kazakhstan and Xinjiang. In 1628, the Torghut moved further west and the Choros assumed a hegemonic position among the remaining Jungars. Inspired by the memory of Genghis khan, they sought to renew his epic by preparing for a military expansion (Grousset 2000). Prior to embarking on a war against the Chinese Emperor, they sent an envoy to Tauke, the khan of Kazakhs (reigned 1680–1718) with the intention of securing their home base. But the khan had no plans to cooperate with the Jungars whose leaders had no particular status on the steppe and put the entire envoy and all 500 men escorting them to death.[25]

---

[24]The term derives from Jagun-ghar, a 'people of the left wing,' a name reflecting a key principle of Genghis Khan's military organization. They were also known as the Dörben Oirat.

[25]He did so in violation of diplomatic immunity that was instituted by Genghis Khan himself, which made it especially hurtful to the Jungars. It is hard to determine why Tauke Khan, otherwise known for his wise political and legal decisions did this. A likely possibility is that the Jungar's leader was not from Genghis Khan's lineage and this is why his title was Hongtaiji and not a khan (Perdue 2005: 53).

This brutal act prompted immediate retaliation in the course of which the Kazakhs were defeated (1698) and set the stage for the events of 1723 (*Aktaban shubirindy*) when the Jungars claimed their livestock, pastures, and towns.[26] The Jungars were more powerful than the Kazakhs since they not only built a centralized political authority and strong military, but expanded their subsistence base, previously including herding only, through the introduction of agriculture, crafts, and construction (Millward, 2007; Perdue, 2005). By the mid-18th century, the Jungars had gained strength based on this gradual shift to a more sedentary orientation of their economy that, we may argue, stimulated Ablai's thinking about moving in a similar direction with his nomadic people.

The Jungars achieved their desired security by demoralizing the Kazakhs and attacked the Chinese in 1731. Four years later, they signed a peace pact with the Emperor. But in 1745, Galdan Ceren passed away prompting a fierce competition among his heirs. The Chinese used this situation and crushed the Jungars in 1757 causing the downfall of the Jungar political and even demographic dominance in the area. The Chinese army wiped out almost the entire Choros tribe to make sure that the ghost of Genghis khan would never reappear (Grousset, 2000).[27] Twenty years later, the Torghuts, who had nothing to do with this conflict, returned to the Tarbagatai from the Lower Volga helping China to repopulate its New Frontier – Xinjiang.[28]

The annihilation of Jungars ended the long-standing trouble for the Kazakhs. The new political disposition, however, opened the steppe for new players. During the 16th century the interaction between the Russians, who were still recovering from the Mongol bondage, and the Kazakhs was limited to sporadic encounters. The presence of Jungars facilitated the establishment of regular contacts between Russia and the khans of Kazakhs who sought its assistance but the Russians remained disengaged observing the explosions of hostility between the two nomadic people (Khodarkovsky, 2002).[29]

---

[26]The towns of Tashkent, Turkistan and Sayram (Grousset 2000: 531–532).

[27]The massacre was followed by a small pox epidemics in 1758, which amplified human loss (Khodarkovsky 2002: 168).

[28]They came to be called Kalmyk. For more on the Torghuts and Jungars see: Perdue (2005: 209–227) and Millward (2007: 78–123). Not all Torghuts moved away from Russia, only some 150 thousand of them. The others stayed behind where they still live today forming an autonomous region in Russia (Perdue 2005: 293).

[29]The Russians seemed to have their interests on the Kazakh side, but they did not confront Jungars, perhaps realizing their strength. Bokeikhanov comments that in "1739, Jungars attacked Kazakhs and chased them until the Ural River, in the course of which many Russian Bashkirs were killed; yet, Russian state did not punish them for the latter ([1903] 1995: 50).

The situation changed in the 17th century following the growth of Russia's interest in Asian markets. The Kazakhs populated 'a transit hall' between Russia and its newly articulated ambition. By the time the Jungars launched the war against China in 1731, the Russians were ready to act. Abulkhair, the khan of Qushi *jüz* (1693–1748), during the same year was taken to oath and confirmed his loyalty to the Russian Empress. This development did not produce faithful subjects as was expected on the Russian side. But it added a new dimension to the steppe politics. The Russians sought control over military and political undertakings by the Kazakhs while the Kazakhs used their relationship with Russia against the Jungars (ibid: 152–163).

This is when Ablai emerged on the political scene. He swore loyalty to the Russian Empress in 1740 and then was captured by Galdan Ceren. Oral tradition highlights Ablai's status and political skills as the factors that motivated Galdan Ceren to let him go. In the film, it is an apex of his struggle ending with Ablai being rescued by the Kazakh woman. In fact, it was the Russian authorities who made this rescue happen in 1743.[30] Two years later, Galdan Ceren died. A power shift occurred among the Kazakhs as well: Barak sultan killed Abulkhair khan in 1748 in a final stroke of their disagreement on the choice of political partners. He subsequently died two years later. Barak's death cleared the field for Ablai but he was not in position to become a khan due to his distant location within the Töre genealogy.[31]

Nevertheless, Ablai remained a powerful figure perhaps the most powerful man in the Orta *jüz* (Valikhanov 1985). During the early 1750s, he secretly offered sanctuary to Amursana, a promising contestant for the Jungar throne. The Chinese wanted Amursana dead and did not want an alliance of Jungars and Kazakhs. They threatened Ablai but as the Emperor admitted belatedly he "made fools of them" (Perdue, 2005). Once Ablai realized that Amursana had no chance of victory, he had him leave, engaging with the Chinese who opened the Urumchi market for Kazakhs (Benson and Svanberg, 1998; ibid: 287). In 1756, Ablai swore loyalty to the Chinese Emperor becoming a subject of two empires simultaneously. A year later, in 1757, the Chinese massacred the Jungars leaving the Kazakhs the sole players in a buffer zone between Russia and China.

---

[30]Suleymenov and Moiseev (2006: 175). The source of information is Kazakhsko-russkie otnosheniya v XVI–XVIII vv. Alma-Ata (1961: 258–262).

[31]Ablai came from a junior line of Orta jüz sultans (Valikhanov 1985: 111).

The latter development motivated Russia to increase its presence on the steppe and, finally, to incorporate the unruly Kazakh neighbors into its political orbit (Khodarkovsky, 2002). Before this occurred, Ablai finally fulfilled his dream of becoming the khan. The ritual took place in 1771, i.e., ten years before he died at the age of 80, and, in 1778, he was confirmed by the Russians who wanted to demonstrate that he was a subject of the Russian Empire (Appolova, 1960). In a Russian discourse, his title received an interpretation as the khan of all three Kazakh *jüzes*, a position that the Russians thought would have granted Ablai definite power over his people and made his politics more disciplined.[32] And yet, Ablai khan continued his usual course, receiving salary and gifts from the Russians and using green pastures and markets that belonged to the Chinese. In 1824, less than 40 years after his death, the Russians who were disillusioned about the steppe leaders and their politics abolished the institution of traditional authority altogether dispelling the Töre as a political stratum among the Kazakhs and, more broadly, the Mongol supremacy in Central Asia.[33]

The story of Ablai thus is a story of one of the most critical periods in the history of Mongol domination in Central Asia. The power of Genghis Khan and his house was rock-hard at the time of the centralized empire but by the 18th century it outlived its relevance as the individual khans and sultans grew apart. Their governance techniques and their claims to exclusive power, which among other things made the alliance of Töre with Jungars impossible, became outdated. Personified by Ablai, his story is about the Töre's frantic attempts to uphold their power and the dignity of their house. But the situation dictated that their rule and their societies were to be reformed. In the Soviet thought, cultural and political change on the steppe was a key function of the Russian civilizing mission, a hegemonic view that blocked other visions. And yet, the idea of change had emerged long before the colonial power came to define this mission. In the Yessenberlin's novel, it originated within the society, among the Töre. Here is Ablai's part from his final dialog with Bukhar zhirau to which I referred earlier:

---

[32]Not all Kazakhs of the Orta jüz accepted Russian suzerainty. Bokeikhanov argues that "naimans and the kereits ... moved from the present day Akmolinsk oblast to their old lands – the Tarbagatai and Black Irtysh, and from there to China" ([1903] 1995: 49); similar information is provided in Khodarkovsky (2002: 172).

[33]Babur's descendants reigned in India until 1857 and Alim Khan, the emir of Bukhara, until 1920 (Weatherford 2004: xx).

All those people who sowed land and were afraid of our tumens [regiments] now organize their lives in a similar way. But they are settled and, in this, is their great strength, their ... future. See, they even build their settlements in a complete order, like tumens. Russians call it 'blocks.' ... they can't leave them, ride away... And we ride on the steppe, feeling happy that it's big. But from all sides, a different life stifles us. And we disappear if ... we don't learn how to build those blocks, sow land and mine ([1973] 1985).

From a Russian/Soviet perspective, the appropriation of the elements of the sedentary way of life by the Kazakh nobility was a sign of their growing dependency on colonial patronage. But Ablai had no desire to surrender; instead, he hoped to strengthen his domain. His appreciation of foreign borrowing was a strategy for collective survival within the new context of power relations. Whether this conversation between Ablai and Bukhar zhirau indeed took place or not is hard to say, but it has been inscribed with "a palpable awareness of what could be truth" (Hecht, 2007).[34] What this dialog and, more generally, the novel, have accomplished is that they repositioned Kazakhs vis-à-vis Russia, reclaiming their role as the actors who were able to define themselves and produce critical reflections on their society. The reflections that open a space for debate and potential arguments that the Russian colonization in the 19th century and the Soviet forced sedentarization project in the twentieth century that had the most devastating impact on the Kazakhs were not inevitable.

In sum, Kazakh oral tradition and history literature tell different stories. The former focuses on Ablai glossing over the active role of other historical actors, especially Russia and China. The latter, on the other hand, attributes so much retrospective significance to Russia and China that it subordinates the local actors to their politics. Despite this disparity, these storylines are compatible, both helping to create a more complex picture of the historical period from the perspective of the Kazakh steppe.[35] In this regard, where does the *Nomad* film fit in? Its final episode has been designed to stir up nationalistic feelings: the globe is being shown to Galdan

---

[34]We should bear in mind that, in Edwards' words, "all historical narratives reflect to some degree a sense of what ought to have happened rather than what did" (1996: 55).

[35]Consider, for example, the interpretations of Ablai's release from the Galdan Ceren's imprisonment. Russians indeed made an effort to have him go; but, at the same time, Ablai indeed could impress Galdan Ceren, which is the interpretation in the oral tradition, who might have thought that he could use Ablai, once he is free, for his purposes.

Ceren and in place of his old domain he sees new contours: "The Land of Kazakhs." This cinematic phrase completes the transformation of Kazakhs from victims to winners. On a historical plane, however, the opposite was the case. The end of Jungars was the beginning of colonization of the Kazakh society and it was China and Russia that began the aggressive redrawing of their imperial borders. This fabricated twist denies this history erasing over two centuries of Kazakhs' resistance and accommodation to shifting political realities that radically transformed their society and shaped the nation of Kazakhstan as it is today.

CONCLUSION

In this chapter, I have critically examined *Nomad* by juxtaposing its storyline with the interpretation of oral tradition and historical evidence. I have argued that the streamlined narrative in the cinematic version is at great odds with both. This film, rather than being a timely effort to reflect on the world through the lens of the old story to stimulate public debate and history research, poses as the reiteration of Ablai's 'curse' that, as Valikhanov said, made the future generations regard him as a saint. To be fair, *Nomad* is not the only film that misconstrued historical reality. *Alexander the Great* and *Troy* are no closer to the events as documented in history literature than *Nomad*. Yet, the former were made from a distance and not with the intention of introducing modern Greece or Italy to the world or shaping the national understandings of the past. In this sense, *Nomad* has more in common with *Borat* because neither film is about Kazakhs or Kazakhstan. Why then does one film fail while the other is a total success?

As a character, Borat has been described as an "incarnation" of a trickster, a "clever fool" from tales and myths around the world. But not a true one: as the authors of *Borat the Trickster* have argued, "though he borrows … from his mythical counterparts, [Borat] lacks rootedness and traditionality" (Kononenko and Kukharenko 2008: 8, 17). I would make a reverse comparison. Borat as a trickster is what Ablai is as a heroic warrior (*batyr*) – neither character is "rooted in a particular culture" (ibid: 17). The shared fault has not compromised the success of *Borat*, which is the genuine attempt of an artist to expose the problems of his world (although we may disagree about his strategies and taste). The lack of cultural authenticity of Ablai's character, on the other hand, is caused by the approach taken to the *Nomad* film by the state in the first place. As opposed to mobilizing local talent, the state simply delegated the task of *national storytelling* to the foreign partners in a fashion similar to the way they negotiated international oil contracts – 'we've got the material; you deliver a sellable product to the global market.' This parochial approach, which is not the most responsible in the resource domain either, defeated the very purpose of the project, which was to create a stamp for the country as a creative economy.

"Creative environment" has become an attractive 'place' image in the world, especially among the Asian states and the countries of Eastern Europe. In business management, this concept connotes a "democratic space" that has a "room to experiment, to disagree with the status quo and to express thoughts freely" and, therefore, is conducive of business and innovation, the conditions attractive to global investors (Ooi, 2008). The association with the 'creative environment' offers a strong competitive advantage to the states in international relations benefiting their economies in particular (Anholt, 2005, cited in Fullerton et al., 2008). The function of *Nomad* was to add this 'creative' dimension to the image of the country, so far known for its hydrocarbon resources and only within professional circles, in order to shape investor sentiment, diversify the national FDI portfolio, and stimulate international tourism. It is argued that if state-sponsored projects are to be successful in sending a desired message they must involve the citizens of the featured place, making up its environment (Fullerton et. el. 2008: 162). This strategy lends authenticity to these projects and distinctiveness to the place. The Kazakhstan's leadership has consistently ignored this strategy so their public diplomacy endeavors missed the target.[36] *Nomad* is a case in point: the only image that this film could succeed in attaching to the country is the opposite of what constitutes the 'creative environment.' It renders visible the authoritarian regime and the patronizing tone of the state that sidelined the public from decision-making and participation in important venues, including the making of the first national epic motion picture.

Nomad is not the only film made in post-Soviet Kazakhstan. *The Road* (1992), *Leila's Prayer* (2002), *Little Men* (2003), *Schizo* (2004), *The Hunter* (2004), *Tulpan* (2008), *Kelin* (2009), and other films have demonstrated

---

[36]When they run TV commercials in the U.S., the content included and the emphasis was made on "natural scenery rather than the Kazakhstani people." This is a key reason why those ads did not help to improve attitudes among Americans about either Kazakhstan's government or its people (Fullerton et. el., 2008: 167).

the skill and creative potential of the country in recent years. These films were not contrived to push a political agenda in their critical depiction of local social life. They are humble noncommercial projects that have been generously acknowledged at international festivals and some of them were screened across Europe, Canada, and the United States. After *Nomad* gathered no awards, as opposed to trying to build on these home grown initiatives and their success, the Kazakhstan's leadership went on to sponsor another blockbuster cinema: *Mongol* by Sergey Bodrov (a codirector of *Nomad*), a film about the life of Genghis Khan, which became the country's first Oscar nominee for the Best Foreign Language Film in 2008. The society learned about this and the film itself at the same time, from the national news agency.

Mongol was not a public diplomacy project; rather it was the state's attempt to save face in the eyes of the society for its previous failure. On the international plane, Kazakhstan's politicians now attempt to capitalize on *Borat* (or showing to the world that their country is not the comedian invention). By inserting Borat's expressions in official statements and publications intended for the Western audience and featuring Borat-themed vacation packages on state websites, they have been using his "brand" as a platform for "rebranding" their country in the future.[37] Time will tell whether Sacha Cohen's film indeed 'put the country on the map,' as they came to believe, or to the contrary, whether it "hijacked Kazakhstan's ability to define itself to the western world" (Michaels, 2008). But if we shift the focus away from *Borat*, then the key issue is that unless the politicians learned to place their trust in the citizens and actively engage them in what they thought was important for their nation, that their country would not only remain an obscure place but its potential international image would always be murky.

As opposed to mobilizing local talent, the state simply delegated the task of national storytelling to the foreign partners in a fashion similar to the way it is done in the international oil industry: a multinational oil company exploits local material delivering a sellable product to the global market. This parochial approach, which is not the most responsible in the resource domain either, defeated the very purpose of the project which was to create a stamp for the country as a creative economy.

---

[37]Saunders (2008: 77–78). His article offers an extended discussion of Kazakhstan's officials views and the change of their relation to Borat.

As a character, Borat has been described as an 'incarnation' of a trickster, a 'clever fool' from tales and myths around the world. But not a true one: as the authors of *Borat the Trickster* have argued, 'though he borrows … from his mythical counterparts, [Borat] lacks rootedness and traditionality.' I would make a reverse comparison. Borat as a trickster is what Ablai is as a heroic warrior – neither character is 'rooted in a particular culture' (Kononenko and Kukharenko, 2008). Why then one film fails and the other is a total success? *Borat* was a genuine attempt of an artist to expose the problems of his world (although we may disagree about his strategies and taste).

KEYWORDS

- **Ablai**
- **Kazakhstan**
- **Nomad the Warrior**
- **Place branding**
- **Public diplomacy**

REFERENCES

Anholt, Simon Brand New Justice Elsevier, Oxford, UK, 2005.

Appolova, N. G. Ekonomicheskiye I politicheskiye svyazi Kazakhstana s Rossiey v XVIII – hachale XIX v. Moscow, 1960.

Benson, Linda and Ingvar Svanberg China's Last Nomads: The History and culture of China's Kazakhs. M.E. Sharpe: An East Gate Book, 1998.

Bokeikhanov, Alikhan (1995). 'Istorichesliye sud'by Kirghizkogo kraya i kul'turnye ego uspehi' In: Rossiya. Polnoye geographicheskoye opisanie nashego otechestva (SPb, 1903, volume XVII). Reprinted in Alikhan Bokeikhanov: Izbrannoye, Almaty: Kazakh entciklopediyasy, 45– 65.

Burt, Ben (1998). 'Writing Local History in Solomon Islands' in: Jurg Wassmann (ed.) Pacific Answers to Western Hegemony: Culture Practices of Identity Construction Berg: Oxford and New York, 97–118.

Cruikshank, Julie (1998). The Social Life of Stories: Narrative and Knowledge in the Yukon Territory Vancouver: UBC Press.

Davis, Natalie (2001). 'Polarities, Hybridities: What Strategies for Decentering?' In: De-centering the Renaissance: New Essays on Early Modern Canada Germaine Warkentin and Carolyn Podruchny, eds. Toronto: University of Toronto Press, 1–32.

Dzharmagambetov K., Ismailov E., Musrepov G. (1958). Antalogiya kazakhskoy poezii Moscow, Gos. Izdatel'stvo tvorcheskoy literatury

Edwards, David Heroes of the Age: Moral Fault Lines on the Afghan Frontier, Berkeley: University of California Press, 1996.

Fischer, Michael M. J. Emergent Forms of Life and the Anthropological Voice Duke University Press, Durham and London, 2003.

Fullerton, Jami, (2008). Alice Kendrick and Courtney Wallis 'Brand Borat? Americans' reaction to a Kazakhstani Place Branding Campaign' Place Branding and Public Diplomacy, Vol. 4/2, 159–168.

Ginsburg, Faye D., Lila Abu-Lughod, Brian Larkin. (2002). 'Introduction' in: Media Worlds: Anthropology on New Terrains by (eds.) Faye D. Ginsburg, Lila Abu-Lughod, and Brian Larkin, University of California Press, Berkeley and Los Angeles, 1–36.

Grousset, René The Empire of the Steppes: a History of Central Asia Rutgers University Press: New Brunswick, New Jersey, and London, 2000.

Hecht, Tobias (2007). 'A Case for Ethnographic Fiction' Anthropology News, Feb. 17–18.

Kasymbaev, Zhanuzak (1999a). 'Smert' I bessmertiye Ablaya' in: Gosudarstvennye deyateli kazakhskih hanstv (XVIII v.), vol. 1 Almaty: Bilim, 130–140.

Kasymbaev, Zhanuzak. (1999b). 'Cblizhat'sya s kitayem, no hranit' soglasiye s Rossiyeey' in: Gosudarstvennye deateli kazakhskih hanstv (XVIII v.) Volume 1, Almaty: Bilim, pp. 216–130.

Kasymbaev, Zhanuzak Ablai Khan. Aruna, Almaty, 2003.

Khodarkovsky, Michael Russia's Steppe Frontier: The Making of a Colonial Empire, 1500–1800 Indiana University Press: Bloomington and Indianapolis, 2002.

Kononenko, Natalie, and Svitlana Kukharenko (2008). 'Borat the Trickster: Folklore and the Media, Folklore in the Media' Slavic Review, vol. 67, Spring, pp. 8–18.

Kudayberdy-Uly Shakarim Rodoslovnaya tyurkov, kirgiziv, kazahov I khanskih dinastiy [1911] 1990, Almaty: Sana. Russian translation, reprint from Karimov, Husainov and Co.

Michaels, Paula, (2008). 'If the Subaltern Speaks in the Woods and Nobody's Listening: Does he make a Sound?' Slavic review, vol. 67/1, spring: 81–83.

Millward, James A. Eurasian Crossroads: A History of Xinjiang, Columbia University Press, New York, 2007.

Morantz, Toby The White Man's Gonna Getcha: The Colonial Challenge to the Crees in Quebec McGill-Queen's University Press, Montreal & Kingston, London, Ithaca, 2002.

Mukanov, M. S. Iz istoricheskogo proshlogo: rodoslovnaya plemen kerey i uak Almaty, Kazakhstan: 1998.

Ooi, Can-Seng (2008). 'Reimgining Singapore as a creative Nation: The Politics of Place branding' Place Branding and Public Diplomacy, vol. 4/4: 287–302.

Perdue, Peter C. China Marches West: The Qing Conquest of Central Eurasia, The Belknap Press of Harvard University Press, Cambridge, Massachusetts, London, England, 2005.

Rossabi, Morris (1994). "The Legacy of Mongols" in Beatrice Manz ed. Central Asia in Historical perspective, Boulder, Westview Press, 27–44.

Saunders, Robert A. (2008). 'Buying into Brand Borat: Kazakhstan's Cautious Embrace of its Unwanted 'Son' Slavic Review, vol. 67, Spring, 63–80.

Sobolev, Leonid Pesni stepey, antologiya kazahskoy literatury, Moscow, 1940.

Suleymenov, R. B., Moiseev, B. A. (2006). Kazahsko – oyratskiye otnosheniya v 30e – 40e gg. XVIII v. in: Kasenov E. B. Kochevniki: Vek kazahsko-dzhungarskogo protivostoyaniya, volume 4, Pavlodar: TOO NPF "Eko", pp. 174–178.

Sultanov, Tursun (1999). The People of a White Bone and the People of a Black Bone in the History of Kazakhstan. Energiya, IPA House 2: 58–66. Almaty.

Thackston, Wheeler M. 'The Genghisid and Timurid: Background of Iran and Central Asia,' in The Baburnama: Memoirs of Babur, Prince and Emperor New York: Modern Library, 2002.

Tolybekov, Sergali (1971). Kochevoye obshestvo kazahov v XVII -- nachale XX veka: politico-economicheskiy analiz, Alma-Ata, Nauka.

Valikhanov, Chokan (1985). 'Ablai' Sobranie sochineny; volume 4, Alma-Ata: Glavnaya redaktsia Kazakhskoy Sovetiskoy entsiklopedii, 111–116).

Valikhanov, Chokan (2006). 'Istoricheskiye predaniya o batyrah XVIII v.' In: Kasenov E. B. Kochevniki: Vek kazahsko-dzhungarskogo protivostoyaniya, volume 4, Pavlodar: TOO NPF "Eko", pp. 12–16.

Weatherford, Jack Genghis Khan and the Making of the Making of the Modern World, Three Rivers Press, New York, 2004.

Winner, Thomas G. The oral Art and Literature of the Kazakhs of Russian Central Asia Duke University Press, Durham, N.C. 1958.

Yessenberlin, Illias Köshpendiler [Kochevniki: Istoricheskaya trilogiya, translation in Russian by M. Simashko] Alma-Ata Zhazushi, [1973] 1989.

Yessenova, Saulesh (2005). "'Routes and Roots' of Kazakh Identity: Urban Migration in Post-socialist Kazakhstan" The Russian Review, October 64/4: 2–20.

CHAPTER 9

CLUSTERING SILK ROAD COUNTRIES BASED ON COMPETITIVENESS FACTORS IN TOURISM INDUSTRY

KAZIM DEVELIOGLU and KEMAL KANTARCI

CONTENTS

INTRODUCTION

Macroeconomic figures in global economies reveal that the volatility of the macroeconomic environment will persist. In this environment, governments' primary concern is to balance macroeconomic figures. In this sense, tourism has been paid special attention due to its contribution to GDP and being a source of employment and foreign currency. As stated in WTTC's 2012 report, over the next ten years the tourism industry is expected to provide 10% of the global GDP and to account for 1 out of 10 jobs in the world.

Leadership of United Nations World Tourism Organization (UNWTO) played a key role in organizing 28 countries from Asia, Europe, and Africa and forming a Silk Road Project. The Silk Road countries are aware of the importance of the tourism industry for the development of their macroeconomics. For a project to be successful, it should be competitive and sustainable in the long run. In this chapter, we intend to disclose how Silk Road countries can be more competitive and sustainable by analyzing UNWTO's Travel & Tourism Competitiveness Index variables. Analysis of T&T Competitiveness Index is expected to offer us both the strengths and the weaknesses of these countries. Furthermore, we aim to cluster the Silk Road countries and then compare the potential clusters based on T&T Competitiveness Index variables in order to attain an opinion on which factors should be more emphasized to be competitive and sustainable in the long run.

WHY DOES COMPETITION MATTER?

According to Porter (2004) "competitive strategy is the search for a favorable competitive position in an industry, the fundamental arena in which competition occurs. Competitive strategy aims to establish a profitable and sustainable position against the forces that determine industry competition" (1). Regarding the national level, "the competitiveness of a nation is defined as the degree to which it can, under free and fair market conditions, produce goods and services that meet the standards of international markets while simultaneously expanding the real income of its citizens" (Artto, 1987; Onsel et al., 2008; Sala-i Martin and Artadi, 2004). While traditional firms focused mainly on internal productivity, the increased globalization made it imperative for contemporary firms to become competitive whether they are from developed or developing countries. As Vietor (2006) states, as a result of globalization, at the national level, countries compete with each other in terms of market, technology, skills, and investment to grow and raise their standards of living. As Onsel et al. (2008) indicate at the firm level, "the capability of firms to survive and to have a competitive advantage in global markets depends on, among other things, the efficiency of public institutions, the excellence of educational, health and communication infrastructures, as well as on the political and economic stability of their home country."

Nations are struggling to remain competitive by having regional specializations in terms of higher value-added nonmanufacturing industries and Research and Development intensive manufacturing niches (OECD, 2007). Similarly, Porter (2009) indicates that competitiveness depends on the productivity with which a nation uses its human, capital, and natural resources. Economic coordination with neighboring countries can significantly enhance competitiveness. Consisting most of the developing and under-developed countries, economic collaboration among Silk Road countries is expected to enhance sustainable competition. In this sense, tourism, being a significant source of income, would help countries to regulate their balance of payments and create new jobs for the society, which in turn will contribute to economic prosperity. Many the countries use tourism as a strategic tool to increase the income of their citizens. In doing this, the problem is that it is relatively difficult to meet the international standards in tourism services and therefore quality issues are likely to arise. Considering the case of Silk Road countries, the level of competitiveness is expected to be relatively lower for underdeveloped and under-developed Silk Road countries.

In the following sections, we begin with analyzing the importance of tourism and contemporary trends in tourism industry. Secondly, we review the geographical, historical, cultural, natural, and economical aspects of Silk Road countries to comprise a theoretical base for our analysis of competitiveness index factors.

TRENDS IN TOURISM INDUSTRY

Tourism has been a significant strategic tool for policy makers at national and firm levels. Growth of the tourism industry depends on its potential and ability to provide economic growth and development for countries worldwide. The global tourism movement has grown from 25 million global tourists in 1950 to 983 million in 2011. International tourism receipts for 2011 are estimated at US$ 1,030 billion worldwide setting new records in most destinations despite economic challenges in many source markets (Olsen, 2003; UNWTO Tourism Highlights, 2012). According to the UNWTO report, "the number of international tourist arrivals worldwide is expected to increase by 3.3% a year on average from 2010 to 2030. This may represent 43 million more international tourist arrivals every year, reaching a total of 1.8 billion arrivals by 2030.... The market share of emerging economies has increased from 30% in 1980 to 47% in 2011, and is expected to reach 57% by 2030, equivalent to over 1 billion international tourist arrivals. Globally, as an export category, tourism ranks fourth after fuels, chemicals and food" (Artto, 1987; Buyers, 2003).

Visitor expenditure on accommodations, food and drinks, local transportation, entertainment and shopping is an important contributor to the economy of many destinations, creating much needed employment and opportunities for development (UNWTO Tourism Highlights, 2007). Thus, the sector is an important driver of growth and prosperity, particularly for developing countries. It also has a key role in the reduction of poverty (Travel & Tourism Competitiveness Report, 2011).

In terms of emerging destinations, based on 2020 estimations, the East Asia and Pacific Region is expected to continue its strong performance and hold a 25% market share in 2020. Similarly, the Middle East, with an expected growth rate of 7.1% a year, is projected to be the fastest growing region in the world. Another trend in tourism movement is emanated from the increasing number of potential travelers from large population countries (India, China, Indonesia, etc.) and emerging new economic powerhouses (Korea, Taiwan, Hong Kong, Singapore, and Malaysia). It is also anticipated that there will be a new mass tourism wave arising from developing Asian economies. Intraregional travel is also expected to increase in Europe and East Asia and the Pacific region, resulting from Open Sky agreements and low cost airlines, which will influence tourist travel patterns (CRC Report, 2008).

The Sustainable Tourism Cooperative Research Center's (CRC) 2008 report summarized global trends affecting tourism. This summary divided these trends into five categories, namely, long-term economic, social, political, environmental, and technological trends affected by globalization.

Globalization makes it easier to cross borders, which will result in the flow of more foreign tourists and increased global competition from international tourist destinations. This is caused by political pressures for higher living standards, diffusion of information technology, and increasingly dynamic private sectors. Economic growth and greater purchasing power are expected to allow more people to travel worldwide. In addition, dissemination of technology will have a great impact on the competitive advantage of destinations.

The main social trends that influence travel and tourism movements are growing populations in developing countries, aging, urbanization, a more stringent health concern, a considerable change in household structure, cultural values, work patterns and gender roles, and an educated society and workforce. As a result of these demographic changes, new tourists are expected to have such characteristics as money rich-time poor, hedonistic, discerning, quality conscious, individualistic, desiring self improvement, more critical and less loyal, seeking authentic tourism experiences, participators not spectators, and seeking optional experiences.

In the CRC report (2008) it is indicated that political trends have a great influence on tourism flows globally. More specifically, these trends include concerns about safety, security, political instability, terrorism, conflicts among nations and minorities, cybersecurity and biosecurity, stricter border control, health risks and climate change. In terms of climate change, Silk Road countries are likely to be influenced by the shortage of water resources and the decrease in the degree to which tourism attractiveness factors depend on.

Environmental concerns in the tourism industry consist of climate change and global warming, rising population affecting the availability of food, water and energy, loss of biodiversity, water shortages, demands for higher food production, and increasing soil salinity. These concerns are extremely important as they influence which destinations will be preferred by tourists.

Technological trends can be evaluated as opportunities as well as threats for the tourism industry, which depends on information and transportation technologies and innovations to discover new products and services. Technological trends include networking to tie tourism industry shareholders and new Internet technologies as agents of consumers and e-communities. These developments are expected to add value to products and services, which will eventually create competitive advantage for a certain destination.

SILK ROAD COUNTRIES AND PROJECT

The ancient Silk Road is perhaps the greatest and well-known route in history, which connected China and Europe and directed trade in ancient times (Akayev, 2001; Buyers, 2003; Kantarci, 2006; UNWTO Silk Road Action Plan, 2012/2013). The Silk Road formed the first bridge between East and West and increased trade among the ancient Empires of China, India, Persia, and Rome. "The route dating back to 200 B.C. was a channel for contact between people and cultures, inspiring the exchange of dialog, art, religion, ideas, and technology. This ancient route has a very rich diverse cultural heritage and natural tourism attractions along its 12,000 kilometers" (UNWTO Silk Road Action Plan 2012/2013). "The huge area from Japan and China, through Central Asia, to Turkey and Europe is connected by one single string—the Silk Road" (WTO, 1998).

Nowadays, the Silk Road has a chance to get its popularity back again. To do this, the World Tourism Organization (WTO) is playing a distinguishing role. The Organization initiated a Silk Road program in 1991 when the newly independent Central Asian republics came into the political arena. By the same token, Central Asian countries play a critical role in this project like in old days (Silk Road Action Plan, 2012/2013).

The aim of the Silk Road Program is to focus on the establishment of collaborative and sustainable tourism growth for the states on the route. Member states of the Silk Road program bear big differences in terms of economic structure, cultural aspects, infrastructure, geography, policy, rules and regulations and so forth.

In 1993, WTO initiated a long-term project to organize and promote the Silk Road as a tourism product concept. In 1994, 19 participating nations arranged a meeting and developed the historic Samarkand Declaration on the Silk Road Tourism. At the Bukhara Declaration participants stressed the benefits of sustainable tourism and outlined specific steps to develop and sustain cultural and ecological tourism along the Silk Road Route. Afterwards, certain important developments and arrangements were accomplished (Silk Road Action Plan, 2012/2013).

The Member States currently involved in the Silk Road Program include: Albania, Armenia, Azerbaijan, Bulgaria, China, Croatia, DPR Korea, Rep. Korea, Egypt, Georgia, Greece, Iran, Iraq, Israel, Italy, Japan, Kazakhstan, Kyrgyzstan, Mongolia, Pakistan, Russia, Saudi Arabia, Syria, Tajikistan, Turkey, Turkmenistan, Ukraine and Uzbekistan (Silk Road Action Plan 2012/2013, 2012).

Although there are 28 member countries, it is necessary to differentiate among participating countries according to their different degrees of commitment. Hence, three concentric circles were identified: The first circle of the program consisted of the Turkestan countries that had just started opening up their borders for tourism. The WTO's main effort is to prepare these countries' action plans and training facilities and to formulate legislation, frontier formalities, and statistics for the projected growth in tourism. The second circle was comprised of countries that had already opened up their sites of the Silk Road and had gained certain experiences with this tourism product. These countries include China, India, Pakistan, Iran, and Turkey. The third circle covered the terminals of the road on both ends such as Japan, the Korean peninsula, ASEAN countries, Arab countries, and Europe (UNWTO, 1998).

The Silk Road Program aims to develop a collaborative framework for the Silk Road tourism and generate a sustainable and globally competitive tourism product. In achieving this aim, the major activities projected are a comprehensive marketing strategy and capacity building as well as creating a framework for Silk Road tourism. Realizing the Silk Road Program requires comprehensive and successful tourism destination management and marketing programs. Goeldner et al. (2000) pointed out that the two major parameters of tourism destination management are competitiveness and sustainability. For a destination to be successful these two parameters must be realized. Neither of them is sufficient alone and both of them are essential and mutually supportive. In this sense, the competitiveness of a destination refers to its "ability to create and integrate value-added products that sustain its resources while maintaining market position relative to competitors" (Hassan, 2000). By a similar token, "sustainability pertains to the ability of a destination to maintain the quality of its physical, social, cultural, technological and environmental resources while it competes in the marketplace" (Goeldner et al., 2000).

Dwyer and Kim (2003) postulate that industry and governments can increase the number of tourists, expenditures and economic impacts by developing a model of destination competitiveness and certain indicators that will help them to identify the relative strengths and weaknesses of different tourist destinations. To solve this issue, destination competitiveness has to be linked to the ability of a destination to deliver goods and services that perform better than other destinations on those aspects of the tourism experience considered to be important by tourists. Therefore, it is extremely crucial to choose a proper strategy to develop a competitive and sustainable Silk Road Program. In this chapter, we used a model developed by the World Economic Forum (WEF) as a primary framework to determine potential strengths, weaknesses, values, and other characteristics of the Silk Road countries.

What could contribute to a competitive and sustainable tourism management on the Silk Road route might include historical, cultural, and natural resources. The Silk Road countries are traditionally very rich in these resources and can provide certain unique experiences for potential travelers and profitable investment opportunities for investors. Especially, prioritization efforts of the first circle countries create a potential to attract foreign investments.

A UNWTO report (2009) reveals that historical resources offered to foreign visitors consist of fascinating structures and monuments, which include ancient mosques, madrasahs, tombs, and relics. The other potential tourism subsector is ecotourism, especially in Central Asian countries because of the most scenic landscapes and ample spaces. High mountains, glaciers, caves, lakes, rivers, hot springs and steppes provide an extremely attractive environment for ecotourists. Similarly, Tajikistan's National Park is classified as one of the largest and most diverse parks in Central Asia.

While the region is rich in natural, historical, and cultural resources, the infrastructure is extremely insufficient, creating a major weakness for the Central Asia region. Shortages in the number and quality of hotels, transportation infrastructure, communication systems and camping and other facilities can be classified as major shortcomings. Weak branding can also be added to the weakness list of the Silk Road region.

In Table 1, below, international tourist arrivals and receipts are summarized for the years between 2009–2011. As it can be inferred from the Table 1, 28 countries as a whole share a high percentage of international tourists (around 1 out of every 4 tourists) and international tourism receipts (1 out of 5) in the world.

TABLE 1   International Tourist Arrivals and Receipts for the Silk Road Countries.

The Silk Road Countries	International Tourist Arrivals (1000)			International Tourism Receipts (US$ million)		
	2009	2010	2011	2009	2010	2011
Albania	1,792	2,347	-	1,816	1,626	1,628
Armenia	575	684	758	334	408	445
Azerbaijan	1,005	1,280	1,562	353	621	1,287
Bulgaria	5,739	6,047	6,324	3,728	3,637	3,967
China	50,875	55,664	57,581	39,675	45,814	48,864
Croatia	8,694	9,111	9,927	8,898	8,259	9,185
DPR Korea	-	-	-	-	-	-
Rep. Korea	7,818	8,798	9,795	9,819	10,359	12,304
Egypt	11,914	14,051	9,497	10,755	12,528	8,707
Georgia	1,500	2,032	2,820	476	659	936
Greece	14,915	15,007	16,427	14,506	12,742	14,623
Iran	-	-	-	2,012	2,707	-
Iraq	1,262	1,518	-	-	-	-
Israel	2,321	2,803	2,820	3,741	4,768	4,849
Italy	43,239	43,626	46,119	40,249	38,786	42,999
Japan	6,790	8,611	6,219	10,305	13,199	10,966
Kazakhstan	3,118	3,393	4,093	963	1,005	1,209
Kyrgyzstan	2,147	1,316	-	459	284	-
Mongolia	411	456	456	235	244	218
Pakistan	855	907	-	272	305	358
Russia	19,420	20,271	22,686	9,366	8,830	11,398
Saudi Arabia	10,897	10,850	17,350	5,995	6,712	8,459
Syria	6,092	8,546	5,070	3,757	6,190	-
Tajikistan	-	-	-	2	4	3
Turkey	25,506	27,000	29,343	21,250	20,807	23,020
Turkmenistan	-	-	-	-	-	-
Ukraine	20,798	21,203	21,415	3,576	3,788	4,294
Uzbekistan	1,215	975	-	99	121	-
Total	248, 898	266, 496	270, 262	192, 641	204, 403	209, 719

Source: UNWTO, 2012, Tourism Highlights.

In certain studies (Dwyer and Kim, 2003; Hassan, 2000), different models were used to classify competitive factors in the tourism industry. In this analysis, we used the World Economic Forum's (WEF) classification of Travel & Tourism Competitiveness factors to examine resources that are expected to influence sustainable competition in the industry. WEF's classification consists of three sub indexes and 14 factors that measure these subindexes, as indicated below:

- T&T regulatory framework
- (Policy rules and regulations, Environmental sustainability, Safety and security, Health and hygiene, Prioritization of Travel & Tourism)
- T&T business environment and infrastructure
- (Air transport infrastructure, Ground transport infrastructure, Tourism infrastructure, Information and Communication Technology (ICT) infrastructure, Price competitiveness in the T&T industry)
- T&T human, cultural, and natural resources
- (Human resources, Education and training, Availability of qualified labor, Affinity for Travel & Tourism, Natural resources, Cultural resources).

METHODOLOGY AND FINDINGS

In this section of the chapter, to be able to classify Silk Road countries, we benefited from the United Nations World Tourism Organization's (UNWTO) Silk Road Action Plan for the years 2012–2013. This report includes the list of Silk Road Countries, which consists of 28 countries: Albania, Armenia, Azerbaijan, Bulgaria, China, Croatia, DPR Korea, Egypt, Georgia, Greece, Iran, Iraq, Israel, Italy, Japan, Kazakhstan, Kyrgyztan, Mongolia, Pakistan, Republic of Korea, Russia, Saudi Arabia, Syria, Tajikistan, Turkey, Turkmenistan, Ukraine, and Uzbekistan. Although there are 28 countries included in this list, we used the data for 23 countries and excluded the remaining five because of lack of data. Countries that are excluded from the list are DPR Korea, Iran, Iraq, Turkmenistan, and Uzbekistan.

For the 23 countries, we first employed a cluster analysis to examine how they will be clustered and which T&T Competitiveness Index pillars would contribute to classify each cluster. The reason for cluster analysis is that we would like to reveal the position of each Silk Road country as a member of a cluster. Second, we employed t-test analyzes to portray the difference of each cluster's performance on T&T Competitiveness Index pillars and variables. Third, we compared each Silk Road country's global rank for each T&T Competitiveness Index pillar and determined the best performing three countries for each pillar, and fourth, we demonstrated graphically international tourist arrivals and tourism receipts of each cluster for the years 2007, 2008, 2009, and 2011. Because of the lack of data, we did not include that of 2010 in our analyzes.

CLUSTER ANALYSIS RESULTS

In order to cluster 23 Silk Road countries, we employed a k-means cluster analysis and obtained findings as reported below in Table 2. Findings in Table 2 reveal that these 23 countries can be grouped in two clusters. Cluster 1 countries include Albania, Armenia, Azerbaijan, China, Egypt, Georgia, Kazakhstan, Kyrgyztan, Mongolia, Pakistan, Saudi Arabia, Syria, Tajikistan, and Ukraine. The second cluster (Cluster 2) countries consist of Bulgaria, Croatia, Republic of Korea, Greece, Israel, Italy, Japan, Russia, and Turkey.

TABLE 2   Countries in Clusters.

Cluster 1	Cluster 2
Albania	Bulgaria
Armenia	Croatia
Azerbaijan	Rep. of Korea
China	Greece
Egypt	Israel
Georgia	Italy
Kazakhstan	Japan
Kyrgyzstan	Russia
Mongolia	Turkey
Pakistan	
Saudi Arabia	
Syria	
Tajikistan	
Ukraine	

Figure 1 shows the map of the Silk Road countries after cluster analysis is employed. In the map, Cluster 1 countries have been shown in dark yellow and Cluster 2 countries in blue.

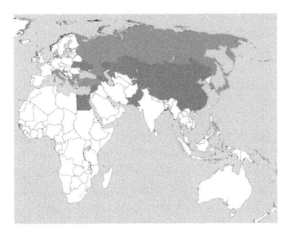

FIGURE 1   Map of clustered Silk Road countries.

One of the other aims of this analysis is to compare both clusters in terms of T&T Competitiveness Index pillars and variables. For this purpose, we employed five t-test analyzes the results of which are reported in Tables 3–6.

RESULTS OF T-TEST FOR TRAVEL & TOURISM COMPETITIVENESS PILLARS

The results of t-test (see Table 3) for cluster membership and Travel & Tourism Competitiveness pillars revealed that Cluster 2 countries performed better than Cluster 1 countries in ten out of 14 competitiveness pillars, which are *policy rules and regulations* ($\text{Mean}_1 = 4.04$, $\text{Mean}_2 = 4.45$; $t = -2.530$; $p = 0.019$), *environmental sustainability* ($\text{Mean}_1 = 3.86$, $\text{Mean}_2 = 4.44$; $t = -4,148$; $p = 0.002$), *health and hygiene* ($\text{Mean}_1 = 4.78$, $\text{Mean}_2 = 6.01$; $t = -3.512$; $p = 0.002$), *air transport infrastructure* ($\text{Mean}_1 = 2.72$, $\text{Mean}_2 = 3.83$; $t = -4.2789$; $p = 0.000$), *ground transport infrastructure* ($\text{Mean}_1 = 3.20$, $\text{Mean}_2 = 4.34$; $t = -3.548$; $p = 0.002$), *tourism infrastructure* ($\text{Mean}_1 = 2.28$, $\text{Mean}_2 = 4.98$; $t = -5.460$; $p = 0.000$), *ICT infrastructure* (Mean$_1$ = 2.40, Mean$_2$ = 4.20; t = −5.962; p = 0.000), *human resources* (Mean$_1$ = 4.89, Mean$_2$ = 5.21; t = −2.652; p = 0.015), *natural resources* (Mean$_1$ = 2.98, Mean$_2$ = 3.76; t = −2.847; p = 0.010), *cultural resources* (Mean$_1$ = 2.42, Mean$_2$ = 4.60; t = −5.590; p = 0.000).

As can be noted in Table 3, Cluster 1 countries have a higher score (Mean$_1$ = 4.82, Mean$_2$ = 4.10; t = 3.595; p = 0.002) in *price competitiveness in T&T industry pillar* than Cluster 2 countries. This result implies that in attracting travelers Cluster 1 countries offer more advantageous prices in terms of goods and services, airfare ticket taxes, airport charges, fuel prices, relative cost of hotel accommodations, and traveler related taxation in the country. To understand which countries in this cluster caused the difference in price competitiveness, we averaged the 4-year score of the T&T Competitiveness Index (TTCI) for all the 23 countries in both the clusters.

TABLE 3   t-test Results for Cluster Membership and Travel & Tourism Competitiveness Pillars.

Pillars	Cluster	Mean	Std. Deviation	t	P
T&T Regulatory Framework					
Policy rules and regulations	1	4.04	0.257	−2.530	0.019
	2	4.45	0.508		
Environmental sustainability	1	3.86	0.181	−4.148	0.002
	2	4.44	0.387		
Safety and security	1	4.71	0.620	−0.288	0.776
	2	4.78	0.560		
Health and hygiene	1	4.78	0.922	−3.512	0.002
	2	6.01	0.614		
Prioritization of travel & tourism	1	4.00	0.628	−1.911	0.070
	2	4.47	0.485		
T&T Business Environment and Infrastructure					
Air transport infrastructure	1	2.72	0.551	−4.279	0.000
	2	3.83	0.689		
Ground transport infrastructure	1	3.20	0.568	−3.548	0.002
	2	4.34	0.970		

TABLE 3 *(Continued)*

Pillars	Cluster	Mean	Std. Deviation	t	P
Tourism infrastructure	1	2.28	0.760	−5.460	0.000
	2	4.98	1.348		
ICT infrastructure	1	2.40	0.412	−5.962	0.000
	2	4.20	0.845		
Price competitiveness in the T&T industry	1	4.82	0.529	3.595	0.002
	2	4.10	0.339		
T&T Human, Cultural and Natural Resources					
Human resources	1	4.89	0.278	−2.652	0.015
	2	5.21	0.271		
Affinity for travel & tourism	1	4.83	0.672	0.119	0.906
	2	4.79	0.673		
Natural Resources	1	2.98	0.728	−2.847	0.010
	2	3.76	0.452		
Cultural Resources	1	2.42	0.880	−5.590	0.000
	2	4.60	0.964		

Comparison of the scores for both clusters revealed that countries in Cluster 1, namely China (Mean = 5.28), Egypt (Mean = 5.80), Pakistan (Mean = 5.15), Saudi Arabia (Mean = 5.57), and Syria (Mean = 5.10) have relatively lower prices to attract travelers.

T-TEST RESULTS FOR T&T REGULATORY FRAMEWORK SUBINDEX

As mentioned before in the interpretation of Table 3, Cluster 2 countries had higher scores in three out of five *T&T regulatory framework* pillars, which are *policy rules and regulations, environmental sustainability,* and *health and hygiene.*

TABLE 4 t-test Results for Cluster Membership and Travel & Tourism Regulatory Framework Variables.

Variable	Cluster	Mean	Std. Dvt.	t	p
Policy rules and regulations					
Prevalence of foreign ownership	1	4.15	0.557	−0.868	0.395
	2	4.33	0.370		
Property rights	1	3.80	0.814	−1.238	0.229
	2	4.23	0.827		
Business impact of rules on FDI	1	4.38	0.620	1.290	0.211
	2	4.05	0.563		
Visa requirements	1	26.14	25.461	−3.890	0.001
	2	69.22	26.649		
Openness of bilateral Air Service agreements	1	7.60	2.131	−2.723	0.013
	2	10.67	3.189		
Transparency of government policymaking	1	4.20	0.508	0.788	0.439
	2	4.04	0.374		
Time required to start a business	1	15.07	10.224	−0.542	0.594
	2	17.44	10.296		
Cost to start a business	1	10.39	12.130	−0.078	0.938
	2	10.74	7.140		
GATS commitments restrictiveness index of T&T services	1	64.24	18.906	1.587	0.133
	2	51.86	11.988		
Environmental Sustainability					
Stringency of environmental regulations	1	3.19	0.599	−2.962	0.007
	2	4.10	0.874		
Enforcement of environmental regulations	1	3.00	0.663	−2.043	0.054
	2	3.70	0.968		
Sustainability of T&T industry development	1	3.87	0.730	0.003	0.998
	2	3.87	0.417		
Carbon dioxide emissions	1	4.59	4.999	−1.982	0.061
	2	8.13	2.299		
Particulate matter concentration	1	66.58	36.688	2.593	0.017
	2	33.75	10.844		
Threatened species	1	5.72	2.030	−0.897	0.380
	2	6.65	2.940		
Environmental treaty ratification	1	17.35	2.977	−1.839	0.080
	2	19.88	3.586		

Health and Hygiene					
Physician density	1	2.41	1.248	−1.411	0.173
	2	3.17	1.294		
Access to improved sanitation	1	80.53	22.269	−2.179	0.041
	2	97.11	4.986		
Access to improved drinking water	1	89.71	8.844	−3.138	0.005
	2	99.11	1.364		
Hospital beds	1	43.71	25.727	−1.942	0.066
	2	68.00	34.256		

The first pillar, *policy rules and regulations*, consists of nine variables (See Table 4). Out of these nine, only two show statistically significant difference scores between the two clusters, which are *visa requirements (Mean$_1$ = 26.14; Mean$_2$ = 69.2; t = −3.890; p = 0.001)* and *openness of the bilateral Air Service Agreements (Mean$_1$ = 7.60; Mean$_2$ = 10.67; t = −2.723; p = 0.013)*. Visa requirements are described as "average number of countries entirely or partially exempt from visa requirements" in the TTCI index (TTCI; p. 97). In this context, certain countries in Cluster 2 a have relatively high number of visa exemptions, such as Republic of Korea (110), Israel (85), Turkey (83), Croatia (70), Bulgaria (68), Greece (68), Italy (68), and so forth when compared to Cluster 1 countries, such as Albania (55), Egypt (61), Azerbaijan (12), Armenia (10), Pakistan (8), and Saudi Arabia (5). Cluster 2 countries' higher average (Mean$_2$ = 69.2) of visa exemption is likely to attract travelers when choosing a certain country as a destination by making it easier to enter the country. In terms of openness of bilateral Air Service Agreements, in which two nations sign an agreement to allow each other to use commercial air services within their territories, Cluster 2 countries have a statistically significant difference score (Mean$_2$ = 10.67), which implies that travelers will be benefitting when they choose a certain country which has a bilateral air service agreement with many countries. The other seven variables of the policy rules and regulations pillar did not produce any statistically significant difference scores between the two clusters (See Table 4). Thus, it can be concluded that all countries have relatively medium scores, which have to be improved by government authorities to develop T&T industry in their countries.

The analysis of the second pillar of the T&T regulatory framework, *environmental sustainability*, revealed (See Table 4) that Cluster 2 countries performed better in 2 out of 7 variables, which are *stringency of environmental regulation (Mean$_1$ = 3.19; Mean$_2$ = 4.10; t = −2.962; p = 0.007)* and *enforcement of environmental regulation (Mean$_1$ = 3.00; Mean$_2$ = 3.70; t = −2.043; p = 0.054)*. Because the policies and factors contributing to environmental sustainability are important to provide tourists an attractive location, the stringency of environmental regulations and the enforcement of environmental regulatory rules stated by governments and local authorities are crucial. Comparative advantage of Cluster 2 countries in these variables is expected to contribute to the attractiveness of these countries as a potential destination for travelers. Besides this finding, Cluster 1 countries have a higher score in the *particulate matter concentration* variable *(Mean$_1$ = 66.58; Mean$_2$ = 33.75; t = 2.593; p = 0.017)*.

The last pillar of the T&T regulatory framework is *health and hygiene*, which consists of 4 variables. *t*-test results in Table 4 reveal that Cluster 2 countries have higher scores for *access to improved sanitation (Mean$_1$ = 80.53; Mean$_2$ = 97.11, t = −2.179; p = 0.041)* and *access to improved drinking water (Mean$_1$ = 89.71; Mean$_2$ = 99.11; t = −3.138; p = 0.005)* variables. Because access to improved sanitation refers to the percentage of population with access to excreta disposal facilities, such as pit latrines and flush toilets, Cluster 2 countries have superior conditions to provide travelers a more sustainable environment. In terms of access to improved drinking water variable, which refers to the percentage of population with access to an adequate amount of water from an improved source, Cluster 2 countries have statistically higher scores and provide superior drinking water from improved sources to citizens and travelers. Besides these findings the two clusters did not show any statistically different results in physician density and hospital beds variables.

T-TEST RESULTS FOR T&T BUSINESS ENVIRONMENT AND INFRASTRUCTURE SUBINDEX

The results in Table 3 show that Cluster 2 countries have relatively more competitive advantage in the T&T business environment and infrastructure pillars, namely, *air transport infrastructure (Mean$_1$ = 2.72; Mean$_2$ = 3.83; t = −4.279; p = 0.000), ground transport infrastructure (Mean$_1$*

= 3.20; Mean₂ = 4.34; t = −3.548; p = 0.002), *tourism infrastructure* *(Mean₁ = 2.28; Mean₂ = 4.98; t = −5.460; p = 0.000)*, and *ICT infrastructure (Mean₁ = 2.40; Mean₂ = 4.20; t = −5.962; p = 0.000)*. Cluster 1 countries scored higher only in *price competitiveness in the T&T industry* pillar *(Mean₁ = 4.82; Mean₂ = 4.10; t = −3.595; p = 0.002)*. Along with these findings, *t*-test results in Table 5 indicate that Cluster 2 countries have higher scores in 5 out of 7 variables for air transport infrastructure pillar. These variables include *quality of air transport infrastructure (Mean₁ = 4.17; Mean₂ = 4.92; t = −2.173; p = 0.041), available international seat kilometers (Mean₁ = 313.32; Mean₂ = 1023.95; t = −2.283; p = 0.033), departures per 1.000 population (Mean₁ = 1.53; Mean₂ = 5.38; t = −4.555; p = 0.000), number of operating airlines (Mean₁ = 35.60; Mean₂ = 77.16; t = −3.022; p = 0.006)* and *international air transport network (Mean₁ = 4.25; Mean₂ = 4.95; t = −2.389; p = 0.026)*.

TABLE 5   t-test Results for Cluster Membership and T&T Business Environment and Infrastructure Variables.

Variable	Cluster	Mean	Std. Dvt.	t	p
Air Transport Infrastructure					
Quality of air transport infrastructure	1	4.17	0.829	−2.173	0.041
	2	4.92	0.752		
Available seat kilometers, domestic	1	516.19	1823.226	0.031	0.976
	2	496.42	722.957		
Available seat kilometers, international	1	313.32	603.779	−2.283	0.033
	2	1023.95	895.215		
Departures per 1.000 population	1	1.53	1.371	−4.555	0.000
	2	5.38	2.690		
Airport density	1	0.76	1.233	−0.544	0.592
	2	1.33	1.019		
Number of operating airlines	1	35.60	27.466	−3.022	0.006
	2	77.16	38.656		
International air transport network	1	4.25	0.663	−2.389	0.026
	2	4.95	0.735		
Ground Transport Infrastructure					
Quality of roads	1	3.37	0.976	−1.930	0.067
	2	4.28	1.304		

TABLE 5 *(Continued)*

Variable	Cluster	Mean	Std. Dvt.	t	p
Quality of railroad infrastructure	1	3.20	0.866	−1.468	0.157
	2	3.88	1.370		
Quality of port infrastructure	1	3.49	0.984	−2.200	0.039
	2	4.31	0.645		
Quality of ground transport network	1	4.47	0.522	−1.876	0.075
	2	4.97	0.777		
Road density	1	25.63	20.056	−2.938	0.008
	2	99.91	92.412		
Tourism Infrastructure					
Hotel rooms	1	0.17	0.205	−3.745	0.001
	2	1.23	1.042		
Presence of major car rental companies	1	3.07	1.899	−4.345	0.000
	2	6.22	1.301		
ATMs accepting VISA cards	1	195.90	187.618	−3.482	0.002
	2	719.53	517.628		
ICT Infrastructure					
Extent of business Internet use	1	4.45	0.468	−3.734	0.001
	2	5.33	0.659		
Internet users	1	24.45	11.653	−4.659	0.000
	2	52.98	17.855		
Telephone lines	1	14.82	7.786	−6.275	0.000
	2	37.98	9.873		
Broadband Internet subscribers	1	2.28	2.324	−7.010	0.000
	2	18.70	8.370		
Mobile telephone subscribers	1	87.94	35.408	−2.544	0.019
	2	123.16	26.807		
Price Competitiveness in the T&T industry					
Ticket taxes and airport charges	1	76.13	11.414	−0592	0.560
	2	78.63	6.674		
Purchasing power parity	1	0.47	0.072	−4.265	0.000
	2	0.78	0.266		
Extent and effect of taxation	1	3.65	0.653	2.262	0.034
	2	3.08	0.462		
Fuel price levels	1	89.42	31.595	−4.111	0.000
	2	144.11	30.370		
Hotel price index	1	158.93	61.337	1.096	0.287
	2	134.52	29.734		

These results show that Cluster 2 countries have a comparative advantage over Cluster 1 countries in most of the air transport infrastructure variables except for *available domestic seat kilometers* and *airport density* variables. Because most of the tourism movements are realized by air transport infrastructure, this pillar is expected to contribute to the attractiveness of Cluster 2 countries by providing travelers a higher number of operating airlines and international flights in addition to the quality of air transport infrastructure and network.

In terms of the ground transport infrastructure pillar, Cluster 2 countries have advantages in quality of port infrastructure *(Mean$_1$ = 3.49; Mean$_2$ = 4.31; t = −2.200; p = 0.039)* and road density *(Mean$_1$ = 25.63; Mean$_2$ = 99.91; t = −2.938; p = 0.008)* variables (see Table 5). The two clusters did not show any statistically significant difference in quality of roads, quality of railroad infrastructure, and quality of ground transport network variables. These findings reveal that especially the road density variable is expected to benefit more from tourism resources, such as sea, mountains, rivers, lakes, rural sites, caves, etc., by improving accessibility for travelers.

It can be observed from Table 5 that Cluster 2 countries have performed better in all tourism infrastructure variables, namely hotel rooms *(Mean$_1$ = 0.17; Mean$_2$ = 1.23; t = −3.745; p = 0.001)*, presence of major car rental companies *(Mean$_1$ = 3.07; Mean$_2$ = 6.22; t = −4.345; p = 0.000)*, and ATMs accepting VISA cards *(Mean$_1$ = 195.90; Mean$_2$ = 719.53; t = −3.482; p = 0.002)*. All these three variables are expected to increase the chance for selecting from available alternatives and make it easy for travelers to choose among. For instance, increasing the number of hotel rooms might imply that travelers would choose from more alternatives in terms of different types of hotels, prices, locations, and services.

Similar to the above mentioned T&T infrastructure results, Cluster 2 countries have a comparatively significant advantage in all the 5 ICT infrastructure variables (see Table 5), which are extent of business Internet use *(Mean$_1$ = 4.45; Mean$_2$ = 5.33; t = −3.734; p = 0.001)*, number of Internet users *(Mean$_1$ = 24.45; Mean$_2$ = 52.98; t = −4.659; p = 0.000)*, telephone lines *(Mean$_1$ = 14.82; Mean$_2$ = 37.98; t = −6.275; p = 0.000)*, broadband Internet subscribers *(Mean$_1$ = 2.28; Mean$_2$ = 18.70; t = −7.010; p = 0.000)*, and mobile telephone subscribers *(Mean$_1$ = 87.94; Mean$_2$ = 123.16; t = −2.544; p = 0.019)*. If a country improves its ICT infrastructure, more travelers are expected to reach the required information in deciding on a certain destination. This information is related to general publicity, publishing the local tourism products, e-mail booking, online payment, e-mail enquiry, tourism guide, and the like. Cluster 2 countries are expected to benefit from their advantageous ICT infrastructure to attract tourists from all over the world.

After the analysis of price competitiveness in the T&T industry, the results revealed that Cluster 1 countries have a higher score in the extent and effect of taxation variable *(Mean$_1$ = 3.65; Mean$_2$ = 3.08; t = 2.262; p = 0.034)*, which makes tourism products cheaper and provides a competitive advantage. Contrary to this finding, Cluster 2 countries bear a disadvantage in the fuel price variable *(Mean$_1$ = 89.42; Mean$_2$ = 144.11; t = −4.111; p = 0.000)*, which makes tourism related products and services more expensive. These findings are consistent with our previous discussion that Cluster 1 countries have a competitive advantage in price competitiveness in the T&T industry pillar.

T-TEST RESULTS FOR T&T HUMAN, CULTURAL AND NATURAL RESOURCES SUBINDEX

Analysis results in Table 6 show t-test results for three T&T human, cultural, and natural resources subindex variables. In Table 3, we had observed that concerning four pillars, only *affinity for travel and tourism* did not show statistically significant difference between Cluster 1 and Cluster 2 countries. Thus, we included individual variables of the rest of the three pillars in t-test analysis and portrayed the results in Table 6.

TABLE 6   t-test Results for Cluster Membership and T&T Human, Cultural and Natural Resources Variables.

Variable	Cluster	Mean	Std. Dvt.	t	p
Human Resources					
Primary education enrollment	1	89.65	8.689	−2.492	0.021
	2	97.20	3.012		
Secondary education enrollment	1	85.55	19.043	−1.163	0.258
	2	93.33	7.333		
Quality of educational system	1	3.27	0.586	−1.133	0.270
	2	3.53	0.458		

TABLE 6 *(Continued)*

Variable	Cluster	Mean	Std. Dvt.	t	p
Local availability of research and training services	1	3.55	0.721	–3.075	0.006
	2	4.43	0.583		
Extent of staff training	1	3.55	0.498	–0.992	0.332
	2	3.83	0.842		
Hiring and firing practices	1	4.43	0.453	4.253	0.000
	2	3.52	0.573		
Ease of hiring foreign labor	1	4.28	0.868	1.969	0.062
	2	3.66	0.444		
HIV prevalence	1	0.135	0.302	–0.063	0.950
	2	0.144	0.353		
Business impact of HIV/AIDS	1	5.307	0.713	–2.517	0.020
	2	5.977	0.440		
Life expectancy	1	69.000	3.352	–4.868	0.000
	2	77.444	5.002		
Natural Resources					
Number of world heritage natural sites	1	1.142	3.158	–1.117	0.277
	2	2.555	2.603		
Protected areas	1	8.585	7.465	0.059	0.953
	2	8.422	4.379		
Quality of the natural environment	1	3.892	0.652	–1.425	0.169
	2	4.333	0.826		
Total known species	1	589.14	454.514	0.232	0.819
	2	552.33	162.300		
Cultural Resources					
Number of world heritage cultural sites	1	8.71	15.779	–1.772	0.091
	2	19.55	11.555		
Sports stadiums	1	19823.28	17152.081	–3.497	0.002
	2	52998.77	28565.252		
Number of international fairs and exhibitions	1	24.51	70.307	–2.708	0.014
	2	131.55	115.568		
Creative industries exports	1	1.66	5.751	0.179	0.860
	2	1.30	2.145		

Test results for the human resources pillar show that Cluster 2 countries performed better in five variables, which are namely primary education enrollment $(Mean_1 = 89.65; Mean_2 = 97.20; t = -2.492; p = 0.021)$, local availability of research and training services $(Mean_1 = 3.55; Mean_2 = 4.43; t = -3.075; p = 0.006)$, hiring and firing practices $(Mean_1 = 4.43; Mean_2 = 3.52; t = 4.253; p = 0.000)$, business impact of HIV/AIDS $(Mean_1 = 5.30; Mean_2 = 5.97; t = -2.517; p = 0.020)$, and life expectancy $(Mean_1 = 69.00; Mean_2 = 77.44; t = -4.868; p = 0.000)$. These results indicate that Cluster 2 countries provide advantages for tourism firms via a higher level of education, especially primary education, and local research and training services. To be able to develop a talented and motivated workforce, level of education in a certain country plays a significant role. Aside from this finding, availability of research and training opportunities, such as human resource agencies providing hiring and training services for firms, make it easier for countries to have a more skilled and motivated workforce. As a result, it is expected that the quality of services and customer satisfaction in tourism industry will be improved. Similarly, the level of negative impact of HIV/AIDS on business is lower in Cluster 2 countries, which indicates that deaths, disabilities, absenteeism, and medical, funeral, recruitment and training expenses will be lower and productivity and revenues will be higher. Although the score of hiring and firing practices is higher for Cluster 1 countries, the result proves that it is easier and has no formal rules when hiring and firing personnel, which means that these countries have no systematic human resource practices and institutional standards.

Findings for the natural resources pillar revealed mixed results. In the interpretation of natural resources (see Table 3), we postulated that Cluster 2 countries had higher scores and more advantageous conditions to develop nature-based tourism products and attract tourists. Contrary to this prediction, t-test results in Table 6 revealed that individual variables of natural resources pillar did not produce statistically significant different scores, which makes further interpretation difficult for individual variables.

The third pillar, cultural resources, revealed certain meaningful results (see Table 6) in two out of four variables, namely, sport stadiums $(Mean_1 = 19823.28; Mean_2 = 52998.77; t = -3.497; p = 0.002)$ and number of international fairs and exhibitions $(Mean_1 = 24.51; Mean_2 = 131.55; t = -2.708; p = 0.014)$. These findings may imply that the number of sport stadiums and international fairs/exhibitions have the potential to create a positive destination image and attract more tourists from all over the world. In this sense, we can conclude that Cluster 2 countries have an advantageous competitive position compared to Cluster 1 countries.

COMPARISON OF COUNTRIES' PERFORMANCE FOR T&T INDEX

To make it more meaningful for readers to understand the performance of each country comparatively, we summarized the Silk Road countries' global rankings for all the pillars in Table 7. In the table, we presented the top three performing countries in a shaded framework for ease of understanding.

Table 7 shows the rankings of Cluster 1 and Cluster 2 countries for 14 pillars of the T&T Competitiveness Index. Overall, it can be inferred from the table that Cluster 2 countries exhibited a better performance compared to Cluster 1 countries (please see the dotted areas for each cluster). Specifically, Japan in Cluster 2 performed the best in 8 out of 14 pillars, which are environmental sustainability, safety and security, air transport infrastructure, ground transport infrastructure, ICT infrastructure, human resources, natural resources, and cultural resources. Out of these 8 pillars, Japan's competitiveness depends mainly on ground transport infrastructure (rank: 6), cultural resources (rank: 12), safety and security (rank: 19), air transport infrastructure (rank: 22), and human resources (rank: 13).

TABLE 7 Top Three Performing Countries per Pillar.

Cluster	Country	Policy rules and regulations	Environmental sustainability	Safety and Security	Health and hygiene	Prioritization of T&T	Air transport infrastructure	Ground transport infrastructure	Tourism infrastructure	ICT infrastructure	Price competitiveness in the T&T industry	Human resources	Affinity for T&T	Natural resources	Cultural resources
1	Albania	46	72	44	66	55	96	97	77	71	94	57	3	113	83
1	Armenia	92	111	51	37	76	95	106	92	97	61	81	38	124	85
1	Azerbaijan	74	92	57	54	54	83	58	96	88	76	49	98	109	81
1	China	80	95	58	96	35	35	59	95	73	24	39	124	5	16

1	Egypt	49	113	135	56	22	55	76	88	93	5	93	29	85	65
1	Georgia	54	69	47	31	31	105	69	87	82	91	30	46	120	80
1	Kazakhstan	95	129	108	9	93	86	96	81	61	92	80	126	107	118
1	Kyrgyzstan	96	100	120	51	118	132	129	135	91	64	101	16	97	103
1	Mongolia	87	138	67	76	96	77	133	121	99	59	99	36	84	71
1	Pakistan	106	133	138	107	121	98	71	119	113	11	122	137	83	62
1	Saudi Arabia	43	131	52	93	88	45	53	46	51	6	34	102	48	97
1	Syria	123	126	69	90	79	110	92	115	106	51	108	23	128	88
1	Tajikistan	119	90	55	63	122	117	117	138	110	58	82	128	115	120
1	Ukraine	107	88	82	17	101	93	74	53	68	119	68	117	119	86
2	Bulgaria	94	99	81	10	71	89	90	6	43	46	71	51	78	37
2	Croatia	77	46	33	32	72	66	54	4	35	101	83	20	75	31
2	Greece	82	68	73	20	17	19	61	5	39	123	59	47	61	25
2	Israel	62	74	46	16	75	51	47	44	22	115	31	56	74	67
2	Italy	84	60	48	27	56	29	39	1	34	129	45	91	49	8
2	Japan	51	52	19	22	50	22	6	48	28	137	22	131	36	12
2	Rep. of Korea	53	81	60	28	94	40	18	56	8	96	38	120	103	5
2	Russia	126	98	113	11	102	30	95	45	46	75	78	136	27	35
2	Turkey	34	85	97	67	61	37	60	54	59	108	69	35	81	21

Japan's strength in the safety and security pillar results from the reliability of police services and road traffic accidents variables. Ground transport infrastructure of Japan ranks 6th in the world and this is due to the country's advantageous conditions in the quality of railroad infrastructure, quality of ground transport network, and road density. Another pillar that makes Japan the third best performer among Cluster 2 countries is cultural resources. The country's rank for creative industries exports and the number of world heritage cultural sites and international fairs and exhibitions are relatively lower than other countries and makes the country competitive in terms of cultural resources.

Among Cluster 2 countries, Italy and Croatia performed well in 4 out of 14 T&T competitiveness index pillars. Considering the tourism infrastructure pillar, Italy is the best performing country in the world by having a sufficient number of hotel rooms, presence of major car rental companies, and ATMs accepting VISA cards. Italy ranks 8th in the cultural resources pillar and this position mainly depends on the country's advantageous conditions in the number of world heritage cultural sites, international fairs and exhibitions, and creative industries exports. The other Cluster 2 country, Croatia, is the 4th best country in the world in terms of the tourism infrastructure pillar. The country's number of hotel rooms, presence of major car rental companies, and ATMs accepting VISA cards are quite sufficient and this provides the country a competitive advantage not only among the Silk Road countries but also throughout the world.

Considering Cluster 2 countries' competitive positions, Greece and Republic of Korea performed well for 3 pillars. Greece's tourism infrastructure provides the country a competitive advantage by having a sufficient number of hotel rooms and major car rental companies. A supporting government prioritization and expenditure of the T&T industry make it possible for the country to achieve a favorable position in prioritization of the T&T pillar. Additionally, airport density and the number of operating airlines of the country provide a competitive advantage among the Silk Road countries. Rankings of the Republic of Korea are quite low for cultural resources, ICT infrastructure, and ground transport infrastructure pillars. In terms of the cultural resources pillar, the country has the advantages of having a high number of world heritage cultural sites and international fairs and exhibitions. The country's ICT infrastructure is quite sufficient and has a leading position in business Internet use, number of Internet users, extent of telephone lines, and broadband Internet subscribers' variables. These variables are expected to provide the country ease of communication, speed of reaching information in reservations and banking, and quality of tourism marketing activities, and so forth.

INTERNATIONAL TOURIST ARRIVALS AND TOURISM RECEIPTS FOR THE SILK ROAD COUNTRIES

The comparison of international tourist arrivals for Cluster 1 and Cluster 2 demonstrates a big difference in the performance of both clusters in attracting tourists worldwide (See Fig. 2). In 2011, the number of tourists that visited Cluster 1 countries was around 80 million whereas it was around 150 million for Cluster 2 countries. Comparing by years, the increase in international tourist numbers does not show any big difference in either cluster. Overall, Cluster 2 countries' performance in attracting international tourists has an absolute advantage over Cluster 1 countries.

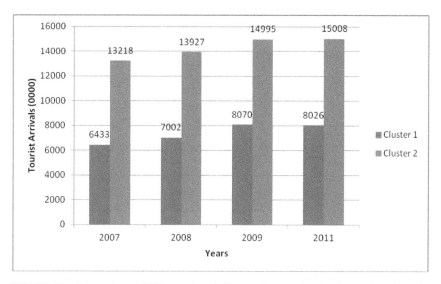

FIGURE 2   Comparison of Cluster 1 and Cluster 2 countries by International tourist arrivals.

Comparison of tourism receipts for Cluster 1 and Cluster 2 countries is displayed in Fig. 3 below. It can be deduced from the figure that Cluster 2 countries' tourism receipts are relatively higher than Cluster 1 countries. For example, for the year 2011, while tourism receipts of Cluster 2 countries is $130 billion, it is $49 billion for Cluster 1 countries. As seen in Fig. 2, while the number of tourists for Cluster 2 countries was double that of Cluster 1 countries in 2011, for the same year tourism receipts of Cluster 2 countries was almost triple. It shows that Cluster 2 countries' revenue per tourist and the value of tourism products are much higher.

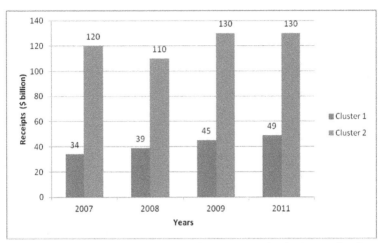

FIGURE 3   Comparison of Cluster 1 and Cluster 2 countries by International tourism receipts.

CONCLUSION

Because the Silk Road Project is a promising and strategically significant one for the aforementioned countries, there is a need for more studies on it. As one of the pioneer studies on the subject, this chapter focused on clustering and comparing the Silk Road countries to determine potential risks, advantages, and disadvantages for today and the future.

Our results postulated that two clusters can be derived as a result of cluster analysis. Diffusion of clusters shows us that Cluster 1 countries mainly consist of Central Asian countries, which can be classified as symbolical Silk Road countries and have the spirit of the ancient Silk Road. Even though Central Asian countries bear critical importance in the project, competitiveness performances are found to be relatively lower compared to Cluster 2 countries. This determination is critically important because if the poor performance of Cluster 1 countries could not be corrected, the project would be strategically unsuccessful in the long run.

In this context, major disadvantages of Cluster 1 countries are related to environmental sustainability, health and hygiene, air transport infrastructure, ground transport infrastructure, tourism infrastructure, ICT infrastructure, human resources, natural resources, and cultural resources.

As almost none of the Cluster 1 countries holds a place in the rankings of 14 competitiveness pillars, they can be described as disadvantageous.

More specifically, Cluster 1 countries should improve their environmental sustainability by passing laws related to stringency and enforcement of environmental regulations. Tougher environmental rules should also be established regarding particulate matter concentration. Health and hygiene conditions should be improved by increasing the degree of access to improved sanitation and drinking water. On the other hand, Cluster 1 countries should improve the quality of air transport infrastructure and international air transport network. They should also increase the number of available international seat kilometers, departures per 1.000 population, and the number of operating airlines. Cluster 1 countries bear the disadvantages of not possessing quality port infrastructure and adequate road density. Any improvement in these conditions would improve the accessibility of travelers to touristic attractions in different locations.

In terms of the tourism infrastructure pillar, we propose that Cluster 1 countries should invest to increase the number of hotel rooms because of the big gap between both cluster countries' possession of hotel room numbers. In these countries, the number of major car rental companies and ATMs accepting VISA cards should be increased. ICT infrastructure of Cluster 1 countries bear another disadvantageous position and should be improved by investing in the Internet infrastructure, whether it is for business or individual consumers. To attract more tourists, telephone lines and mobile telephone infrastructure are other alternatives to invest in.

Because the tourism industry depends mainly on services provided by human capital, Cluster 1 countries should pay greater attention to human resources variables. In this context, education systems must be revised and tourism-related schools must be established. Local availability of private research and human resource consulting agencies must be fostered. Considering the natural resources pillar, Cluster 1 and Cluster 2 countries do not possess good rankings and do not have statistically significant differences. To improve their conditions in this pillar, both clusters should have comprehensive plans to increase the number of protected natural areas and improve the quality of the natural environment. Cultural resources can be considered as one of the major sources for attracting domestic and international tourists. To establish a more attractive cultural environment, Cluster 1 countries should add more sport stadiums to their portfolios and organize an increasing number of international fairs and exhibitions.

Cluster 2 countries should revise their policy rules and regulations because of their poor overall rankings in the world (see Table 7). To achieve this aim, prevalence of foreign ownership and property rights should be encouraged by passing laws. It is also necessary to reduce the time and expenses required to start a business. These countries also have to give greater importance to government prioritization of travel and tourism by increasing government expenditures on them and establishing an effective marketing and branding strategy. One the biggest disadvantages for Cluster 2 countries is the low level of price competitiveness in the travel and tourism industry. To correct this, governments should give higher priority to lowering related taxes and adjusting fuel prices at an optimum level.

In order to establish competitive and sustainable tourism cooperation among the Silk Road countries and increase the welfare of the member countries, sound strategies must be developed by increasing collaboration among them. Discussions and suggestions made above might shed light on potential alternatives in strategy development processes. We would hereby like to suggest as well that while these countries complete the missing parts, they should also protect their unique characteristics especially in natural and cultural resources.

KEYWORDS

- **Cluster Analysis**
- **Silk Road Countries**
- **Strategic Marketing**
- **Tourism Industry**
- **Tourism Performance**
- **Travel & Tourism Competitiveness Index**

REFERENCES

Akayev, A. (2001). Kyrgyzstan. Australia: Asia Pacific Press.

Artto, E.W. (1987). Relative total costs—An approach to competitiveness measurement of industries. Management International Review, 27, 47–58.

Buyers, L. M. (2003). Central Asia in Focus. New York: Nova Science Publishers Inc.

CRC (Cooperative Research Center). (2008). Megatrends Underpinning Tourism to 2020 Report, Australia.

Dwyer, L., Kim, C. (2003). Destination competitiveness: Determinants and indicators, Current Issues in Tourism, 6, 369–414.

Goeldner, C.R., Ritchie, J. R. B., Macintosh, R. W. (2000). Tourism, Wiley, USA.

Hassan, S. (2000). Determinants of market competitiveness in an environmentally sustainable tourism industry, Journal of Travel Research, 38, 239–245.

Kantarci, K. (2006). Perceptions of Central Asia travel conditions: Kyrgyzstan, Kazakhstan, Uzbekistan, and Turkmenistan. Journal of Hospitality & Leisure Marketing, 15:2, 55–71.

OECD. (2007). Competitive Regional Clusters: National Policy Approaches, (http://www.oecd.org/document/2/0,3746,en_2649_33735_38174082_1_1_1_1,00.html), (22.04.2012).

Olsen, M. (2003). Tourism themed routes: A Queensland perspective. Journal of Vacation Marketing, 9, 331–341.

Onsel S., Ulengin F., Ulusoy G., Aktas E, Kabak O., Topcu Y. I. (2008). A new perspective on the competitiveness of nations. Socio-Economic Planning Sciences, 42, 221–246.

Porter, M. E. (2004). Competitive Advantage. Free Press: New York.

Porter, M. E. (2009). The Competitive Advantage of Nations, States, and Regions, Harvard Business School, Advanced Management Program.

Sala-i-Martin, X and Artadi, E.V. (2004). The Global Competitiveness Index. In: The Global Competitiveness Report 2004–2005. New York: Oxford University Press for the World Economic Forum, 2004.

UNWTO. (1998). How to Source Japan-A Major Tourist Market for the Silk Road, Madrid, Spain.

UNWTO. (2007). Tourism Highlights Report.

UNWTO. (2009). Investment Guide to the Silk Road.

UNWTO. (2012). Tourism Highlights Report.

UNWTO. (2012–2013). The Silk Road Action Plan.

Vietor, R. H. K. (2006). Strategy, Structure, and Government in the Global Economy. Harvard Business School Press: Boston, Massachusetts.

World Economic Forum (WEF). (2007). The Travel & Tourism Competitiveness Report.

World Economic Forum (WEF). (2008). The Travel & Tourism Competitiveness Report.

World Economic Forum (WEF). (2009). The Travel & Tourism Competitiveness Report.

World Economic Forum (WEF). (2011). The Travel & Tourism Competitiveness Report.

WTTC Report. (2012). Travel and Tourism Economic Impact (Kazakhstan).

CHAPTER 10

VISA REGIMES AND REGULATORY DOCUMENTS AS AN OBSTACLE FOR TOURISM DEVELOPMENT IN CENTRAL ASIA

SLAVOMÍR HORÁK

CONTENTS

"A Dutch tourist dies and goes to heaven. In heaven he's bored because everything is perfect. He wonders how hell is, so one day he writes a request to God that he wants to go to hell. God reads his request and discards it. The Dutch tourist doesn't take rejection well and submits a request to God every day that he wants to go to hell. Finally god gives in and grants him a 3-day Tourist visa, the gates to Hell open for him and he enters hell. The first thing he sees are beautiful women everywhere and there's drinks and drugs. The three days pass quickly as time flies when you're having fun. So on his last day, he says goodbye to his friends in hell and passes through the gates of Heaven where his other friends await him. He tells them about his wonderful experiences in hell and that he wants to go back. All his friends want to join him and they all send requests to God. God is annoyed that everybody wants to go, so to get rid of all the requests, he grants them a group visa for an indefinite stay in Hell. So they all enter hell and there are no beautiful women, no drinks, no drugs. Only fire and torture. So the Dutch tourist asks God, "What have you done, where are all the beautiful women? And the drinks? And the drugs?" God answers, "Your first visit was on a tourist visa. Now you're in reality."
(http://www.travbuddy.com/travel-blogs/2397/Uzbek-Tourist-Visa-2)

INTRODUCTION

The Central Asian area has been unjustly neglected by global tourism and is home to a wide variety of medieval historical monuments, as well as great natural beauty. At the same time, it forms a traditional meeting place for people of varying nationalities and for the mutual exchange of labor and goods, serving as a center for transit trading between Eastern and Southern Asia on the one hand, and the Near East, Northern Asia and Europe, on the other. Indeed, a number of tourist attractions could hardly have come into existence without the presence of waves of migration and transit trading.

After the collapse of the Soviet Union, Central Asia made it onto the map of international tourist destinations, albeit only marginally. The text that follows will analyze the reasons for its marginalization, highlighting visa regimes and other regulatory documentation as seen by the tourism community. In particular, the focus will be on the introduction of visas for foreigners from "distant lands" in the countries of the region, their attempts to enhance the visa simplification process for tourists from abroad and the impact this has had on the development of tourism. Two diametrically opposed approaches have been taken to tourism in the region. Kyrgyzstan has been more or less liberal on the issue, while Turkmenistan operates under a system of almost total control. Other countries may be located somewhere between these two extremes. Obviously, regulatory documentation and visas (together with the area's distance from the primary outbound tourism countries and lack of available means to get there) are the main obstacles for incoming tourism development in the region. This follows from the arguments of B. Whyte that greater visa incentives encourage greater tourist flows (Whyte, 2008).

The basis of the chapter consists of long-term observations and interviews at Central Asian borders during border crossings. The interviews were not structured and were normally based on everyday conversation with locals. Thus the text is a sort of "sideline" survey resulting from working in the region for approximately 12 years. Such an approach is of a qualitative nature. But long-term observation can show the dynamics and changes occurring at Central Asian borders. The most visited frontiers are those, which lie between Kazakhstan and Kyrgyzstan, between Kyrgyzstan and Uzbekistan, Uzbekistan and Tajikistan, and Tajikistan and Kyrgyzstan. The situation described at the borders of Turkmenistan and the Kazakhstan-Uzbekistan borders are mostly based upon the experience of other sources.

I argue that visa policy and regulatory mechanisms ordinarily mirror the character of the particular Central Asian regime in question. The harsher the regime, the more problematic the tourist bureaucracy becomes (in terms of visas and other regulatory documentation). Of course, the overall bureaucratization of Central Asian regimes and their mass corruption have also had a significant impact on the procedures. The main approach taken is to survey the situation on various Central Asian borders, see how it has evolved over time and the different approaches taken to differing categories of people who cross the border.

Two principal categories of people must be distinguished: locals (meaning mostly Central Asians and CIS citizens) on the one hand, and citizens of third countries (those from "distant lands" noted above) on the other. The membership of these two individual groups, however, cannot be considered homogeneous.

Reports from various borders indicate that corruption is much more evident in dealing with locals. The character of the regimes themselves is considered as the principal reason. In this article, however, I will discuss mostly the problems of third-countries incomers as it represents the major segment, which the regimes are aimed on.

GETTING INTO CENTRAL ASIA PROBLEM

Central Asia has traditionally been a relatively complicated place to gain access to, for both foreigners and local residents. Migration has been blocked by significant distances, which must be traveled over inhospitable deserts and mountains lying between Central Asia and other centers of civilization. To this must be added the distrust displayed by many in authority toward the outside world, including on the part of local leaders, who have many times taken advantage of travelers for their own enrichment (Hopkirk, 2001; Morrier, 1895; Vambery, 2010). For this reason, for example, the Hungarian Orientalist Arminius Vambery (2010) traveled disguised as a dervish pilgrim for safety reasons as late as 1863–64 (i.e., the year before Tashkent was occupied by the Russians). The relatively late development of modern infrastructure in the region (railroads and later aviation) also impacted on the region's accessibility to travelers. Although the Turkestan region was declared a military district in the latter years of the nineteenth century, a number of European travelers visited the area (Curtis, 1911; Curzon, 1889; Donovan, 1883; Fait, 1907; Graham, 1916; Hedin, 1903; Olufsen, 1911; Schuyler, 1877; Skrine, 1899). The Russian authorities of the time took a relatively benevolent stance toward similar visits, even if they intervened at the slightest sign of espionage activity taking place on "their" territory (Hopkirk, 2001).

After the establishment of the Soviet regime, access to Central Asia was permitted only to selected groups of foreign tourists, as well as to journalists loyal to the Soviet regime (Hughes and Mikosz, 2006). The goal for the latter was to build positive references to the regime. Their trips were coordinated with the local NKVD and, later, the KGB. Another category of foreigners who went to Central Asia was the so-called Interhelp Brigade, aid teams who visited the area during the 1930s.

After the WWII, the region began to open up to organized tourism as part of the opening taking place to tourism within the Soviet Union in general. Several favored routes for foreign tourists were established including the "exotic" area of the Soviet Muslim East (i.e., Central Asia). Aside from border and military zones, it was not even necessary to have a special permit for tours organized by the state tourist agencies Inturist or Sputnik. Border checks at the Soviet border were sufficient in this case (Kostiainen, 2002).

Starting in the 1950s, tourism in Central Asia began to include so-called "wild" tourism, not directly connected to organized groups. In addition to scientific expeditions, this type of travel primarily involved nature lovers, hikers and tourists engaging in other kinds of sport (Maurer, 2006). Participants in these trips got a much better view of the real situation of the local people and life under the Soviet regime. These tourists made frequent complaints about controls and attempts by militias and tourism organizers to include them in the officially permitted trips (at the very least by including them in organized expeditions) (Janouch, 1966; Maťašák, 1981, 1983). One of the chief problems for this type of tourism was the obligation that both foreign tourists and domestic Soviet tourists had to register.[1] Despite the bureaucratic difficulties imposed, however, sport and hiking expeditions were increasingly arriving at mountain camps in the Pamir, Fan and Tan-Shan mountains.

Another important source of foreign tourism has been student exchanges from the socialist and, later, capitalist countries as well. These have led to word-of-mouth recountings an official reports (Blazek et al., 2012).

CONSEQUENCES OF VISA POLICY IN THE CENTRAL ASIAN COUNTRIES

After the breakup of the Soviet Union and the rise of the independent states of Central Asia, new border controls and border crossings appeared along borders which had heretofore been only formal. Visa requirements and other bureaucratic demands were introduced for citizens of countries outside the CIS. Particularly in the early years, however, these requirements were subject to a high degree of ambiguity. No embassies were established at which it would be possible to obtain a visa, and the conditions and payment required for visas to be issued varied considerably.[2] Normally,

---

[1]Residents of the so-called Socialist Bloc had it better in this regard; normally an official paper written in Russian and issued by an institution sending the tourists was adequate. (This institution might even be the tourist's university.) Similar looking documents were often falsified and carried fake stamps (so-called potato stamps).

[2] A colleague of mine who traveled to Central Asia in 1992 (to Uzbekistan, Tajikistan and Afghanistan) indicated that his group was held at the border between Uzbekistan and Afghanistan, where border agents demanded an Uzbek visa that was impossible to obtain formally. By contrast, at the still open borders with the former Soviet republics, no one was interested in such a formality.

however, the old system, which had mandated an invitation from the local tourist office remained in place. This has remained true to the present in Uzbekistan and Turkmenistan, as well as in Tajikistan and Kazakhstan in some cases. For the majority of tourists from developed countries, the institution of the written invitation presents a complication in terms of both time and money. The invitation may lead to greater control over the activities of foreigners, but from the tourist's standpoint, it is a factor that may play into the choice of destination in a decisive fashion. For local tourism organizations, this may mean additional bureaucracy to some extent, but it adds up to good business for the facilities that process the invitations.

Rules set up for entry and residency visas in Central Asia also underwent a period of marked chaos in the 1990s, which opened the opportunities for corruption although tourists from foreign countries had fewer such possibilities than tourists from CIS countries.[3] In addition, until the end of the 1990s it was generally true that the holder of a visa to one CIS country could remain up to 72 h in other CIS countries (especially neighboring ones). But this rule was acknowledged only selectively and it was never clear which visa could be used in which countries. Particularly in the first half of the 1990s, there were no border controls between post-Soviet states.

A number of tourists went, for example, to Kazakhstan or Kyrgyzstan on a Russian visa, which was often (but not always) recognized by border guards. What's more, in the 1990s the Russian Embassy was authorized to issue visas to selected post-Soviet countries in some states (Kazakhstan, Kyrgyzstan).

In general, it may be stated that the visa situation and the situation regarding border crossings began to stabilize during the second half of the 1990s, firming up over the subsequent decade. At the same time, pronounced differences between individual states in terms of visa issuance rules have resulted. Standard border crossings have been constructed at the borders between states, which impact foreigners and domestic tourists alike.

TRAVELING IN CENTRAL ASIA WITHOUT A VISA

An interesting exception regarding the visas used to include several incentives for members of the former Socialist bloc. As noted above, trips

---

[3]One Czech tourist at the end of the 1990s was able to gain entry to Uzbekistan without a visa, traveling in a cargo train for a small bribe. Once inside the country, no further bribes were necessary and it was possible to exit the country in the same manner.

involving the Soviet Union and these states were formally visa-free, based upon a decision by bodies in the outgoing country. For this reason, for example, residents of Central and Eastern European countries were able to travel to all Central Asian countries except Uzbekistan without a visa long after the breakup of the USSR. This was conditional upon the issuance of a "AB Sluzhebnaia" stamp (for business travel) or a "AB Obmen" stamp for private travel by the pertinent body of the Central or Eastern European country concerned.[4] A similar advantage was enjoyed by citizens of the Czech Republic, Slovakia, Poland, Hungary, Romania and Bulgaria. These mutual agreements were confirmed or done away with, depending upon the era. Visa-free travel for holders of ordinary passports was interrupted as part of the preparations for entry of these countries into the EU and the harmonization of their laws with the *acquis communautaire*.[5] Paradoxically, by the end of 1999, holders of Czech, Slovak or Polish passports could enter Turkmenistan without a visa (although with some complications), while residents of surrounding countries and the countries of the Commonwealth of Independent States were already subject to visa requirements. To this day, passport holders from Cuba, Vietnam and North Korea can, for example, go to Kyrgyzstan without a visa, even if such visits are quite improbable. Until 2008, residents of the majority of countries of Central and Eastern Europe were able to travel there without a visa (on the basis of a unilateral decision by the Kyrgyzstan authorities). Only after this year were rules unified for all EU citizens. Exemption from visa requirements under these agreements also concerns short-term stays for holders of diplomatic passports.[6]

The lack of visa requirements for these special categories of tourists, however, has not come close to gaining unilateral acceptance by local au-

---

[4]While the issuance of this stamp was connected with marked difficulties during the communist period, involving gaining authorizations and submitting invitations from the Soviet Union, getting a certificate from the workplace or school of the individuals involved and one from the housing administration, etc., after the fall of communism in the 1990s, issuance of this stamp became a formality.

[5]The Czech Republic took this action in 2000, Poland not until 2004, and Romania and Bulgaria as part of their own entry into the EU in 2007.

[6]The Uzbekistan Ministry of Foreign Affairs indicates on its website that short-term stays (normally of 30 or 90 days) may be made by holders of diplomatic passports from Slovakia, Hungary and Romania. Visa-free access to Turkmenistan is available to diplomats from Slovakia and Hungary. Holders of service passports and diplomatic passports from Slovakia, Hungary, Romania, Bulgaria, Vietnam and Cuba do not need a visa to travel to Kazakhstan, nor do diplomatic passport holders from Slovenia, Estonia and Poland. Kyrgyzstan continues to impose no visa requirements on diplomats from Hungary, while Tajikistan offers the same to all citizens of Hungary.

thorities. To the contrary: the number of exceptions and the ambiguity of the rules has been an invitation for attempts to force bribes. The author of this article has experienced a number of passport controls and luggage checks during his stay in Kyrgyzstan, particularly in Bishkek in 1999–2003. In spite of advisories of the visa-free relationship and registration in our passports, we were subjected to interrogations on several occasions and verification of the visa-free relationship. This was done in order to obtain a bribe ("We won't make any problems for you regarding visas if you share with us in a brotherly way," that is, give us "something").

Tourists from CIS countries should theoretically be in the most advantageous position in terms of visa policy (including those from Georgia, which recently exited the organization). Most CIS countries have mutually recognized visa-free relationships based upon treaties.[7] This makes it much easier for CIS citizens to move within the visa-free zone. However, the embassies of the CIS states' failure to protect their own citizens makes the border guards and militiamen prefer to extract bribes from the much more vulnerable former citizens of the USSR. Citizens of developed countries may call upon their own consuls for assistance if problems should arise (EU citizens have recourse to the authorities of any Member State of the Union), but those of CIS countries may not be allowed to do so by local authorities because the laxity of consular staff from these countries is well known.

A significant shift in visa-free regimes between states of the former USSR arose when travel between selected states became possible using just internal passports or internal identification cards. In Central Asia, this option is available for travel between citizens of Kazakhstan and Kyrgyzstan, as well as between citizens of Kazakhstan, Russia and Belarus (as parts of the Custom Union). The measure had already been in effect regarding Russia before introduction of this treaty.

By contrast, since 1999 Turkmenistan has withdrawn from joint treaties and introduced visa requirements for all CIS citizens without exception, slightly easing visa requirements only for border areas along the Uzbekistan border. After the invasion of armed groups belonging to the Islamic Movement of Uzbekistan in Central Asia, Uzbekistan introduced visa requirements for citizens of Kyrgyzstan and Tajikistan, with lesser

---

[7]Soglasheniie o bezvizovom peredvizhenii grazhdan gosudarstv Sodruzhestva Nezavisimykh Gosudarstv po territorii ego uchastnikov ot 9 oktiabria 1992 g.

requirements for movement by citizens from border regions. The introduction of visas significantly complicated the relationship between Kyrgyzstan and Uzbekistan and the movement of citizens, particularly in the Fergana Basin with a number of extraterritorialities, enclaves, etc. This was reflected in restrictions on movement between the two countries. Automobiles and busses from Kyrgyzstan, for example, were allowed only sporadic entry to the country in the Uzbekistan enclave of Soch and had to go around the enclave using a dusty roadway which prolonged the trip and made it more expensive. At the same time, intercity busses and minibusses from Osh to Jalalabad or northern areas of the Fergana Basin which, prior to that time, had been entered routinely by traveling through Uzbek territory, now had to be gotten to via a long detour.

As regards Uzbekistan-Tajikistan relationships, this action continued to deepen the isolation of both countries. By the end of the 1990s, direct transport connections between the two countries (in terms of direct flights, railway connections or bus connections) were canceled. The only exception consisted of some rail transit links (Dushanbe-Moscow, Dushanbe-Khudzhand) where Tajikistan citizens have no right to step foot on Uzbek soil.

COMPLICATIONS IN ACQUIRING VISAS FOR CENTRAL ASIA

Since 2008, when Kyrgyzstan unified conditions for the issuance of visas, virtually all citizens of countries outside the CIS have required a valid visa for entry into any Central Asian state. With regard to the paucity of direct connections between Central Asian countries (with a few exceptions) and the need for transfers at borders with thorough passport checks, it is no longer a realistic possibility to enter/exit without a visa, even taking corruption into account.

With the significant current differences in visa issue policies, it is interesting to take a look at shifts in the visa policies of individual Central Asian countries to see how they correlate with the nature of the regime. As has been noted, in general terms visa issuance rules have been stabilized, as has their actual implementation at various locations (border checkpoints, etc.).

Kyrgyzstan undoubtedly has the most liberal visa policy, with President Akayev's intent being to attract tourists and investors. The influx of tourists has not been particularly strong, but in spite of this, Kyrgyzstan has become one of the first countries in the post-Soviet area to substantially lighten its visa policy requirements. Most significant of all, soon after the fall of the USSR, the requirement to submit an invitation from a local travel organization was dropped for citizens of developed countries. As has been gone into in some detail above, Kyrgyzstan also retained its faithfulness to the treaties between the Soviet Union and former states of the Soviet bloc. This was a step in the right direction, because, during the 1990s, a significant number of tourists came from these countries (particularly from the Czech Republic, Slovakia, Poland and the Baltic countries). Over time, this liberal policy regarding visas and the attractive mountain areas within the country, along with its relative political stability, resulted in an influx of new tourists from other developed markets. In spite of the fact that harmonization of visa policy regarding the developed world somewhat worsened Kyrgyzstan's position in the Central and Eastern European marketplaces, the liberal policy was maintained and confirmed by the formal cancelation of former, theoretically functional limitations for travelers, including permissions to visit the mountain border regions and registration. The option to obtain a visa to Kyrgyzstan at the airport (and not at border crossings) made Kyrgyzstan an attractive destination for foreign visitors and a good base country for getting to know the region. Although easing the visa issue into formal bureaucratic step at the airport, the Kyrgyzstan government went even further. Visa-free regime was established for major developed countries in July 2012 (Kabar, 2012). The result of this policy should be clearly visible in 2013 statistics (the tourism in 2012 season was partly visa regime).

Kazakhstan is gradually liberalizing its own visa policy in small steps. At the start, visas for the country could be issued by Russian authorities. But in the mid-1990s, this practice was abandoned and visas were issued only by Kazakh authorities. By the late 1990s, express visas became available at the airport in Almaty (very expensive and for short periods of time only). Otherwise, however, requirements for a letter of invitation were still in force. Kazakhstan began to liberalize this (cautiously) only in recent years. A list was created for the first time in 2004 of developed countries (Western Europe, Japan, the USA, Australia, etc.) whose citizens would be allowed to obtain a visa for up to 30 days without an invitation from the

Ministry of Foreign Affairs. In 2009, this list was expanded to include other European and Asian countries (mostly OECD member states) and today it includes 47 countries.[8] At the same time, the registration procedure for 28 selected countries was simplified. This had been a further unpleasant (and in the view of developed countries unnecessary) barrier to access and their citizens' ability to stay in Kazakhstan (see further). But for the time being, Kazakhstan has taken no steps toward further simplification of its visa policy for selected countries. Although a short-term visa may be acquired today for a single access at the airport, an invitation is still required, which means the visa policy has still not been simplified very much. In the future, however, Kazakhstan intends to completely do away with short-term visas for citizens of the most developed (OECD) countries.[9] But, so far this trial has not been implemented into the practice.

Noteworthy and progressive for Central Asia is the agreement between Kazakhstan and Kyrgyzstan for mutual recognition of visas within border areas. In practice, this means that holders of a Kazakh visa may stay in northern Kyrgyzstan and vice versa. This is complicated though by the fact that an exit stamp was issued at the border, for single-entry visas, which means the tourists cannot return to the country.[10] In spite of the fact that the treaty has the inadequacies noted, overall it may be seen as a highly positive step, which may strengthen tourism in border areas (a tourist with a Kazakh visa may thus visit Bishkek, Issyk-Kul and other attractive locations for tourists in Kyrgyzstan within the period of the visa's validity without further bureaucratic obstructions). However, introducing the visa-free regime for developed countries in Kyrgyzstan, the rule became useless as tourists need the visas for Kazakhstan anyway unless they have Kyrgyz ones in their passports.

Tajikistan is in a similar situation to that of Kazakhstan. Since 2006, the country has simplified its visa policy for approximately 67 countries, for which it has become possible to issue a single-entry or double-entry visa after arriving at the Dushanbe Airport. For a long period, the problem

---

[8]A document from the Ministry of Foreign Affairs of Kazakhstan.

[9]Kazakhstanlive.com, July 19, 2011; Pavlovskaya, Olga: Kazakhstan courts tourists with visa-free regime. Central Asia Online. July 11, 2012.

[10]Author's experience, 2010. My single-entry Kazakh visa was marked as invalid for Kazakhstan at the Kazakhstan-Kyrgyzstan border. I was let into Kyrgyzstan without problem (the visa was still valid) but upon returning to Kazakhstan, I was forced to arrange a new visa.

Tajikistan was unclear rules for the issuance of visas. At the start of the 1990s, the visa policy was completely paralyzed by the Civil War. Crossing the Tajikistan border during this period depended greatly upon the will of individual border guards, as well as on the ability of the tourist to negotiate entry without a visa. But as late as 1997, for example, there were no border controls along most of the Uzbekistan-Tajikistan frontier.[11] Some Russian embassies also issued visas to Tajikistan (this practice was accepted by the Tajiki authorities). The visa required that all cities to which the visitor planned to travel be listed on the visa itself.

Only after the conclusion of the civil war in 1997 did the policy stabilize and at least partially become unified. Based upon experience with various embassies, it appears that issuance of a visa to Tajikistan depends to a great degree upon the embassy, or the particular consular employee doing the job. In submitting a request for a visa to Tajikistan, this author has been asked to pay a bribe to the consular employee for issuing a visa to the country without an invitation.[12] On the other hand, some Tajikistan consulates at the turn of the century issued visas without any further documentation (traditionally open consulates included those in Vienna and Bishkek, Kyrgyzstan); strict requirements for a letter of invitation were made in other places (Brussels).

The above-indicated procedure for simplifying Tajikistan visas did not, however, lead to a complete, clear unification of requirements. The practical implementation of new measures has run into considerable roadblocks—the presence of consular employees at the airport was not guaranteed with every flight. At the start, it was unclear whether anyone could obtain the visa (according to a decree by the Ministry of Foreign Affairs of Tajikistan) or only citizens of countries without direct diplomatic representation in Tajikistan (an interpretation of the Commission for Tajiki Border Control), or whether a letter of invitation would be required upon arrival (information from IATA). In the latter case, air carriers would theoretically not check passengers in who were bound for Tajikistan and do not possess a visa or letter of invitation. This lack of comprehensive information led to very careful use of the Visa on arrival institution and shortly after this information was published, it seemed this undoubted advantage

---

[11]Interview with Czech journalist working in Tajikistan during the civil war. See also Hannafin, M., King, J., Noble, J., Humphreys, A., p. 83.

[12]I withhold the consulate, period of issuance and name of the consular employee for security reasons.

would be revoked. Over time, the implementing regulations for the decree were specified and unified. Tourists got used to being issued a 30-day single-entry tourist visa at the Dushanbe airport since 2010. However, Tajik officials may issue, for example, a private visa at the airport requiring further bureaucratic procedures, including compulsory registration. The full visa-free regime with developed countries is still under the consideration. Although Tajikistan Lower Chamber of the Parliament approved the respective bill, the rule has not been signed by President yet.[13]

Both Kyrgyzstan and Tajikistan and, to some extent, Kazakhstan have managed to employ the liberalization of their visa policies to create the impression that visas do not represent significant obstacles. In particular, the opportunity to obtain a visa at the airport had a decidedly positive impact on the number of tourists in both mountainous countries and the impact of 2012 visa-free regime introduction in Kyrgyzstan could serve as positive example for other two countries. Kyrgyzstan, in particular, ranked among countries offered as tourist destinations by European tourist agencies (especially those offering adventure or active tourism). In the case of Tajikistan, its situation is complicated both by its isolated location and the lack of transport access, as well as by other bureaucratic obstacles analyzed further in this text.

While the three aforementioned states have gradually more or less successfully sought to liberalize their visa policies, the two remaining states of Central Asia have continued to maintain rigid visa policies or even complicated them further. Any steps taken toward liberalization have been minor in nature.

Since the beginning of its existence, Uzbekistan has established a clear visa regime with all countries except those of CIS. The issuance of a visa was tied to a letter of invitation by an Uzbek travel agency (initially, this was a monopoly of Uzbektourism, the former UzbekIntourist). Starting in the mid-1990s, however, visas could also be issued by other travel agencies and at the airport, upon prior agreement. But Uzbekistan was the first country in Central Asia to consolidate its embassies and brought relatively clear rules issuance of visas, something which was rare in the 1990s. In addition, a relatively effective system was introduced in which travel agencies arranged an invitation for a fee and, upon doing so, were able to send

---

[13]Tajik Lower Chamber Approves Visa-Free Travel Bill for Western tourists. RFE/RL, May 25, 2012. *http://www.rferl.org/content/tajik-lower-chamber-approves-visa-free-travel-bill-for-western-tourists/24592819.html*

the invitation to the client via fax or e-mail, while the Ministry of Foreign Affairs of Uzbekistan sent its consent for a visa to be granted to the applicable consular section of the pertinent embassy. The tourist thus only required a single visit to the consulate and a visa was normally issued on the spot. This removed the need for a several day wait for issuance of the visa itself. In addition, in 1994 Uzbekistan introduced an option to have the visa granted in Tashkent at the airport, upon prior arrangement. While the consular section at the Tashkent airport had certain problems to deal with and worked only upon request, the issuance of a visa was definitely possible. After relaxing the visa rules, Uzbekistan also allowed tourists to buy only the letter of invitation at a tourist agency, without the necessity to reserve accommodation and other services. This practice has remained in force after almost 20 years, and its relaxation is taking place only cautiously. List of countries whose citizens could receive short-term tourist visas without letters of invitation was released in 2009 only. The list included several developed countries, while many others were not mentioned (e.g., Latvia was included, while other Baltic countries not; Czech Republic is also included, but other Visegrad countries not). Nevertheless, Uzbekistan's visa policy thus remains stable and its tourism trades primarily on attractive locations, which make travelers to the region not want to miss visiting Uzbekistan, despite some problems processing the visa.

Turkmenistan remains one of the most closed-off countries in the world, with one of the most restrictive visa policies on earth. Despite a promising start in the 1990s, when it was possible to obtain a visa to Turkmenistan at several consulates in Europe even without an invitation, from the mid-1990s a letter of invitation has become essential for visits. Until 2003, however, a system remained in effect in which the tourist was able to pay for a relatively formal letter of invitation which could then be taken to any Turkmenistan Embassy. Travel agencies included the automatic registration fee in the price of the visa, or permission to enter the border zone (including popular destinations such as Konya-Urgench). After 2003, Turkmenistan's visa policy changed significantly in the direction of tightening visa procedures. Requests for a tourist visa began to be examined much more closely (currently the visa issue and requests for visas are a focus for the presidential administration)[14], which forms a significant filter and brings about the rejection of a substantial number of requests. But

---

[14]Author's interview people close to migration agency in Turkmenistan. Moscow, September 2010.

the most important filter on the development of tourism in Turkmenistan is the strict requirement to purchase accommodation, transportation and other services, without which a visa will be refused. The Turkmenistan government uses this to attempt to obtain total control over the movement of all foreigners. Deviations from the designated program may be made only with the regime's consent by an authorized travel agency. The reason for requiring a guide during travel in Turkmenistan (outside of Ashgabat), which also applies to individual tourists, is to prevent locations prohibited by the state from being seen. Experience shows that this gives rise to a significant increase in travel expenses, especially for individual tourists, in addition to creating a psychological and financial obstacle, which makes entry to Turkmenistan more difficult. On the one hand, the official guides are—especially for individual tourists—the sole mediators of life in Turkmenistan. In practice, though, it is they who can present that side of life in the country which power demand to be hidden (impoverished areas, corruption etc.). In reality, the person working as a guide and his/her self-critical observations is very important.

Tourists who, normally from lack of funding, do not wish to or cannot pay for a full program in Turkmenistan must rely instead upon being granted a transit visa, which is normally issued for a five-day period. This is enough time to transit the country, but only allows trips to one or two locations and thereby fails to take advantage of Turkmenistan's full potential for tourists. Most tourists take advantage of the fact that granting a visa is not tied to further services by travel agencies. Turkmenistan's visa policy thus focuses primarily on very strict control of foreigners. For this reason, Turkmenistan's policy is the most reminiscent of all the post-Soviet countries of what travel had been during the Soviet era. This significantly impacts the tourist potential of Turkmenistan as an attractive, exotic tourist destination. A short-term transit visa does not allow tourists to make adequate use of all the options that should be available to them, and the tourist visa is not available for the majority of people.

In looking at the visa policy of Central Asian countries overall, a general equality relation may be seen between the internal character of the regime, the amount of effort it puts into isolating itself from the external world, and its visa policy. On the one hand there is Kyrgyzstan, whose regime is much more liberal (in the context of the region) and whose visa policy is the most open. On the other hand, there are the strong authoritarian systems of Uzbekistan and Turkmenistan, whose conditions for granting visas and permitting movement within the country are much more convoluted. Kazakhstan and Tajikistan are somewhere in between these two extremes. They, too, may be characterized as lacking freedom; nevertheless their visa policy is much more open for a number of reasons. Kazakhstan attempts to declare its attractiveness to foreign investors and show the world that is an open democratic state. Tajikistan sees tourism (and the corresponding visa policy) as one of its very few options to overcome its significant isolation.

Because getting a visa is a major obstacle which figures significantly into decisions of where to travel, the countries of Central Asia significantly reduce tourist inflows by virtue of their visa requirements (Han et al., 2011). If the sparse nature of the embassy network is taken into account, which in Europe, for example, provides coverage only for key countries, the significance of this factor grows even more. For many EU citizens, obtaining a visa represents additional travel costs for the visa process, postal charges or fees paid to mediators etc.). Tourists would be willing to put up with this—the visa stamp becomes an interesting souvenir in the passport—were it not for further paperwork. But traveling to Central Asia requires a number of other documents. This is one of the reasons for the underlying low rate of tourism in the region as a whole, even compared to authoritarian regimes like Iran.

REGISTRATION PROCESSES AS AN OBSTACLE TO TOURISM IN CENTRAL ASIA

In addition to visas, tourism in Central Asia is complicated by a number of other regulatory measures, which do not significantly limit movement within the country but are often tied to delays and costs (considered unnecessary by tourists). From the point of view of the purpose they allegedly serve (usually safeguarding tourist and checking them), the measures are considerably inefficient. But it must be acknowledged that, while the countries of Central Asia are not willing to do away with the regulations, in many cases they are willing to approach the issue pragmatically and try to simplify things to the extent possible. But this does not apply in every case and persistent inconsistencies in interpreting the law and enforcing it must also be taken into consideration. This inconsistency of interpretation and discrepancies in the law form the basis for rampant corruption and lead to those in the tourism industry accepting nonstandard and semilegal solutions.

Registration of foreigners (*propiska*) is one of the most significant relics of the Soviet system, under which it served not only as a tool for controlling foreign tourists (particularly those coming to the country on an individual basis) but also for regulating movement within the empire. Currently, registration of foreigners in the post-Soviet area is required even for short-term stays (aside from Russia and Belarus) in Uzbekistan, Turkmenistan, and to some extent in Tajikistan and Kazakhstan. This registration is another factor, which complicates individual tourism in Central Asia. Some regimes require tourists to join organized groups and stay in official hotels.[15]

In spite of the effort to transform tourism into an organized framework, the demand for individual tourism generates a semilegal offer of registration or disproportionately increases the price of individual tourist services. This particularly applies to Turkmenistan, where the system has exceeded the best traditions of the Soviet Inturist agency. A full program, which includes accommodation in official hotels, a guide and arranged transportation is necessary for registration to be successful and a visa to be granted.

Registration requirements in Uzbekistan are somewhat milder, but also less clear-cut. But the rule has been maintained. Although the granting of tourist visas is tied to tourism agencies, which theoretically bear responsibility for each of their clients, in actual fact these agencies are not authorized to register foreigners. The holder of the tourist visa is thus ordinarily forced to take care of his own registration. For standard states in which the tourist stays in a hotel, the problem solves itself, since the hotels are obligated to register tourists.[16] If a tourist wishes to follow a nonstandard program in Uzbekistan (by staying in the mountains, being unofficially invited to stay with a family, couchsurfing, cycling, etc.), he may not then theoretically demonstrate registration for the night's accommodation and may be fined at spot checks or upon leaving the country. For tourist visas, the tourist may not obtain registration from private persons.

---

[15]When the author of this text asked the OVIR office in Uzbekistan why tourists cannot stay with a host family, he received the terse reply "because tourists come here to stay in hotels."

[16]Some hotels are authorized and licensed to do this. Other, cheaper, hotels are unlicensed and do not have the option. In addition to leading to high regulation of hotel services in Uzbekistan, it also cuts available accommodation capacity in smaller towns lying off the beaten path.

In this case, the system ends up mandating that the tourist be included in the organized tourism category (including accommodation at a licensed facility) or risk problems with Uzbek authorities. In the past, registrations were a good source of business for hotels and their employees. It was those not at all unusual for tourists living in private apartments to be formally registered with hotels for a lesser fee. The Uzbek government has tried to bring some semblance of order to the system and Uzbek authorities have substantially strengthened controls on registration and tried to ensure that guests are actually staying in licensed facilities. But the result has been to increase complications for the individual tourist. Unofficial registrations have for the most part ceased to be issued, now limited only to a few small facilities, which tolerate similar practices.[17] In addition, a number of facilities have lost their attractiveness for tourists lacking complete registration for the entire period of their stay in Uzbekistan recently (particularly in Tashkent).[18]

The ambiguity and often contradictory nature of Uzbekistan's laws on tourist registration have led to a range of possible interpretations and, understandably, opened the door for corruption. Actions taken by the authorities to regulate the lowest levels of the tourism trade (hotels, etc.) may seem to have reduced corruption, but in reality, as with Tashkent, they have reinforced ties of corruption between selected local institutions and even selected individuals.

In Kazakhstan, citizens of most developed countries may obtain registration upon entry to the country at the international airport by getting stamps on their migration card (it must contain two stamps).[19] If for any reason a stamp is not obtained (particularly at overland border crossings), individual registration is necessary at a local visa and registration office within five days at the latest. This registration is then valid for the entirety

---

[17]In Tashkent in 2010, for example, there was one small hotel which accepted tourists without registration and was also willing to register tourists for a payment who did not actually intend to stay in the hotel. According to unofficial information, this hotel was in touch with OVIR, the local registration authority, whose head had good ties with the Ministry of Interior. If this otherwise unconfirmed information is indeed true (which is possible), the real face of the Uzbek system is showing through.

[18]Author's personal experience, 2010 and a number of discussions on tourist forums at Thorn Tree Lonely Planet (e. g. http://www.lonelyplanet.com/thorntree/thread.jspa?threadID=2029294).

[19]Rules of entry into Kazakhstan, stay and exit from Kazakhstan. Ministry of Foreign Affairs of Kazakhstan, http://portal.mfa.kz/portal/page/portal/mfa/ru/content/consular_info/foreigners. It is remarkable that the website of Kazakhstan's Ministry of Foreign Affairs does not include most countries of Central and Eastern Europe on its list. The websites of the Czech, Polish and Bulgarian Ministries of Foreign Affairs indicate the rule applies even to these countries (something confirmed by practice).

of Kazakhstan for the entire period of time the visa is valid. Travel agencies may arrange this registration for a fee, as well. The sense of this action is questionable, particularly when one remembers that Kazakhstan has increasingly opened itself to the world. But the country's strategy for foreign tourism shows that a comprehensive approach is lacking. Kazakhstan has eased its registration process but not enough, and clarification is still lacking.

By contrast Tajikistan and Kyrgyzstan are both countries, which completely did away with registration for short-term stays (up to 30 or 90 days, respectively). Kyrgyzstan had in fact already done so in the 1990s, when it officially ceased to require foreigners to register. But the country's public safety authorities determined that the absence of this registration could become an opportunity for corruption.[20] In 2002, therefore, Kyrgyzstan's Ministry of Foreign Affairs published information on its website concerning the cancellation of registration requirements.[21] Currently, this fact is generally accepted. In Tajikistan, tourists are allowed to stay up to 30 days with a tourist visa. It should be noted that this concerns tourist visas: private visas still require registration.

As is clear from the above overview, the registration of foreigners (like visa policy) reflects the general character of the bureaucracy and the existing regime, while the reasons behind the requirements and their implementation vary widely. In Turkmenistan, which is an example of a "hard regime," there is an attempt to gain total control over the populace, including foreign tourists, while in Uzbekistan, there is significant disparity in the way the regulations are interpreted, leading to the temptation for corrupt dealings between tourists and Uzbek authorities. By contrast, the softer regime of Kyrgyzstan does not require any further paperwork of tourists. But cancelation or weakening of the registration rules, as well as their enforcement, has been inconsistently carried out (except in Turkmenistan). From the standpoint of developing the tourist trade, it would therefore be advisable to completely do away with registration formalities. From the regime's viewpoint, this would be an understandable step. It therefore holds true that the greater attempt made by the regime to control activities within its borders, the greater the attempt will be to control foreigners and tourists, as well.

---

[20]Author's experience, 1999.

[21]Author's archive, the content of the website was later removed.

FURTHER BUREAUCRACY AND BARRIERS TO FOREIGN AND DOMESTIC TOURISM

But registration is not the only example of documentation, which makes traveling harder for foreign tourists. Also present are a number of further entry permissions to border zones where particular areas which, paradoxically, are often highly attractive for the country's tourism. The greatest paperwork demands in this regard are made by Tajikistan, which in other respects presents itself as opening to tourism. Mountain areas in the country are among the most attractive for tourism in the country. At the same time, these are areas in which most movement involves individual tourists. Any further bureaucracy significantly interferes with their movement. In 2005, fees for former permission to visit the mountains cost tens of dollars, with a per diem ecological tax of approximately 1 US dollar. The experience of tourist suggests that these fees have served partially to increase the profit of travel agencies, with only minimal impact on Tajikistan's state budget. A number of tourists came into Tajikistan's mountains without any travel agencies support. Checks on payment of fees were very restrictive and there was often no unified receipt to show payment of the fees in any event. Currently, the officially designated fee is 10 Tajiki somoni for entry to the national parks and protected areas. But there is often nowhere to pay these fees, which make them a target for corruption by some, often self-appointed, park rangers.

The last remaining bureaucratic barrier in Tajikistan is permission to enter the Badakhshan Autonomous Region. Although the logic of this remaining in place is based upon the presence of a border zone, it nevertheless represents one more unnecessary burden for travel into this otherwise very attractive area for tourism. The Badakhshan border regime remains in force as one of the last survivors of the Soviet system in Central Asia. It must also be stated that the existence or lack thereof of permission to stay in the Badakhshan has no effect on security problems in the area (narcotic trafficking, terrorism, etc.), which typically do not involve tourists. It only serves as another formality for tourists to arrange. On the other hand, requiring permits to visit Lake Sarez in the Badakhshan Mountains is entirely legitimate. In environmental and security terms, this is an area at relatively high risk.[22]

---

[22]The natural dam of Sarez Lake (the so-called Usojsky Mass) was created in the 1911 earthquake and its fracture (which could occur after another earthquake or in a terrorist attack) might herald catastrophe for the entire Central Asia region.

On the other hand, the Tajiki government has significantly simplified the issuance of this confirmation. Several years ago, two weeks were required, but today it can be issued within a single day in Dushanbe. Some Tajiki embassies will issue the permit at the same time as the visa.

Another problem is the inconsistent interpretation of regulations and their application in practice. A permit to visit Sarez Lake is required when going the usual route to see the dam. If an alternative route from the south is taken, the permit is unnecessary because there are no controls. Significant ambiguity arises regarding permits to visit Zorkul Lake in the border region along the Tajikistan-Afghanistan-China frontier, which is also the source of the Pyandzh-Amu Darya River. A permit is technically required, but in practice is not enforced.

It is evident that Tajikistan's tourism policy is tending in the direction of liberalization but certain elements of corruption continue to persist in practice even if only a small number of foreigners come into contact with it.

Other Central Asian countries have, thankfully, done away with restrictive measures. In the past, for example, Kyrgyzstan theoretically required a permit for entry to the border area in the south of the country (along the border with Tajikistan). In practice, this permit for moving in the area of the Kyrgyzstan-Tajikistan border was not required and free movement was possible through Alayska Basin, where a favored route to the Lenin Peak base camp is located.

The exception is Turkmenistan, which has preserved the permit requirement for border zones. This permit is ordinarily included as part of the package of services for the tourist visa. A problem may arise with transit visas, since the border zone also includes locations in the north of the country attractive for tourists. But if the transit visa shows the entry point or exit point within this region, the problem disappears. The Entry Travel Pass is a nonsensical document in its own way, one which tourists perceive from their guide at the country's border. This permit covers tourist travel and is also included in the price calculated by the institution issuing the invitation. Nevertheless it appears to simply double the visa. One possible reason for introducing this certificate is an attempt to avoid abuse of the visa process at Turkmenistan's embassies abroad.[23]

---

[23]This measure was introduced after the so-called assassination attempt on President Turkmenbashy in November, 2002, after which Turkmenistan's former ambassador to Turkey and others remained abroad as the opposition in exile. The stricter visa policy in Turkmenistan was dictated by the circumstances of this event.

In addition to a number of problems with documentation, tourists may also encounter problems in crossing the border itself. In the past, this has been one of the chief trials associated with traveling in Central Asia. In some extreme cases, it was even possible to cross the border illegally, without a visa, on the strength of a bribe.[24]

The low pay of officials at border stations, bureaucratic chaos and inadequate enforcement of mutually contradictory regulations has led to the authorities demanding bribes from tourists. The greatest degree of protection was afforded tourists coming from outside the CIS countries, for whom documentation was normally in order (or seemingly so). Tourists from the CIS countries, however, were often seen as "ours" and lacked the protection of Western consulates and possible diplomatic notes.

Airport border crossings, the usual gateway into Central Asia, are ordinarily problem-free. Nonstandard procedures on the part of border guards ordinarily equate to bribes being demanded from tourists. The most frequent location at which this takes place is customs control and is connected to customs declarations. The custom declaration, which is available in a number of locations only in local languages and Russian, may be a great aggravation for tourists who are not fluent in either language. And a potential source of misunderstanding occurs during the customs procedure.[25] Normally, however, a bribe will be requested during discussions with the customs official, particularly at smaller border crossings or places where corruption is an everyday part of life.[26] In spite of great progress in administering border crossings, the situation has changed only very slowly.

Chaotic organization at border crossings often acts as a stimulus for corruption. At one of the largest border crossings between Russia and Kazakhstan, at Petropavlovsk, it is first necessary to run to the train station for a migration card for entry to Kazakhstan. Only after having done so can one address the border guards. Because of the frequent border crossings, which take place at night, a number of people are unable to arrange

---

[24]In 2000, my colleagues got into Turkmenistan in a cargo train from Uzbekistan and back for a few dollars.

[25]The customs declaration also does not allow for money to be taken from an automatic teller, a problem chiefly with Uzbeck customs agents.

[26]In spite of the fact that the extent of corruption cannot be quantified, Zhibek Zholy remains one of the most problematic border crossings. Being located between Kazakhstan and Uzbekistan close to Tashkent, it also has the most traffic. Tourists may encounter efforts to find an excuse for asking for a bribe on both the Kazakh and Uzbek sides.

an entry stamp into the country and become easy victims for controls inside Kazakhstan.

Internal checks are another problem faced by Central Asian tourism. Because of the low pay of local officials, corruption and attempts to earn money off of foreign tourists are routinely practiced by police units in practically all Central Asian countries. These practices include demanding proof of identity from foreign tourists in the Tashkent Metro, at GAI posts (transport inspections), in trains (particularly in Kazakhstan) and other locations. Normally this is just a formality and militiamen are satisfied with checking documents and visas, but the reaction of militiamen is not always completely predictable. Document checks are, of course, not a bad thing but during the 1990s and later, for example, tourists were selectively targeted by militiamen and, under the ruse of control checks, taken to closed-off locations where their luggage, finances, etc. were gone through.[27] Although Uzbekistan, for example, has forgotten its militiamen to aggravate tourists in this fashion and demand bribes, problems of this type are eliminated only very slowly, and travelers' forums like Thorn Tree Lonely Planet are full of similar stories.

In some places the requirements imposed by police reach the point of absurdity. One example would be the permission required to photograph some modern memorials (which are in no way connected to the government or in any way sensitive). In the past, foreigners have traditionally been stopped at the Ismoil Somoni monument in Dushanbe (where even most locals have photographs taken). After photographing the monument, foreigners were asked to prove their identity and a demand was made for a permit allowing the monument to be photographed (which, of course, did not exist) and to be produced.[28] As a continuation of Soviet propaganda, tourists from countries lying outside the CIS could be considered spies, particularly if they know at least a little Russian or a little of the local language.

But even in this there has been significant apparent progress. There are fewer and fewer complaints on websites about police demanding bribes

---

[27]Especially famous for this was Bishkek, where the author and others encountered this detailed "control check."

[28]It was at this location that the author encountered one of the most absurd interpretations of the law. When we did not wish to divulge the address at which we were staying (in spite of being registered with the local travel agency which was theoretically the guarantor of our stay), we were informed that not knowing the address at which we were staying was subject to a significant fine, which might be reduced by making a payment on the side.

(Lonely Planet Thorn Tree, Travel Buddy, Trip Advisor, etc.). Uzbek police have issued an unofficial directive not to bother foreign tourists with valid visas. This has now gone so far that the majority of tourists leaving Uzbekistan do not have their registration checked at all. Of course the possibility that tourists may be bothered by local authorities is not completely ruled out, but the likelihood of it is getting smaller and smaller. This gives tourists from countries outside the CIS significant advantages over the locals, whose everyday reality is interwoven with encounters with corrupt local authorities.

In this, however, the rule involving the degree of hardness of the regime does not always apply. To the contrary: direct encounters with unpleasant police officers are much less likely in Turkmenistan. There are fewer tourists, who are thus more easily guarded by the secret police. In softer regimes like Kyrgyzstan's and Tajikistan's, by contrast, police exceed their powers more often. Weak working morale and the impossibility of calling on one's own embassy in traveling for illegal or semilegal work leads to much more widespread corruption in practice in border areas and at transport posts (Tajikistan: what about tourism? 2007). For the locals, border crossing represents a special issue, especially in places where two countries with poor mutual relationships are concerned (e.g., Turkmenistan/Uzbekistan, Tajikistan/Turkmenistan and others.) The isolated nature of individual countries and national/nationalistic propaganda lead to isolation between locals who until recent times had lived together in one village (Reeves, 2010). A feeling of alienation leads to several reactions on both sides of the border: closed borders and complicated crossings, and ever stronger feelings of alienation and nostalgia for the Soviet Union, resulting in reinforcement of the influence of those groups declaring for the elimination of these barriers. These include radical Islamic groups like Hizb-ut-Tahrir (Liberation Party) (Starr, 2011).

CONCLUSION

20 years after the breakup of the Soviet Union, the approach taken by Central Asian states the visa policy and other tourist documentation is as diverse as their political, economic and social development has been. The more open the economy (and, to some extent, the political system), the more open the country is about visas and other tourist documents. In the

case of Kyrgyzstan and Tajikistan, this is often the only possibility for making the country attractive to tourists. At the same time, however, both countries are among the most criticized in terms of corruption and nepotism, because of the absence of laws or the failure to enforce them.

Visa policy and services in the more isolated countries in the region primarily insist upon group tourism, which allows them greater control over the movement of tourists within the limits they desire, similar to what was the case during the Soviet era. Any individuals or small groups are discouraged by the high price associated with fixed costs for arranging visas (in Turkmenistan, a guide and other program costs, etc.). Key tourism segment in Central Asia – expedition and active tourism – is regulated by restrictions placed on free movement making them too highly overpriced. Travelers in this segment may also encounter other obstacles, particularly in the form of registrations and other paperwork.

It should be noted that bureaucratic requirements placed upon tourists from developed countries have begun to be simplified over the last decade. Further amelioration of visas and bureaucratic demands may certainly be expected. In some cases, this could lead to the complete removal of visas (as was the case of Kyrgyzstan in 2012) or their formalization (the cases of Tajikistan or Kazakhstan in some segments).

KEYWORDS

- Borders
- Central Asia
- Permits
- Registration
- Soviet Union
- Tourism
- Travel documentation
- Visas

REFERENCES

Hopkirk, P. (2001). *The Great Game. On Secret Service in Higher Asia*. Oxford, England: Oxford University Press.

Morier, J. (1895). *The Adventures of Hajji Baba of Ispahan*. London, England – New York, USA: Macmillan and Co.

Vámbery, Á (2010). *Travels in Central Asia*. London, England: J. Murray, 2010 (reprint).

Schuyler, E. (1877). *Turkistan: notes of a journey in Russian Turkistan, Kokand, Bukhara and Kuldja*. New York, USA.

Skrine, F. H. B. (1899). The heart of Asia: a history of Russian Turkestan and the Central Asian khanates from the earliest times. New York, USA: Methuen & Co.

Hedin, S. (1903). *In the Heart of Asia. Central Asia and Tibet : towards the Holy City of Lassa*. London, England: Hurst and Blackett.

Curtis, W. E. (1911). *Turkestan: the heart of Asia*. New York: Hodder & Stoughton.

O'Donovan, E. (1882). *The Merv Oasis: Travels and Adventures East of the Caspian during the Years 1879-80-81 Including Five Months' Residence Among the Tekks of Merv*. London, England: Smith, Elder & Co.

Curzon, G. N. (1889). Russia in Central Asia in 1889. London, England: Routledge.

Graham, S. (1916). *Through Russian Central Asia*. New-York, Toronto and Melbourne.

Fait, E. (1907). Národové středoasijští. Prague, Austro-Hungaria: Matice česká.

Olufsen (1911). *The emir of Bokhara and his country: journeys and studies in Bokhara (with a chapter on my voyage on the Amu Darya to Khiva)*. Stockholm, Sweden: Nordisk forlag.

Kabar.kg (2012). Kyrgyzstan introduced a visa-free regime for citizens of 44 countries up to 60 days. Kabar News Agency, July 24, 2012. http://www.kabar.kg/eng/politics/full/4828.

Hughes, L., Mikosz, D. (2006). *A Negro looks at Soviet Central Asia*. Bishkek, Kyrgyzstan: Al-Salam Printhouse

Kostiainen, Auvo (2002). The Soviet Tourist Industry as Seen by the Western Tourists of the Late Soviet Period. *XIII International Congress of Economic Historians*, Buenos Aires, July 22–26, 2002. Retrieved from http://users.utu.fi/aukosti/Soviet%20Tourism.html.

Janouch, F. (1966). *S občanským průkazem na střechu světa*. Prague, Czechoslovakia: Svět Sovětů.

Maťašák, M. (1981). *Vrcholy přátelství*. Prague, Czechoslovakia: Naše vojsko.

Maťašák, M. (1983). *Na streche sveta*. Bratislava, Czechoslovakia: Šport.

Maurer, E. (2006). Al'pinizm as Mass Sport and Elite Recreation. In A. E. Gorsuch, D. Koenker (Eds.), *Turizm: the Russian and East European Tourist under Capitalism and Socialism* (pp. 141–162), New York: Cornell University Press.

CHAPTER 11

TOURISM IN KYRGYZSTAN

PINAR AKÇALI

CONTENTS

INTRODUCTION

This chapter basically aims to describe the opportunities and obstacles within the tourism sector in post-Soviet Kyrgyzstan, within the framework of the basic economic and political challenges that the country faces in the independence era. The first part of the chapter is a brief introduction of Kyrgyzstan from geographical, economic and social perspectives, all of which either directly or indirectly affect the tourism sector in the country in the post-Soviet era. The second and third parts describe the opportunities and obstacles to the development of tourism in Kyrgyzstan, respectively. The conclusion focuses on the comparative advantage of the country for the development of tourism despite all odds, and briefly comments on the possible bright future of this sector.

Kyrgyzstan is a small Central Asian country which shares borders with the Sinkiang Uygur Autonomous Region of the People's Republic of China on the east, Tajikistan on the south and west, Uzbekistan on the west and Kazakhstan on the north. The capital city of the country is Bishkek (Frunze during the Soviet era). According to July 2012 estimates, the population of Kyrgyzstan is approximately 5.5 million in which the ethnic Kyrgyz composes 64.9%. However, the country has several minority groups as well: the Uzbeks compose 13.8%, Russians 12.5%, Dungans 1.1%, Ukrainians 1%, Uyghur 1%, and others 5.7% of the population.[1] The Kyrgyz are Turkic, speaking the Turkic dialect of Kipchak that belongs to the Altaic family of languages.

The ancestors of today's Kyrgyz were nomads who had migrated to these lands around the late 90s from Siberia (Roudnik, 2007). They used the pasturelands in the Western Tien Shan Mountains herding their horses and camels and traveling with their yurts (McMann, 2006). They would lead a very traditional life that revolved around "the seasons and animals" (Anderson, 1999). Even though by the late 15th century the Kyrgyz had formed a large tribal union that would not prevent them from being attacked by the Uzbeks and Kazakhs. They would eventually fall under the rule of the Russians, first as part of the Tsarist Empire in the 1860s (Roudnik, 2007), and then as part of the Soviet Union after the Bolshevik Revolution in 1917. The Kyrgyz nomads would settle in the late 1930s when the Soviet administration started to implement sedentarization policies.

---

[1]https://www.cia.gov/library/publications/the-world-factbook/geos/kg.html

However, not all Kyrgyz would adopt a settled and urban way of life. Even today some Kyrgyz continue to live as nomads (McMann, 2006).

In terms of topography, Kyrgyzstan is a very mountainous country, with "a few isolated lowlands" in the western and northern parts of the country.[2] Mountain ranges (especially the Pamir-Alai and Tien Shan) cover approximately 95% of the country's lands (Kort, 2004). Most of Kyrgyzstan lies more than 1,500 meters above the sea level,[3] the average elevation being 2,750 meters. A 40% of Kyrgyzstan are more than 3,000 meters above sea level (Kort, 2004). Due to this mountainous topography, there are several mountain streams and rivers in Kyrgyzstan that flow into and feed some 3,000 lakes of the country. Kyrgyzstan also has some of the world's largest glaciers, such as the Inylchek, Kainda, Semenov and Mushketov.[4]

Between these high mountains lie also some important valleys, such as the Chu, Kemin and Talas. However, the most important among these is the Fergana Valley that Kyrgyzstan shares with Tajikistan and Uzbekistan. The Mountain Rivers and streams flow into the valley, making it quite rich in terms of agricultural land and pastures. It is mostly in the Fergana Valley that the Kyrgyz produce cotton. In Chu, Kemin and Talas, animal husbandry is a major activity. In addition to this, tobacco and other agricultural products such as grain, fruits and vegetables are raised (Saray, 2004).

Kyrgyzstan has some light industry as well, mostly revolving around electrical devices and appliances, textile, shoes, refrigerators, canned food, wool and silk (Roudnik, 2007; Saray, 2004). These industries are mostly concentrated in the major cities of Bishkek, Osh and Tokmak. The country is not as rich as Kazakhstan, Uzbekistan and Turkmenistan. Together with Tajikistan, Kyrgyzstan has the smallest economy of the region, making it highly dependent on foreign help (Mahnovski, Akramov, and Karasik 2007, xv). The country has some deposits of mineral resources such as gold, mercury, uranium, antimony, zinc, tin, lead, coal, and tungsten, as well as small amounts of oil and natural gas (Kort, 2004; McMann, 2006; Özcan, 2010; Roudnik, 2007).

Kyrgyz industry would develop during the Soviet era when the Soviet administration started to make certain investments in Kyrgyzstan to

---

[2]*Kyrgyzstan: Then and Now.* 1993. USA: Lerner Publishing Company, Geography Department, 13.
[3]*Kyrgyzstan: Then and Now.* 1993. USA: Lerner Publishing Company, Geography Department, 12.
[4]*Kyrgyzstan: Then and Now.* 1993. USA: Lerner Publishing Company, Geography Department, 12, 17.

develop metal working and to exploit the mineral and energy resources there. The Soviets also developed the hydro-electric potential of the region by using the fast-flowing rivers of the country (Anderson, 1999). Despite these changes, the Kyrgyz mostly continued to live in rural areas, preserving their traditional values. Even during the Soviet era, "harshly imposed social reforms" (Öraz, 2006) could eradicate this structure. As such, one of the most visible characteristics of the Kyrgyz people would be kinship-based solidarity mechanisms in which "respect to the elders" is "one of the most fundamental principles of intergenerational interaction" (Beyer, 2010). These solidarity mechanisms would then be enlarged into clan-based or tribal loyalties and have a deep impact on the post-Soviet political processes and rivalries as well (Abdibaitova, 2009; Juraev, 2010).

In the post-Soviet era, all of these geographical and historical conditions influenced the development of tourism in the country. The next part will focus on the opportunities of Kyrgyzstan to have a vibrant and progressing tourism sector.

OPPORTUNITIES OF KYRGYZSTAN FOR DEVELOPING ITS TOURISM SECTOR

The tourism sector, being "the world's largest industry" according to some accounts (Kennedy and D'Arcy, 2009) is considered to have great potential for the economies of developing countries in a competitive and globalized world (Özdil and Yılmaz, 2008). According the W.T.O. (World Trade Organization), "tourism has every reason to become a major economic alternative for Central Asian countries."[5] This seems to be especially the case for Kyrgyzstan in which tourism is one of the fastest growing sectors (Boz, 2008). As indicated by Oktay (2011) "As a tourist destination, Kyrgyzstan can truly lay claim to the title of Pearl of Central Asia." Likewise, being a country of rare natural beauty, Kyrgyzstan has been referred as "the Switzerland of Asia" (Gleason, 2003). The country has an unspoiled and undiscovered nature (Capisani, 2000) with a clean air and relatively

---

[5]"According to the World Tourism Organization (WTO), Tourism has Every Reason to Become a Major Economic Alternative for Central Asian Countries," *Newspaper Source Plus*, M2PressWIRE, February 7, 2006, http://ehis.ebscohost.com/eds/detail?sid=c745fb73-aa04-45ba-afac-58f1333fd7fa%40sessionmgr12&vid=5&hid=116&bdata=JkF1dGhUeXBlPWlwJnNpdGU9ZWRzLWxpdmUm%3d#db=n5h&AN=16PU52217872 (accessed December 9, 2011).

unpolluted environment.[6] It has great biodiversity in terms of flora and fauna with its "extensive snow-capped mountains" (The World Bank, 1993) that contribute a lot to the image of the country. There are also many green forests and rivers as well as many highland lakes (Oktay 2011).

As elsewhere, in Kyrgyzstan too, tourism is considered to have great potential for poverty reduction and foster economic growth, as it creates opportunities for investments, jobs, and communal and regional development (Kennedy and D'Arcy, 2009). As such, the tourism sector also becomes crucial for the poor people by creating the conditions in which they can make a better life for themselves. Known as "pro-poor tourism" this sector may significantly help reduce poverty in the country (Özdil et al., 2008).[7]

Considering the geographic conditions of Kyrgyzstan, such a goal may be quite attainable, as it offers a rich variety of activities for tourists. The country is ideal for certain tourism activities such as canoeing, sailing, rafting, skiing, scuba diving as well as hunting, fishing, horseback riding and camping. In addition to these, it is also possible to be engaged in health tourism and ecotourism in Kyrgyzstan, a country with a warm climate and rich fauna and flora. Last, but not least, cultural tours (commonly known as the "Silk Road tours") are also highly demanded, as the country is located on this legendary route (Oktay, 2008; Werner, 2003).

As Seval et al. (2003) suggest, Kyrgyzstan can be divided into six different regions in terms of its tourism opportunities: Issyk-Kul, Chui, Osh, Talas, Naryn and Batken. Each of these regions has the potential to contribute to the development of the tourism sector in the country. The Issyk-Kul region takes its name from the Issyk-Kul, the world's second largest alpine lake at 1,608 meters high (Özcan, 2010). The lake, being 170 km long (Anderson, 1999), covers an area of 6,000 square km (Kort, 2004), and it is the deepest lake on earth with 695 meters (Balbay, 1999). According to the local legend, the lake extends to the center of the earth (Kort, 2004).

---

[6]However, uranium mining, a legacy of the Soviet Union, is one source of environmental pollution that affects regional rivers (Sievers 2003, 31). According to some accounts, "Kyrgyzstan is littered with 49 uranium dumps that hold 145 million tons of radioactive waste" (Kort 2004). As will be mentioned below, in the post-Soviet era, Lake Issyk-Kul was also faced with the challenge of pollution.

[7]This is one of the basic reasons why young people in Kyrgyzstan who are being educated in the field of tourism believe that their profession will be one of the most important ones for their country in the future (Batman and Oktay 2008, 108).

Issyk-Kul is a "wonder of nature" (Kantarcı, 2006) and sometimes called "the pearl of Central Asia" (Azizova, 2010). It has a very unique characteristic: although it lays at the top of a very high mountain with very low temperatures, it never freezes. This is mostly due to the hot springs flowing into the lake, making the water temperature always above zero. So the lake never freezes even in the winter, easing the temperature along its coasts (Capisani, 2000). There are also high levels of underground thermal activity in the region, warming the waters of Issyk-Kul (Kort, 2004). The lake is one of the most important tourist attractions in Kyrgyzstan. Along its shores, there is a particular location, Cholpan-Ata, known as the "Montreux" of the Issyk-Kul (Capisani, 2000). Cholpan-Ata is the most famous place along the Issyk-Kyl, offering opportunities for climbing, skiing and swimming. There are several summer resorts and health spas as well as many rocky terrains to attract tourists here (Balbay, 1999; Capisani, 2000). The town of Karakol is another important location along the banks of the Issyk-Kul, becoming more important with its newly opened ski resorts, national park and developing nature tourism (Werner 2003).

One unfortunate incident that negatively affected Issyk-Kul's post-Soviet prospects was the accident in which trucks of the Canadian-Kyrgyz joint venture operating the Kumtor goldmine crashed and dumped highly poisonous cyanide that they were carrying to the rivers flowing into the lake (Kort, 2004; Sievers, 2003; The World Bank, 2001). As a result of the accident, there was some ecological damage to Issyk-Kul and fish, birds and other small animals ended up dead (Balbay, 1999).

The Chui region, where Bishkek is located, is excellent in terms of eco and mountain tourisms as well as rafting within the boundaries of Ala-Archa National Park. The park is also used for daily picnics. One of the most important historical artifacts in the country, the Burana Minaret (or Burana Tower) is also in Chui.

The Osh region takes its name from the ancient city of Osh, which comes second after Bishkek in terms of its population. The city lies across the banks of the Ak-Buura ("White Camel") River and at the footsteps of the Pamir-Alai Mountains (Özcan, 2010).[8] As such, Osh also offers opportunities for winter sports and mountain tourism. Furthermore, the Kara-Koi Valley, with its clean air, is a convenient location for health tourism (Seval et al., 2003). However, Osh is also important for historical reasons.

---

[8]*Kyrgyzstan: Then and Now*. 1993. USA: Lerner Publishing Company, Geography Department, 19.

It is the oldest urban settlement in Kyrgyzstan, dating back to the third century B.C. The local people claim the city to be older than Rome. Historically, Osh was one of the most important commercial centers on the Silk Road (Özcan, 2010). Osh is also famous as one of the most important centers of Sufism in Central Asia and is known for centuries as the "Second Mecca," attracting many Muslim pilgrims who wanted to see the city's holy places such as Solomon's Throne (Capisani 2000). One other such attractive place in Osh is the Arslanbob site. Believed to be a servant of Prophet Muhammad, Arslanbob came to Osh upon the request of the Prophet himself to find the most beautiful place on earth. Upon his arrival, Arslanbob saw that there were beautiful waterfalls but no trees in the valleys of Osh. Upon hearing this, the Prophet sent a bag of seeds and nuts, which Arslanbob scattered throughout the vast valleys, beautifying them as they are today (Özcan, 2010).

The Talas region is rich in terms of rivers that account for more than 250 in number. However, what makes Talas more interesting in cultural and historical terms is the Manas Museum and Manas Dome. Talas is the region in which most of the events described in the Manas story took place (Seval et al., 2003). Being the "legendary home of the epic hero Manas" this region enjoys a growing reputation (Anderson, 1999). In 1995, UNESCO sponsored a three-day festival that celebrated the 1,000th anniversary of the Manas epic poem, the origins of which go back to the ninth century (Kort, 2004). Describing the strength, bravery, virtue as well as military skills of Manas, the epic is considered to be a folk story of the national history of Kyrgyzstan. As put forward by a Kyrgyz diplomat in Bishkek, "This legend will continue to be recited until the last Kyrgyz on earth perishes" (Balbay, 1999).

The Naryn region is renowned for its valleys, caves, the Naryn River and Lake Song-Kul that are suitable for a variety of sportive activities such as horse riding, trekking, outdoor activities and rafting. This region is also known by its beautiful alpine lake, the Chatyr-Kul (Seval et al., 2003).

Finally, Batken is famous for the Aygul, a kind of rose that can only be found in Afghanistan and Batken in the world (Seval et al., 2003). The Aksu Valley, which is known as the "Patagonia of Central Asia," also offers great opportunities for rock climbers (Dlugy, 1999). A huge Manas sculpture located here is another tourist attraction.

Such advantages that these regions offered acquired a new meaning in the post-Soviet era. Soon after independence, the Kyrgyz government, acknowledged the potential of and the need for tourism in the country, as it had "few other alternatives for development" (Werner, 2003). For President Askar Akaev, it was detrimental to realize the importance of tourism as one of the most critical sectors to contribute to the development of the country (Seval et al., 2003). Certain policies and programs to improve tourism in Kyrgyzstan began as early as 1994 (Boz, 2008). Starting with 2000s, however, the Kyrgyz government started to take some important steps to reduce restrictions on travel and encourage local entrepreneurs to be actively involved in developing tourism (Werner, 2003). The year 2001 was declared as the "Year of Tourism" indicating the political will and commitment to develop the country's tourism potential (Azizova, 2010). A year later, upon the initiative of President Akaev, the United Nations declared 2002 as the "International Mountain Year," a big advantage for the mountainous country.

During the 2000s, Kyrgyzstan started to regularly attend international tourism conferences such as International Tourism Exchange Berlin (Werner, 2003) and further learn how to develop an organizational infrastructure both at the state and civil society levels. In this context, the country encouraged its citizens to get involved in developing this sector. As such, official bodies like the State Committee of Tourism, Sport and Youth (the basic responsible organ for tourism) as well as the Issyk-Kul Agency for Tourism became more active (Seval et al., 2003). In addition to these state agencies, unofficial organizations such as the Kyrgyzstan Tour Operations Association and the Silk Road Tour Operators Association emerged as other influential agencies (Werner, 2003).

During the 2000s, the government also started to cooperate more with international companies as well as investors. For example, in the year 2005 together with the Norwegian Trekking Association (Den Norske Turistforening, DNT), the Trekking Union of Kyrgyzstan was established in 2000.[9] However, the most successful attempt in that sense was the Community Based Tourism (CBT) project, the aim of which was to provide benefits to the local population, especially the economically disadvantaged people from rural communities (Boz, 2008). In the year 2000, the Swiss Association for International Cooperation (Helvetas) set up a CBT network in Kyrgyzstan. Over the course of years, the project would become quite successful with a relatively small budget and few international consultants. Ten towns and villages across the country were identified in

---

[9]http://www.tuk.kg/index.php?lang=english (accessed 29 February 2012).

addition to the central office in Bishkek. In these places, local families would run their guest houses for tourists, making modest but steady contributions to the family income (Özcan, 2010).

In the year 2003, the Kyrgyz Community Based Tourism Association (KCBTA) "Hospitality Kyrgyzstan" was created as an umbrella organization in order to "improve living conditions in remote mountain regions by developing a sustainable and wholesome ecotourism model that uses local natural and recreational resources."[10] The overall goal of the program is defined as follows: "Community driven development initiated by communities contributes to diversification of local economies in the selected regions (of the Kyrgyz Republic) through poverty alleviation, enhanced access to assets, strengthening and empowerment of civil society and social partnership."[11]

In addition to such projects, in some rather interesting cases, the authorities designed certain ideas to attract tourists to the country such as the "International Winter Festival of Santa Claus and His Friends" which was first organized in 2008 (Tokbaeva, 2009). The reason why "a predominantly Muslim and former communist republic [is] honoring the jolly old elf" was simply the desire to develop the tourism industry of the country.[12] So, Santa ("Ayaz Ata" or Grandpa Frost) was seen as a good way to do that (Tokbaeva, 2009).

These policies have actually contributed to the development of the tourism sector in Kyrgyzstan. More and more people are visiting the country on a yearly basis and the share of tourism in the G.D.P. (Gross Domestic Product) of the country is also increasing (Boz, 2003; Duran, 2002; Werner, 2003). Furthermore, the country has become more of a center of interest for some tour operators in some European countries such as Switzerland, Italy and France (Capisani, 2000). However, as is explained in the next part of the study, the country also faces several obstacles for further improvements.

---

[10]Kyrgyz Community Based Tourism Association Yearly Report. 2006. Bishkek, 6.

[11]Kyrgyz Community Based Tourism Association Yearly Report. 2006. Bishkek 8.

[12]"Mount Santa' to Join Lenin, Yeltsin Among Peaks in Central Asia's Kyrgyzstan," The Canadian Press, December 20, 2007, http://ehis.ebscohost.com/eds/detail?sid=c745fb73-aa04-45ba-afac-58f13 33fd7fa%40sessionmgr12&vid=5&hid=116&bdata=JkF1dGhUeXBlPWlwJnNpdGU9ZWRzLWxpcmd mU%3d#db=n5h&AN=MYO142215254807 (accessed December 9, 2011).

OBSTACLES OF KYRGYZSTAN FOR DEVELOPING ITS TOURISM SECTOR

Despite the fact that Kyrgyzstan has several advantages for developing tourism, there are certain obstacles that limit the country's potential. In this part, these obstacles will be analyzed under four headings: 1) the Soviet legacy, 2) economic problems, 3) political problems, and 4) legal problems. All three are in fact closely related and sometimes influence each other.

THE SOVIET LEGACY

One basic challenge that Kyrgyzstan has to face is related to the general perception of the tourism sector in the former Soviet Union. One of the basic characteristics of the Soviet era tourism was heavy state control over the tourism sector (Özcan, 2010). There was no real mechanism for private initiatives, as the system was not working on the principle of profit-making (Yılmaz et al., 2008). Central agencies of the Soviet state, such as the Central Council for the Administration of Health Resources, the Central Council for Tourism and Excursions, and the Central Children's Excursion and Tourism Station, were responsible for managing tourism activities (Özcan, 2011). Furthermore, tourism was basically seen as an activity related to health: "the workers of the country had a right to leisure and good health that would stimulate high achievements" (Özcan, 2010). As for Central Asia, the region was officially opened for foreign tourism only in the early 1970s for sightseeing, cultural tourism, health travel, and sports (Özcan, 2010). However, foreign tourists, especially the ones from capitalist countries were strictly controlled upon their arrival. As Werner (2003) suggests: "Generally tourists who visited Central Asia did so on a comprehensive tour of the Soviet Union, rather than a specific tour of Central Asia" with the exception of Uzbekistan, "the crown jewel" having within its borders the historical sites of Samarkand, Bukhara and Khiva.

Although tourism in Kyrgyzstan is neither new nor unprecedented, the Soviet rule had "created artificial tourism trading conditions within Kyrgyzstan" (Palmer 2007, 651). The post-Soviet era conditions, however, would bring a totally different perspective to tourism activities in the republic. As was the case in all of the other Central Asian republics, in Kyrgyzstan too, the sector would be negatively affected by the worsening economic conditions and decreased incomes created by the dissolution of the Soviet Union (Özcan, 2010). As Kantarcı (2007b) emphasized, Central Asian republics, including Kyrgyzstan, "had to adjust to shift in tourism flows. In spite of their tourism structure and their previous links to the communist system, after the collapse of the Soviet Union, these countries could not adapt to the changes in the fast pace of the global tourism market."

In this context, one of the most important consequences of the Soviet legacy is seen in the field of tourism-promoting and image-building activities that are the basic prerequisites of introducing Kyrgyzstan to the outside world. Despite the fact that the country has considerable tourism potential, it is not represented well neither academically (in the tourism literature) nor in the world tourism sector market. As Kantarcı (2007b) suggests, Central Asian countries, including Kyrgyzstan, "have done little to determine their image as a tourist destination. ... [They] have little knowledge, if any at all, about the effect [the] travelers' perceptions have on the selection of a tourist destination. ... [These] countries are weak and lack of knowledge and skills to effectively develop and manage tourism facilities and tourism." The fact that advertising activities are very weak in the country is a major obstacle for the development of tourism (Azizova, 2010). Advertising activities become much more important when the already existing negative image that the country suffers from is taken into account. As will be explained below, Kyrgyzstan is sometimes associated with conflicts, radical Islam and instability, and put into the same category with countries such as Afghanistan and Pakistan. It has also been pointed out that in some cases, "potential clients" may even "confuse Kyrgyzstan with Kurdistan" (Werner, 2003).

One other important issue that needs to be taken into account is the Soviet legacy of "state monopoly in provision of transport services" (Muhambetov, 2003). As there were no commercial considerations in the operations of transportation facilities, the government would subsidize these services and connect Central Asian republics to each other in a centralized manner (Muhambetov, 2003). As such, being one of the neighboring republics of Uzbekistan during the Soviet era, in some cases, airline and railroad travel have to be done via Uzbekistan, making Kyrgyzstan even farther away and isolated (Anderson, 1999). A related problem is the poor and inadequate infrastructure that the country suffers from, especially in terms of transportation facilities, another basic requirement for the development of the tourism potential. Airline travel is still under modern standards and the airports are insufficient (Capisani 2000). Likewise, roads are also of poor quality and inadequate (Azizova, 2010). This "weak transportation infrastructure" (Mahnovsi et al., 2007) is partly due to the mountainous terrain that limits and sometimes hinders both domestic and international travel (Capisani, 2000; The World Bank, 2005). For example, in Issyk-Kul, one of the most important tourist attractions in Kyrgyzstan, there is only one "dilapidated paved road" and no functional airports (Oktay, 2011). Likewise, in Cholpan-Ata, due to lack of fuel, the airport is often closed (Capisani, 2000).

Another important problem that the country took over as part of the Soviet legacy is the poor quality of accommodation facilities (Oktay, 2011). Hotels and guest houses are not comfortable and suitable enough when compared with international standards (Capisani, 2000; Dlugy, 1999). Furthermore, they are also not of sufficient quantity in case there is an intensive tourism demand for the country (Kızılırmak and Oktay, 2008).

One other related problem is the level and quality of services that are below modern standards. Despite the fact that many Western tourists have mentioned the Kyrgyz being "friendliest people they've run into" and the "warmth of the welcome" they have encountered there (Dlugy, 1999), most of the services in the guest houses and hotels are well behind in meeting their expectations (Azizova, 2010; Oktay, 2011). The people serving in these facilities generally lack professional knowledge and skills, as well as the mastery of foreign languages (Seval et al., 2003).

One final issue that needs to be taken into account is how the Soviet legacy still has a deep impact on the general framework in which the civil society institutions, which can be seen as one of the main actors to contribute to the development of the tourism sector, function in Kyrgyzstan. These institutions, even when they get their funding and advice from the Western countries, still seek assistance from the state. The government, however, "neither interferes with their activities nor provides support for them" (McMann, 2004). The civic sphere is, to a large extent, working under the Soviet economic legacies of "party-state ownership of municipal buildings and minimal production of consumer goods" which in turn forces the civic activists in the country "to seek office space, facilities, free utilities and transportation from local authorities" (McMann, 2004). This rather peculiar understanding of civil society in the country is another characteristic that has to be considered in terms of developing the tourism sector in the country.

THE ECONOMIC PROBLEMS

In addition to and in close relation with the problems that stem from the Soviet legacy, certain economic developments of the post-Soviet era also limit the country's potential for developing its tourism sector. At the time of independence, Kyrgyzstan was "confronted by highly adverse circumstances in which to initiate the transition to a market economy" (The World Bank, 1993). Its options were quite limited, taking into account the geographic and economic conditions of the country. Being a tiny, landlocked, mountainous and isolated country with little resource potential other than water, gold and natural beauty, the country had to establish as many diplomatic ties with the outside world as possible (Pomfret, 2006; Capisani, 2000). It was hoped that "a rapid adoption of market reforms [and] the welcoming of foreign investors with open arms ... would give the country a pivotal role in a region wary of reform" (Anderson, 1999). Being one of the poorest republics of the former Soviet Union with a highly dependent and specialized economy, independent Kyrgyzstan found no other option than getting as much international assistance as possible (Özcan, 2010). As Askar Akaev put in December 1991, the country's future depended on "the development of private interest, private life, and private property" (Kort 2004, 159). Therefore, despite the fact that tourism was considered to be an important sector that would develop the Kyrgyz economy, it was not the number one priority from the perspective of the governments. Gas industry, electricity sector, aviation, urban transport, telecommunications, water management, agriculture, mining and metallurgical sectors occupied the major place when it came to economic policies. At best, tourism was just one "source of potential growth" (The World Bank, 1993) for the Kyrgyz economy among many others.[13] When combined with the economic problems that are analyzed below, such an attitude would be another obstacle for the development of tourism.

---

[13]For the importance and priority given to other sectors, see The World Bank (1993, 123-148) and The World Bank (2001).

In the first couple of years after independence, Kyrgyzstan seemed to have a good potential for economic development (The World Bank, 1993). Akaev was quite enthusiastic about the reform process himself, promising to make his country "the Switzerland of Central Asia" with its beautiful mountains and future goal of becoming a financial center and a transport hub (Olcott, 2005). Akaev's reforms began as early as January 1992 with price liberalization (Kort, 2004) as a result of which all prices would be liberalized by 1994 (Anderson and Pomfret, 2003). Kyrgyzstan was also successful in curbing hyperinflation and bringing the annual inflation rate below 50% by 1995 (Anderson and Pomfret, 2003). A 85% of 4,700 state enterprises were privatized between 1991 and 1994 (Anderson and Pomfret, 2003). The country became a member of the World Bank on 18 September 1992 (The World Bank, 1993) and was the first post-Soviet republic to introduce its own convertible currency, the som, to replace the ruble (Anderson, 1999; Capisani, 2000). Likewise, Kyrgyzstan was the first country to be a member of the World Trade Organization (W.T.O.) in 1998. It seemed as if the country would succeed in adopting a liberal trade and investment policy as "the most dynamic reformer" of the Soviet successor states (Anderson and Pomfret, 2003). Kyrgyzstan was also heavily supported by Western countries and international financial institutions such as the World Bank and the IMF.[14] Some international firms preferred Kyrgyzstan for their investments, such as the Canadian-run Cameco Company that became interested in the Kumtor gold mine as early as 1992.[15]

Despite the fact that these reforms were initially successful in terms of GDP growth, increased investments, and successful fiscal adjustments (The World Bank, 2001), "the outcome during the first decade has been at best mixed" (Anderson and Pomfret, 2003). As some reports indicated (The World Bank, 2005), "Favorable national circumstances, such as supportive macroeconomic conditions, friendly investment climates and market-expanding trade agreements, contribute to competitiveness, but they do not guarantee success." In time, the country started to have serious economic, political and social problems stemming mostly from the failed economic reforms. At the end of the first decade of independence, Kyrgyzstan had 1.7 million dollars debt, approximately 130% of its GDP

---

[14]For a detailed analysis of economy in the first couple of years in Kyrgyzstan, see The World Bank (1993).

[15]This joint venture provides a significant part of the country's GDP and is one of the most successful enterprises in Kyrgyzstan (Mahnovski, Akramov, and Karasik 2007; Özcan 2010; Pomfret 2006).

(Anderson and Pomfret, 2003). Between 1991 and 1995, output fell by 50%, triggering a loss of tax revenues amounting up to 7.5% of the GDP (The World Bank, 2001). The real GDP decline for the same period was about 45% (Anderson and Pomfret, 2003). Agricultural production fell by around one-third and industrial production by two-thirds (Anderson, 1999). In early 1990s, levels of inflation were very high: 200% in 1991, 900% in 1992 (Anderson, 1999) and 1,300% in 1993 (Anderson, 1999). Although between 1995 and 1997 there was about 15% economic growth rate, that growth was mostly due to the Kumtor goldmine project. Furthermore, the 1998 economic crisis in Russia as well as poor agricultural performance in that year once again slowed down the economic growth (Anderson and Pomfret, 2003).

These economic problems resulted in a sharp decline in the living standards of a majority of the people in Kyrgyzstan most of whom had already been lacking modern conveniences, living in rural areas and being employed in agriculture (McMann, 2006). Due to the fact that health care, education, and social welfare networks organized by the Soviet state were also no longer provided, increasing numbers of people started to live below the poverty line (Kort, 2004). In addition, economic inequality also increased (Anderson and Pomfret, 2003). A small class of new rich "whose lifestyle contrast[ed] sharply with that of substantial sections of the population" emerged in major cities (Anderson, 1999). This "sharp socioeconomic stratification" (Kuehnast and Dudwick, 2004) shrank the informal social networks which had always functioned as the "safety nets" for the people, making the poor even more desperate and dependent on the non-poor.[16] Shortly after independence, poverty alleviation would become one of the highest priorities of the Kyrgyz government (Kasybekov, 1999).[17]

Furthermore, it must also be kept in mind that nepotism and clientalism are very much ubiquitous in Kyrgyzstan, where personal contacts play a major role in social, economic, and political matters (Demirel and Seçkin, 2009). This resulted in increased levels of corruption in the post-Soviet era (Pomfret, 2006). During the first decade of independence, there were many scandals in which politically powerful people bought state enterprises "at absurdly low prices" such as a silk factory in Osh that was sold

---

[16]For a detailed analysis of how the poor is negatively affected see Kuehnast and Dudwick (2004).
[17]For a detailed analysis of poverty in Kyrgyzstan, see Ackland and Falkingham (1997).

for only 2% of its real value (Kort, 2004). Kupatadze (2010) further mentions of a mechanism of "collaboration between politicians and criminals based on an exchange of various favors" that complicated things further. As such, anticorruption efforts rarely work and organized crime is on the rise (Marat, 2010). This is considered to be one of the major reasons why the original foreign aid and debt relief were sometimes withheld. It was suggested that loans given for the development of certain industries or sectors sometimes disappeared and that in certain cases it was actually the political elites who "siphoned off" them into their own personal accounts (Djoroev, 2003).[18]

Corruption has also been a major problem in Kyrgyzstan's hydropower endowments which had already been suffering from problems of accessibility and reliability of supply due to "the lack of a coherent energy policy and poor management" (The World Bank, 2005). According to certain reports, in early 2000s, there was a deeper crisis in Kyrgyzstan's hydro-energy sector, this time mostly due to "large-scale corruption in the energy sector that benefit[ed] only the few among the ruling elites, but caus[ing] the destruction of the sector at large" (Marat, 2010). When President Bakiev privatized KyrgyzGaz, the major hydro-energy site in the country without any public discussion on the parliamentary scrutiny, most people believe that "the primary beneficiaries would be the same officials, not the national economy" (Marat, 2010).

One final point that needs to be taken into account is about the intensive out-migration from Kyrgyzstan, mostly due to the economic problems such as poverty, low living standards and unemployment (Edilova and Zhetibaeva, 2008). Some experts suggest that today, "the problem of migration is one of the most significant issues in Kyrgyzstan" (Dzhumaeva, 2008). As of early 2000s, about 11.3% of Kyrgyzstan's working population was outside their country providing about 10% of the GDP (Mahnovski et al., 2007). By then, it had already become "a mass phenomenon" for the young people between the ages of 18–35 as well as low-skilled migrants from the rural southern provinces (Tajibaeva, 2008). Some experts suggest that in about 15–20 years the country "will face a situation in which the most basic qualified labor needed to drive national economy" (Dzhumaeva, 2008).

---

[18]This may have a direct impact on the tourism sector as well. According to a former analyst with the SNB (Kyrgyz National Security Service), the structure officially in charge of fighting human trafficking would most probably sell protection to legal tourist companies unofficially engaged in human smuggling (Kupatadze, 2010, 65).

To conclude, it is possible to suggest that being very much a part of the economy of Kyrgyzstan, the tourism sector was also negatively affected by the ups and downs of the economic conditions that considerably exacerbate economic corruption. Increasing corruption is considered to be another major problem that hinders the development of tourism (Oktay, 2011). There are some reported cases of corruption in the field of tourism, such as the Ak Keme (White Boat) Hotel that took its name from the famous novel of Chinghiz Aitmatov. The hotel, built by a Turkish firm as a joint partnership between Kyrgyzstan and Turkey, soon became very popular with a rate of occupancy of at least 75%. However, soon, some mafia groups (among whom, allegedly were top Kyrgyz officials from the intelligence service of the country as well as some ministers) started to threaten the Turkish managers of the hotel to demand a share from the profits. Eventually these managers were deactivated and the new partners of the hotel were determined by the mafia groups (Balbay, 1999).

THE POLITICAL PROBLEMS

Political problems also sometimes have a negative impact on the potential of Kyrgyzstan to develop its tourism sector, despite the fact that in early 1990s, Kyrgyzstan seemed to be different than other Central Asian countries in terms of its commitment to democracy. Askar Akaev, who was elected to the newly created post of presidency by the deputies of the Supreme Soviet on 28 October 1990, soon would be renowned for his commitment to liberal democracy and market economy calling his country "an oasis of democracy" and "an island in the midst of a tempest, which could, however, be suppressed by high seas" (Capisani, 2000). Akaev was quick to realize several elections and referendums for democratic transition, and in the early years of independence Kyrgyzstan was far ahead of other Central Asian countries in terms of basic freedoms such as freedom of speech, freedom of the press and freedom of association. The judiciary was also more independent and the legislature more representative. Akaev was quick in realizing many legal reforms to guarantee the protection of property rights too (Roudnik, 2007).[19] However, in time he shifted to more authoritarian policies and started to concentrate more and

---

[19]For a detailed analysis of some of the major political events in the first decade of Kyrgyzstan's independence, see Anderson (1999).

more power in his hands albeit via seemingly democratic methods, such as referendums for constitutional amendments, to increase presidential powers. The resentment created by this change of attitude would culminate in March 2002, when an influential parliamentary deputy from the southern town of Aksy, Azimbek Beknazarov, was prosecuted as a result of a political dispute with Akaev over a border agreement with China. The police opened fire against the demonstrators in Aksy protesting the prosecution, killing five people (Lewis, 2010). The shootings caused greater resentment among the people, resulting in further protests and demonstrations in other parts of the country. Although eventually Beknazarov was released and the government resigned after a series of investigations, "the crisis had demonstrated the weakness of the regime and emboldened opposition to Akaev" (Lewis, 2010).

The fall of Akaev, however, would take place after the fraudulent 2005 parliamentary elections. People started protesting the results of the elections and eventually forced Akaev to step down and be replaced by Kurmanbek Bakiev, a leadership change referred as the "Tulip Revolution."[20] However, despite his initial popular support, Bakiev was also forced to leave power as a result of another popular uprising in 2010. During Bakiev's five years of rule, political, economic, and social problems of the country deepened and the unfulfilled expectations of the people created even more reaction. Bakiev was ousted in June 2010 to be replaced by the interim president Rosa Otunbayeva.[21] The fall of the two presidents by popular uprisings in just five years caused great concerns about political stability of the country, a major impediment to tourist inflows.

One other important factor that contributed to political problems in Kyrgyzstan was the regional attachments among the people, commonly known as the north-south divide, which, historically and geographically speaking is the result of the mountainous terrain. The country is naturally divided by the high mountains into two having a direct impact on how the northern and southern regions developed culturally, traditionally and economically (Sarı, 2010). The north has a more advanced economy, a highly Russified population with a more secular and cosmopolitan outlook. The south, on the other hand, is economically backward with high levels of

---

[20]For a detailed analysis of the impact of March 2005 elections on the Tulip Revolution, see Kulov (2010) and for a detailed analysis of the Tulip Revolution in general, see Cummings (2010).

[21]For a detailed analysis of events that took place prior to the fall of Bakiev see Sarı (2010).

unemployment as well as narcotics trafficking. The radical Islamic groups concentrate their activities in the south as well (Kort, 2004; Sarı, 2010). This division is reflected in the political arena too: northern and southern elites compete with each other in order to have access to resources and political positions (Lewis, 2010). The elites from the north and the south have been acting differently since 1991, based on their regional interests (Luong, 2002). This has been given as one of the main reasons behind Akaev's and Bakiev's fall (Ryabkov, 2010).

Another important problem is related to the ethnic tensions and bloody ethnic conflicts in Kyrgyzstan, some of which took place even during the Soviet era despite the fact that centralized state power at the hands of Moscow would prevent most ethnic tensions to escalate into full-fledged violence. The Osh conflict between the Kyrgyz and the Uzbeks in June 1990, however, was an exception, as it was "one of the largest and most violent riot-type conflicts on the territory of the former USSR" (Roudnik, 2007).

The Osh conflict had both economic and political reasons. The Kyrgyz in Osh resented the Uzbeks who lived in relative wealth and controlled about 80% of the city's trade (Huskey, 1993). They believed that the Uzbeks were taking "all of the best jobs in the retail and consumer sector" (Anderson, 1999). A severe shortage of land in Osh also contributed to the rise of tensions between the two groups. The city is "squeezed between mountains" and the available land that can be used for agricultural, industrial and housing purposes "have been in a perpetual zero-sum deadlock" (Liu, 2007). The Uzbeks in the city, on the other hand, felt that they were underrepresented in the local governmental institutions in Osh, despite the fact that demographically and economically they were the dominant group (Huskey, 1993; Kort, 2004). The Uzbeks also resented the rejection of their demand about their language to be given the same official status alongside Kyrgyz and Russian in Osh and Jalalabad (Anderson, 1999).

The event, which triggered the conflict, was the decision of the local authorities to allocate some land from an Uzbek collective farm to the Kyrgyz rural migrant families in Osh to be used for housing purposes (Anderson, 1999; Liu, 2007). The Uzbeks in the city severely opposed this decision and called for "the incorporation of predominantly Uzbek territories [in Kyrgyzstan] into Uzbekistan" (Anderson, 1999). The tensions would soon escalate into violent clashes that lasted for about a week. The riots could be stopped by the troops of the Interior Ministry and the Soviet Army (Anderson, 1999). During the conflict, 120 Uzbek, 50 Kyrgyz and one Russian were killed and over 5,000 crimes including rape, assault, and burning of houses were committed (Roudnik, 2007).

The Osh conflict would leave behind "a legacy of tension between the Kyrgyz and Uzbek communities" in Kyrgyzstan (Anderson, 1999) that has an impact on the post-Soviet era as well. When combined with some other negative factors such as unbalanced income distribution, unemployment, regional inequalities and public riots that ousted two leaders in 2005 and 2012, this legacy further increased tensions in the country (Sarı, 2010). The second bloody ethnic conflict between the Kyrgyz and the Uzbek took place in April 2010 in Osh and Jalalabad, which started soon after Bakiev's fall from power. These clashes that took place between the Kyrgyz and Uzbeks in the cities of Osh and Jalalabad started on the night of June 10th in a casino in Osh. An argument between the Kyrgyz and Uzbek youth gangs was "spilled out onto the street," then quickly spreading to other parts of the city as well as to Jalalabad.[22] When the events were finally taken under control, there were 400 dead and 2000 wounded people from both sides.[23] Although there are different and conflicting accounts of what really happened that night and who were behind these events, one thing remains certain: the clash indicated how small incidents could turn into full-fledged ethnic violence in the region.[24]

One other important issue is the potential threat of infiltration of radical Islamic groups from the Kyrgyz-Uzbek border. In fact in 1999, the militants of the I.M.U. (Islamic Movement of Uzbekistan) would pose such a threat, especially when they killed 18 Kyrgyz soldiers and took four American tourists, four Japanese geologists, and some Kyrgyz police officers hostage (Kort, 2004). The raids continued throughout the first half of 2000 and when the Kyrgyz troops failed to stop the IMU guerillas who had infiltrated into the Batken region of Kyrgyzstan, the Kyrgyz government had to ask for help from other regional countries to stop the raids. It

---

[22]"Deadly Clashes in Kyrgyzstan's Southern City of Osh," http://www.bbc.co.uk/news/10290717 (accessed February 7, 2012).

[23]"Kyrgyz Speaker Proposes Admitting Head of International Commission Probing June 2010 Clashes" Interfax, Russia & FSU General News, http://ehis.ebscohost.com/eds/detail?sid=683dd724-8e36-41c0-8676-a18c66b22e65%40sessionmgr12&vid=5&hid=2&bdata=JnNpdGU9ZWRzLWxpdmU%3d#db=n5h&AN=62173826 (accessed February7, 2012).

[24]For more information on the subject, see, Bruce Pannier "Audio menu Internet TV Kyrgyzstan: Anatomy of A Conflict," 2 Temmuz 2010, http://www.rferl.org/content/Kyrgyzstan_Anatomy_Of_A_Conflict/2089464.html (accessed February 7, 2012); "War in Kyrgyzstan: What is Causing the Violence?." http://www.guardian.co.uk/world/2010/jun/14/kyrgyzstan-conflict-background (accessed, February 13, 2012).

has been suggested that this failure would negatively affect the country's image as a weak state that cannot even protect its own borders and turn into one of the major reasons behind Akaev's eventual fall (Sarı, 2010).

Such incidents, when combined with other domestic disturbances further damage Kyrgyzstan's image as a tourist destination country. As Oktay (2011) indicates, "It is obvious that tourists place great emphasis on security and peace aspects of the countries they prefer to travel. People are not inclined to visit those countries at risk." In addition to its own domestic instabilities, Kyrgyzstan is also negatively affected by the spill-over effects of the cross-border issues, especially as regards to Tajikistan, a country that suffered heavily from civil war, unrest and lawlessness (Kinzer, 1999).

THE LEGAL PROBLEMS

A final group of problems that hinders the development of tourism in Kyrgyzstan is related to the insufficiencies of the legal framework of the country, having a negative impact on the development of tourism in Kyrgyzstan.[25] For example the laws regulating the banking system are inadequate to support the tourism sector and/or meet the financial needs of foreign tourists (Azizova, 2010). Furthermore, despite the fact that Kyrgyzstan is one of the most liberal countries in terms of opportunities for foreign investment, there are still certain bureaucratic obstacles for foreign investors who want to develop the tourism sector in the country (Seval et al., 2003). For example, there are restrictions on land property rights for such potential foreign investors (Oktay, 2011).

One other very important problem for foreign tourists is the customs and visa procedures for entering the country. First of all, not all countries have a Kyrgyz Embassy or consulate. Furthermore, "there is a good amount of paperwork and waiting time involved when obtaining a visa" making it quite "a hassle" for many foreign tourists (Oktay, 2011). It has also been indicated that the cost of tourist visas is too high. Furthermore, in addition to paying the visa cost, tourists also have to pay fees for entering recreational places such as national parks and/or participating to the "alpine tours" (Werner, 2003).

Such problems resulting from the lack of a sufficient, coordinated legal framework to support tourism is another obstacle that the country faces.

---

[25]Some scholars also suggest that there are several problems in the implementation of the existing laws passed for the purpose of developing tourism, further exacerbating the situation (Seval et al., 2003).

CONCLUSION

Shortly after independence, an American diplomat would say the following about Kyrgyzstan: "... a good President [Akaev] ... beautiful mountains ... then what? The Kyrgyz are lucky enough to have an enlightened President and splendid mountains, but they have nothing else" (Capisani, 2000). This rather realistic comment had a tone of pessimism in it but that "enlightened President" allowed the functioning of an environment in which economic, political, cultural, and religious rights and freedoms were more extensive as compared to other Central Asian countries (Pomfret, 2006). It may be suggested that although eventually Akaev turned out to be authoritarian and ousted by a popular riot, he set up an example and left behind a legacy in terms of democratization. Today, despite all sources of domestic instability, the country "retains a considerable degree of social pluralism and a more open political space than any of its Central Asian neighbors" (Anderson, 1999). Kyrgyzstan is also doing much better in terms of development of civil society (Kasybekov, 1999; Marat 2010; McMann, 2004).

In terms of economic conditions, Kyrgyzstan has its own advantages as well, despite all odds. It has a "relatively free market economy ... and vibrant markets" (Pomfret, 2006). It has also been suggested by specialists in the international financial community that it is easier to work with the Kyrgyz officials due to their "supportive attitude" (Olcott, 2005). Furthermore, in Kyrgyzstan, environmental problems are not as severe as other postcommunist countries, not posing "immediate threats to human health or sustainable development" (The World Bank, 1993).

Kyrgyzstan has the potential of using such comparative advantages in the field of tourism. However, in order to be more successful in the sector, certain major steps need to be taken. First of all, as was mentioned before, the legal infrastructure of the country has to be strengthened. To that end, a comprehensive tourism law has to be adopted in order to provide a comprehensive and coordinated legal framework. The tourism sector has a complex structure and is influenced by laws on transportation, customs, land use, environmental protection and trade (Kızılırmak and Oktay, 2008). Therefore, such a framework would provide a smoother legal environment for the tourism sector.

Likewise to make "an integrative and comprehensive development plan" for the future of the sector is of utmost importance (Kantarcı, 2007a).

In this framework, tourism statistics have to be systematically updated in order to provide reliable data for the formulation of long-term policies (Kızılırmak and Oktay, 2008).

One other area that has to be dealt with is to create a better image of the country by more active campaigns of promotion and advertising. This can be realized to a great extent by stressing the unique qualities of the country in terms of its tourism potential. As Palmer (2007) suggests, "... Kyrgyzstan needs to project a distinctive identity and position for its place brand. To do this, those involved in the destination marketing of Kyrgyzstan must identify the country's unique selling point (USP) and differentiate the destination, most notably from the neighboring competition destinations, such as Mongolia, to avoid substitutability." In this framework, an interesting way to promote tourism in Kyrgyzstan can be "niche marketing" in which certain marketing strategies are designed in order to meet specific demands of smaller groups of tourists who more or less need the same types of services. As was mentioned above, Kyrgyzstan has the opportunity of offering a diverse set of services in different parts of the country. This potential can be used more by niche marketing (Boz, 2008).

Another very important point is tourism education in Kyrgyzstan. There has to be a coordinated effort to standardize tourism education so that the personnel that the tourists come into contact with in their visa and customs operations as well as hotel accommodations would be competent enough to provide quality service (Oktay, 2005). Part of such quality service also includes better travel conditions including lower costs. Likewise, safety and security conditions need to be satisfied (Kantarcı, 2006).

Finally, in order to develop a better long-term policy, Kyrgyzstan needs to find a balanced position in which it will both provide better incentives for those people who want to invest in the tourism sector and to protect the environment. As its unspoiled beauty is one of the most attractive features in terms of attracting tourist, sustainable development becomes critical.

Being a country with great tourism diversity (Tunca, 2006) Kyrgyzstan has good potential for developing its tourism sector. Tourism is portrayed as "one of the prioritized branches of the republic's economy with which "the republic's rich natural, recreational and ecological potential could be put at the disposal of domestic and international tourists."[26] Therefore, the

---

[26]*Tourism in Kyrgyzstan: 2006–2010.* (2011). Bishkek: National Statistical Committee of the Kyrgyz Republic, Yearly Publication, 15.

more this sector is really "prioritized," the better the chances of Kyrgyzstan to have its deserving place as an attractive tourist destination in the region.

KEYWORDS

- Health Tourism
- Issyk-Kul
- Kyrgyzstan
- Mountain Tourism
- Tourism Policy
- Tourism Sector

REFERENCES

"According to the World Tourism Organization (WTO), Tourism has Every Reason to Become a Major Economic Alternative for Central Asian Countries," *Newspaper Source Plus*, M2Press-WIRE, February 7, 2006, http://ehis.ebscohost.com/eds/detail?sid=c745fb73-aa04-45ba-afac-58f1333fd7fa%40 sessionmgr12&vid=5&hid=116&bdata=JkF1dGhUeXBlPWlwJnN pdGU9ZWRzLWxpdmUmc2NvcGU9c2l0ZQ%3d#db=n5h&AN=16PU52217872 (accessed December 9, 2011).

"Mount Santa' to Join Lenin, Yeltsin Among Peaks in Central Asia's Kyrgyzstan," *The Canadian Press*, December 20, 2007, http://ehis.ebscohost.com/eds/detail?sid=c745fb73-aa04-45ba-afac-58f1333fd7fa%40 sessionmgr12&vid=5&hid=116&bdata=JkF1dGhUeXBlPWlw JnNpdGU9ZWRzLWxpdmUmc2NvcGU9c2l0ZQ%3d#db=n5h&AN=MYO142215254807 (accessed December 9, 2011).

Abdibaitova, Burulkan. (2009). "Avrupa Birliği ve Kırgızistan İlişkilerinde Sorunlar ve Fırsatlar." *Orta Asya ve Kafkasya Araştırmaları*, 8 (8), 95–119.

Ackland, Robert, Jane Falkingham. (1997). "A Profile of Poverty in Kyrgyzstan." In *Household Welfare in Central Asia*, eds. Jane Falkingham, Jeni Klugman, Sheila Marnie, and John Micklewright. Great Britain: MacMillan Press, 81–99.

Anderson, John. (1999). *Kyrgyzstan: Central Asia's Island of Democracy*. The Netherlands: Harwood Academic Publishers.

Anderson, Kathryn H., Richard Pomfret. (2003). *Consequences of Creating a Market Economy: Evidence from Household Surveys in Central Asia*. USA: Edward Elgar Publishing Inc.

Azizova, Nargız. (2010). "Kırgızistan Tanıtımında Turizm Potansiyeli." *Alatoo Academic Studies*, 5 (1), 172–179.

Balbay, Mustafa. (1999). *Ortadaki Asya Ülkeleri*. Istanbul: Çağ Pazarlama A.Ş.

Batman, Orhan, ve Kutay Oktay. (2008). "Kırgızistan'da Turizm Eğitimi Alan Öğrencilerin Meslek ile İlgili Algılamalarına Yönelik Bir Araştırma." In *Kırgızistan'da Turizm Eğitiminin Mevcut Durumu, Sorunlar ve Çözüm Önerileri*, Bishkek: Kırgızistan-Türkiye Manas Üniversitesi Yayınları: 104, Kongreler Dizisi: 13, 105–112.

Beyer, Judith. (2010). "Authority as Accomplishment: Intergenerational Dynamics in Talas, Northern Kyrgyzstan." In *Eurasian Perspectives: In Search of Alternatives*, eds. Anita Sengupta and Suchadana Cahatterjee. India: Shipra Publications, 78–92.

Boz, Mustafa. (2008). "The Impact of Community Based Tourism in Economic and Social Development of Local Population: Kyrgyzstan Case." In *Kırgızistan'da Turizm Eğitiminin Mevcut Durumu, Sorunlar ve çözüm Önerileri*, Bishkek: Kırgızistan-Türkiye Manas Üniversitesi Yayınları: 104, Kongreler Dizisi: 13, 94–104.

Capisani, Giampaolo. (2000). *The Handbook of Central Asia: A Comprehensive Survey of the New Republics*. London: I. B. Tauris.

Cummings, Sally N., ed. (2010). *Domestic and International Perspectives on Kyrgyzstan's Tulip Revolution: Motives, Mobilization and Meanings*. London: Routledge.

"Deadly Clashes in Kyrgyzstan's Southern City of Osh," http://www.bbc.co.uk/news/10290717 (accessed February 7, 2012).

Demirel, Yavuz and Zeliha Seçkin. (2009). "Örgüt İçi Politik Davranışların Tespiti Üzerine Kırgızistan'da Sağlık Sektöründe Bir Araştırma." *Orta Asya ve Kafkasya Araştırmaları* 4 (7), 143–161.

Djoroev, Erkinbek. (2003). *The Roots of Corruption in the Kyrgyz Republic*. Ankara: METU.

Dlugy, Yana. "Way Off the Beaten Path," *Newsweek*, 134 (2), 70–71.

Duran, Meltem. (2002). *Kırgızistan Ülke Etüdü*. Istanbul: Istanbul Ticaret Odası Yayınları.

Dzhumaeva, Asel. (2008). "Migration Trends in Central Asia: Migration Flows in Southern Kyrgyzstan." In *Rethinking Global Migration: Practices, Policies and Discourses in the European Neighbourhood*, eds. Helga Rittersberger-Tılıç, Aykan Erdemir, Ayça Ergun and Hayriye Kahveci. Ankara: METU/KORA, 220–226.

Edilova, Mariam, Gulzat Zhetibaeva. (2008). "Labor Migration from Kyrgyzstan to Russia and Kazakhstan: Human Rights and Security Challenges." In *Rethinking Global Migration: Practices, Policies and Discourses in the European Neighbourhood*, eds. Helga Rittersberger-Tılıç, Aykan Erdemir, Ayça Ergun and Hayriye Kahveci. Ankara: METU/KORA, 236–248.

Gleason, Gregory. (2003). *Markets and Politics in Central Asia: Structural Reform and Political Change*. London: Routledge.

https://www.cia.gov/library/publications/the-world-factbook/geos/kg.html

http://www.tuk.kg/index.php?lang=english (accessed 29 February 2012).

Huskey, Gene. (1993). "Kyrgyzstan: the Politics of Demographic and Economic Frustration. In *Nations and Politics in the Soviet Successor States*, eds. Ian Bremmer and Ray Taras. Cambridge: Cambridge University Press, 398–418.

Juraev, Shairbek. (2010). "Kyrgyz Democracy? The Tulip Revolution and Beyond." In *Domestic and International Perspectives on Kyrgyzstan's Tulip Revolution: Motives, Mobilization and Meanings*, ed. Sally N. Cummings. London: Routledge, 30–42.

Kantarcı, Kemal. (2006). "Perceptions of Central Asia Travel Conditions: Kyrgyzstan, Kazakhstan, Uzbekistan, Turkmenistan." *Journal of Hospitality and Leisure Marketing*, 15 (2), 55–71.

Kantarcı, Kemal. (2007a). "Perceptions of Foreign Investors on the Tourism Market in Central Asia Including Kyrgyzstan, Kazakhstan, Uzbekistan, Turkmenistan." *Tourism Management*, 28 (3), 820–829.

Kantarcı, Kemal. (2007b). "The Image of Central Asian Countries: Kyrgyzstan, Kazakhstan, Uzbekistan, Turkmenistan." *Tourism Analysis*, 12 (4), 307–318.

Kasybekov, Erkinbek. (1999). "Government and Nonprofit Sector Realtions in the Kyrgyz Republic." *Civil Society in Central Asia*, eds. M. Holt Ruffin and Daniel Waugh. USA: University of Washington Press, 71–84.

Kennedy, Kathleen, Dornan D'Arcy. (2009). "An Overview: Tourism Non-Governmental Organizations and Poverty Reduction in Developing Countries." *Asia Pacific Journal of Tourism Research*, 14 (2), 183–200.

Kinzer, Stephan. "Tourism From Scratch In Central Asia's Wilds," *New York Times*, 31 October, 1999.

Kızılırmak, İsmail, Kutay Oktay. (2008). "Kırgızistan Turizm Sektörüne İlişkin Genel Bir Analiz ve Geleceğe Yönelik Öngörüler." In *6.Türk Dünyası Sosyal Bilimler Kongresi 25–28 Mayıs 2008*. Calalabad, Kırgızistan.

Kort, Michael. (2003). *Central Asian Republics*. New York: Facts on File, 2004.

Kuehnast, Katleen, Nora Dudwick. (2004). *Better a Hundred Friends than a Hundred Rubles: Social Networks in Transition – The Kyrgyz Republic*. Washington D.C: The World Bank.

Kulov, Emir. (2010). "March 2005: Parliamentary Elections as a Catalyst of Protests." In *Domestic and International Perspectives on Kyrgyzstan's Tulip Revolution: Motives, Mobilization and Meanings*, ed. Sally N. Cummings. London: Routledge, 112–122.

Kupatadze, Alexander. (2010). "Organized Crime Before and After the Tulip Revolution: the Changing Dynamics of Upperworld-Underworld Networks." In *Domestic and International Perspectives on Kyrgyzstan's Tulip Revolution: Motives, Mobilization and Meanings*, ed. Sally N. Cummings. London: Routledge, 56–76.

Kyrgyz Community Based Tourism Association Yearly Report. (2006). Bishkek.

"Kyrgyz Speaker Proposes Admitting Head of International Commission Probing June 2010 Clashes" Interfax, Russia & FSU General News, http://ehis.ebscohost.com/eds/detail?sid=683dd724-8e36-41c0-8676-a18c66b22e65%40 sessionmgr12&vid=5&hid=2&bd ata=JnNpdGU9ZWRzLWxpdmU%3d#db=n5h&AN=62173826 (accessed February 7, 2012).

Kyrgyzstan: Then and Now. (1993). USA: Lerner Publication Company.

Lewis, David. (2010). "The Dynamics of Regime Change: Domestic and International Factors in the 'Tulip Revolution'." In *Domestic and International Perspectives on Kyrgyzstan's Tulip Revolution: Motives, Mobilization and Meanings*, ed. Sally N. Cummings. London: Routledge, 43–55.

Liu, Morgan Y. (2007). "A Central Asian Tale of Two Cities: Locating Lives and Aspirations in a Shifting Post- Soviet Cityscape." In *Everyday Life in Central Asia: Past and Present*, eds. Jeff Sahadeo and Russell Zanca. Indiana: Indiana University Press, 66–83.

Luong, Pauline Jones. (2002). *Institutional Change and Political Continuity in Post-Soviet Central Asia: Power, Perceptions and Pacts*. Cambridge: Cambridge University Press.

Mahnovski, Sergej, Kamil Akramov, and Theodore Karasik. (2007). *Economic Dimensions of Security in Central Asia*. California: Rand Corporation.

Marat, Erica. (2010). "March and After: What has Changed? What has Stayed the Same?." In *Domestic and International Perspectives on Kyrgyzstan's Tulip Revolution: Motives, Mobilization and Meanings*, ed. Sally N. Cummings. London: Routledge, 7–18.

McMann, Kelly M. (2004). "The Civic Realm in Kyrgyzstan: Soviet Economic Legacies and Activists' Expectations." In *The Transformation of Central Asia: Sates and Societies from Soviet Rule to Independence*, ed. Pauline Jones Luong. USA: Cornell University Press, 213–245.

McMann, Kelly M. (2006). *Economic Autonomy and Democracy: Hybrid Regimes in Russia and Kyrgyzstan*. USA: Cambridge University Press.

Muhambetov, Omurbek. (2003). *Transition Period and Decentralization in the Kyrgyz Republic.* Ankara: METU.

Oktay, Kutay. (2005). "Kırgızistan Turizm Sektörünün Gelişiminde Yönetim, Danışmanlık ve Eğitim Hizmetlerinin Önemi." *Ülkümüz,* 2 (3), 209–214.

Oktay, Kutay. (2011). "The Role of Tourism in the Integration of Central Asia." In *Traditional and Non-Traditional Threats to Central Asian Security,* eds. Ajay Patnaik and Anuradha M. Chenoy. New Delhi: Knowledge World Publishers, 349–359.

Olcott, Martha Brill. (2005). *Central Asia's Second Chance.* Washington D.C: Carnegie Endowment for International Peace.

Öraz, Seçil. (2006). "Tribal Connections within the Political Processes: the Case of Kyrgyzstan." *Orta Asya ve Kafkasya Araştırmaları,* 1 (2), 78–91.

Özcan, Gül Berna. (2010). *Building Markets and States: Enterprise Development in Central Asia.* Great Britain: Palgrave Macmillan.

Özdil, Tuncer, and Cengiz Yılmaz. (2008). "Turizm Sektörünün Ülke Ekonomisi İçindeki Öneminin Girdi-Çıktı Analiziyle İncelenmesi." In *Kırgızistan'da Turizm Eğitiminin Mevcut Durumu, Sorunlar ve çözüm Önerileri,* Bishkek: Kırgızistan-Türkiye Manas Üniversitesi Yayınları: 104, Kongreler Dizisi: 13, 71–82.

Özdil, Tuncer, Gonca Yılmaz, and Doğan Demir. (2008). "Sosyolojik Düşünmenin Turizme Etkileri." In *Kırgızistan'da Turizm Eğitiminin Mevcut Durumu, Sorunlar ve Çözüm Önerileri,* Bishkek: Kırgızistan-Türkiye Manas Üniversitesi Yayınları: 104, Kongreler Dizisi: 13, 59–70.

Pannier, Bruce. "Kyrgyzstan: Anatomy of A Conflict." 2 July 2010, http://www.rferl.org/content/Kyrgyzstan_Anatomy_Of_A_Conflict/2089464.html (accessed February 7, 2012).Palmer, Nicola. (2007). "Ethnic Equality, National Identity and Selective Cultural Representation in Tourism Promotion." *Journal of Sustainable Tourism,* 15 (6), 645–662.

Pomfret, Richard. *The Central Asian Economies Since Independence.* New Jersey: Princeton University Press.

Roudnik, Peter L. (2007). *The History of Central Asian Republics.* Connecticut: Greenwood Press.

Ryabkov, Maxim. (2010). "The North-South Cleavage and Political Support in Kyrgyzstan." In *Domestic and International Perspectives on Kyrgyzstan's Tulip Revolution: Motives, Mobilization and Meanings,* ed. Sally N. Cummings. London: Routledge, 77–92.

Saray, Mehmet. (2004). *Modern Kırgızistan'ın Doğuşu.* Ankara: TİKA Yayınları.

Sarı, Yaşar. (2010). "Kırgızistan'da İktidarın El Değiştirmesi: Akayev ve Bakiyev'in Düşüşü." *Orta Asya ve Kafkasya Araştırmaları,* 5 (9), 27–47.

Seval, Halil, Kutay Oktay, and Cıldız Kurmanaliyeva. (2003). *Kırgızistan Turizmi: Pazarlama Problemleri ve Çözüm Önerileri.* Bishkek: Kırgızistan-Türkiye Manas Üniversitesi Yayınları: 37, Yardımcı Ders Kitapları Dizisi: 20.

Sievers, Eric W. (2003). *The Post-Soviet Decline of Central Asia: Sustainable Development and Comprehensive Capital.* London: RoutledgeCurzon.

Tajibaeva, Nazgul. (2008). "Labor Migration and Home State Responses in the Post-Soviet Era: the Cases of Ukraine and Kyrgyzstan." In *Challenges of Global Migration: European Union and Its Neighbourhood,* ed. Ayşe Güneş-Ayata. Ankara: METU/KORA, 56–75.

The World Bank. (1993). *Kyrgyzstan: The Transition to a Market Economy.* USA: Washington D.C.

The World Bank. (2001). *Kyrgyz Republic: Fiscal Sustainability Study.* USA: Washington D.C.

The World Bank. (2005). *Enhancing the Prospects for Growth and Trade of the Kyrgyz Republic*. USA: Washington D.C.

Tokbaeva, Dina. "Kyrgyzstan: Here Comes Santa Claus," *Transitions Online*, July 13, 2009 http://ehis.ebscohost.com/eds/detail?sid=259e0ec8-641c-420d-927f-f344c17253db%40 sess ionmgr112&vid=6&hid=116&bdata=JkF1dGhUeXBlPWlwJnNpdGU9ZWRzLWxpdmU%3 d#db=a9h&AN=43380325 (accessed December 9, 2011).

Tourism in Kyrgyzstan: 2006–2010. (2011). Bishkek: National Statistical Committee of the Kyrgyz Republic, Yearly Publication.

Tunca, Elif Asude. (2006). "Ülke İmajının ve Tanıtımının Yabancı Yatırımlara Etkisi: Kırgızistan Örneği." In *Uluslarası Girişimcilik Kongresi*. Bishkek: Kırgızistan-Türkiye Manas Üniversitesi Yayınları: 86, Kongreler Dizisi: 11, 257–265.

"War in Kyrgyzstan: What is Causing the Violence?." http://www.guardian.co.uk/world/2010/jun/14/kyrgyzstan-conflict-background (accessed, February 13, 2012).

Werner, Cynthia. (2003). *The New Silk Road: Mediators and Tourism in Central Asia*." *Ethnology*, 42 (2), 141–59.

Yılmaz, İlham, Seyil Nacimudinova, and Günce Yılmaz. (2008). "Niş Pazarlamanın Turizm Sektöründe Uygulanması ve Bir Manisa Spil Dağı Turizmi Örneği." In *Kırgızistan'da Turizm Eğitiminin Mevcut Durumu, Sorunlar ve çözüm Önerileri*, Bishkek: Kırgızistan-Türkiye Manas Üniversitesi Yayınları: 104, Kongreler Dizisi: 13, 83–93.

CHAPTER 12

ICT DIFFUSION AND THE DIGITAL DIVIDE IN TOURISM: KAZAKHSTAN PERSPECTIVE

VLADIMIR GARKAVENKO and GUILLAUME TIBERGHIEN

CONTENTS

ICT AND TOURISM

Information and communication technologies (ICTs) can be defined as manufactured products and services intended to enable or stimulate information processing, communication, use of electronic means to detect, measure or record physical phenomena or to control physical processes (OECD, 2001). Starting from the first Computer Reservation System (CRS) in the 1950s, information technology has both transformed the way in which customers plan and purchase their holidays and how the tourism industry promotes and sells its products and services.

The fast and efficient exchange of information between the players in the tourism is essential for efficient distribution, sales and customer service. This information dependence has placed the industry at the forefront of ICT adoption (Mason and Milne, 2002). The Internet and electronic commerce development in the late 1990s and their adoption by tourism as one of the prime business to business (B2B) and business to consumer (B2C) applications has changed the industry and has shifted the traditional way tourism and travel products are distributed (Buhalis, 2003; O'Connor, 1999; O'Connor and Frew, 2002).

Tourism suppliers (particularly airlines, car rental firms and hotel chains) have taken advantage of the new opportunities offered and have developed e-commerce applications by allowing users to directly access their reservation systems. This includes single supplier providers such as British Airways (britishairways.com), Marriott Hotels (marriot.com), Avis (avis.com), and multi-supplier web pages that support airlines (opodo.com; orbitz.com). In addition, destinations have developed management systems to distribute their smaller properties and present the destination as a holistic entity (tiscover.com; holland.com). A number of web-based TAs have also emerged (e.g., Expedia.com, ebookers.com, Travelocity.com), and some off-line agencies have developed on-line provision (thomascook.com; lunnpoly.com). Moreover, Internet portals (Yahoo, Altavista, Excite) and vertical portals (or vortals—web site portals that provide information and resources for a particular industry) have also developed on-line travel distribution systems, often by sourcing their content from external on-line agents and suppliers (ski.com; golfonline.com; tennis.com).

The effective use of ICT is pivotal in the tourism industry. Commentators have noted that "A whole system of ICT is being rapidly diffused throughout the tourism industry and no player can escape its impact" (Poon, 1993, p.123).

Unlike durable goods, intangible tourism services cannot be physically displayed or inspected at the point of sale before purchasing. They are bought before the time of their use and away from the place of consumption. Hence they depend exclusively upon representation and descriptions, provided by the travel trade for their ability to attract consumers. Timely and accurate information, relevant to consumers' needs, is often the key to satisfaction of tourist demand. Therefore, ICT provides the information backbone that facilitates tourism (Buhalis, 1998, p. 411).

The cyberspace travel market is characterized by steady growth in different countries. On-line sales accounted for 14.4% of the American market—a massive shift to online travel, which is being repeated in other parts of the world. However, online services have yet to take off in the huge Asian market. Global Internet users reached 1.4 billion, of which 65% was located in Asia, by 2009, according to Yahoo! South-east Asia at the Travel Distribution Summit Asia 2006 (European Travel Commission—New Media Review, 2006). Yahoo! South-east Asia believes that Asia Pacific is expected to account for 423 million Internet users, excluding China, of the total 1 billion base. In Europe online services were growing rapidly (Economist.com, 2005). In 2005, the number of visitors to travel websites in America grew by 12.7%. This compares with an increase of almost 30% in the number of visitors to British websites.

The wider availability of e-tickets should speed the development of online travel everywhere. It spread even faster once paperless tickets became more widely accepted for so-called 'interline agreements,' in which a ticket issued by one carrier is valid on another carrier for part of the journey (Economist. com, 2005). Furthermore, all major airlines switched to e-ticketing by 2007.

There are, of course, variations between countries, with the UK accounting for 39% of the European on-line travel market followed by Germany in second place at 23%. According to the research, Germany had the fastest growing on-line travel market in Europe; the breakdown by type of service was: air travel 57.3%, hotels 14.4%, package tours 16.5%, rail 8.4%, rental cars 2.1%, and other services 1.5% (Marcussen, 2004).

Different sectors of the tourism industry are characterized by different levels of ICT adoption. Airlines realized fairly early the need for efficient, quick, and inexpensive systems. In 1962, American Airlines introduced its Sabre Computerized Reservation System (CRS), a project that was described as a technical marvel (French, 1998; O'Connor, 1999). Subsequently, the CRS expanded rapidly into a gigantic computerized network. In the 1990s, CRS evolved into Global Distribution Systems (GDS), which offered a wide range of tourism products and provided a mechanism for communication between principals and travel agencies. GDSs effectively became travel supermarkets offering information and reservation capabilities for the entire range of travel products, including accommodation, car rentals and schedules for nonair transport. GDSs are at the heart of airline operational and strategic agendas as they control and distribute the vast majority of airline seats (Buhalis, 2004).

The development of the world wide web (www) in the late 1990s provided both a challenge and an opportunity for airlines (American Airlines, 2000; French, 1998; Smith & Jenner, 1998; Buhalis, 2000a,b). By 1998, most airlines already had web sites, which not only informed consumers but also enabled itinerary building, fare construction, and reservations. In turn, this enabled interactivity with consumers and the development of relationship marketing strategies. It also assisted airlines in launching another communication and purchasing channel to reduce the power and costs of conventional intermediaries.

Overall, it would appear that the establishment of new distribution channels by airlines in the Asia-Pacific region is following recent trends elsewhere—but will more likely be similar to those in Europe than in the US.

The development of the Internet has made information easily accessible to consumers, and has therefore established a direct link between consumers and suppliers. As a result, traditional travel distribution channels are changing rapidly. A major feature of this change is "disintermediation," with principals such as airlines, hotels and rental car chains bypassing intermediaries to sell directly to consumers. A number of web-based travel agents have also emerged (Expedia.com, Travelocity.com) while off-line agencies have developed their on-line provision. Internet portals (Yahoo, Altavista, Excite) and vertical portals (or vortals) have also developed on-line travel distribution, often by sourcing their travel contents from external online agents and suppliers.

On-line travel agencies are moving into Asian markets. Travelocity, one of the two leading on-line agencies in Canada, Europe and the US, is reported to be establishing an on-line distribution system in Asia (Kirby, 2001).

There has been little research on the impact of ICT on the tourism industry outside European and North American settings. Some research has been done on the ICT impact on the travel agent sector in Singapore (Tse, 2003) and in New Zealand (Garkavenko, 2008a, 2008b). In our previous research (Garkavenko et al., 2010; Rybina, and Garkavenko, 2009; Garkavenko et al., 2009a; Garkavenko et al., 2009b; Garkavenko et al., 2010) a clear digital disparity was established between the global travel industry and Kazakhstan's tourism industry. The need for countries to measure and bridge domestic and international digital divides is a general consensus in academic circles (Minghetti and Buhalis, 2010). However, there is very little research focusing on the reduction of the digital gap between tourism markets and destinations within and between countries. Studies on the digital divide in tourism appear particularly relevant in countries where tourism is considered to be very important for socioeconomic development. The Kazakhstan travel industry is emerging. At this stage there is a lack of academic research into the industry in general and specifically on any ICT impact or its integration into the global travel industry system. The study aims to analyze ICT adoption by the Kazakhstan tourism industry and the digital divide in the industry and its implementation for global tourism industry integration.

Business and academic literature on Kazakhstan Internet and ICT adoption, literature on Kazakhstan tourism industry as well as official statistics were used as sources of the secondary data. The researchers also summarized their primary data on the Kazakhstan's tourism industry (Garkavenko et al., 2009a,b, 2010a,b; Garkavenko and Tiberghien, 2011a,b; 2012; Rybina and Garkavenko, 2009; Tiberghien and Garkavenko, 2011). A series of research projects supported by KIMEP University (Almaty, Kazakhstan) have been conducted on different aspects of the Kazakhstan's tourism industry—its structure, ICT adoption by different tourism industry sectors, consumer adoption of ICT and readiness to go on-line for ticketing and bookings.

METHODOLOGY

The presented exploratory study adopts qualitative methods. The goal of qualitative research is to locate the understanding of a phenomenon within the context of another (Oppenheim, 1992; Rubin and Rubin, 2005; Silverman, 2004; Seymour, 2001).

The research uses two types of data collection and analysis: case study and in-depth interviews. Case studies are broadly used in tourism research (Aneshensel, 2002; Beeton, 2005; Horner, and Swarbrooke, 2004). Unlike more specifically directed research, case studies investigate a problem that seeks a holistic understanding of the event or situation in question. According to Flyvbjerg (2006), a case study can be used to both generate and test hypotheses. Suggested sources of secondary data are business and academic literatures on Kazakhstan Internet and ICT adoption, literature on Kazakhstan tourism industry, official statistic as well as ICT use by tourism industries in other countries.

It is well accepted that in-depth interviews are applied to enhance knowledge of newly emerging, under-researched phenomena (Kwortnik, 2003). Until the researcher is relatively clear on what is to be studied and how, the objective of the interview should be discovered, and enhanced understanding of the phenomena. Such an understanding is derived from data grounded in the informant's experience—what they say about what they did, felt, or thought.

A total of 30 industry specialists were interviewed. A sampling method was adopted that enabled the researcher to include a cross-section of tourism businesses, including franchise/chain retail operations, small independent enterprises, and wholesalers. Each the in-depth interview was about an hour long each. The interviews were designed to produce a considered response to certain issues including: background about the firm, the use of ICT and associated issues.

In addition a total of 50 in-depth interviews were held with prospective consumers. A judgmental technique was applied to select interviewees. The criteria of selection were at least one trip (overseas and/or domestic) per year, and at least basic PC skills. A brief questionnaire preceded the interview that included demographic data, and PC skills. The interview was focused on the questions: PC and mobile phone ownership, general attitude towards PC, buying on-line, usage of the Internet in searching of the information and in preparing, booking and buying a trip, and attitude towards TA.

Notes were taken during the interviews, which were also taped recorded and summarized. Subsequent analysis of the interviews was employed to identify common themes.

KAZAKHSTAN TRAVEL INDUSTRY AND ICT DIFFUSION

Before the collapse of the Soviet Union, the Kazakhstan's travel industry was integrated into the Soviet Union under *Intourist* (a contraction of the Russian words for 'foreign tourist'). *Intourist* was responsible for managing the great majority of foreigners' access to, and travel within, the Soviet Union and grew into one of the largest tourism organizations in the world. *Intourist* also owned its own hotels, destinations and means of transport, Travel Agencies, Tourist Offices and transport agency in one large enterprise. *Sputnik* was another big travel agency in the Soviet Union, responsible for inbound and outbound youth tourism and *Intourbureau* was organizing the trips for trade unions' members. After the 1990s' perestroika, those agencies left Kazakhstan and the tourism industry was left to develop its own businesses and infrastructure.

The development of Kazakhstan's tourist industry began with so called "shopping tours"—organized trips from Almaty, the former capital, to Turkey, China, Emirates and Pakistan. Multiple travel agencies formed spontaneously to organize charter trips, which led to further agencies forming, and selling air tickets. These were mainly small businesses under the auspices of banks and other corporate organizations to service their own business-trip needs. So called "seasonal" tour companies also sprang up to take domestic tourists to summer destinations such as Issuk Kul Lake (Kyrgyzstan) or to winter attractions like the Medeo (Kazakhstan) skating rink.

At that time there was no one official carrier and private airlines were organizing charters and regular flights abroad. In February 2004 Air Astana became the national carrier after the government closed Air Kazakhstan. Currently they service 21 domestic and 23 international destinations. The airline is a joint venture owned by the Government of the Republic of Kazakhstan (who hold 51%) and BAE Systems of Britain (a British firm of defense and airline contractors who hold 49%). Kazakhstan's private airlines such as Scat and Sayakhat were left mainly with the niche market servicing private clients, cargo or charter tours.

According to official statistics, there were 16.6 million tourists in Kazakhstan in 2010. Twelve million were domestic and outbound tourists. There are 1250 registered tourism businesses in Kazakhstan.

According to our original research data (Garkavenko et al., 2009a, 2009b, 2010a, 2010b, 2011a, 2011b, 2012; Kadyrova et al., 2011) more than 95% of tourism businesses in Kazakhstan are travel agencies. Almaty is the biggest urban center where the majority of travel businesses are situated. Before the financial crisis, there were about 800 Travel Agencies. They were mainly small businesses—from 3 to 10 employees, often family-owned and operated. According to Kazakhstan's legislation, one must be licensed in order to operate as a travel agent or tour operator. The Travel Agencies' main activity is selling holiday packages for groups. Seasonal tourism organizations also still exist, operating without licenses in summer for lakeside holidays or in winter for skiing. The structure and function of these agencies are rudimentary—just an organized bus, often with a nonprofessional guide. These agencies work with domestic tourists and such 'wild' tours meet strong opposition from licensed travel agencies.

Very often Travel Agents are acting as operators trying to develop their own tour packages to fill the gaps in infrastructure and to promote tourist destinations. These agencies are mainly concerned with outbound tours, although some handle both outbound and inbound tourists. For instance, an agency would sell a package tour to Turkey, but also organize cultural and food tours in the country. Outbound Travel Agencies prefer to liaise directly with foreign partners representing their own facilities like hotels and resorts. These agencies market themselves mainly at international travel fairs in Europe and Asia.

An average travel agent cannot afford to sell airline tickets directly—the airlines' deposits are too expensive—so they prefer to purchase fares through bigger agencies. Approximately 30–40 Travel Agents in Almaty have a distributor's agreement with the airlines.

According to our research on TA businesses in Almaty (Garkavenko et al., 2009a, 2009b, 2010a, 2010b, 2011a, 2011b, 2012), not all agencies have access to the Global Distribution System (GDS). If they do it is Amadeus. Travel agents often are not aware of any other GDS or Computer Reservation System (CRS). The majority of the travel agents uses the Internet for e-mails. If an agency has a website—it is only for the web presence—the majority of websites are not functionally active. Founders and owners of travel agencies are entrepreneurs with no special education in tourism. Personnel are drawn from such former occupations as engineering or political activists etc. However, a new type of agency is on the rise—on-line Travel Agencies. Kazakhstan operates a scholarship program known as *Bolashak* whereby graduate students are sent abroad on government grants to complete their education in different fields. Young postgraduates bring back international trends to the country. One such trend is online commerce and business. One online travel business owner believes that even now the country has a market for online commerce—in young people, the well-traveled and the well-off, white-collar strata. However, the majority of TAs believes that there is no demand for on-line services; they believe marketing is not essential; this is especially true in family-run small TA with loyal clientele. Regarding prospective consumers, TAs think that clients differ in terms of ICT readiness, but it can be taken as true that a traveler is more sophisticated and Internet savvy nowadays and is likely to do a lot of research on the Internet.

The data on ICT adoption by TA in Kazakhstan is summarized in Table 1.

TABLE 1   TA—ICT adoption.

ICT adoption	Status
Connection to global systems	No GDS/CRS for the majority of TAs
Internet use	Mainly for e-mails, rudimentary web presence
ICT perception	No demand for on-line services
Overall ICT adoption	Low

There are several big travel operators such as KazTour (Kazakh owned), Tez Tour (Russia/Ukraine), Zhana Nur (Kazakh ownership), On Travel (with Bulgarian ownership) and Gulnar Tour (Kazakh/Turkish ownership). The characteristic feature of Kazakhstan's Tourist Operator business is to sell directly to consumers. Operators normally do not have any agency agreement with travel agents, although an exception is Tez Tour from Russia. Its relationships are more structured—they work with and sell tours only through travel agencies. This more structural approach earns them loyalty from their agents. Tez Tour forms packages in every country they work—they have branches in Turkey, for instance. Tez Tour also has its own airplane (Sky Bus) and performs charter flights. They also brought to Kazakhstan "last minute" packages with low prices. The Internet adoption is reasonably high especially in TO with foreign participation—Kaztour, Tez Tour, Gulnar Tour, Zhana Nur, On Travel. ICT adoption by Kazakhstan TO is summarized in Table 2.

TABLE 2   ICT adoption by TO in Kazakhstan.

ICT adoption	Status
Connection to global systems	Amadeus only
Internet use	E-mails, web presence, B2B
ICT perception	Necessary tool
Overall ICT adoption	High

The Hospitality industry in Kazakhstan is presented by various types of hotels—from small family operated to big international chains such as Intercontinental, Hyatt, Rixos, Royal Tulip. ICT diffusion by hospitality industry varies from high in international chains (GDS, front and back stage systems, often CRM) to low in small hotels with old systems of running business (phone bookings, direct orders from TA and TO). ICT adoption by hotels in Kazakhstan is summarized in Table 3.

TABLE 3   Hotel industry and ICT adoption.

ICT adoption	Status
Connection to global systems	GDS, front and back stage systems, often CRM
Internet use	Variable, high in international franchises and chains, low in small local hotels
ICT perception	Necessary tool for international chains, franchises
Overall ICT adoption	Variable

Destinations in Kazakhstan do not have a very strong presence on the web. Only websites of big cities such as Almaty or Astana can be found. Smaller cities and especially the towns and local communities in rural areas do not have any websites because very often there is no Internet access. Some destinations in rural locations are trying to have more exposure on the web with the help of international experts (Garkavenko and Tiberghien, 2011, 2011a). Thus, there is a huge disparity between cities and rural areas in terms of Internet and PC diffusion—high adoption in big cities and very low in rural and small town areas. Data on ICT adoption by tourism destinations in Kazakhstan is summarized in Table 4.

TABLE 4 Destinations and ICT adoption.

ICT adoption	Status
Websites	Only in big cities. Small towns and local communities do not have websites and very often Internet access
ICT perception	Variable
Overall ICT adoption	Variable

Regarding airlines—the national carrier Air Astana has a monopoly on flights in sectors through Asia. 51% of its shares belong to the state and 49% belongs to the BAE Systems in Great Britain. It has 3000 employees, including 100 flight staff; it has 21 aircraft. Air Astana sells tickets through its call centers and own travel agencies as well as through its website. It also has distributor agreements with some major travel agencies. Other companies such as Sayakhat offered (ceased operations in 2005) and Scat offers charter flights. Smaller airlines also exist, serving mainly private clients. Kazakhstan's airlines follow the international tendency in terms of ICT adoption. Data on airlines ICT adoption is summarized in Table 5.

TABLE 5 ICT adoption by Kazakhstan airlines.

ICT adoption	Status
Connection to global systems	GDS, CRS
Internet use	High B2B, only 2% ticketing on-line, strong web presence
ICT perception	Necessary tool
Overall ICT adoption	Very high

ICT ADOPTION BY KAZAKHSTAN CONSUMERS

Tourism is a dynamic system that must respond quickly to significant environmental changes. Those changes in the international travel market have been introduced by ICTs, which have had an impact not only on suppliers but also on consumers. A new more knowledgeable and sophisticated consumer is emerging who is familiar and comfortable with new technologies such as the Internet, interactive digital television, and mobile phone services or m-commerce (Buhalis and Licata, 2002; Minghetti & Buhalis, 2010; O'Brien, 1999; Rybina and Garkavenko, 2009).

Travellers are also increasingly gathering travel information themselves, forming their own customized holiday packages and making their own bookings. Inevitably, this leads to elimination of the non-value-added segments of the tourist service system. Therefore, changes in market conditions and in tourists' behaviors have created a gap between service suppliers and the volatile demand side of the industry. The development of the Internet has made information easily accessible to consumers and has therefore established a direct link between consumers and suppliers.

There have been dramatic advances in mobile data technologies that allow services to be delivered to a device such as a mobile phone or palm computer (O'Brien, 2002). Consumer adoption of the digital lifestyle differs from country to country (Morrisette et al., 1999). For instance, in 2009, B2C online travel sales reached over $90 billion in the USA alone (eMarketer, 2009). In 2013, it is expected that nearly 70% of the population will be online, which amounts to 221 million people. Retail e-commerce also boomed in Europe during 2008—for instance, in France, according to the Federation du E-commerce et de la Vente à Distance (FEVAD), online sales rose nearly 30%, reaching Euro 20.1 billion (Karin von Abrams, 2008). In Europe, a survey carried out by the computer company IBM and the intelligence unit of the British magazine 'The Economist' indicated that four Nordic countries (Denmark, Sweden, Norway, Finland) and the UK were the most frequent users of the Internet (Economist.com, 2005). According to the Internet market analysis by ROMIR Monitoring (2009), the Kazakhstan and Russian Internet markets are the fastest growing in Europe.

Thus, the travel market is affected not just by the initiatives of principals but also by high levels of ICT adoption by consumers. Increasingly, sophisticated and price conscious consumers have combined with the forces of globalization and electronic commerce to create new challenges for tourism businesses (Dean et al., 2002).

There is inconsistent data on ICT diffusion in Kazakhstan. Different statistic agencies give different figures on PC penetration and Internet adoption (Table 6). The figures on the PC and Internet adoption vary between 15 and 34 percent of the population with only 16% connected to the broadband. The Ministry of Communication and Information in

Kazakhstan has announced that it intends to achieve 100% broadband population coverage by 2013 (International Telecommunication Union, 2011). In 2006, Kazakstan adopted a program of reducing information and digital inequality/divide where ICT is considered to be a strategic tool for economic growth that provides businesses with a competitive advantage by increasing the efficiency of operations. The program aimed to reach 20% computer Internet literacy by 2009 as well as to increase the social and economic importance of ICTs (Electronic government of the Republic of Kazakhstan, 2007). According to recent data, the usage of ICT increased by 26%. PC usage increased by 38.5% and Internet usage was raised by 49%. Interestingly, mobile phone diffusion is very high—100 to 130% depending on the statistic agency. BuddeCom gives 21 million subscribers for the mobile phone services (2012).

TABLE 6   PC penetration and Internet adoption by different agencies.

Agency	PC, Internet Adoption (% population)	Mobile Phone Adoption (% population)
GISWatch	15	-
CIA The World Factbook	30	100
Internet World Stats	34	-
KZ Stat Agency	7 (Internet subscribers)	123
BuddeCom	16 (Internet subscribers)	130

In the presented study all respondents emphasized that PC and the Internet penetration in the country is still in its infancy. Among the factors slowing ICT adoption, business respondents pointed to high cost and low-speed Internet. Just getting online for a business can cost between $111 and $22,000 a month, depending on the desired connection speed and not including hardware. The average monthly wage in Kazakhstan is just $399. That means large swaths of the population are cut off from the online world completely. The high cost can be explained by the fact that there is only one major Internet provider in this country – KazakhTelecom. However, KazakhTelecom doubled Internet speed by the end of 2011 (Tengrinews.kz, 2011a).

Those who do find their way onto the net face a number of restrictions in what they can publish. According to marketingvox.com (2007a), Kazakhstan residents face both very high Internet access costs as well as restrictions on their online publishing freedoms. The government often slows down the loading speed of pages it finds offensive to discourage visitors (marketingvox.com, 2007b). Censorship of the Internet recently enforced by the government was also named by the respondents as a factor having a negative impact on the ICT adoption and usage.

Kazakhstan's Ministry of Communications and Information has set a goal to raise Internet speed to 16 Mbit per second in three years' time (Tengrinews.kz, 2011b). Now 4G is available in some major Kazakhstan cities. In 2011, it was reported that this particular format is available in 20 cities of Kazakhstan.

There are considerable differences in ICT adoption between big cities and rural areas: major cities such as Almaty and Astana show high Internet and PC adoption, but there is very slow PC/Internet adoption in rural areas. According to the interviewees, consumers in rural areas do not have access to PCs, nor are they connected to the Internet. Pronounced differences in ICT adoption were also noted between different age groups. People in the 18–25 year age bracket were much more comfortable with the technology than older generations. Interviewees pointed out that similar differences exist between different social strata with higher incomes predicting an earlier adoption of the technology. On the basis of the obtained data, an early adopters profile was formulated: up to 25 years old, city dweller, above average income bracket, white-collar or student. Early adaptors are also PC owners, Internet adopters and mobile phone(s) owners. The Internet for them is a mainstream medium mainly used for information search.

In our previous pilot research on the comparison of the Russian, Ukrainian and Kazakh markets, considerable similarities in ICT adoption by the younger generation (student or white-collar, 18–35 years old) were found (Rubina and Garkavenko, 2009). Similar to the previous study, it was established that this group of prospective consumers was characterized by a positive attitude towards the Internet. They perceived themselves as very confident ICT users who have no problem searching the Internet for information. However, there were some strong reservations regarding buying online. The privacy issues, security and difficulty of the shopping process were found to be the main reasons for being wary about using the Internet for shopping. It was also shown that there was no association between any of the demographic variables including gender, income, and attitude towards the Internet in general, and shopping online in particular. This group is characterized by a high level of ICT adoption including the Internet and mobile Internet. It was concluded that e-commerce and m-commerce have a great potential with the young generation of students and young professionals in those three markets.

However, the respondents in the present study pointed out the existence of limiting factors in ICT adoption. Specifically regarding the purchase and booking of travel products on-line, it was pointed out by the interviewees that heterogeneity of Internet adoption within the population is a limiting factor for the development of e-commerce. Another important limiting factor is a banking system that does not support on-line purchasing. Credit card transactions are poorly regulated; the banks do not take any responsibility for unauthorized transactions and put limits on on-line transactions. For instance, the credit card from the Popular Bank (Narodnij Bank) imposed a limit for on-line transactions of 200 dollars. It is obvious that most airfares cannot be purchased within this limit. The most popular sites for shopping are www.homeshop.kz.

The most popular algorithm in searching for information on a destination is through social forums (http://ct.kz (tsentr tiazhesti), http://vk.com (v kontakte), http://yvision.kz). The most popular site for purchasing airfares is the Air Astana website. The interviewees pointed out that the website is user friendly and provides a wide range of services. The Air Astana website (www.airastana.com) was awarded "the best Kazakh site" in 2009. However, the very group who are the most advanced technology users (younger than 25 years and eligible for the special category of tickets for young people) is prevented from making such a purchase online. This cheaper fare category can be purchased only through travel agents. According to the respondents, bookings and ticketing through agents will continue and this situation is not likely to change in the near future.

Similarly to the official statistic data interviewees in the presented study talked of very high mobile phone adoption. According to the respondents, "Everyone has a mobile phone." There was no noted disparity between rural and urban areas for mobile phone adoption.

CONCLUSION

The Travel industry is an information intensive one. With the adoption of the Information and Communication Technologies (ICT), and the Internet, in particular, both the distribution chain and the way of doing business have changed. The Internet connects all players directly—airlines, tour operators, travel agents and their consumers, and in this way ICT has become a catalyst of travel industry globalization and integration. However, it has been noted that digital disparities between destinations leads to an asymmetrical development of the global tourism system (Mingetti and Buhalis, 2010). The research on the digital divide in tourism would help to identify appropriate actions to bridge the digital gaps and to develop communication mechanisms between digitally excluded markets, destination and businesses.

There is a little academic and business research on ICT adoption by the Kazakhstan tourism industry (Garkavenko et al., 2009a,b; 2010a,b; Garkavenko and Tiberghien, 2011a,b; 2012). Our previous studies showed considerable disparities between travel industry sectors and businesses within a sector in terms of ICT adoption. The presented study summarizes the ICT adoption by the Kazakhstan tourism industry and consumers using both secondary and primary data. The original exploratory study adopts qualitative methods to seek a holistic understanding of the under-investigated Kazakhstan travel industry.

It was found that the level of ICT adoption by the travel industry in Kazakhstan is variable within the different sectors and between different businesses within one sector, and generally is much lower compared to that of western countries. As one would expect, airlines were the earliest adopters of ICT and they are fully integrated with the international airline network. The hotel industry, however, varies in ICT adoption. The biggest hotels are part of major international chains and keep their systems up to international standards. Small hotels however, are not as motivated in ICT implementation—some of them prefer to connect directly with travel agents to attract tourists, and they do not have any web presence. Regarding tour operators, ICT adoption is restricted to one particular GDS—Amadeus. The travel agents' sector is the biggest sector of the tourism industry in Kazakhstan by the number of businesses. It also varies in the level of ICT adoption—there is a group of TAs that has invested in the GDS system (again Amadeus only) to purchase tickets or to have access to international hotel bookings. Partially they use the Internet for the B2B model, for instance to sell tickets to smaller non-GDS-connected agencies. The majority of travel agencies consist of small businesses (less than 10 employees) that do not have access to any GDS and their usage of ICT is limited to simple e-mails and phones. The majority of them have websites, but TAs are mainly concerned with a web presence rather than website performance. Consumers in their interviews complained about the lack of ICT-savvy tourism specialists. The study reveals that, overall, the Kazakhstan tourism industry is a laggard in ICT adoption.

Consumers' in-depth interviews revealed interesting trends in ICT diffusion. There are considerable geographical, social and age disparities in ICT adoption and perception of Kazakhstan consumers. The early adopters' profile was formulated as a result of the research: up to 25 years old, city dwellers, above the average income bracket, white-collar or students. Privacy issues, security and complexity of the shopping sites were identified as the main barriers for the shopping on-line. High Internet cost, low broadband speed, censorship of the Internet post were barriers for the Internet adoption and further diffusion. Official statistics gives different figures for ICT diffusion in general population—from 15 to 34%. Interestingly both official statistics and primary data indicate a very high level of mobile diffusion—more than 100%. We concluded that mobile phones are the potential media to reach prospective consumers.

KEYWORDS

- **Digital divide**
- **ICT adoption**
- **ICT diffusion**
- **ICT impact on tourism**
- **Tourism in Kazakhstan**
- **Tourism industry**

REFERENCES

American Airlines. (2000). *American Airlines Web site*. Retrieved April 3, June 14, August 20, 2000, from http://www.aa.com/.

Aneshensel, C. S. (2002). Theory-based data analysis for the Social Sciences. Thousand Oaks, California: Pine Forge Press.

Beeton, S. (2005). The case study in tourism research: A multi-method case study approach. In B. W. Ritchie (Ed.), *Tourism Research Methods: Integrating Theory With Practice* (pp. 37–48). Oxford: Oxford University Press.

BuddeCom. (2012). *Kazakhstan—Telecoms, Mobile, Broadband and Forecasts.* Retrieved 16/05/2012 from https://www.budde.com.au/Research/Kazakhstan-Telecoms-Mobile-Broadband-and-Forecasts.html?r=51.

Buhalis, D. (1998). Strategic use of information technologies in the tourism industry. Tourism Management, 19(5), 409–421.

Buhalis, D. (2000a). Conference report: Distribution channels in the changing travel industry. The Dorchester, London, 9–10 December 1998. *International Journal of tourism research, 2*(2), 137–139.

Buhalis, D. (2000b). Tourism and information technologies: Past, present and future. *Tourism Recreation Research, 25*(1), 41–58.

Buhalis, D. (2003). *eTourism: Information Technology for Strategic Tourism Management*. Harlow, England: Pearson Education.

Buhalis, D. (2004). eAirlines: Strategic and tactical use of ICTs in the airline industry. *Information & Management, 41*, 805–825.

Dean, A., Morgan, D., Tan, T. E. (2002). Service quality and customers' willingness to pay more for travel services. *Journal of Travel & Tourism Marketing, 12*(2/3), 95–110.

www.economist.com. (2005). Flying from the computer: The Internet has pitted travel agents against travel providers in an intense battle to win customers. *economist.com, Special Report, Sep 29th 2005.* Retrieved 04.10.2005, from http://www.economist.com/displaystory.cfm?story_id=4455692

Electronic government of the Republic of Kazakhstan. (2007). Program for Bridging Digital Divide in the Republic of Kazakhstan 2007 to 2009. Retrieved 26/04/2011 from http://egov.kz/wps/portal/Content?contentPath=/library2/extra/all%20egov/project%20egov/sin&lang=en.

eMarketer. (2009). US Internet users. Accessed on 20/03/09 at www.emarketer.com/Reports/All/Emarketer_2000561.aspx.

European Travel Commission. (2006). Asia Pacific. New Media Review (ETC CET)–& Regional Overview, 26 May. Retrieved 1/06/2006, from http://www.etcnewmedia.com/review/default.asp?SectionID=10&CountryID=34

Flyvbjerg, B. (2006). Five misunderstandings about case-study research. Qualitative Inquiry, 12(2), 219–245.

French, T. (1998). The future of global distribution systems. *Travel & Tourism Analyst, 3*, 1–17.

Garkavenko, V., Milne, S. (2008a). New Zealand Travel Agents in the Internet Era: Spatial Differences in ICT Impact, Adoption and Perception. In O'Connor P, Hopken W, Gretzel U. (Eds.), Information and Communication Technologies in Tourism—2008. Springer Wien: New York, 298–307.

Garkavenko, V., Milne, S. (2008b). ICT and the travel industry: Opportunities and challenges for the New Zealand travel agents' market. In C. Van Slyke (Ed.), Information Communication Technologies: Concepts, Methodologies, Tools and Applications. Hershey, PA: IGI Global.

Garkavenko, V., Surnina, S., Tiberghien, G., Gimranova, D. (2009a). Kazakhstan's Travel Agent Sector: Main Issues, Impacts and Relationships. VI KIMEP International Research Conference (6th KIRC), 23–24 April, Almaty, Kazakhstan.

Garkavenko, V., Surnina, S., Tiberghien, G., Gimranova, D. (2009b). ICT impacts on the Kazakhstan travel industry. VI KIMEP International Research Conference (6th KIRC), 23–24 April, Almaty, Kazakhstan.

Garkavenko, V., Tiberghien, G., Gimranova, D. (2010a). Kazakhstan Travel Market and ICT Readiness: Consumer Dimension. *VII KIMEP International Research Conference (7th KIRC),* March 25–27, 2010, Almaty, Kazakhstan.

Garkavenko, V., Tiberghien, G., Surnina, S., Gimranova, D. (2010b). Information and communication technologies: Kazakhstan travel market perspective. *Proceedings of ENTER 2010–Information and Communication Technologies in Tourism. The 17th International Conference on Information Technology and Travel & Tourism IFITT's Global Travel & Tourism Technology and eBusiness Forum.* 10th-12th February 2010, Università della Svizzera Italiana, Lugano Switzerland.

Garkavenko, V., Tiberghien G. (2011a). Information and communication technologies adoption by the Kazakhstan travel market. *Proceedings of Eurasia Business and Economics Society (EBES) 2011 Conference–Istanbul,* June 1–3, 2011, Istanbul, Turkey.

Garkavenko, V., Tiberghien G. (2011b). Kazakhstan's travel industry: its history, current structure, and perspective for global integration. *Proceedings of the World Research Summit for Tourism and Hospitality,* 10–13 December 2011, Hong Kong.

Garkavenko, V., Tiberghien, G. (2012). Kazakhstan's travel industry: past and future—perspective for global integration. *Proceedings of IX KIMEP International Research Conference (9th KIRC), April 19–21, 2012,* Almaty, Kazakhstan.

Horner, S., Swarbrooke, J. (2004). International Cases in Tourism Management. Oxford: Elsevier Butterworth-Heinemann.

International Telecommunication Union. (2011). *Measuring the Information Society 2011.* Geneva: ITU.

Kadyrova, D., Maratov, A., Bolatbekuly, O., Laulanov, A., Gimranova, D., Garkavenko, V. (2011). The ICT development Index in Kazakhstan: The Focus on Business Environment. *Proceedings of VIII KIMEP International Research Conference (8th KIRC), April 22–23,* Almaty, Kazakhstan.

Karin von Abrams. (2008). France's e-tailers upbeat. eMarketer. Accessed 20/03/09 at www.Emarketer.com/Article.aspx?id=1006949.

Kirby, M. (2001, May 22). Orbitz boasts healthy prelaunch statistics. *Air Transport Intelligence News,* Washington, DC.

Kwortnik, R. J. (2003). Clarifying fuzzy consumer-research problems with depth interviews and qualitative analysis. *Cornell Hotel and Restaurant Administration Quarterly, 44 (April),* 117–129.

Marcussen, C. H. (2004). Trends in the European Internet distribution—of travel and tourism services. *Report, 27 May 2004.* Retrieved 9/06/2004, from http://www.crt.dk/uk/staff/chm/trends.htm.marketingvox.com. (2007a). *Internet Censorship Strengthens in Malaysia, Kazakhstan and Other Countries.* Retrieved 16/09/2011 from http://www.marketingvox.com/Internet-censorship-strengthens-in-malaysia-kazakhstan-and-other-countries-031803/.marketingvox.com. (2007b). Kazakhstan's Internet Access Not Very Nice. Retrieved 17/09/2011 from http://www.marketingvox.com/kazakhstans-Internet-access-not-very-nice-031795/.

Mason, D., Milne, S. (2002). E-Commerce and Community Tourism. In: P. C. Palvia, S. C. Palvia & E. M. Roche (Eds.), Global Information Technology and Electronic Commerce: issues for the New Millenium (pp. 294–310). Marietta, Gerogia: Ivy League Publishing Ltd.

Minghetti, V., Buhalis, D. (2010). Digital Divide in Tourism. *Journal of Travel Research, 49*(3) 267–281.

Morrisette, S., Gazala, M. E., Green, E. N., Reitsma, R., Metzger, T. (1999). Europe's digital decade. *The Forrester Report Quick View, November 1999.* Retrieved July 23, 2000, from http://www.forrester.com/

O'Brien, P. F. (1999). Intelligent Assistants for retail travel agents. *Information Technology & Tourism, 2*(3/4), 213–228.

O'Brien, P. F. (2002). *An architecture for ubiquitous travel service delivery.* Paper presented at the European Conference on Information Systems, Gdansk, Poland.

O'Connor, P. (1999). *Electronic information distribution in tourism and hospitality.* Wallingford: CABI Publishing.

O'Connor, P., Frew, A. J. (2002). The future of hotel electronic distribution: expert and industry perspectives. *Cornell Hotel and Restaurant Administration Quarterly, 43*(3), 33–45.

Oppenheim, A. N. (1992). *Questionnaire Design, Interviewing and Attitude Measurement* (2nd ed.). New York: Continuum.

Organization for Economic Cooperation and Development (OECD). (2001). Understanding the Digital Divide. Paris: OECD.

Poon, A. (1993). Tourism, Technology and Competitive Strategies. Oxford: CAB International.

ROMIR Monitoring. (2009). Russian Internet Advertising Report. Accessed 20/03/09 at www.mediarevolution.ru/english/231.html.

Rubin, H. J., Rubin, I. (2005). *Qualitative Interviewing : The Art of Hearing Data* (2nd ed.). Thousand Oaks, California: Sage Publications.

Rybina, L., Garkavenko, V. (2009). Internet adoption by prospective consumers: example of Kazakhstani, Russian and Ukrainian markets. VI KIMEP International Research Conference (6th KIRC), 23–24 April, Almaty, Kazakhstan.

Selwyn, N. (2004). Reconsidering Political and Popular Understandings of the Digital Divide. New Media Society, 6(3), 341–362.

Seymour, W. S. (2001). In the flesh or online? Exploring qualitative research methodologies. *Qualitative Research, 1*(2), 147–168.

Silverman, D. (Ed.). (2004). *Qualitative Research: Theory, Method and Practice* (2nd ed.). London: SAGE Publications.

Smith, C., Jenner, P. (1998). Tourism and the Internet. *Travel & Tourism Analyst, 1*, 62–81.

Tengrinews.kz. (2011a). *KazakhTelecom introduces new Internet tariffs from 1 October 2011.* Retrieved 10/12/2011 from http://tengrinews.kz/kazakhstan_news/kazahtelekom-1-oktyabrya-zapuskaet-novyie-tarifnyie-planyi-Internet-polzovateley-197968/.

Tengrinews.kz. (2011b). *Internet speed in Kazkahstan to reach 16 Mbit per second by 2014.* Retrieved 04/03/2012 from http://en.tengrinews.kz/Internet/Internet-speed-in-Kazakhstan-to-reach-16-Mbit-per-second-by-2014-1126/.

Tiberghien, G., Garkavenko, V. (2011). Exploratory study on contributions of Information and Communication Technologies to the development of ecocultural tourism in Central Kazakhstan. *Proceedings of ENTER 2011—Information and Communication Technologies in Tourism.* The International Conference on Information Technology and Travel & Tourism IFITT's Global Travel & Tourism Technology and eBusiness Forum. 26th–28th January 2011, Innsbruck, Austria.

Tse, A. C.-B. (2003). Disintermediation of travel agents in the hotel industry. International Journal of Hospitality Management, 22, 453–460.

CHAPTER 13

PERCEPTIONS OF FOREIGN INVESTORS ON THE TOURISM MARKET IN CENTRAL ASIA

KEMAL KANTARCI

CONTENTS

INTRODUCTION

Central Asia (CA) has a rich history, to which numerous tribes and nationalities have contributed over the last 2500 years. A vital factor in the history of the southern part of the region was its location astride the most direct trade route between China and Europe, the so called Silk Route which began to develop in the Roman times (Buyers, 2003; Akayev, 2001). CA countries—Kazakhstan, Kyrgyzstan, Turkmenistan, Uzbekistan, and Tajikistan—contain a large and rich untapped tourism market that has great potential for foreign tourism investors and in particular for Turkish tourism investors. At the same time CA, as a new destination, has been gaining importance in the travel and tourism international market (Ghosh et al., 2003a, 2003b; Jeffries, 2003; Jenkins, 1997; Qu and Zhang, 1997).

This chapter examines the foreign investors' perceptions of general investment, tourism specific investment, and sustainability investment consideration factors in four of the five CA states (CAS) of Kazakhstan, Kyrgyzstan, Turkmenistan, and Uzbekistan. Due to a lack of tourism information and infrastructure Tajikistan was excluded from this research. The s t u d y also tested if overall investment conditions of the four CAS can be explained as a function of general investment, tourism specific investment, and tourism sustainable investment consideration factors.

After the collapse of USSR in 1991, the five Soviet Republics of CA were faced for the first time with the prospect of existence as independent states (Culpan and Akcaoglu, 2003; Curtis, 2003a and 2003b; Gurgen, 2000; Nowak and Steagall, 2003). CA is being touted as terribly significant to the entire world (Buyers, 2003). The five CA countries occupy a territory of some 3,994,400 km² and have a total population of nearly 60 million (Gleason, 2003). The region stretches from the Caspian Sea in the west, to China in the east, and from central Siberia in the north to Afghanistan, Iran and Pakistan in the south (Buyers, 2003). Kazakhstan, the largest of the four, occupies 2.7 million km² with a population of 14.8 million (2001) (Curtis, 2003a, 2003b). Kyrgyzstan occupies 198,500 km² and has a population of 5 million (2001). Turkmenistan has a landm a s s of 488,100 km² with a population of 5.5 million and Uzbekistan occupies 447,400 km² with a total population of 25.1 million inhabitants (2001) (Gleason, 2003). One of the main examples of cultural, historical and infrastructural proximity is the Silk Road project (Cabrini, 2002); established over many hundreds of years between Turkey and the CA countries. Now Turkey and the CA countries are in the same project (WTO, 2005a, 2005b). Infrastructural proximity such as highways, railways and airports also provides relatively comfortable and easy accessibility between Turkey and the CA region. There appears to be sufficient resources to expand opportunities for investment in tourism infrastructure at all levels (www.Adb.org/CAREC, 2005). For example, Uzbekistan with 33 airports with paved runways, Turkmenistan with 23, Kazakhstan with 67, and Kyrgyzstan with 16 airports (2004). All have fairly easy access from major airports and market areas to the entire region (The World Factbook, Country listing, 2005).

A review of literature on investment confirms that foreign direct investment (FDI) is largely influenced by the earlier trade relations and by the geographical and cultural proximity to host countries (Culpan and Akcaoglu, 2003). The rate of cultural change between the host country vis-à-vis its home country orientation is probably one of most important factors transnational corporations (TNCs) must fully comprehend. Similarities in culture and language between the host country and the home country of the TNC tend to facilitate the process of planning, development, managing and controlling hotels, resorts and tourist facilities located abroad (Go et al., 1990). Naturally, geographical proximity along with cultural proximity has helped some Turkish companies to expand their investment into these countries (Culpan and Akcaoglu, 2003).

The nature of such collaboration and expansion of investment into these countries by Turkish companies can be best explained by an eclectic paradigm of international production theories, which is also known as Ownership–Location–Integration (OLI) paradigm that combines theories into a general eclectic framework (Fig. 1; Culpan and Akcaoglu, 2003).

The eclectic paradigm suggests that FDI depends upon three advantages. The TNC has some specific ownership advantage (O) as compared to the domestic/local firm, thus making it more competitive. There has to be a location advantage (L) of production in the foreign country rather than producing at home for export. There also has to be some internalization advantage (I) meaning risk sharing and scale economy benefits. Ownership advantages or firm-specific assets can be patents, trademarks, human capital, managerial superiority or reputation for quality.

These confer cost advantages and market power sufficient to overcome the costs of producing abroad.

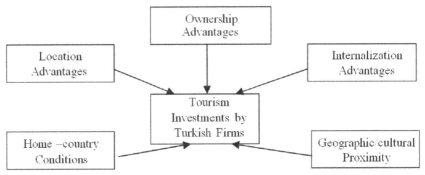

FIGURE 1   Enhanced OLI model for Turkish tourism investors, adapted from Culpan, and Akcaoglu (2003). An examination of Turkish direct investments in Central and Eastern Europe and the Commonwealth of Independent States. In: S. T. Marinova, and M. A. Marinov (Eds.), Foreign direct investment in Central and Eastern Europe (pp. 181–197), Ashgate: USA.

Location advantages, which are external to the firm, depend on the host country's economic characteristics. They can be analyzed in three categories, namely economic, social, and cultural and political. Economic factors include the quantity and quality of the production factors, size and scope of the market, and transport and telecommunication costs. Social and cultural factors consist of psychic distance between the home and host country. Psychic distance implies the geographical, cultural, political and linguistical distance between the home and the host country. Political factors include the government policies that affect inward FDI flows, international production and intrafirm trade. Based on this theory of ownership advantages, Culpan and Akcaoglu (2003) explain that Turkish firms possess both tangible and intangible assets such as capital, strategic leadership, talented and skilled human resources, and domestic and overseas experience to penetrate CA as general and tourism markets. These resources combined with Turkey's geographic and/or cultural proximity to the CA countries give Turkish tourism firms an advantage over other competing companies. This advantage has resulted in around $561 million in direct investment (1980–2005) and $42 million in tourism investment between 1980 and 2005 in the four states of CA (http://www.treasury.gov.tr/stat/yabser/sermaye_ihraci.xls, 2005). There are many investment opportunities for different sectors. In the tourism sector, not only hotel investments but also opportunities such as logistic and communication, health and thermal tourism, camp-caravan, shopping centers, tourism education centers, transportation facility for the TTIs are also part of the investment opportunity portfolio. Naturally, the rapidly expanding markets of Asia, a region in which cultural similarity impact might be expected, would encourage the development of tourism projects in different forms, whether it be investment or number of arrivals between Turkey and CA countries (Williams, 1998).

Go and Ritchie (1990) point out that TNCs usually determine marketing opportunities in a foreign country by way of a four-step process—analysis of the general environment determining market potential, forecasting sales and estimating and weighing prospective profitability vs. risk. The search for a location with a lower risk and greater return will be aided by a location study. For a greater return, various business environmental factors, market potential and capital budgeting should be studied. The ideal site, besides having a larger net present value (NPV) and a higher internal rate of return (IRR), should have high scores in the screening criteria, which encompass risk, incentives, repatriation, foreign investment restrictions, tax, market and the hotel industry growth rate.

Thus, this particular study attempted to include three major areas of investment consideration factors—general investment consideration factors, tourism-specific investment considerations, and sustainability investment considerations. More specifically, this particular study is one of the first attempts to understand how Turkish companies perceive the investment conditions and the investment process using a conceptual framework of market entry opportunities in CA countries. It is hoped that information generated from this study could be of further help for investors, tourism developers and government officials.

TOURISM INVESTMENT CONDITIONS

Kazakhstan is considered the most successful Central Asian country in terms of both economic and political reform. The government actively encourages international trade and foreign investment (Gleason, 2003). For purposes of tourism promotion in the Republic of Kazakhstan, the country has developed a certain standard-and-legal basis. It embraces virtually all types of tourism and specifies legal, economic, social and organizational fundamentals of undertaking tourism activities. In addition, in 1997 Kazakhstan has developed a strategy for tourism development up to 2030. Over 370 hotels of various types and 430 tourism agencies function in the Republic of Kazakhstan (Voronina, 2005, http:// www.bis-nis.doc.gov). Investment areas cover sectors such as hotels, health centers, business tourism, adventure tours, sport tourism, museums and parks, equipment for hotels and event tourism.

Uzbekistan has many historical, archeological and ecological sites along the Ancient Silk Road, offering great potential for development and various incentives to attract investors. Tourism's contribution to Gross Domestic Product (GDP) is currently only 0.4 percent, but it is set to become a more important income-generating sector in the future. The government plans to create free economic tourist areas as well as new hotels, camping sites and activities. Uzbek tourism hopes to attract foreign investors to the privatization plan, which will be implemented under three different categories: hotels for sale, hotels for reconstruction and upgrade of services, and construction of new hotels. Creating some new theme parks and enhancing the quality of tourist services are also part of their privatization plan. With the population exceeding 25 million, Uzbekistan has the potential to benefit from the growth of jobs and revenue that a more developed tourism infrastructure could bring. There are over 500 registered tourist firms and agencies in Uzbekistan. Training of tourism staff will be a priority. Since independence, Uzbekistan has been modernizing its airports, air fleet, railroads and roads. Some big projects include: modernization of the Tashkent's airport infrastructure, the works associated with the modernization of the regional airports, the construction of tourist class hotels in cities along the Great Silk Road, the construction of hotels and related infrastructure in Chimgan mountains, and the construction of theme parks throughout Uzbekistan (Cabrini, 2002; DEIK, 2004; Ebrd, 2005; Investment Policy Review of Uzbekistan, 1999; WTO, 2005a, b).

Kyrgyzstan, with its many unique places and distinctive nature, has an eventful and interesting history with over a thousand historical and cultural monuments (http://www.sairamtour.com, 2005). Lying between China and Kazakhstan, Uzbekistan and Tajikistan, Kyrgyzstan is a country of rare natural beauty, sometimes referred to as the "Switzerland of Asia" (Gleason, 2003). The Kyrgyzstan government has made good progress in establishing the legal and regulatory foundation for a market economy (Akayev, 2001). A comprehensive foreign investment law was adopted in September 1997. Kyrgyzstan has 172 hotels, approximately 293 travel agents (2005) and 1925 hotel rooms (2003). The total employment figure in the tourism sector is 6635 (2004) (http://stat-gvc. bishkek.su, 2004; http://www.tsm.kg, 2005).

Turkmenistan was known for most of its history as a loosely defined geographic region of independent tribes (Nichol, 2003a, b). The Government has now completed a full year of implementation of its strategy for Turkmenistan's economic, political, and cultural development for the period up to 2020. In an effort to attract foreign investment and tourism to Turkmenistan, the government has focused on infrastructure, construction of quality accommodation, including several 4-star hotels, and the development of conference and business facilities. Turkmenistan now hosts the largest and most modern airport in CA (www. turkme-nistanembassy.org, 2005). A rail link to the Iranian network, which enables train travel from Turkmenistan to Turkey (Istanbul), was completed in 1996. The railway system also connects to highways and airports (www.sitara.com, 2005). Tourism has been designated a priority area of economic development. In 2001, hotel rooms numbered 2616 with 6571 beds (1997) (www.nationsencyclopedia.com, 2005).

Today, the number of tourist arrivals in the CA countries is around 3.304 million and tourism receipts are $726 million (excluding Turkmenistan, 2004) (WTO, 2005a, b). It is clear from the efforts of these countries that they are making tourism one of their strategic initiatives in their development plans.

DATA SAMPLE

This study examines foreign investors' perceptions of tourism investment conditions in CAS. This study specifically examines investors' perceptions of overall foreign investment conditions with respect to tourism and the most attractive investment area in tourism for foreign investors from the Turkish tourism investors' point of view. The investigation-involved members of the Turkish Tourism Investors Association (TTIA), established in 1988 by the principal tourism investors in Turkey. TTIA is a private nongovernmental organization initiative whose main objective is to bring together entrepreneurs investing in the tourism sector and provide assistance in their present and future plans. TTIA presently has 178 members representing over 200 thousand beds in the up market accommodation sector. The member establishments are mostly 4- and 5-star hotels, and 1st class holiday villages. TTIA members have also invested in marinas and yachting, tourism-oriented land and air trans port, tour operating, touristic shopping centers, entertainment and recreation facilities and golf courses. The total investment portfolio is around US$18 billion representing 3/4 of the private investment in tourism in Turkey. Besides, TTIA members offer services in the tourism sector, such as turnkey project contracting, tourism related equipment and material manufacturing and representation. So far TTIA members have constructed and are operating several touristic facilities in various countries, mainly in the Commonwealth Independent States (CIS) and the Balkan region. One of the TTIA's activities is to assist and achieve collaboration for foreign entrepreneurs with their local counterparts, who are interested in tourism investment and management in Turkey or in third world countries. In this context, international cooperation is vital for TTIA to be considered as a reference institution (http://www.ttyd.org.tr, 2005).

The study population consisted of all members of the TTIA, approximately 178 investors. The questionnaire was sent by fax, mail and in some cases by hand as face-to-face delivery. The first wave of questionnaires was sent out in the last quarter of 2005 with a 3-month data collection period. Nearly 90% of the questionnaires were returned within the first two months of the 3-month data collection period. This data collection effort resulted in 61 usable questionnaires for the study with a response rate of 34%. Since the unit of the analysis was the organization and that the study used the entire sample population, the generated response rate was deemed appropriate. The number was considered large enough to yield a sizeable base for examining investor perceptions of tourism investment conditions in the CAS. Given the fact that since the study had a minimum 1–4 ratio for every factor analysis variable to the number of observations, the total number (n – 61) was large enough to conduct factor analysis on the three types of investment consideration items (Hair et al., 2002). The study used a proportionally stratified random sampling technique based on the distribution of investors by origin.

SURVEY INSTRUMENT

The survey questionnaire was divided into five parts. **Part I** comprised questions about investment types, magnitude, and the intention of future investment in the CAS. **Part II** had a list of 15 general investment consideration items that were generated based on a review of related literature and the opinions of a select group of investors. This was in order to evaluate the conditions that were suitable for general investment and choosing a place for investment in the CAS. These general market conditions reflected concerns and conditions about market situations and structures, the nature and existence of incentives and workforce conditions. The questions were rated on a 5-point Likert type scale ranging from 1 (not at all suitable) to 5 (very suitable). The information collected in this section included such items as: conditions for entering the market, fiscal regime conditions, stable growth in the market place, understanding business environment, past experience with the sector, safety and security issues in general, level of responsiveness of government institutions, sufficiency in the all other investment criteria, direct and indirect incentives, provision of investment land/property, competitions, local business environment, workforce, and logistic matters. **Part III** mainly concerned questions regarding the evaluation of tourism specific investment factors as areas of direct tourism facilities such as rural tourism, camp and caravan, health and thermal tourism facilities, winter tourism, renovation and modernization of facilities; and areas of tourism support facilities such as shopping centers, serves concessionaries at airports, entertainment centers, accommodation and support services for Silk Road issues. **Part IV** collected information on tourism sustainable investment factors that included positive investment conditions such as appropriate tourism policies, growing tourism market, attractive incentives relative to other competing investment and facilities, degree of liberalism in the economy, low construction costs compared with European countries, long-term use of public land with infrastructure in place, appropriate law and regulations system and attractive investment cost options for sustainable tourism investment. These items were rated on a 5-point Likert type scale ranging from 1 (strongly disagree) to 5 (strongly agree).

The last section, **Part V**, generated information concerning the general conditions for overall investment suitability in each of the four CAS; Kyrgyzstan, Kazakhstan, Uzbekistan and Turkmenistan. This question was rated on a 5-point Likert type scale ranging from 1 (not at all suitable) to 5 (very suitable).

STATISTICAL ANALYZES

The analysis of data in this study consisted of three stages. Descriptive runs were firstly employed to investigate the frequency distribution of responses to the stated questions. These questions were composed of issues about investment types, magnitude, and intention about future investment in the CAS. Secondly, the items of general investment, tourism specific investment, and tourism sustainable investment were factor analyzed separately to identify the underlying dimensions of investment consideration factors. Based on the results of factor analysis, independent t-tests were used to examine the general investment factors, tourism specific investment factors and tourism sustainable investment factors with regard to general questions. Then the resultant factors of investment considerations were used in regression analysis in which the overall investment condition for each of the four countries was used as the dependent variable.

FINDINGS

CHARACTERISTICS OF TURKISH TOURISM INVESTORS

The descriptive analysis of the data revealed that almost 64% of the investors were in tourism and 36% were in non tourism-related areas of business. Almost 51% of the participants expressed that they have an investment or business facility in CA countries, 49% of the participants expressed that they had no investment and any business facility in the countries. Almost 43% of the investors who have invested in CAS made their investments in businesses directly related to the tourism field. The remaining investors, who invested in the CAS, made their investments in areas not directly related to tourism or nontourism businesses. The distribution of companies which have an investment or business facility in the CAS is as follows: 3% in Kyrgyzstan, 34% Kazakhstan,

11% Uzbekistan, and 3% Turkmenistan. It is also interesting to note that 21% of the participants who currently had no investments in these countries expressed that they would like to invest in the CAS.

FACTOR ANALYSIS OF GENERAL INVESTMENT FACTORS

Fifteen general investment conditions were factor analyzed using principal components with varimax rotation. The overall significance of the correlation matrix was 0.00, with a Barlett Test of Sphericity value of 607.8. The statistical probability and the test indicated that there was a significant correlation between the variables, and the use of factor analysis was appropriate. The Kaiser– Meyer–Olkin value was 0.669. The data was, therefore suitable for the proposed statistical procedure of factor analysis. The eigenvalues suggested that three-factor solution be identified, representing approximately 64.5% of the total variance in general investment factors. All retained factors had an eigenvalue greater than 1 and all factor loadings were above 0.53. The factors were labeled: "General Market Condition," "Incentives," and "Workforce Condition." The "General Market Condition" factor explained the highest percentage of the total variance (25.2%). The reliability coefficients (Cronbach's-a) ranged from 0.643 to 0.886. Table 1 presents the results of the factor analysis with its associated statistics.

Eleven tourism specific investment factors were also analyzed to delineate the underlying dimensions of tourism specific investment consideration. This analysis resulted in two factors, which explained almost 66.7% of the total variance in tourism specific investment (Table 2). The overall significance of the correlation matrix was 0.00, with a Barlett Test of sphericity value of 485.8 and a Kaiser–Meyer–Olkin value of 0.785. All retained factors had an eigenvalue greater than 1 and all factor loadings were greater than 0.52. The two factors were identified as "Direct Tourism Facilities,' and "Tourism Support Facilities." The areas of direct tourism facilities factor explained the highest percentage of the total variance (52.5%). The reliability coefficients (Cronbach's-a) ranged from 0.727 to 0.925. Table 2 presents the results of the factor analysis with its associated statistics.

The nine tourism sustainable investment factors were also analyzed to delineate the underlying dimensions of sustainable investment consideration and resulted in two factors, which accounted for almost 61.5% of the total variance in tourism sustainable investment (Table 3). The overall significance of the correlation matrix was 0.00, with a Barlett test sphericity value of 212.5. The Kaiser–Meyer–Olkin value was 0.714. All retained factors had an Eigen-value greater than 1 and all factor loadings were greater than 0.60 with the exception of one item—"adequate tourism legal system" with a loading value of 0.40. The two factors were identified as "Positive investment conditions for sustainability," and "Attractive investment cost." The positive investment conditions for the sustainability factor was almost 40% of the total variance with a reliability coefficient of Cronbach's-a 0.774. The Attractive investment cost factor was almost 22% of the total variance with a reliability coefficient of Cronbach's-a 0.791. Combined, these two factors accounted for almost 62% of the variance in tourism sustainable investment variables.

The study also compared the seven delineated factor groupings of general investment, specific tourism investment, and sustainability investment consideration variables with respect to three descriptive questions: (1) type of business area—direct tourism related vs. indirect or nontourism-related areas of business; (2) whether or not, the selected companies already had some investment or business activities in the four CAS countries; and (3) if the ones that did not have business activities in the four countries of the CAS whether they would consider making an investment there. The study used an independent t-test to do the comparisons. Table 4 presents the results of the t-test analyzes with mean scores, associated t-values and significant levels.

TABLE 1 Factor analysis of the general investment consideration factors.

Investment consideration	Factor loading	Eigenvalue	Explained variance	Reliability coefficient
Factor 1: General market condition	0.855	3.024	39.10%	0.886
Conditions for entering the market				
Fiscal regime (tax, incentives, etc.)	0.755			

TABLE 1 *(Continued)*

Investment consideration	Factor loading	Eigenvalue	Explained variance	Reliability coefficient
Stable growth in the market place	0.734			
Understanding business environment	0.701			
Past experience with the sector	0.673			
Safety and security conditions in general	0.593			
Level of responsiveness of government institutions	0.581			
Sufficiency in the all other investment criteria	0.533			
Factor 2: Incentives	0.883	1.765	14.70%	0.869
Incentives (indirect effect)				
Incentives (direct effect)	0.77			
Provision of investment place/ property	0.751			
Competition conditions from the domestic market	0.733			
Local business environment (tax, incentives, cost base)	0.673			
Factor 3: Workforce condition	0.822	1.283	10.70%	0.643
The skills of workforce				
Logistic and communication possibilities	0.729			
Total variance explained			64.5	

Note: Extraction Method—principal component analysis; Rotation Method—Varimax with Kaiser normalization; KMO (Kaiser–Meyer–Olkin measure of sampling adequacy) – 0.669; Bartlett's test of sphericity: p – 0.000.

Scale rating: 1 – not good condition at all, 2 – slightly good condition, 3 – somewhat good, 4 – good, and 5 – very good.

TABLE 2   Factor analysis of the tourism specific investment factors.

Tourism specific investment consideration	Factor loading	Eigenvalue	Explained variance	Reliability coefficient
Factor 1: Areas of direct tourism facilities	0.922	5.77	52.50%	0.925
Rural tourism facilities				
Officially registered and restored, historical/cultural sites	0.825			
Camp and caravan facilities	0.813			
Health and thermal facilities	0.786			
Tourism education facilities	0.76			
Winter tourism options and facilities	0.747			
Renewed and modernization of tourism and investment improvement	0.697			
Factor 2: Areas of tourism support facilities	0.923	1.56	14.20%	0.727
Shopping centers				
Service concessionaires at airports	0.793			
Entertainment centers	0.573			
Accommodation and support services for the silk road	0.522			
Total variance explained			66.70%	

Note: Extraction Method—principal component analysis; Rotation Method—Varimax with Kaiser normalization; KMO (Kaiser–Meyer–Olkin measure of sampling adequacy) – 0.785; Bartlett's test of sphericity: p – 0.000.

Scale rating: 1 – not good condition at all, 2 – slightly good condition, 3 – somewhat good, 4 – good, and 5 – very good.

A closer look at the mean differences with respect to three questions suggests that those companies that already have some investment or business activities in the four CAS countries seem to have more favorable responses to investment conditions. However, significant differences were found across the three questions in relation to general investment conditions. The companies that already have direct tourism related businesses in general had a perceived higher mean ($\times$ –3.68) score for "positive investment conditions for sustainability" than the ones that did not ($\times$ –3.65). The difference was statistically significant at the 0.027 probability level. It is also interesting to see that the companies that already had some investment and business activities in the four CAS countries had a lower perceived mean score ($\times$ −2.54) for "areas of direct tourism facilities" than did those companies ($\times$ −3.02) that had no investment or business activities at the time of the study The difference was statistically significant at the 0.026 probability level. This finding may be attributed to the fact that companies that have experience with the CAS countries may know the situation of business and investment conditions better. These companies may be the ones that take risk, as venture capitalists often do in unexplored markets.

TABLE 3   Factor analysis of the tourism sustainable investment factors.

Sustainability investment consideration	Factor loading	Eigen-value	Explained variance	Reliability coefficient
Factor 1: Positive investment conditions for sustainability Appropriate tourism policies	0.813	3.59	39.90%	0.774
Conducive market conditions for tourism market growth and expansion	0.796			
More attractive incentives relative to other investment options and facilities	0.73			
Wide market possibilities as a result of geographic location	0.708			
Degree of liberalism in the economy	0.62			
Appropriate law and regulations system	0.405			
Factor 2: Attractive investment cost Low construction cost compare with European countries	0.887	1.94	21.50%	0.791
Long term use of public land with infrastructure in place	0.8			
Relatively low capital cost and expenses	0.783			
Total variance explained			61.50%	

Note: Extraction Method—principal component analysis; Rotation Method—Varimax with Kaiser normalization; KMO (Kaiser–Meyer–Olkin measure of sampling adequacy) − 0.714; Bartlett's test of sphericity: $p − 0.000$.
Scale rating: 1 − strongly disagree; 2 − disagree; 3 − neither disagree nor agree; 4 − agree; and 5 − strongly agree.

TABLE 4 Results of the *t*-test analyzes.

Variables	Direct tourism-related (63.9%)	Indirect tourism-related (36.1.2%)	t-value	Significance level
General investment conditions	3.62	2.99	2.21	.032*
Incentives	3.26	3.13	.744	.461
Workforce conditions	2.89	3.09	-1.08	.285
Areas of direct tourism facilities	2.75	2.82	-.291	.772
Areas of tourism support facilities	3.46	3.18	1.61	.114
Positive investment conditions for sustainability	3.68	3.35	2.28	.027*
Attractive investment cost	3.22	3.54	-1.52	.135
Investor profile	Yes	No	t-value	Sig.
General investment conditions	3.46	2.98	3.46	.004*
Incentives	3.27	3.16	.714	.478
Workforce conditions	2.91	3.01	-.549	.585
Areas of direct tourism facilities	2.54	3.02	-2.27	.026*
Areas of tourism support facilities	3.40	3.32	.453	.652
Positive investment conditions for sustainability	3.65	3.47	1.29	.201
Attractive investment cost	3.16	3.52	-1.77	.082
Investor Attitudes about investing in CA countriesa	Planned (21.3%)	Not planned (27.9)	t-value	Sig.
General investment conditions	3.25	2.78	2.01	.055*
Incentives	3.07	3.22	-649	.522
Workforce conditions	3.19	2.88	1.31	.199
Areas of direct tourism facilities	2.96	3.06	-355	.726
Areas of tourism facilities	3.53	3.16	1.64	.111
Positive investment conditions for sustainability	3.44	3.49	-223	.825
Attractive investment cost	3.64	3.43	.928	.362

"*" indicates significant level at .05 or better probability level.

aThe values do not add up to 100 since the figures represent only those who did not have investment in CAS countries.

TABLE 5 Regression analysis: prediction of perceived overall investment conditions.

Variables	Kyrgyzstan	Kazakhstan	Uzbekistan	Turkmenistan
	b coeff. (sig.)	b coeff. (sig.)	b coeff. (sig.)	b coeff. (sig.)
Investment consideration				
General investment conditions	.218	.642*	0.068	−.371*
	(148)	(.000)	(0.649)	(.028)
Incentives	−.268*	−222	.000	.105
	(.071)	(.137)	(1.000)	(.517)
Workforce conditions	.575*	(−.062)	.354*	.573*
	(.000)	(.599)	(.004)	(.000)
Tourism specific investment consideration				
Areas of direct tourism facilities	.159	.044	.045	.176
	(.196)	(.723)	(.712)	(.198)
Areas of tourism support facilities	−.375*	−.048	.192	.078
	(.019)	(.758)	(.219)	(.651)
Sustainability investment consideration				
Positive investment conditions for sustainability	−.216	.145	−.310*	−.141
	(.139)	(.322)	(.036)	(.380)
Attractive Investment cost	.443*	.442*	.544*	.240*
	(.001)	(.001)	(.000)	(.078)
Adjusted R^2	0.456	0.448	0.458	0.335
F-test value	8.194	7.946	8.248	5.314
F-test sig.	.00	.00	.00	.00

Dependent variable: overall investment condition; 1 – not good condition at all, 2 – slightly good condition, 3 – somewhat good, 4 – good, and 5 – very good.
"*" indicates significant level at 0.05 or better probability level.

REGRESSION ANALYSIS

In order to further understand and predict overall investment conditions for each of the four CAS countries—Kyrgyzstan, Kazakhstan, Uzbekistan and Turkmenistan (as a function of general investment, tourism specific investment and tourism sustainable investment consideration factors) the resultant factors of investment considerations were used as predictors (7 independent variables) in four regression models. In these, the overall investment condition of each of the four countries was used as the dependent variable (Table 5). An examination of the results of the four models revealed that overall the models were significant at a probability level of 0.05 and better, and the adjusted R^2 values ranged from 0.335 for Turkmenistan to 0.458 for Uzbekistan. The adjusted R^2 values were 0.448 and 0.456 for Kazakhstan and Kyrgyzstan, respectively. These significant R^2 values indicate that a significant portion of the variance in evaluating the overall investment conditions of the CAS countries could be explained as a function of the included investment consideration factors.

With significance (as measured by p-value) and importance (as measured by standardized b coefficients) the study indicated that attractive investment cost options as one of the predictors of overall evaluation of investment conditions for the CAS countries for sustainable tourism investment, is significant at the probability level of 0.07 and better. This variable had a positive sign and was significant for the four countries included in the study. The standardized b coefficients were 0.544 for Uzbekistan, 0.443 for Kyrgyzstan, 0.442 for Kazakhstan, and 0.240 for Turkmenistan. With the exception of the model for Kazakhstan, the factor of workforce conditions, as one of the independent variables of the overall evaluation of investment conditions, exerts positive significant influence on explaining the overall evaluation of investment conditions for each of the four CAS countries. The standardized beta coefficient for this variable was 0.575 for Kyrgyzstan, followed by 0.573 for Turkmenistan, and 0.354 for Uzbekistan. The study also indicated that the significance and relative importance of variables showed variation from one country to country. The significant variables for the model of Kyrgyzstan were workforce with a beta coefficient of 0.575 (p – 0.00), followed by attractive investment cost with a beta coefficient of 0.443 (p – 0.00), and areas of tourism support facilities with a negative b-value of –.375 (p – 0.01). On the other hand, the significant variables for the model of Kazakhstan were general investment conditions with a b coefficient of 0.642 (p – 0.00), followed by attractive investment cost with a b coefficient of 0.442 (p –.00). However, the variables of attractive investment cost with a b coefficient of 0.544 and workforce conditions with a b coefficient of 0.354 (p −.004) exerted positive effects and the variable of investment conditions for sustainability with a b coefficient of −.310 (p − 0.036) exerted a negative effect, on the overall evaluation of the investment conditions in Uzbekistan. The significant and important variables for the Turkmenistan model were workforce conditions (b − 0.573; p − 0.00), attractive investment cost (b − 0.240; p − 0.078), and general investment conditions (b − 0.371; p − 0.028). The first two variables had a positive relation with overall investment evaluation and the last variable—general investment conditions—had a negative relation with overall investment evaluation.

CONCLUSION

This particular study attempted to examine Turkish investors' perceptions of general investment, tourism specific investment, tourism sustainability investment consideration factors in the four selected Central Asian countries. More specifically, this particular study is one of the first attempts to understand how Turkish companies perceive investment conditions and investment process using a conceptual framework of market entry opportunities in the CA countries. The study also generated information on the prediction level of the overall perceived investment condition in each of the four CA countries as a result of the perceived evaluation of three investment consideration factors.

The results indicated that the delineated three-factor groupings of general investment conditions explained almost 65% of the variance, two factor groupings of tourism specific investment conditions explained almost 67% of the variance, and two factor groupings of tourism sustainability investment conditions explained almost 62% of the variance in investment consideration variables. Combined, these three types of investment conditions predicted 0.335% of the perceived overall investment condition in Turkmenistan, 0.448% in Kazakhstan, 0.456% in Kyrgyzstan, and 0.458% in Uzbekistan, suggesting that these investment conditions are reasonably robust and represent a majority of market entry (investment into a new place) barriers and considerations.

It is also observed, from the findings of the regression models for each country, that the significance and relative importance of the delineated factor groupings of investment conditions show variation from country to country. Thus, each should develop country specific invest-ment strategies and incentives to attract more foreign investment in tourism industries. These incentives may cover a range of incentives, including lower taxes, low interest rates, higher ownership options for foreign investors, long-term land lease options and similar. However, making investment cost attractive with incentives seems to apply to all four countries. This point needs to be carefully incorporated into the investment strategies of the four CA countries. Trained workforce and favorable general investment conditions are also regarded important in considering further investment into such countries, thus, these factors also need to be part of investment-based development strategies in the four countries of CA.

Although the findings of this study are about Turkish investors, this may be one of its limitations in terms of generalization of the study's findings. It is logical to suggest that similar studies with a similar ques-tionnaire can be easily conducted for investment companies located in different countries. It is hoped that the information generated from this study could be of further help for investors, tourism developers and gov-ernment officials. It is equally important to mention that this study did not directly assess the strength and importance of demand and market considerations for these countries, which is very important. However, this is beyond the scope of this current study and this point needs further research and careful investigation in order to augment supply driven stud-ies such as this one. Most of the general findings from this study about the perceived importance of investment consideration variables could also help prospective investors regardless of their location with their future investment plan in the CA countries. The study also revealed that investment companies that already had business activities in the selected CA countries are likely to further explore and expand investment activi-ties. These companies, unlike the ones that have limited experience in the four CA countries, seem to have much more favorable perceptions of the investment conditions. Thus, the officials of the selected CA countries could use currently active companies in their respective countries to encourage them to team up with other companies to further attract more investment capital. Naturally, this would force the CA countries to be more creative and innovative in their efforts to obtain foreign investment. They need to develop creative, future oriented, sustainable investment incentive packages and plans to promote their countries. Such efforts on the part of the CA countries would also mean developing an integrative and comprehensive development plan for their countries.

ACKNOWLEDGMENT

This article was originally published in *Tourism Management* in 2007, vol. 28, pp. 820–825. With the Publisher's permission dated December 14, 2013, this article as Chapter 13 is reprinted in the book.

KEYWORDS

- **Central Asian States**
- **Foreign Direct Investment**
- **Foreign Investor**
- **Geographic/Cultural Proximity**
- **Home-Country Conditions**
- **Tourism Investment**

REFERENCES

About TYD (2005). http://www.ttyd.org.tr/english/engmain.htm.

ADB, Central Asia Regional Economic Cooperation—CAREC (2005). http://www.adb.org/CAREC/default.asp.

Akayev, A. (2001). Kyrgyzstan. Australia: Asia Pacific Press.

Buyers, L. M. (2003). Central Asia in Focus. New York: Nova Science Publishers, Inc.

Breakdown of Capital Export of Turkey by Country and Sector (2005). http://www.treasury.gov.tr/stat/yabser/sermaye_ihraci.xls.

Cabrini, L. (2002). Review and prospects of the WTO Silk Road project. In Fourth international meeting on the silk road. Bukhara, Uzbekistan (pp. 1–3).

Culpan, E., Akcaoglu, E. (2003). An examination of Turkish direct investments in Central and Eastern Europe and the Commonwealth of Independent States. In S. T. Marinova, & M. A. Marinov (Eds.), Foreign direct investment in Central and Eastern Europe (pp. 181–197). USA: Ashgate.

Curtis, G. E. (2003a). Kazakhstan: A country study. In L. M. Buyers (Ed.), Central Asia in focus (pp. 37–116). New York: Nova Science. Curtis, G. E. (2003b). Kyrgyzstan: A country study. In L. M. Buyers

(Ed.), Central Asia in focus (pp. 117–195). New York: Nova Science.

DEIK Ozbekistan ulke bulteni (Aralik, 2004), Ankara.

Ebrd and transport (2005). http://www.ebrd.com/country/sector/trport/index.htm.

Ghosh, R. N., Siddique, M. A. B., Gabbay, R. (2003a). Tourism, ecotourism and economic development: An overview. In R. N. Ghosh, M. A. B. Sıddıque, & R. Gabbay (Eds.), Tourism and economic development (pp. 1–8). Burlington, USA: Athenaeum Press, Ltd.

Ghosh, R. N., Siddique, M. A. B., Gabbay, R. (2003b). International

tourism and economic development. In R. N. Ghosh, M. A. B. Sıddıque, & R. Gabbay (Eds.), Tourism and economic development (pp. 19–30). Burlington, USA: Athenaeum Press, Ltd.

Gleason, G. (2003). Markets and politics in Central Asia. New York: Routledge. Transnational hotel expansion. Tourism Management, 11(4), 297–304.

Go, F., Ritchie, J. R. B. (1990). Tourism and transnationalism. Tourism Management, 11(4), 287–290.

Gurgen, E. (2000). Central Asia: Achievements and prospects, finance and development. A Quarterly Magazine of the IMF, 1–7.

Hair, J. F., Jr., Anderson, R. E., Tatham, R. L., Black, W. C. (2002). Multivariate data analysis (6th ed.). Englewood Cliffs, NJ: Prentice-Hall.

Investment Policy Review of Uzbekistan (1999). United Nations conference on trade and development. United Nations, New York, Geneva.

Jenkins, C. L. (1997). Impacts of the development of international tourism in the Asian region. In F. M. Go, & C. L. Jenkins (Eds.), Tourism and economic development in Asia and Australia (pp. 35–48). New York: Pinter.

Jeffries, I. (2003). The Caucasus and Central Asian Republics at the turn of the 20-first century. New York: Routledge.

Kyrgyzstan (2005). http://www.sairamtour.com/ca/ca_06_1.html.

Nowak, A. Z., Steagall, J. (2003). Foreign direct investment in Central and Eastern Europe in the period 1990–2000: Patterns and consequences. In S. T. Marinova, & M. A. Marinov (Eds.), Foreign Direct Investment in Central and Eastern Europe (pp. 59–92). Burlington, USA: Athenaeum Press Ltd.

National Statistical Committee (2004). http://stat-gvc.bishkek.su/.

Nichol, J. P. (2003a). Turkmenistan: Current developments and US interests. In L. M. Buyers (Ed.), Central Asia in Focus (pp. 9–16). New York: Nova Science.

Nichol, J. P. (2003b). Uzbekistan: Current developments and US Interests.

In L. M. Buyers (Ed.), Central Asia in Focus (pp. 1–9). New York: Nova Science.

Qu, H., Zhang, H. Q. (1997). The projection of international tourist arrivals in East Asia and the Pacific. In F. M. Go, & C. L. Jenkins (Eds.), Tourism and Economic Development in Asia and Australia (pp. 35–47). New York: Pinter.

Tourism & Travel in Turkmenistan (2005). http://www.turkmenistanembassy.org/turkmen/travel/travel.html.

The State Committee of the Kyrgyz Republic for Tourism, Sport and Youth Policy, Tourism (2005). http://www.tsm.kg/.

Turkmenistan, Tourism, Travel, and Recreation (2005) http://www.na-tionsencyclopedia.com/Asia-and-Oceania/Turkmenistan-TOURISM-TRAVEL-AND-RECREATION.html.

Voronina, S. (2005). The market for tourism, hospitality & recreational services in Kazakhstan, http://www.bisnis.doc

Welcome to Turkmenistan, General information (2005). http://www.sitara.com/turkmenistan/general.html#Religion.

WTO Silk Road Project (2005a). http://www.world-tourism.org/projects/silkroad/silkroad.html.

WTO, Facts & Figures, Tourism Indicators, (2005b). http://www.world-tourism.org/facts/menu.html.

Williams, S. (1998). Rotledge contemporary human geography tourism geography, USA and Canada. New York: Clays Ltd.

FURTHER READING

Report of the intergovernmental meeting to develop an intergovernmental agreement on the Asian highway network, Bangkok, 17–18 November 2003. Economic and social commission for Asia and the Pacific. United Nations Economic and Social Council.

Review of developments in transport and communications in the ESCAP region (2001). Economic and Social Commission for Asia and the Pacific. New York.

http://tourism.unctad.org/QuickPlace/sustainable-tourism-for-development.

CHAPTER 14

A CHRONOLOGY OF CENTRAL ASIA

AYHAN PALA

CONTENTS

---

*Turkish to English translation: Ayşegül Amanda Yeşilbursa.

INTRODUCTION

This chronology covers the history of Central Asia from ancient times to the modern day (Table 1). The events, which occurred on this ancient continent, form an important part of world history. The chronology will help those studying the political history, economy, culture and other aspects of the region to grasp the subject matter from all aspects. It presents political history and cultural history together, and thus shows in which political conditions certain cultural artifacts arose. Given its scope, it is impossible to present this chronology in detail within the structure of an article; thus, only the most significant historical events have been presented. The dates of certain events are given differently in various sources. In the current study, the main sources of each period were used, and the researches of certain important historians were referred to, and a single date was chosen without reference to different opinions. It would be otherwise impossible to present a study, which aims to present a general idea. Readers must refer to the sources for each period for more detailed dates.

CHRONOLOGICAL LIST

In the chronology, a period of time has been given for events for which there are no definite dates, and for those events, which continued over a long period of time. On some occasions the beginning date of the historical event has been given, a + sign indicates that these events continued for some years after. Unity of spelling has been taken into consideration in the transcription of names. The most frequently occurring forms of names, which appear in different forms in different sources, have been accepted, and where necessary alternative forms have been given in parentheses. A number of these names have been given in accordance with the most recent research. However, because this chronology is aimed at the general reader, forms, which are not familiar to the general audience, have not been used. These names are the subject matter for specialized research. For example, the Asian Hun leader, Me-te's name appears in different forms in such studies, such as Motun, Mao-tun, Beğtun or Bagatur. In the current study, the two forms have been given.

TABLE 1 A Chronological List that Covers the History of Central Asia

Period	Events
4000–1000	Afanasyevo culture: In the environs of Ashkhabad, Turkmenistan. Horse, sheep and cattle breeding prevalent. Adobe houses.
3000	Kelteminar culture: Around the Aral Sea.
2000	Indo-Iranians pass through Central Asia on the way from the Indo-European homeland in southern Russia to India and Persia.
1700–1200	Andronovo culture: Yayik and Lake Balkhash, along the banks of the River Irtysh and the head of the River Obi. Predominantly horse and sheep breeding culture.
1200	The Cimmerians begin to occupy the South Russian Steppe.
1200–700	Karasuk culture: The head of the River Yenisey. Southern Siberia and the environs of Altai, the middle region of the Yenisey area. Thin-faced mongoloid features. Agriculture around Altai. Four-wheeled carts, houses made of felt.
1200–700	The Proto-Turks to the south-west of the Altai-Sayan mountains start to move toward Ordos in the east, and Volga in the west.
1050–256	Chou dynasty in China. Influences of Turkish culture: horse rearing, cult of the sky *(gök)*, military characteristics in administration, animal styles in art.
705–400	Scythians: In the region including the environs of the Azak Sea, to the north of Crimea and the Black Sea, central Don and Dneiper rivers up to the Danube. The Saka: Around the Syr Darya and Aral Sea.
700–330	The Parsi state in Persia.
700–100	Tagar culture: Bronze and bone objects decorated with animal heads. Bronze knives, daggers and arrow heads. Iron forging in the Minusinsk region and the environs of Altai in the 5th-fourth century B.C.
624–543	Buddha, the founder of Buddhism.
Sixth century	Zoroastrianism in Persia. Massagets between the Aral and Caspian Seas.
Sixth century	The Invasion of Transoxiana by the Achaemenids of Persia under Darius I and Cyrus and the establishment of three satrapies: Sogdiana, Khorezm and Saka.
516–513	Persian King Darius' campaign against the Scythians.
400– + 200	Sarmatian occupation from Central Asia to the Danube, including the region north of the Black Sea, central Dnieper as far as the Carpathian mountains.

330	Alexander the Great defeats the last Achaemenid, Darius III, in Mesopotamia.
329–28	The invasion of Transoxiana and capture of Samarkand by the Greeks under Alexander the Great, resulting in the rule of the Greek Seleucids in both Bactria and Sogdiana.
318 B.C.–216 A.D.	The Asian Hun state.
318	Treaty alliance between the Huns (Hsiung-nu) and the five feudal Chinese states against the Ts'in state. The first information about the Huns in Chinese records.
300	Pazyryk culture: In the south-eastern Altai mountains.
256	The Ch'in dynasty takes over power from the Chou dynasty and unifies China.
250	The Parthians take Sogdiana from the Greeks, leaving the latter to rule on Bactria.
230–221	The weakening of the Huns, progress of China, and Parthians against the Greeks in Persia.
221–210	The Ch'in emperor Shih Huang-ti built the 1845 km long Great Wall of China against raids from the north.
220–210	China's control of the Ordos region, and Chinese sovereignty in the steppes. Yuezhi (Sogdian?) sovereignty in Eastern Asia.
209–200	Mo-tun (Bagatur) (209–174) fights with his father T'u-man and accedes to the head of the Hun state. He gains the obedience of his neighbors. The Huns' golden age. Battles between the Huns and the Vusun and Yuezhi (Sogdians?)
206	The Han dynasty is established in China by Kao-ti (206–195).
203	The Huns defeat the Indo-European Yuezhi in the region of the Tienshan (Tengri mountains)-Kansu.
201	The Huns defeat the army of the Han Empire. A peace and friendship treaty is signed. China accepts to give taxes to the Huns.
189–180	Sarmations attack the Scythians. The Huns take control over the Western Region, northern Turkestan and the Vusun lands. All the Turkish peoples of Asia are united under one flag.
	The borders of the Hun Empire reach as far as Korea in the east; Lake Baykal, and the rivers Ob, Iyrtysh and Ishim in the north; the Aral Sea in the west; and the Wei river—Tibetan plateau-Qaraqoram mountains in the south.
169–160	The Parthians take Merv from the Greeks.
174–161	Driven from their homelands, Dzungaria and Yedisu, by the Huns, the Yuezhi go the Afghanistan. They bring the Greek state established by Alexander the Great in Bactria to an end.

174–161	A branch of the Yuezhih attack the Vusuns in Eastern Tienshan. They later progress to the Issyk Lake region toward the Saka.
174–161	The Hun Emperor Ki-ok enters the Chinese capital, Ch'ang-an. A trade agreement was made. The competition between the two countries for control over the Silk Road continues over the ensuing years.
169–160	The Parthians take Merv from the Greeks.
160	The Huns and Vusuns remove the Yuezhih from the Sakas' land.
155	T'an Shih-huai, leader of the Hsien-pi tribal union, established the Hsien-pi state in Mongolia.
141–128	On arrival in Bactria, the Yuezhih occupy the Greco Bactrian kingdom.
140–87	As from the Han dynasty emperor Wu-ti (140–87BC), the Chinese begin to form a world empire by taking sovereignty of their neighbors, whom they referred to as barbarians, and to propogate Chinese culture these peoples.
139–130	The Sakas invade the Parthian country. Hun-Han wars.
138–125	The first Chinese diplomatic mission to the Ferghana Valley, led by Chang Chien.
121	The Chinese, under General Ho Chu-ping, defeat the Hsiung-nu.
119–110	The Parthians defeat the Sakas. Control by the Han victory over the caravan route from Yin-Shan to Lubnor.
109–100	A counterattack by the Hun. The Chinese walk to Fergana against foreign armies.
106	Diplomatic ties are established between the Chinese and the Persians.
102	The Chinese capture Kokand.
55	When the Hun leader, Ho-han-yeh (58–31BC), requests Chinese protection, his brother Chi-Chi, the leader of the left wing, does not recognize the leader. The state splits into two.
54	Chi-Chi becomes emperor of the Western Hun Empire (43–36BC). On losing the capital city, Ho-Han-yeh retreats to Ordos in north-western China.
54	Chi-Chi takes control of the whole western region as far as Aral. He forms a new capital city between the rivers Chu and Talas.
36	The Chinese enter Hun territory and destroy the capital city on the banks of the Talas. Chi-Chi and the palace members die in battle.
29–20	The Huns are freed from the sovereignty of the Han Empire. They repossess their land from Manchuria in the east to Kashgar in the west.

0 +	Roman-Parthian peace. The Huns are freed from Chinese rule. The rise of Kang-chu. The Sarmatians are along the banks of the river Don. The Scythians are in Crimea.
	The Kirghiz ancestors, the Kienku, go the Upper Yenisey region from the north of Lake Balkhash.
10	Kujula Kadphises I established the Kushan dynasty on Bactrian/Trocharian land (now north-eastern Afghanistan).
21–30	Wars between the Kushan dynasty and the Sakas and Parthians. Rebellion and civil war in Parthia. The Huns establish superiority over Chinese.
48	The Huns split into the Northern Huns and the Southern Huns. The Southern Huns become bound to China. Some of the Southern Huns go to Ordos and become Chinese subjects.
50	Kujula Kadphises unites the Yuezhih to establish the Kushan Empire, stretching from Persia to Transoxiana to the Upper Indus.
71–80	Kanishka of the Kushans continues his conquest of India. Buddhism becomes the predominant religion.
71–80	China, Hsienpi, Ting-ling and the Southern Huns unite against the Northern Huns.
81–90	China defeats the Yuezhih (Kushan) in Kashgar.
91–100	Some of the northern Huns go to Western Tienshan and later retreat to the west.
97	Chinese armies reach the Caspian Sea.
141–150	Hsienpi, China, Ting-ling and the Vusuns attack the Huns. The Huns come to the steppes of southern Kazakhstan and Turkmenistan from Orhon.
151–160	The defeat of Hsienpi causes the Hun to divide into four branches. Some of them mix with the Kipchak in the Altais to form the Cuman (Poloves). Those going to China are known as the "Sha-t'o Turks."
155	Tan Shih-huay establishes the Hsienpi Empire in what is now Mongolia.
155–390	Hsienpi rule in Estern Central Asia.
216	The Southern Hun state collapses. Their land is annexed to China.
216–394	The Hsienpi rule over parts of the Hun territory.
220	The end of the Han dynasty in China.
224	The Parthians destroy the Persian-Arshakids. The Sassanids in Persia.

224	Ardashir I (224–241) becomes the first Sassanid ruler of Persia. During his rule, the land of Kushan (today's north-east Afghanistan and West India: Kasmir, Pakistan and Punjab) come under Persian control.
226	The Sassanids overthrow the Parthians in Persia.
271–280	The alliance of the Hun tribes at Yedisu.
276	The killing of Mani.
Fourth century	The Chionites dwell in the lower parts of Syr Darya.
320–550	The Gupta Empire in India.
311	The Southern Huns occupy Loyang. The Hun Chanyu, Liu Yüan, establishes the Early Chao dynasty in China.
331–340	The collapse of the Kushan kingdom. The Muvung and Tabgach become stronger. Juan-Juans, escaping from the Tabgach, Teleut Bozkıra Tabgaç, Teleut and north China settle in the steppes.
350	The nomadic Hyon/Uar-Huns (Ak Hun-Hephthalite) settle in Eastern Tocharistan. Some of the Persian Kidarids moved further west from here, others went to the vicinity of Peshawar.
350 +	The Tielö/Ogur of the Irtysh region migrate to the Kazakh steppes.
351–360	The Persians first fight then makes an alliance with the Hionites. The Hun massacre in China.
351–360	The Mongolian Juan-Juan Empire is formed in Mongolia.
386–534	The Northern Wei dynasty of Topa origins is established in Northern China.
394	Sholun established the Juan-Juan Empire.
420	The name "Turk" is first recorded in a Persian source as an Altaic tribe.
431–440	The Tabgach of Northern China unite and become Chinese.
439	The last Hun state, Northern Liang, is destroyed by the Tabgach leader T'ai-wu. The Achina army, which fled from here to form the Göktürk State, arrive in the Altais. They became subjects of the Juan-Juans.
440	The Hephthalites (White Huns, later known in the West as the Avars) move south from the Altai region to occupy Transoxiana, Bactria, Khurasan, and eastern Persia.
448	Sin-Yuepan (Hun origin) alliance against the Juan-Juan.
451–460	Hun occupation of Azerbaijan.
451–460	End of the Eastern Huns.

456–457	Hephthalite dynasty sovereignty after the Hyon/Uarhon migrations in Eastern Tocharistan. The Hephthalite defeat the Kushan kingdom.
471–480	The Persians exile the Kidaris of Tocharistan to India. The Hephthalites take over Central Asia and Western India.
Sixth century	Byzantine sources (Menandros) use the name Turkhia for Central Asia.
545	War between the Western and Eastern Wei Empires. The Turks are under Juan-Juan sovereignty. An ambassador comes to Bumin from Western Wei.
546	An Hephthalite ambassador in Western Wei. An ambassador was sent from the Turks to Western Wei.
552	Bumin, the founder of the Gokturk Khaganate, rebels against the Juan-Juan. A-na-kui, the Juan-Juan king, commits suicide after his defeat.
554	The Juan-Juan who were raiding Ch'i are defeated by the Chinese. Istemi Khan's western campaign.
555	The Turks defeat the Avars. Their first battles with the Hephthalites.
557	The Gokturks arrive in the Caspian region.
562	Turk-Sassanid alliance against the Hephthalites. Persian-Byzantine peace.
563	The Persians defeat the Hephthalites.
564	The Turks take over Tashkent.
565	The Turks defeat the Hephthalites outside Nesef.
566	The Hephthalite land is divided between the Turks and the Sassanids. The Hephthalites move west to the Russian steppe to form the Avar Khanate.
570	The birth of Prophet Muhammad.
579	The Turks invade China. The death of Khusrev Anushirvan.
571–580	Persian-Byzantine war. Internal struggles within the Göktürk Khaganate. The partition of the Khaganate.
576	The Turks invade the Caucasus and establish the Khazar Khanate.
581	The establishment of the Sui dynasty in China.
582	The Turks invasion of China repels. The Göktürk Empire divides into Eastern and Western Khanates.
588	Regions of free trade are formed on the Turkish-Chinese border.

589	The Turks' campaign in Persia. They are defeated at the battle of Herat. The Persians take control of Paykend. Turk-Sassanid peace.
603	The Kushan rebellion against the Persians with Turkish help. Tocharistan breaks off from Persia.
618	The collapse of the Sui dynasty in China. The establishment of the T'ang dynasty (618–907).
620	The birth of the great power of Tibet.
624	The T'ang dynasty unites the whole of China under one administration.
625	Mutual exchange of ambassadors between the Byzantine Empire and the Western Turkic Khaganate.
630	The Eastern Göktürk Khaganate becomes subject of the Tang Empire.
632	The death of Prophet Muhammad and beginning of the expansion of the Arab Muslim Empire.
642	The Sassanid Shah Yazdigird is defeated by the Arabs at the Battle of Nahavand.
642–651	The collapse of the Sassanid Empire under the pressure of Arab raids.
650	The Khazars defeat the Alans and Bulgars, resulting in their domination of the Caucasus and the Volga region.
652	The Arabs first capture Khurasan.
658–659	The Western Turkic Khaganate comes under the sovereignty of the Tang Empire.
663	Eastern Turkestan is held by the Tibetans.
667	The Arabs defeat Peroz, the last Sassanid shah, and first cross the Oxus River (Amu Darya).
670–692	The Tibetans destroy the Tuyuhun/Aja Empire.
671–680	The Arabs attack Bukhara, Samarkand and Khwarezmı. Tang Empire controls Asia.
679	The Eastern Turks rebel against the Chinese.
681	Kutlug Ilterish Khagan makes the Eastern Göktürk State independent.
689	The Arab occupation of Termez.
691–700	The establishment of the Türgish Khaganate.
696–697	The Göktürks defeat the Kitay with help from the Chinese.
701–710	Arab conquest of Central Asia. The Türgish clash with the Tibetans and Chinese.

705	The Arabs, under Qutayba ibn Muslim, launch a holy war against Transoxiana from Merv.
709	The Arabs capture Bukhara and Samarkand.
711	The Arabs capture Khiva.
711–720	The Türgish are defeated by the Göktürks.
711	The Pechenek-Türgish war.
712	The Arabs subdue Khwarezm and recapture Samarkand.
713	The Arabs sack Kashgar.
714	The Chinese, under emperor T'ai-tsong, defeat the Turks at Lake Issuk-kul.
715	The end of the Arab conquest of Transoxiana as a result of the death of Qutaiba.
726–727	Bilge Kaghan, the vezier of the Göktürk Khagan, erects a monument in the name of Tonyukuk in Mongolia. This is one of the first Orkhun monuments, which constitute the first example of Turkish history, language, and literature.
728	Arab attempt to forcibly convert Transoxiana to Islam, resulting in general revolt.
731–740	The break of the Soghdian resistance against the Arabs.
731	Kul Tigin's death. The second Orkhun monument erected in the name of Kul Tigin, Bilge Khagan's brother and vizier.
734	The death of Bilge Kaghan, the Eastern Göktürk ruler.
735	The third Orkhun monument erected in the name of Bilge Khagan.
737	The defeat of the Hazars by the Arabs.
741–750	The collapse of the Türgish khaganate.
744	The Basmyls kill Ozmish, the last khagan of the Eastern Göktürks.
745	The Uighur-Basmyl-Qarluq coalition destroy the Göktürk Empire.
745	Kutlug Bilge Kul (745–747) becomes the first Uighur kaghan.
748	The Chinese invade the Ferghana Valley.
750	The Abbasids seize the Caliphate from the Umayyad's and subsequently transfer the capital to Baghdad.
751	Arabs defeat the Chinese in the Talas valley with the help of the Turks and the Tibetans. Tang sovereignty in Central Asia comes to an end. Central Asia becomes part of the Islamic world.

751	Chinese prisoners teach the Arabs how to make paper. Paper production starts in Samarkand.
755–797	Tibet's golden age.
759–779	Bügü Kaghan: The golden age of the Uighur Empire. Manichaeism becomes the state religion.
765–785	Semirechye and the eastern Syr Darya come under the rule of the Qarluqs while the western Syr Darya comes under the rule of the Oghuz (Ghuzz).
779	Buddhism becomes the state religion of Tibet.
790	The Tibetans and Qarluqs defeat the Uighur-Chinese coalition at Peying.
790–860	Eastern Turkestan passes once more to the Tibetans.
791–800	The defeat of the Qarluqs in Fergana by the Arabs.
815–819	Samanid state established in Samarkand and Herat.
821–830	The establishment of the Tahirid Emirate in Khurasan.
840	The Kirghiz destroy the Uighur Empire. The Uighurs migrate from the Orhun river to Inner Asia. Some of them settle in north-western Kansu, others settle in the cities of Eastern Turkestan.
840	Kul Bilge Khan establishes the Qarakhanid state.
840–920	Kirghiz Empire in the land of modern Mongolia and Tuva.
845–911	Eastern Turkestan (Turfan) Uighur state established.
850	The Pecheneks live in the environs of Issyk Lake and Balkash.
851–860	The Oghuz defeat the Pecheneks, who went to the area near the Emba, Ural and Volga rivers.
860–880	The Pecheneks cross the Volga and go to Don and Kuban.
867–869	The rise of the Saffarid dynasty (Shi'ite) in Persia.
870–950	Turkish philosopher Farabi.
873	The Saffarid victory in Khurasan.
875	The Persian Samanid dynasty (Sunni) obtains the administration of Transoxiana, with its capital in Bukhara, from the Caliph.
900	The Samanids overthrow the Saffarids, thus extending their rule into all of Persia.
906	The end of the Tang dynasty in China.
10th century	China divides and loses land in the north. In north-western China, Tankut (Hsi-Hsia) establishes the Leao states in the north-east.
907–960	The Five Dynasty period in China.
920	The Mongol Khitans defeat the Kirghiz.

921–922	The ambassador to the caliph of Baghdad, Ibn Fadlan, goes to the Volga Bulgars.
930	The Turkic Qarakhanid dynasty is established, with its initial center in Kashgar.
930–950	The Qarakhanid leader, Satuq Bughra Khan, accepts Islam. The birth of the first Muslim Turkic dynasty in Central Asia.
932–1055	The Buwayhid dynasty in Western Persia.
947–1125	The Liao dynasty (Kitay origin) in Northern China.
950	The Pecheneks live in the environs of Emba ve Yayik.
951–960	The Qarluqs accept Islam. The Hazars are defeated by the Russians, Guz and Pecheneks.
962	The Turkic Ghaznavid dynasty is established in Afghanistan.
965	The Kievan ruler Svyatoslav crushes Khazar political power in the Russian steppe region.
973–1048	Islamic scholar Biruni. He wrote astronomy, mathematics, physics, chemistry, medicine, history books.
980–1037	Islamic philosopher and thinker Avicenna. His work *The Canon of Medicine* studied for centuries.
985	The Khwarezms leave Hazar. Volga Bulgar-Pechenek alliance against the Rus-Uz alliance.
985	The Seljuq Turks, a ruling tribe of the Oghuz, move to the vicinity of Bukhara.
990+	The pro-Shi'ite Persian Buwayhids end the political power of the Abbasid Caliphate by seizing control of Iraq and much of Iran.
995–1017	The Mamunids in Khwarezm.
999	The Ghaznavids defeat the Samanids in Khurasan and the Qarakhanids capture Bukhara, the Samanid capital.
1000 +	200,000 Qerait and the khans in the vicinity of the Orhun and Selenge rivers accept Nestorian Christianity.
1001–1010	The strengthening of Ghazna. The division of Central Asia.
1008	The Belkh war: Mahmud of Ghazni defeated the Qarakhanid armies. Khurasan remained in the hands of the Ghaznavids.
1017–1034	Ghaznavid sovereignty in Khwarezm.
1021–1030	The Mongols and Merkits of Siberia arrive in the steppes.
1028	The Tanguts occupy Kanchou. The Kansu Uighurs lose their independence.
1028–1029	The Seljuqid leaders Chaghri and Tughrul invade Nishpour and Merv.

1034	Khwarezm passes onto Seljuqid control.
1040 +	Migration of the Kipchak/Cuman tribes. The Qays forced the Cumans, who in turn forced the Sharids, who in turn forced the Turkmen, who in turn forced the Uz, who in turn forced the Pecheneks westward.
1040+	The Qarakhanid Empire splits in two: one rules over Western Turkestan (Transoxiana), the other over Eastern Turkestan (the Tarim Basin).
1040	The war of Dandanakanı: Khurasan comes under Seljuqid control. The Ghaznavis are forced into Afghanistan and Northern India.
1041–1050	Control over Persia by the Seljukids.
1044–1179	Abdul Khaliq Ghujdawani: an important name in Central Asian Islamic sufism. His tomb is in Bukhara Ghujdewan.
1048–1140	Abu Yusuf Hamadani: An important name in Central Asian Islamic sufism.
1055	The Seljuqs, under Tughral Beg, capture Baghdad, the Abbasid capital, from the Buwayhids, establish the Seljuq Sultanate, and become the official protectors of the Caliphate.
1058	Tughrul Beg takes the title of Sultan.
1060	The pagan Cumans move into the Russian steppe.
1063	On the death of Tughrul Beg, Chagri Beg's son, Alp Arslan, becomes the Seljuqid sultan.
1068	The Cumans defeat the South Russian princes.
1069–1070	Kutadgu Bilig written in Kashgar by Yusuf Balasaguni.
1071 +	The Seljuqs, under Alp-Arslan, defeat the Byzantine emperor Romanus Diogenes at the Battle of Manzikert and establish the Turkish sultanate of Rum in Anatolia.
1072	Melik Shah (1072–1092) becomes the Seljuqid sultan. The golden age of the Seljuqids.
1072–1074	Divanu Lughati't-Turk written in Baghdad by Mahmud Kashgari.
1073	The Seljuqs defeat the Qarakhanids.
1091–1100	The establishment of the Ismailid state in Persia.
1092	The death of the Seljuq sultan Malik-Shah, resulting in the division of the Sultanate into three parts: Nicaea (Anatolia), Hamadan (Persia), and Merv (Transoxiana and Khurasan).
1093–1166	Ahmed-i Yesevi, founder of the first Turkish tariqa, lives in Turkistan (Kazakhistan).
1097–1231	The Khwarezm State.
1122	The Russians defeat the Cumans.

1124	The Tungusic Juchen drive the Mongol Khitans (Liao dynasty: 916–1124) from China, resulting in the creation of the Qarakhitai state in Semirechye.
1137	The Qarakhitai defeat the Qarakhanids (now vassals of the Seljuqs) at Khojent.
1125–1234	The Qin dynasty (Jurjen origins) in Northern China.
1130	Seljuqid sultan Senjar defeats Samarkand.
1141	The Qarakhitai defeat the Seljuq Sultan Sanjar at the Battle of the Qatwan Steppe, thus gaining power in Transoxiana.
1153	The overthrow of the Seljuq Sultanate of Merv by Oghuz mercenaries.
1166–1175	The Qarakhitai invade Belkh and Khwarezm.
1157	The death of Sultan Sanjar, resulting in the breakup of the remaining Seljuq Sultanate.
1167	The birth of Ghengiz Khan under the name of Timuchin in Mongolia on the banks of the river Onon.
1187	Ghaznavid state overturned by the Ghurlu.
1194	The death of Tughrul III, the last Persian Seljuq ruler, resulting in the end of Seljuq power in Iran and the rise of the Turkic Khwarezmians (Khwarezm Shahs) in Transoxiana.
1199	Qerait leader Tughrul defeats the Tartars in Peking with the help of the Qin and becomes the strongest leader in Mongolia. Tughrul is given the title Wang (king) by the palace in Peking. He is known as Wang-han.
1200	Tekesh's son, Muhammed (1200–1220) becomes shah of Khwarezm.
1206	Ghengiz Khan is announced as Khan by all the Mongols and Turks.
1206–1413	The Delhi Sultanate (Turkish Mamelukes) in India.
1207	Ghengiz Khan takes over the whole of Mongolia.
1207–1273	Former of the Mawlawi tariqa, Mawlana Jalal al-Din Rumi. Born in Belkh. Dies in Konya.
1209	The Mongols defeat the Kirghiz of the Yenisei, forcing them to flee south to the Tien Shan.
1209	The Uighurs, under Barchuq, submit to Mongol rule.
1210	The Khwarezmians conquer Transoxiana, defeating the Qarakhitai.
1211–1215	Ghengiz Khan's campaign against the Qin Empire.

1215	The Mongols invade northern China, besieging and sacking the Jin capital of Yanjing (later known as Beijing).
1218	The Mongols capture Semirechye and the Tarim Basin, occupying Kashgar and crushing the Qarakhitai.
1219	The execution of Mongol envoys by the Khwarezm Shah Muhammad sets in motion the first Mongol westward thrust.
1219	The Mongols cross the Jaxartes River (Syr Darya) and begin their invasion of Transoxiana.
1220	The Mongols capture Bukhara and Samarkand, defeating the Khwarezmians.
1221	The Mongol conquest of Khurasan and Afghanistan.
1221	The Mongols control Gurgench, the capital of the Khwarezmshah Empire. The collapse of the Khwarezmshah Empire. The Mongols of Turkestan become subjects of the Chagatayid Nation.
1223–1224	The Mongols, in pursuit of the Khwarezm Shah, encounter the Russians on the river Kalka, where they defeat them.
1227	The death of Chingiz Khan, resulting in the division of his empire among his heirs, including Batu (the Kipchak Khanate, on the Russian steppe) and Chagatai (The Chaghatayid Khanate, in Transoxiana, the Tarim Basin, and Semirechye).
1236	The second Mongol westward thrust begins.
1236–1502	Batu Khan's Golden Horde Khanate.
1240	Kiev falls to the Mongols and Russia comes under the Mongol yoke.
1242	The Mongols stop their westward advance at the gates of Vienna.
1243	The Mongols defeat the Seljuqs at the Battle of Kösedagh.
1249–1250	The establishment of the Kipchak Turkic Mamluke dynasty in Egypt.
1256	The Mongol Il-Khanid dynasty is established in Iran under Hülegü.
1258	The Mongols destroy Baghdad and bring the Abbasid caliphate to an end.
1260	The Mamlukes defeat the Mongols at the Battle of 'Ayn Jalut.
1260	The Kipchak Khanate divides into the White Horde and the Golden Horde.
1260	The Mongol Yüan dynasty is established in China under Kublai Khan.
1270	The Uighur Kingdom is defeated by rebels.
1284	The Uighur Kingdom is absorbed into the Chagatayid Khanate.

1294–1295	The Il-Khanids convert to Islam under Ghazan Khan.
1303	The Mamlukes stop the last Mongol invasion of Syria.
1310+	The Chagatayid Khanate splits in two parts: Transoxiana (West) and Moghulistan (East).
1313–1342	The rule of the Golden Horde by Khan Uzbek (1282–1342), under whom the Horde converts to Islam.
1318–1389	Muhammad Baha al-Din Naqshband, founder of the Naqshibandi tariqa.
1326	The conversion of the Chagatayid Khan Tarmashirin to Islam.
1336	The end of the Il-Khanid dynasty in Iran.
1336	Timur is born in the city of Kesh (Shehr-i Sebz).
1346	The rule of the Chagatayid Khan Tughlug Timur in Transoxiana.
1363	Timur expels Khan Tughlug Timur and sets up a puppet Khan under his control.
1368	The end of the Yüan dynasty in China.
1368–1644	The Ming Dynasty in China.
1370	Timur brings an end to the sovereignty of the Chagatayid Nation in Turkestan. The Chagatayid dynasty continues in Eastern Turkestan until 1508.
1377–1395	The rule of the Golden Horde by Khan Tokhtamysh.
1380	The Russians defeat Mamay, Khan of the Golden Horde, at the Battle of Kulikova.
1380	The Golden Horde is amalgamated with the White Horde (together called by the former name).
1380–1387	Timur conquers Iran.
1382	Tokhtamysh sacks and burns Moscow.
1389–1405	Tomb of Hodja Ahmed-i Yesevi built by Timur in the city of Yesi (Türkistan).
1390+	The Turfan Uighurs accept Islam.
1395	Timur defeats Tokhtamysh, destroys the Golden Horde capital of Sarai Berke, and briefly occupies Moscow.
1398–1399	Timur defeats the Delhi sultanate.
1400	Timur defeats the Mamlukes in Syria.
1401	Timur destroys Baghdad.
1402	Timur defeats the Ottoman sultan Bayezid I at the Battle of Ankara.
1405	Timur dies at Otrar when he set of on his campaign against China.

1407–1447	Continuation of the Timurid dynasty with the rule of Timur's son Shah Rukh in Herat.
1407–1449	The rule of Shah Rukh's son Ulugh Beg (1394–1449) in Samarkand.
1408	The emirate of the Karakoyunlu (Black Sheep) Turks is established in western Persia.
1417–1420	Ulugh Bey Madrasah built in Registan Square, Samarkand.
1421	Shahruh's son, Ulug Beg, builds an observatory at Samarkand.
1428	Abu'l-Khayr Khan, one of Genghiz Khan's grandsons, establishes the Uzbek Khanate.
1430	Part of the Golden Horde splits off to form the Crimean Khanate under Hajji Giray Khan.
1430–1460	The Uzbek tribes rebelling against Abul'l-Khayr Khan are called the Kazak.
1434	The rise of the Oyrat (Western) Mongols in Jungaria.
1441–1501	Chaghatai poet and thinker, Ali-Shir Nava'i. Grave in Herat.
1445	Part of the Golden Horde splits off to form the Kazan Khanate.
1446	Abu'l-Khayr Khan moved the center of his government at Syr Darya to Syghnak.
1447	Timur's wise grandson, Ulug Beg, ascends to the throne. Transoxiana is attacked by the Uzbeks.
1449	Ulug Beg is killed.
1451	Abu Said (1451–1469) moved the Timurid center from Samarkand to Kherat.
1456	Abul'l-Khayr Khan is defeated by the Mongol Qalmuqs.
1466	Part of the Golden Horde splits off to form the Astrakhan Khanate.
1467	Timur's nephew, Omar Sheikh, becomes the independent leader of Fergana. He makes Akhsikand his center. On his son's, Babur's, accession to the sultanate, he moves the center to Andijan. Defeated in the battle against the Shaybanidds, he loses Fergana.
1467	The Akkoyunlu (White Sheep) Turks defeat the Black Sheep Turks in Persia.
1468	An internal feud results in the death of Abu al-Khayr, leader of the Uzbeks, in battle and the splitting off of the Kazaks from the Uzbeks.
1469	Sultan Ahmed moves the Timurid center back to Samarkand.
1469–1506	Sultan Hussein Bayqara announces independence at Kherat. He takes over Khurasan and Khwarezm.

1480	Ivan III throws off the Mongol yoke and proclaims himself Czar of Russia.
1480–1511	Burunduq Khan attempts to unite the Kazaks under his sovereignty.
1490	Abu'l-Khayr Khan's cousin at Astrakhan, Muhammed Shaybanid, defeats the Kazak Khan, Burunduq, and becomes the leader of the city of Yes. He fights with the Timurids in order to unite the Uzbeks.
1490+	The decline of the overland trade routes, including the Silk Road, due to a new emphasis on trade by sea.
1497	Babur, the ruler of Ferghana, captures Samarkand.
1500	The Uzbeks capture Samarkand under Muhammad Shaybanid Khan, thus taking over Transoxiana from the Timurids.
1502	The final collapse of the Golden Horde at the hands of the khan of the Crimean Tatar Khanate.
1502	The beginning of the Safavid dynasty in Persia.
1504	Babur establishes himself in Kabul.
1505	Muhammed Shaybanid takes the Khwarezm capital, Urgench. Later, the Shah of Persia, Shah Ismail invades.
1506	The Uzbeks capture Bukhara.
1507	The Uzbek Khan, Shaybanid, controls Kherat and announces himself as caliph. Timurid sovereignty in Turkestan and the vicinity comes to an end. The Uzbek Empire is established from the Caspian Sea to Eastern Turkestan.
1508	Chagatayid sovereignty in Eastern Turkestan comes to an end with the execution of Sultan Ahmed Khan after his defeat by the Uzbeks. Eastern Turkestan breaks up.
1510	Muhammad Shaybanid Khan is killed in the Battle of Merv against Shah Ismail, the Safavid ruler, resulting in the establishment of the Shaybanid dynasty in Transoxiana, with the capital in Samarkand, but political power increasingly centered in Bukhara.
1510–1920	Khiva Khanate in Khwarezm.
1511	The Khwarezm Uzbeks rebel against Persia. The choose Ilbars as Khan.
1514	The Timurid Zahiruddin Babur, who was exiled from Turkestan by the Uzbeks, establishes a Timurid Empire in India.
1514–1533	The rule of the Eastern Chagatayid Khan Sayid, under whom the capital moves from Ili to Kashgar.
1516	The rise of the Khojas in Kashgar, later split into the Aq-Taghliqs (whitecaps) and the Qara-Taghliqs (black-caps).

1522	Babur captures Qandahar.
1523	Qasim Khan unites the Kazaks under his own sovereignty. After his death, the Kazaks divide into three hordes: the Great Horde (east), the Middle Horde (center), and the Lesser Horde (west).
1526	Babur wins the Panipat war and takes control over India.
1552	Ivan IV (the Terrible, reigned 1533–84) subjugates the Kazan Khanate.
1556	Ivan IV defeats the Astrakhan Khanate.
1557–1598	The reign of the last and greatest Shaybanid ruler in Bukhara, Abdullah Khan II (1533–98).
1558–1559	The first Russian commercial contacts with Transoxiana under Anthony Jenkinson.
1558–1582	Russia begins to take over Siberia.
1563–1598	The reign of the last Shaybanid ruler of the Siberian Khanate, Kuchum Khan.
1570	The height of Oyrat Mongol power in Jungaria and Mongolia.
1571	The Crimean Tatars sack Moscow.
1583–1599	The sultanate of the Kazak Tevekkel Khan.
1584	Yermak, the Russian Cossack leader, defeats Kuchum Khan at the Battle of Tobol River.
1598–1599	The Astrakhanid dynasty, related to the Shaybanids by marriage, inherits power in Transoxiana, with their power base in the Khanate of Bukhara.
1597 +	The Uzbek Shahruh becomes the leader in Fergana and establishes a dynasty. The Fergana State is established in place of the Hodja sovereignty. Shahruh's antecedent, Abu Rahim, founds the city of Hokand.
1598	The Uzbek Khan Abdullah Khan II (1560–1598) dies. The Uzbek Khanate splits up. The khanates of Bukhara and Khwarezm (Hive) are established.
1599	Baqi Muhammed, the grandson of the Khan of Astrakhan, announces himself as the Khan of Bukhara.
1599–1640	The sultanate of the Kazak Khan Ishim Khan.
1615	Hive becomes the capital of the Khwarezm Khanate.
1619–1621	The first diplomatic contacts between Moscow and Bukhara.
1620+	The Kalmuks, part of the Oyrat Confederation, migrate from Jungaria to the volga. The Kalmuk-Kazak wars continue until 1730.
1643	The Oyrats who stayed in Jungaria conquered Semirechye.

1644	The Manchu Qing dynasty is established in China.
1644–1663	Abu'l-Ghazi Bahadir Khan becomes the Khan of Khwarezm.
1645	The Russians reach the Pacific Ocean.
1680+	Clashes between Russian and Chinese troops in Manchuria.
1680–1718	The rule of Khan Teuke over the reunited Kazak hordes.
1687	The Khan of Bukhara, Subhan Kulu Khan, invades Khwarezm. The Shaybanid administration in Hive comes to an end.
1690+	The Ferghana valley, under the leadership of the Khojas, separates from the Bukharan Khanate.
1697–1727	The Jungars invade Yarkent during the time of the Jungar Khan, Tsevan Rabdan. Eastern Turkestan is divided into city states.
1700+	Oyrat raids on the Kazaks.
1710	Shahrukh Bey overthrows the Khojas in the Ferghana valley and establishes an independent principality in Kokand, which evolves into the Khanate of Kokand.
1715	The first Russian military expedition to the Kazak Steppe under Peter the Great.
1718	The Oyrats defeat the Kazak Middle Horde north of Lake Balkash.
1718	Abu'l-Khayr fights with the Kazak Khan, Bolot, and declares the independence of the Lesser Horde.
1721	Abilay Khan is elected as the khan of the Middle Horde in Yesi, and then fights with the Kalmuks. He wants to unite the Three Hordes, but is unsuccessful.
1722	The Afghans invade Persia, bringing to an end the Safavid dynasty.
1723	The Great Horde comes under Kalmuk sovereignty. This continues until 1758, after which its lands were divided between China, Russia and the Hokand Khanate.
1729	Nadir Qoli Beg (later Nadir Shah) drives the Afghans out of Persia.
1731	The leader of the Lesser Horde, Abu'l-Khayr Khan enters Russian protection.
1732	Nadir Qoli Beg takes Herat.
1734–1735	The founding of the Russian fort at Orenburg.
1736–1747	The sultanate of Nadir Shah, the Persian Shah.
1739	Nadir Shah takes Ghazna and Kabul and occupies Delhi.
1740	The khan of the Lesser Horde, Abu'l-Khayr Khan, invades Khwarezm with the help of the Russians. The Persian Shah, Nadir Shah, attacks Khwarezm.

1740	The Kazak Middle Horde accepts Russian protection.
1740–1747	The invasion and subsequent domination of Transoxiana by Nadir Shah.
1742	Part of the Kazak Great Horde accepts Russian protection.
1747	The Kalmuk governor of Tashkent, the Uzbek Hakim Beg, declares Tashkent's independence.
1747	The establishment of the Durrani dynasty in Afghanistan.
1747	The Uzbek Mangit dynasty begins to rise to power in the Khanate of Bukhara as a result of the collapse of Nadir Shah's regime in Transoxiana.
1753	The Uzbek Manghit leader, Muhammed Rahim Atalik, accedes to the throne in Bukhara. The Manghit dynasty begins.
1755	The Chinese army takes advantage of the struggle for the throne among the Jungars and enter Turkestan. They take the city of Aksu. The Tashkent Khanate also comes under Chinese control.
1756	Abilay Khan comes under Chinese protection.
1757	The Chinese defeat the Oyrats in Jungaria.
1759	The Chinese conquer the Tarim Basin, resulting in the Khojas fleeing to Kokand.
1759	The Khwarezm (Hive) Khanate comes under Chinese protection.
1763	War between The Manghit, Kipchak and Kungrat tribes for the Khwarezm Khanate. The victorious Kungrat take over the administration of the dynasty.
1768	Eastern (Chinese) Turkestan is officially renamed "Xinjiang" by the Chinese.
1771	The Chinese attempt to bring the Kazaks into a vassal relationship.
1771	Some Kalmuks migrate back to Jungaria and the Ili Valley from the Volga.
1780	The Khan of Tashkent, Yusuf Hodja, takes over cities such as Sayram, Chimkent and Turkestan.
1781	Abilay Khan dies in Yesi, (Turkestan), the capital of the Middle Horde.
1783	The Crimean Tatar Khanate is absorbed by Russia.
1784–1785	The Mangits succeed the Astrakhanids as rulers of the Khanate of Bukhara and adopt the title of Emir.
1798	Alim Bey (1788–1810) of Kokand adopts the title of Khan.
1799	The Hokand army attacks Tashkent.

1804	The Kungrats (in Khiva) adopt the title of Khan.
1808	The Khanate of Kokand captures Tashkent.
1812	The Russians succeed in splitting up the Middle Horde. The leader of the Argyn tribe, Bökey Khan, shares sovereignty with Veli Khan. The Russians proceed as far as Balkash Lake.
1814	The Khanate of Kokand captures the city of Turkestan.
1820–1828	The Khojas revolt against Chinese rule in Altishahr (the Tarim Basin).
1822	The Khanate of the Kazak Middle Horde is abolished by Russia.
1824	Russia abolishes the Lesser Horde and annexes the region to the province of Orenburg.
1824–1840	Kazak revolts against Russian rule.
1826	The establishment of the Barakzai (or Mohammadzai) dynasty in Afghanistan.
1830	Hokand Khan, Muhammed Ali, takes Kashgar back from the Chinese. He expands his land.
1837–1847	Kazak resistance to Russian rule under Kenesary Kasimov.
1839	A Russian expedition to Khiva is forced to turn back due to the extreme cold.
1839–1842	The First Anglo-Afghan War results in the British capturing Kabul and Qandahar and installing a puppet ruler on the Afghan throne.
1848	The Khanate of the Kazak Great Horde is abolished by Russia.
1848	The British absorb the Punjab and the Peshawar Valley into their Indian Empire.
1850	The British put an end to the Timurid state in India.
1854	Russia annexes the regions belonging to the Lesser Horde in the north of the Aral Sea and Balkash Lake to the Russian Empire.
1854	The founding of Fort Vernoe (now Almaty) by the Russians.
1855	Kazakstan comes fully under Russian control, who now hold the Syr Darya line (from the Aral Sea to Lake Issyk Kul).
1861	The abolition of serfdom in Russia results in many settlers coming to the northern Kazak steppe.
1862	The Russians capture Pishpek (Bishkek) from the Khanate of Kokand.
1864	The Russians capture the towns of Turkestan, Aulie-Ata, and Chimkent from the Khanate of Kokand.
1864	Yaqub Beg establishes an independent state in Altishahr, based in Kokand.

1865	The Russians establish the Province of Turkestan, which is connected to the General Governorship of Orenburg.
June 1865	The Russians capture Tashkent.
1867	The Russian Tsar, Alexander II, decides to proceed as far as Persia and India, and thus pressurizes the Bukhara Emirate.
1867	The Russians create the Governorate-General of Turkestan, with Tashkent as its capital.
1867	The Russians capture Kokand.
January 1868	The Russians sign a treaty with the Khanate of Kokand which reduces it to a virtual Russian protectorate.
1868	Russia completes its occupation of Kazak land and declares the lands as Russian property.
1868	The Russians create the Governorate-General of the Kazak Steppe, with Orenburg as its capital.
May 1868	Russia raids Samarkand, which is part of the Bukhara Khanate.
June 1868	The Khanate of Bukhara becomes a Russian protectorate.
1869	The Russians establish a fort at Krasnovodsk on the Caspian Sea.
1869	Russia attacks the Khwarezm Harezm (Hive) Khanate.
1871	Russian forces occupy the Ili Valley.
12 August 1873	The Khanate of Khiva becomes a Russian protectorate.
1876	Russia abolishes the Kokand Khanate, which has weakened as a result of civil war. The Kokand Khanate is annexed to the General Governorship of Turkestan under the name of Fergana Province.
1876	The Chinese begin their reconquest of Xinjiang.
1877–1881	The Goktepe battles between the Russians and the Turkmen.
1878	Kashgar falls to the Chinese, under Tso Tsung-t'ang.
1878–1880	The Second Anglo-Afghan War.
1880	The Transcaspian Railroad is begun at Krasnovodsk.
1881	The Treaty of St. Petersburg between Russia and China results in the return of the Ili Valley to China.
1884	The Russians occupy the Merv oasis.
1884	Xinjiang officially becomes a Chinese province.
1885	Muslim revolt in the Ferghana Valley against Tsarist rule.
1885	The Trans-Caspian Railroad reaches Mary (Merv).
1885	The Russians occupy the Pandjeh oasis on the Afghan border, thus completing their conquest of Turkestan.
1888	The Trans-Caspian Railroad reaches Samarkand.

1897–1898	Muslim uprising in Andijan against the Russians.
1905	Russia is defeated by Japan in Manchuria. The 1905 Russian Revolution and the declaration of the constitution.
1906	The completion of the Orenburg-Tashkent Railroad, linking Turkestan to European Russia.
1911	The Republican Revolution in China brings the Qing dynasty to an end.
1912	The founding of the Alash Orda party among the Kazaks.
1914–1918	World War I
1916	The Russian Tsar asks for soldiers from Turkestan. Rebellion in Turkestan. 200,000 Turkestanis are sent to the front. 160,000 Turkestanis resist and are sent to Siberia. The rebellions continue until 1917.
1917	Famine in Turkestan. A large proportion of the people and livestock die.
12 March 1917	The "February" Revolution in Russia, resulting in the establishment of the Tashkent Committee of the Provisional Government and the Tashkent Soviet of Worker's and Peasant's Deputies.
April 1917	The Bolshevik Party affirms it support of the right of all nations within Russia to separate and form independent states.
April 1917	The First Pan-Kirghiz (Kazak) Congress in Orenburg.
16–23 April 1917	The Turkestan Muslim congress takes place. The decision is made to establish an organization under the name of the Turkestan Central Muslim Council. Mustafa Chokai is elected as president.
1–11 May 1917	The First Pan-Russian Congress of Muslims in Moscow.
21–26 July 1917	The Second Kazak Congress in Orenburg.
3 September 1917	The Second Central Asian Muslim Congress in Tashkent proposes the creation of an Autonomous Federated Republic of Turkestan.
7 November 1917	The Bolshevik "October" Revolution in Russia, resulting in the Tashkent Soviet seizing power from the Tashkent Committee.
15 November 1917	The Third Regional Congress of Soviets in Tashkent decides to exclude Muslims from local government.
25–27 November 1917	The Fourth Central Asian Muslim Congress in Kokand results in the creation of the Muslim Provisional Government of Autonomous Turkestan.
5–13 December 1917	The Third Kazak Congress in Orenburg proclaims a Kazak nationalist government under the leadership of the Alash-Orda in an attempt to halt the spread of Communism into the Kazak steppe.

January 1918	The Fourth Regional Congress of Soviets in Tashkent declares war on the Kokand Government.
February 1918	The Muslim government in Kokand is crushed by the Tashkent Soviet and the Red Army, resulting in the slaughter of many Muslims.
1918–1920	The first phase of the Basmachi Revolt.
21 February 1918	A Russian army consisting of the Red Guards and the Armenian Tashnaks invade Hokand. Members of the government floss the city.
25 March 1918	Peace treaty signed between the Russians and Bukharans. The Soviet Government recognized the independence of the Bukharan Emirate.
April 1918	The Turkestan Autonomous Soviet Socialist Republic (ASSR) is established.
28 May 1918	Independent Republic of Azerbaijan established at Genche. Mehmed Emin Resulzade becomes the president.
May 1919	The First Conference of Muslim Communists of Central Asia proposes a "Unified Turkestan Soviet Republic."
20 January 1920	The Fifth Congress of the Communist Party of Turkestan proposes a Soviet Republic of Turkic Peoples and a Turkic Red Army.
2 February 1920	Soviet troops capture Khiva, resulting in the abolition of the Khanate of Khiva and the end of the Kungrat dynasty.
March 1920	The Alash Orda government gives up resistance to the Bolsheviks.
4 April 1920	The People's Republic of Khorezm (Khiva) is established under the leadership of the Young Khivans.
27 Nisan 1920	The Red Army abolishes Azerbaijan independence. Mehmed Emin Resulzade is arrested.
26 August 1920	The Kazak (then called Kirghiz) ASSR is created.
2 September 1920	Soviet troops capture Bukhara, resulting in the abolition of the Khanate of Bukhara and the end of the Mangit dynasty.
6 October 1920	The People's Republic of Bukhara is established under the leadership of the Young Bukharans and the Bukharan Communist Party, with Faizullah Khojaev (1896–1938) as chairman and then premier.
1920–1923	The second phase of the Basmachi Revolt.
14 March 1921	The Soviets depose the Young Khivan government of the People's Republic of Khorezm.
October 1921	Enver Pasha (1881–1922) arrives in Bukhara to assist the Soviets and switches allegiance to the Basmachis.

February 1922	The Bukharan Communist Party comes under the control of the RCP.
February 1922	Enver Pasha and the Basmachis capture Dushanbe.
4 August 1922	Enver Pasha is killed, resulting in the gradual crumbling of the Basmashi Revolt.
December 1922	The Union of Soviet Socialist Republics is created, with the Turkestan and Kirghiz (Kazak) ASSRs included as parts of the Russian Soviet Federated Socialist Republic (RSFSR).
March 1923	The First Conference of the Turkestan ASSR and the People's Republics of Bukhara and Khorezm establishes the Central Asiatic Economic Council, resulting in the economic and administrative unification of the three republics.
June 1923	Stalin denounces "Sultan Galievism" and the Muslim Communist aspirations for an independent Turkestan.
October 1923	The Khorezmian Soviet Socialist Republic (SSR) is established, replacing the People's Republic of Khorezm.
1923–1933	Intermittent Basmachi operations against the Soviets in Turkestan.
January 1924	The death of Lenin and subsequent rise of Stalin to full power in the USSR.
20 September 1924	The Bukharan SSR is established, replacing the People's Republic of Buhkhara.
October 1924	The National Delimitation of Soviet Central Asia results in the abolition of the Turkestan ASSR, the Bukharan SSR, and the Khorezmian SSR and the establishment of the Turkmen SSR, the Uzbek SSR, and the Tajik ASSR (as part of the Uzbek SSR).
27 October 1924	The Turkmen and Uzbek SSRs are created.
15 March 1925	The Tajik ASSR is created.
April 1925	The "Kirghiz" ASSR is renamed the Kazak ASSR.
1926	The Baku Turkological Congress proposes the adoption of the Latin script for all Turkic languages in the USSR.
February 1926	The Kirghiz ASSR is created.
1927–1928	The liquidation of the Kazak Alash-Orda party by the Communists and the replacement of Kazaks by Russians in the republican government.
1928	Soviet anti-Islamic campaign launched, resulting in the disbanding of Islamic courts and waqfs.
1928–1930	The Latin script replaces the Arabic alphabet in Soviet Central Asia.

1928–1933	The forced collectivization of Soviet Central Asians under the First Five Year Plan.
15 October 1929	The Tajik SSR is created.
1930	The completion of the Turkestan-Siberian Railroad.
November 1933	The Turkish-Islamic Republic of Eastern Turkestan (TIRET) is established in Kashgar.
December 1933	The beginning of Soviet control of Xinjiang under Governor Sheng Shizai.
July 1934	The TIRET falls to Dungan (Chinese Muslim) forces.
1936	The incorporation of the Karakalpak ASSR into the Uzbek SSR.
5 December 1936	The Kazak and Kirghiz SSRs are created.
1937	Muslim revolt in Kashgar, Xinjiang, resulting in Soviet military intervention.
1939–1940	The Cyrillic script replaces the Latin Alphabet in Soviet Central Asia.
1939–1945	World War II
1944	The forced evacuation of Crimean Tatars, Meskhetian Turks, and other Caucasian Muslims to Soviet Central Asia.
12 November 1944	As a result of the Kulja rebellion against China, the Republic of Eastern Turkestan is established in the provinces of Tarbagatay ve Altai. Alihan Türe is elected president.
1945–1949	Civil War in China between the Communists and the Nationalists.
June 1946	The ETR disbands as a result of a treaty with Nationalist China.
1947	The partition of British India and independence of India and Pakistan.
August 1949	Leaders of the Xinjiang Muslim League die in a mysterious plane crash en route to meeting the new Communist leaders in Beijing.
1 October 1949	The People's Republic of China (PRC) is established by Mao Tse-tung.
1955	The establishment of the Xinjiang Uighur Autonomous Region in China.
1962	Mass exodus of Kazaks from Xinjiang to Soviet Central Asia.
1966–1976	The Great Proletarian Cultural Revolution in the PRC.
1973	A military coup in Afghanistan abolishes the monarchy and establishes Muhammad Daud Khan as prime minister of the Republic of Afghanistan.
1976	The death of Mao Tse-tung.

April 1978	A Communist-backed coup in Afghanistan results in the assassination of Daud Khan and the establishment of the Democratic Republic of Afghanistan.
January 1979	The Islamic Revolution in Iran under Ayatollah Khomeini.
December 1979	The Soviet invasion of Afghanistan props up the Afghan regime in its battle against the mujehaddin.
1985	Mikhail Gorbachev is appointed as General Secretary of the CPSU.
1986	The 27th CPSU Party Congress approves the policies of glasnost (openness) and perestroika (restructuring).
16–18 December 1986	Anti-Russian riots in Alma-Ata, Kazakstan, as a result of the Kazak Communist Party chief being replaced by a Russian.
1989	Soviet troops withdraw from Afghanistan.
1989	Birlik (Unity) organized as the first serious non-Communist party in Uzbekistan.
February 1989	Anti-Russian riots in Tashkent, Uzbekistan.
June 1989	Ethnic violence in Uzbekistan between Uzbeks and Meskhetian Turks.
February 1990	Ethnic riots in Tajikistan.
February 1990	Ethnic violence in Osh, Kirghiz SSR, between Uzbeks and Kirghiz.
27 October 1990	Askar Akayev is elected president by the Kirgizstan Parliament.
27 October 1990	Saparmurad Niyazov is elected president of Turkmenistan.
November 1990	Kyrgystan SSR becomes Republic of Kyrgystan.
April–May 1991	The five Soviet Central Asian republics declare their sovereignty.
31 August 1991	Kyrgystan and Uzbekistan are declared independent countries.
9 September 1991	Tajikistan is declared an independent country.
27 October 1991	Turkmenistan is declared an independent country.
1 December 1991	Nursultan Nazarbayev is elected president of Kazakstan. Kazakstan SSR becomes Republic of Kazakstan.
16 December 1991	Kazakstan is declared an independent country.
21 December 1991	Founding of the Commonwealth of Independent States in Almaty.

22 December 1991	The Kirgizstan Commonwealth of Independent States treaty is signed.
29 December 1991	İslam Kerimov is elected president of Uzbekistan.
1993	President Saparmurad Niyazov of Turkmenistan has his presidency extended to 2002 by parliament.
1995	Presidents Nursultan Nazarbarev of Kazakstan and Islam Karimov of Uzbekistan win referendums to extend their presidencies to 2000.

KEYWORDS

- **Central Asia**
- **Chronology**
- **Culture**
- **History**
- **Timeline**
- **Turks**

REFERENCES

Agacanov, Sergey Grigorviç, Oğuzlar, translated by Ekber N. Necef, Ahmet Annaberdiyev, İstanbul. (2002). Selenge Yayınları.

Devlet, Nadir, Çağdaş Türk Dünyası, İstanbul. (1989). Marmara Üniversitesi Yayınları.

Dickens, Mark, Major Events Relevant to Central Asian History, http://www.oxuscom.com/CA_History_Timeline.pdf (12.10.2012).

Diyanet İslam Ansiklopedisi, İstanbul. (1988–2012). Türkiye Diyanet Vakfı Yayınları.

Encyclopaedia of Islam (2nd edition), Leiden. (1960–2005). E. J. Brill.

Erken İç Asya Tarihi, ed. Denis Sinor, İstanbul, (5th edition). (2009). İletişim Yayınları.

Grousset, Rene, Bozkır İmparatorluğu, translated by M. Reşat Uzmen, İstanbul. (1996). Ötüken Neşriyat.

Gumilev, Lev Nikolayeviç, Hazar Çevresinde Bin Yıl, translated by Ahsen Batur, İstanbul. (2002). Selenge Yayınları.

Gumilev, Lev Nikolayeviç, Eski Türkler, translated by D. Ahsen Batur. İstanbul, (2nd edition). (2002). Selenge Yayınları.

Hayit, Baymirza, Türkistan Rusya İle Çin Arasında, translated by Abdulkadir Sadak, İstanbul. (1975). Otağ yayınları.

Hayit, Baymirza, Ruslara Karşı Basmacılar Hareketi, Türkistan Türklüğünün Milli Mücadelesi, İstanbul. (2006). Babıali Kültür Yayıncılığı.

History of Civilizations of Central Asia, Paris. (1994–1996). UNESCO.

Kafesoğlu, İbrahim, Türk Milli Kültürü. İstanbul, (27th edition). (2007). Ötüken Neşriyat.

Sümer, Faruk, Oğuzlar, İstanbul. (1992). Türk Dünyası Araştırmaları Vakfı.

Togan, Zeki Velidi, Umumi Türk Tarihine Giriş, İstanbul (3th edition). (1981). Enderun Kitabevi.

Türkler, ed. Hasan Celal Güzel, Kemal Çiçek, Salim Koca, Ankara. (2002). Yeni Türkiye Yayınları.

Vasary, İstvan, Eski İç Asya'nın Tarihi, translated by İsmail Doğan, İstanbul. (2007). Ötüken Neşriyat.

INDEX

For Product Safety Concerns and Information please contact our EU
representative GPSR@taylorandfrancis.com
Taylor & Francis Verlag GmbH, Kaufingerstraße 24, 80331 München, Germany

www.ingramcontent.com/pod-product-compliance
Ingram Content Group UK Ltd.
Pitfield, Milton Keynes, MK11 3LW, UK
UKHW021605240425
457818UK00018B/402